PRAISE FO[R]

Junípero Serra

STEVEN W. HACKEL

Junípero Serra

Steven W. Hackel is a professor of history at the University of California, Riverside, and the author of the award-winning *Children of Coyote, Missionaries of Saint Francis: Indian-Spanish Relations in Colonial California, 1769–1850*. He also directs a project in digital history, the Early California Cultural Atlas, and was co-curator of the Huntington Library's exhibit *Junípero Serra and the Legacies of the California Missions*. He lives in Pasadena, California.

ALSO BY STEVEN W. HACKEL

Children of Coyote, Missionaries of Saint Francis:
Indian-Spanish Relations in Colonial California, 1769–1850

AS EDITOR
Alta California: Peoples in Motion, Identities in
Formation, 1769–1850

Junípero Serra

Junípero Serra

CALIFORNIA'S FOUNDING FATHER

STEVEN W. HACKEL

HILL AND WANG

A DIVISION OF FARRAR, STRAUS AND GIROUX

NEW YORK

Hill and Wang
A division of Farrar, Straus and Giroux
18 West 18th Street, New York 10011

Copyright © 2013 by Steven W. Hackel
Maps copyright © 2013 by Jeffrey L. Ward
All rights reserved
Printed in the United States of America
Published in 2013 by Hill and Wang
First paperback edition, 2014

The Library of Congress has cataloged the hardcover edition as follows:
Hackel, Steven W.
    Junípero Serra : California's founding father / Steven W. Hackel.
— First edition.
        pages   cm
    Includes bibliographical references and index.
    ISBN 978-0-8090-9531-5 (hardcover)
    1. Serra, Junípero, 1713–1784.   2. Missionaries—California—
Biography.   3. Franciscans—California—Biography.   4. Missions,
Spanish—California—History.   5. California—History—To 1846.
I. Title.

F864.S44 H33 2013
979.4'02092—dc23
[B]
                                                                        2013015253

Paperback ISBN: 978-0-8090-6239-3

Designed by Jonathan D. Lippincott

Hill and Wang books may be purchased for educational, business,
or promotional use. For information on bulk purchases, please contact the
Macmillan Corporate and Premium Sales Department at 1-800-221-7945,
extension 5442, or write to specialmarkets@macmillan.com.

www.fsgbooks.com
www.twitter.com/fsgbooks • www.facebook.com/fsgbooks

1   3   5   7   9   10   8   6   4   2

For Heidi and Anna and Gabriel

Contents

THE WESTERN MEDITERRANEAN, 1300

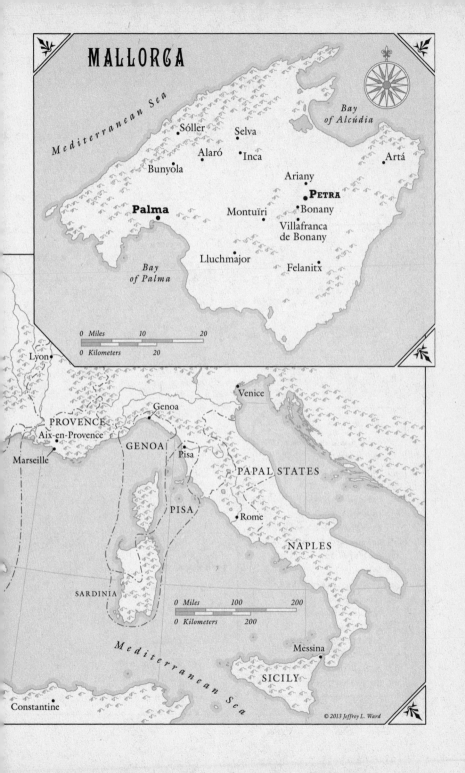

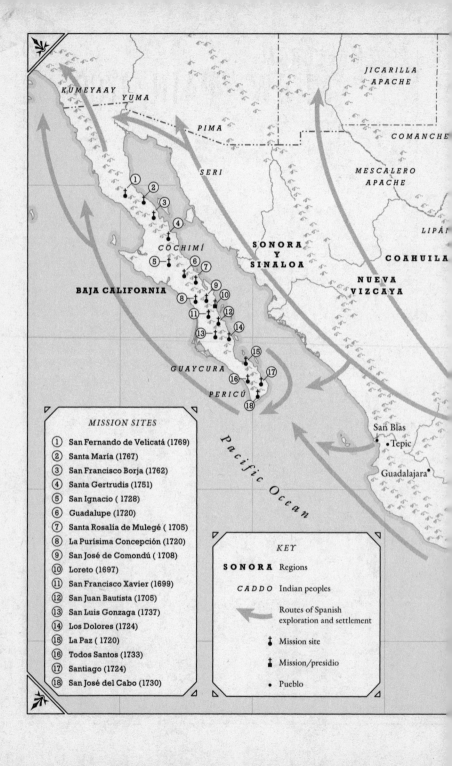

KUMEYAAY

YUMA

PIMA

SERI

JICARILLA
APACHE

COMANCHE

MESCALERO
APACHE

LIPÁN

COAHUILA

SONORA
Y
SINALOA

NUEVA
VIZCAYA

CÓCHIMÍ

BAJA CALIFORNIA

①
②
③
④
⑤ ⑥ ⑦
⑧ ⑨ ⑩
⑪ ⑫
⑬ ⑭

GUAYCURA

⑮
⑯ ⑰
PERICÚ ⑱

San Blas
• Tepic

Guadalajara•

Pacific Ocean

MISSION SITES

① San Fernando de Velicatá (1769)
② Santa María (1767)
③ San Francisco Borja (1762)
④ Santa Gertrudis (1751)
⑤ San Ignacio (1728)
⑥ Guadalupe (1720)
⑦ Santa Rosalía de Mulegé (1705)
⑧ La Purísima Concepción (1720)
⑨ San José de Comondú (1708)
⑩ Loreto (1697)
⑪ San Francisco Xavier (1699)
⑫ San Juan Bautista (1705)
⑬ San Luis Gonzaga (1737)
⑭ Los Dolores (1724)
⑮ La Paz (1720)
⑯ Todos Santos (1733)
⑰ Santiago (1724)
⑱ San José del Cabo (1730)

KEY

SONORA Regions

CADDO Indian peoples

Routes of Spanish
exploration and settlement

✝ Mission site

✝ Mission/presidio

• Pueblo

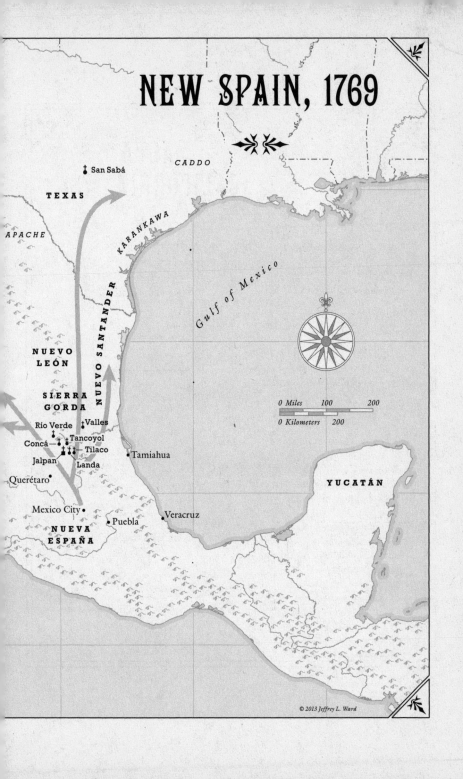

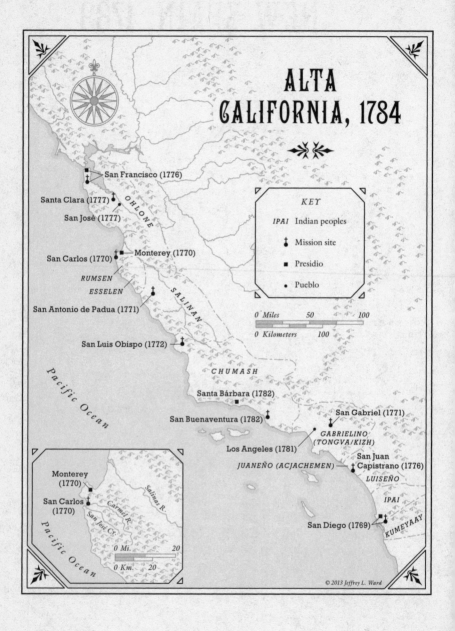

ALTA
CALIFORNIA, 1784

KEY

IPAI Indian peoples

Mission site

Presidio

Pueblo

0 Miles 50 100

0 Kilometers 100

San Francisco (1776)

Santa Clara (1777)

San José (1777)

OHLONE

San Carlos (1770)

Monterey (1770)

RUMSEN

ESSELEN

San Antonio de Padua (1771)

SALINAN

San Luis Obispo (1772)

CHUMASH

Santa Bárbara (1782)

San Buenaventura (1782)

San Gabriel (1771)

*GABRIELINO
(TONGVA/KIZH)*

Los Angeles (1781)

JUANEÑO (ACJACHEMEN)

San Juan
Capistrano (1776)

LUISEÑO

IPAI

San Diego (1769)

KUMEYAAY

Pacific Ocean

Monterey
(1770)

San Carlos
(1770)

Carmel R.

San José Cr.

Salinas R.

Pacific Ocean

0 Mi. 20

0 Km. 20

© 2013 Jeffrey L. Ward

Preface

In 1931, an imposing statue of a man who stood a bit taller than five feet and suffered from a chronically ulcerous leg was unveiled in the U.S. Capitol. It was of Father Junípero Serra (1713–1784), a Mallorcan-born Franciscan, who in 1749 gave up a successful career as a priest and university professor in his homeland and sailed to Mexico to begin his life there as a missionary to Indians. Twenty years later, at the age of fifty-five, Serra played a key role in the settlement and colonization of Alta—or Upper—California, most notably as the founder of the chain of Catholic missions that eventually extended from San Diego to just north of San Francisco. This is why he is one of two Californians represented in the Capitol's Statuary Hall and why a newspaper poll, conducted in 1984, the bicentennial of Serra's death, revealed that two-thirds of Californians considered him the most important individual in the state's history.

Today Serra's statue stands awkwardly alongside bronzes of George Washington, Samuel Adams, and Ethan Allen, men more commonly thought of as founding fathers and whose legacies are less divisive. While they helped the American colonies make a decisive break from England, Serra was a colonizer, and so did something of the reverse, transplanting pre-Enlightenment European institutions, ideals, and hierarchies to a distant corner of the continent. He was not alone in his mission. Spanish missionaries like Serra were enormously important—if largely forgotten today—to the history of America. They were often the ones who made first contact with the continent's indigenous peoples and brought to them unprecedented change. They were also the ones who, both long before and decades after Washington and others were ensuring that England's colonial rule came to an end in British North America, made it possible for Spain to assert control, not only over much of Central and South America but also over vast expanses of North America as well.

Of the thousands of Catholic missionaries like Serra who came to the Americas, nearly all have been forgotten, losers not so much in the contest for North America as in the subsequent battle for a place in American history. Pitted against the founders of Protestant New England and the signers of the Declaration of Independence, they stood little chance. Those few Catholic missionaries who have been remembered—Serra, the Jesuit Eusebio Kino, and a handful of others—are for the most part viewed today through the haze of myth, not with the clarity of historical fact and context. At the same time, only their years in North America are considered, further obscuring their lives and purposes. However, as historians reexamine the historical development of North America, reenvision the geographic and chronological boundaries of colonial America, and reconsider whose early American life is worth telling and teaching, Serra's complete life, and his contributions to the history of California and early America, are especially worthy of study.

Compelling and instructive on its own, Serra's life offers a view into the transformative events of his time. Serra figured centrally in Spain's exploration and colonization of three regions of North America, in the Catholic Church's attempts to convert Native peoples to Catholicism and instill in others a more devoted form of observance, in the rivalries between church and state in the Bourbon era, and in the frustration of Indians' attempts to retain elements of their own culture and society in the face of a relentless onslaught of European men and the diseases they carried. Serra was a visionary, indefatigable and unyielding, who extended Spain's imperial reach, protected the privileges of the Catholic Church against attack, and ushered in a period of dramatic and even calamitous change for many Indians, especially those of California. For the last he is regarded by some as a destructive imperialist. Yet others see in his life evidence that he was a civilizing pioneer or even a virtuous saint.

This book seeks to restore Junípero Serra both to history and to his full complexity, for only by doing both can we come to understand how an island-born Spaniard became one of America's founding fathers and why his legacy divides us like no other's.

⇥✳⇤

A brief explanatory note on translations and sources. Francisco Palou's *Relación histórica* is a hagiographical account intended to portray Serra as heroic and saintly, but it remains the most useful source on the basic chronology and events of Serra's life. Maynard J. Geiger's very elegant translation of the *Relación histórica* from time to time glosses over or shades the meaning intended by Palou. When I disagree with Geiger's translation, I rely on my own translation of the original 1787 version and cite it in the notes. Otherwise, I quote from and cite Geiger's edition. Similarly, Antonine Tibesar's translations of Serra's letters capture Serra's meaning most of the time. However, in some instances I felt the need to provide my own translation, and for those passages I rely on the transcriptions provided by Tibesar. Thus, my quotes from Serra's letters sometimes depart slightly from the translation in Tibesar.

PART ONE

Mallorca

ONE

Mallorca

The man whom Californians know as Father Serra came from Mallorca, an island whose rich and complex history shaped his life and character and gave him direction and identity through all of his days. The largest island in a chain known as the Baleares and equidistant from the coasts of Spain and Africa, Mallorca was for thousands of years a center of trade and thus a place where diverse peoples came into contact with one another. Economically, religiously, and culturally, it was deeply integrated into a larger Mediterranean and European world, yet it did not share the region's characteristic and salutary lushness. For most of its history, and in particular between Serra's birth in 1713 and his departure for Mexico in 1749, Mallorca was in fact an arid and unforgiving land, one stalked by disease and famine and surrounded by enemies both real and imaginary. Rival imperial powers desired Mallorca for its strategic location; conquest and religious conflict marked the island and remade its peoples. Mallorcans alternated between a wary embrace of others and violent attempts to convert, enslave, or expel those with different beliefs and customs. But because of the island's small size and history of famine, Mallorcans also came to look longingly beyond their shores, first across the Mediterranean Sea for material sustenance and then across the Atlantic Ocean for spiritual fulfillment. It is no coincidence that Junípero Serra, an ardent, crusading, and hardened Franciscan missionary, came from Mallorca.

※

Mallorcan summers are warm, and its winters are cool. Summer days stretch to nearly fifteen hours, and winter days bring just over nine hours of light. A dusting of winter snow in the mountains is not uncommon in the northwest and southeast, but it rarely snows on the agricultural plain that stretches between the ranges. In general, precipitation is light. Summer is characterized by drought, and there are no rivers that flow throughout the year. As a result agriculture is precarious: the island has more often than not failed to produce enough food for its inhabitants. Since Mallorca is relatively small, only about fourteen hundred square miles, a man on horseback or foot could traverse the island in a matter of days. Mallorca's best natural harbor, now known as Palma, is in the southwest, away from the mountains and just to the west of the agricultural plain.

Archaeological evidence suggests that people have been living on Mallorca for more than seven thousand years.[1] A turning point in the island's early history came in 123 B.C.E. when Rome conquered the Talaiotic peoples of the Balearic Islands; later, through the Roman Empire, Christianity came to Mallorca. By the beginning of the fifth century C.E., if not earlier, it was the island's dominant religion.[2] Soon after, the Vandals and then the Byzantine emperor Justinian conquered the island. The Byzantines would abandon the Balearics in 624, and for centuries thereafter both African Muslims and European Christians raided the islands. African Muslims had taken most of the Iberian Peninsula by 711, but it was not until 902 that they arrived on Mallorca, introducing not only Islam but also windmills and waterwheels turned by animals, improving irrigation and agriculture, and in other ways helping the island prosper.[3]

Given the island's importance in Mediterranean trade and the growing European commerce with Africa in the Middle Ages, rival European kingdoms desired to retake the island from the Muslims.[4] In 1229, Catalan troops led by the Catholic king of Aragon, James I (1208–1276), "the Conqueror," captured Medina Mayurqa, as Palma, Mallorca's best natural harbor, was then known.[5] As king of Mallorca, James I distributed land to his followers and transported Christian religious orders and mendicant priests to Mallorca. Both the Dominicans and the Franciscans arrived in the 1230s. In 1238, Franciscans received land in Palma to build a convent, but construction of the influential Convento de San Francisco did not begin until 1281.[6] By the middle of the fourteenth century, the convent had more than sixty Franciscans.[7]

Upon his death in 1276, James I divided his kingdom between his two sons, James II of Mallorca (1243–1311) and Peter III, "the Great" (1239–1285). Almost two decades of political unrest ensued. After swearing his allegiance to his brother's son who had become king of Aragon, James II began to carve out a separate existence for the kingdom of Mallorca. He created a standard currency, imposed taxes on Catalan merchants, and formally recognized the governing bodies of the small agricultural communities across the island, ushering in a period of economic expansion. Because of the island's location as a mercantile entrepôt, many Mallorcans made their living as sailors, pilots, fishermen, merchants, shipwrights, and hired hands. Palma soon rivaled Barcelona as a major port, especially after the pope granted Mallorcan merchants the special privilege to trade with non-Catholics in Africa, as long as they traded for food, something that was necessary given that the island was nearly always threatened by famine.[8] As early as 1280, Mallorcan ships had sailed for London loaded with commodities, among the most important of which was wool. And Mallorcans, in particular Jews, cultivated a profitable and busy trade with North Africa.[9] Mallorcan culture flourished during this period as well; Palma's Jewish cartographers, for instance, created some of the most important and widely used atlases of the Middle Ages.

Owing to the influence of the colorful, brilliant, and ascetic Franciscan tertiary Ramon Llull (1232–c. 1315), Mallorca in these years became a center of Catholicism and a breeding ground for Catholic missionaries.[10] After a series of religious visions, Llull committed himself to three pursuits: converting the "unbelievers"; writing a book, the "best in the world, against the errors of the unbelievers"; and encouraging the pope, kings, and "Christian princes" to support monasteries in which missionaries would learn the languages of the "unbelievers." Llull espoused the belief that all non-Catholics— by which he meant primarily Jews and Muslims—could be converted, not by war, but by reason.[11] He traveled to Africa to preach and learned Arabic so that he could do so in the local tongue. He established a missionary college in the hills above Palma, where he trained followers, and Mallorca became a launching point for Catholic missionaries bound for Africa, the Holy Land, or the Canary Islands, off Africa's Atlantic coast.[12] Soon destroyed by slave traders, the Canary Island missions nevertheless helped to set a pattern of Mallorcan Franciscan missionaries venturing far from their home island.[13] Llull himself died in 1315 or 1316, most likely in Mallorca, although some have suggested that he died in Tunis at the hands of Muslims who repudiated his teachings, or on a ship sailing back to his homeland. His bones were interred in the sacristy and then the pulpit of the church of the Convento de San Francisco in Palma.[14]

Mallorcan independence came to an end in 1343 when Peter IV of Aragon, "the Ceremonious" (1319–1387), conquered the island to protect Barcelona's supremacy.[15] The attempt of James III of Mallorca (1315–1349) to liberate the island in 1349 failed, not least because the Black Death had struck the year before, thinning the ranks of his supporters.[16] The island remained under the Crown of Aragon's firm control and was governed from the mainland.[17] Yet the cultural and economic achievements of its period of independence— and its political subjugation at the hands of outsiders—would long remain central to Mallorcan identity.

Loss of its independence coupled with the Black Death made the Middle Ages one of the darkest periods in Mallorca's history. As a center of trade, the island was especially vulnerable to contagious epidemics, and the plague continued to strike, carrying off twenty thousand souls on the island in 1481 alone.[18] Not until 1573 did the island's population top sixty thousand for the first time since 1329.[19] The plague also straitened Mallorca's foreign trade; as a result, the island underwent an economic transformation, turning to the production of textiles and wool,[20] and so becoming ever more dependent on imported grains.[21]

The combined pressures of plague, famine, and economic decline threw much of Spain, including Mallorca, into turmoil, leading many to blame the Jews among them for their hardships; a wave of anti-Jewish violence had begun earlier in Seville, and it soon swept the island. The Jewish quarter of Palma was sacked in August 1391 by a mob of some seven thousand Catholic assailants, who massacred three hundred Jews.[22] In the following months, five hundred Jews converted to Catholicism. Catholic religious authorities forced the mass conversion of many of the island's remaining Jews in 1435.[23] Public displays of Islam had already largely been rooted out of the island, and now Mallorca became among the first Spanish regions in which the open practice of Judaism disappeared.[24] In Mallorca some fifteen hundred conversos (Jews who had been forced to convert to Catholicism) lived apart from Catholics in Palma.[25]

⁕⁕⁕

By the late fifteenth century, with the plague having largely finished its deadly work on the Iberian Peninsula, the kingdom of Castile was ascendant. In 1478 it conquered the Canary Islands, and then in 1492 it took Granada, the last Muslim kingdom on the peninsula, sent Columbus on his voyage across the Atlantic, and expelled from its territories all Jews who refused to convert to Christianity. Mallorca, however, was still part of the Crown of Aragon, which remained largely separate from imperial Spain even after the houses of Castile and Aragon were joined through the marriage of Ferdinand and Isabella in 1469 and later during Spain's unification under a single Hapsburg monarch in the early sixteenth century.[26]

The persistent inability of the Mallorcan economy to feed the island's residents was exacerbated by the Little Ice Age, a drop in temperatures that devastated agricultural production across much of Europe between 1550 and 1700.[27] In these years of recurrent famine, Mallorcans devoted themselves to agriculture but still had to import grains from Sardinia, Naples, Genoa, North Africa, and Castile.[28] The island plunged into debt.[29] As one astute observer noted in 1632, "It is certain, that if the scarcity of Corn did not oblige them sometimes to send Money out of the Countrey, this Kingdom would be one of the richest in Europe."[30] The majority of the people of the countryside saw their own economic condition worsen, and more became renters or simply field hands. Meanwhile, a long period of discrimination against Mallorcan Muslims, many of whom were enslaved, culminated in 1609, when King Philip III forced all Moriscos—Muslims converted to Catholicism—to leave Spain for Muslim North Africa.[31]

※

In the seventeenth century, Spain's trade with American colonies fell off, as did the influx of treasure from the New World, and plague once again reared its head. In 1600, Spain's population was around 8.5 million; a century later it had been reduced to approximately 7.5 million.[32] All told, over the course of the seventeenth century, more than 1.25 million people died from the disease in Spain; another 500,000 immigrated to the Americas.[33] In Mallorca, more than 20,000, or 25 percent of the population, died in the epidemic of 1652 alone.[34] In one of the island's towns, Inca, about 40 percent of the population perished.[35] As the population declined, the burden of taxation on survivors only seemed to increase. Making matters worse, across Spain agricultural production plummeted. In the Mallorcan countryside, the dire economic situation spawned peasant unrest and banditry. Adding to the island's woes were the periodic attacks on coastal towns by Muslim, Turkish, and even French raiders.[36]

The only stable institution in Mallorca across these centuries was the Catholic Church. Mallorca had over three hundred parish priests and hundreds more clergymen who served in the religious orders.[37] The great wealth of the Church was conspicuous amid Spain's general economic malaise. For adult males the priesthood was a common career choice. Outside the priesthood, formal education and literacy were unusual. On Mallorca basic education was limited and overseen by the Church.

One of the principal responsibilities of Mallorcan priests was to teach young children the catechism. Every Sunday and throughout Lent and days of obligation, the rector would ring the church bell to call children to church for instruction. The catechism would be taught and recited in Mallorquí, the Mallorcan variety of the Catalan language, or in Latin, not Castilian. And most likely the children would have been instructed in a very basic catechism, either the Doctrina Christiana of Padre Diego de Ledesma or a translation of the Ripalda Catechism.[38]

In Mallorca, the ritual calendar of the Catholic Church structured village and family life. There were more than one hundred additional Catholic feast days, not including Sundays. Church attendance was expected, if not mandated, on Sundays, and all adults were required to go to confession and receive Communion at least once a year, usually during Lent, when some adults fasted and others abstained from eating meat and all foods prepared with eggs or milk.[39] Church leaders considered many Mallorcans to be lax in their faith and observances, and so welcomed itinerant missionaries who periodically crisscrossed the island trying to reinvigorate the spiritual lives of the laity.[40] Typically, these missions were composed of small groups of traveling friars who spent twenty to thirty days in one of the island's small communities trying to shore up villagers' faith.[41]

During the seventeenth century, as the Hapsburg monarchs struggled to rule Spain in the shadow of the glories of an earlier age, Mallorca felt the pains of Spanish imperial decline. Mallorcans were repeatedly called upon to help defray the costs of lodging troops on their island, and many young Mallorcan men were pressed into military service.[42] Once again, hardship and uncertainty spurred fears about insidious Jewish activity on the island. In 1677 the Inquisition arrested 237 conversos, accusing them of cryptojudaism.[43] Most were given jail sentences of two years or so. A decade later, though, when a group of those previously punished prepared to flee to Holland, and one Raphael Cortés de Alfonso reported to a Jesuit priest that he suspected his cousin and others of "observing the Law of Moses," a cycle of devastating denunciations unfolded. Hundreds were arrested and accused of faking their conversions. In 1691—merely one generation before Junípero Serra's birth—the Inquisition found forty-five men and women guilty of practicing cryptojudaism. Five who had already died or fled were burned in effigy. The remaining condemned were publicly ridiculed in central Palma and then paraded to the outskirts of town, where more than thirty thousand people—a huge proportion of the island's population—thronged to watch the executions. Thirty-seven were strangled and then burned. Three, who refused to renounce their religious beliefs, were set on fire alive.[44] The Jewish community in Palma never fully recovered, and the persecutions became an important part of the island's culture, bringing religious intolerance ever closer to the center of Mallorcan identity.[45]

Despite having to support Hapsburg troops, Mallorca remained relatively free from imperial oversight—until, that is, the victory of the Bourbons over the Hapsburgs in the War of Spanish Succession (1701–1714).[46] By 1710 it was clear that the Bourbon monarch Philip would prevail and consolidate his control over Spain. In 1714 the Bourbons took Barcelona; only Mallorca remained loyal to the Holy Roman Emperor, Charles IV. To defend itself against the inevitable Bourbon invasion, Palma improved its defenses, raised taxes to pay for an army, and enlisted men from the countryside in the army. But when Philip's massive fleet disembarked on the island in June 1715, Mallorcans' resolve evaporated.[47] A Franco-Spanish force of twenty-two thousand easily overran the island's Austrian garrison of one thousand men, and Mallorca once again had a new imperial overlord.[48]

Philip fashioned his Spanish realm after the blueprint devised by the French king Louis XIV, which meant that Mallorca was reminded of its status as a subject land.[49] The Bourbon king introduced a host of changes that collectively altered the relations between ordinary Mallorcans and the imperial capital.[50] The Bourbons published a series of regulations in Mallorca known as the Decrets de Nova Planta on November 28, 1715, two years after Junípero Serra's birth. These laws disassembled the previous institutional system based on local political self-determination and replaced it with one in which power emanated from Castile. Among many other repressive measures, the island was forced to support a standing imperial army.[51] The Bourbons governed Mallorca as if it were a colony: the island had no meaningful political autonomy and found its culture and language under official attack. Political power resided in the hands of non-Mallorcans, and laws mandated that court cases and official documents be presented in Castilian, not Catalan or Mallorquí.

Mallorcans of Serra's generation thus grew up with a healthy suspicion of state authority and a proud sense of Mallorca's distinct culture and history, but also an understanding of the island's constraints. They knew that Mallorca's limitations would not allow a true and lasting separation from the rest of the Mediterranean or the emerging transatlantic world and that Mallorcan survival had for centuries depended upon foods produced in distant lands. For many, this translated into a firm allegiance to the Catholic Church, the only institution that at times met their spiritual and material needs. This Mallorcan worldview would only solidify during a series of devastating crises during the first half of the eighteenth century.

TWO

Petra

Like Mallorca, Petra, the village where Serra was born, has a long and complex history shaped by local and international developments. Situated in the middle of the island's agricultural plain, Petra was a day's travel—about twenty-five miles—from Palma but far enough inland that it was spared the pirate attacks and invasions that periodically imperiled coastal towns. Little is known about the village's early history, though in Serra's time its residents were known to take pride in its ancient origins; Serra himself boasted that Petra was among the oldest communities on the island.[1] By 1251, Petra had its own municipal government, and by 1338 it was officially a Catholic parish within the larger organization of the Catholic Church across the island.[2] The grid of streets that formed the center of Petra, still known today as the Barracar, had some 800 residents by 1329. By 1591, Petra's population had reached 1,882, making it the eleventh-largest village on the island.[3]

Immediately after James I conquered the island in 1229, he redistributed Petra's land to fifty-five of his followers, who sold off their holdings bit by bit for annual payments or agricultural produce. These payments both enriched the seigneur and affirmed the supremacy of the landed elite over commoners, and as subsequent generations of Petrans inherited these small plots of land, their obligations to the descendants of the seigneur persisted. The names of the lands they took possession of, however, echoed the previous era, when Muslims had ruled the island. Such was the case with Son Maimó, Son Homar, and Ca'n Mora, small pieces of land just outside

Petra whose names can be loosely translated as "Place of Muham-mad," "Place of Omar," and "House of the Moors."

Petrans, when the weather cooperated, specialized in the produc-tion of flour; they grew wheat in the fields surrounding the village and then refined it in the town's wind-powered mills. In many years Petra produced more flour than nearly every other community on the island.[4] In the seventeenth and eighteenth centuries Petrans also grew a wide variety of cereals—wheat, barley, and oats—as well as legumes, carob, and figs. The last was especially important as a sub-sistence crop when all others failed and as a substitute for flour.[5] Petra was quintessentially Mallorcan in the frequency with which it was hit by disease and famine. For example, the 1652 epidemic killed some twenty-four thousand people across Mallorca; in Petra the death toll was nearly four hundred, or a fifth of the town's popu-lation. Whole families were wiped out; others fled the pestilence and the deepening poverty that followed in its wake.[6]

In search of a defining and stabilizing institution, town leaders tried to entice one of the religious orders to establish a convent in Petra. In 1607, after the Augustinians had declined, one of the town's officials contacted his brother-in-law and fellow Petran, a friar in the Convento de San Francisco in Palma; later that year some sixteen Franciscans took up residence in Petra. These men found inspira-tion in the life of Saint Francis of Assisi (1181/82–1226), the son of a wealthy Italian cloth merchant who as an adult endured deep spiritual and emotional crises that led him to renounce the high liv-ing and concern for social status that had characterized his youth. Francis repudiated his own biological father and family for what he saw as the Heavenly Father and the brotherhood of like-minded believers, and even as he struggled against physical infirmities, he founded a religious order in 1209 that would be among the most influential religious movements of the early modern period. The Order of Saint Francis did not cloister friars in monasteries as monks even as its members devoted themselves to self-mortification and prayerful contemplation of Christ's crucifixion. Rather, followers of Saint Francis sought to engage the world and reform it through exemplary behavior and evangelical missions. By assuming vows of poverty, chastity, and obedience, Franciscans rejected all that was material, corporeal, and individual in an attempt to critique the excesses of the world and lead society to repentance and salvation.[7]

The nascent Franciscan Convento de San Bernardino de Siena soon became one of Petra's most important institutions, a center of activity in the Barracar, and a magnet that drew in people from the surrounding communities of Sineu, Lloret, San Juan, and Villafranca. The convento brought to the town learned Franciscans who had been educated at Palma's Convento de San Francisco, and it tied the religious life and education of Petrans to the mother convent. Formal religious instruction of some of Petra's children must have commenced soon after the Franciscans arrived, for by 1610 the padres had successfully petitioned the town for two tables for their school.[8] Twenty years later they were raising funds and organizing labor to complete a cistern that would afford the town's residents freshwater year-round.[9] With their school and cistern completed, the Franciscans raised a new building and completed the church edifice and their living quarters by the 1670s.[10]

Furnishing the church interior proceeded slowly and would not be finished for another half century. But by the early eighteenth century the Convento de San Bernardino had become a major center of Catholic worship in Petra, overtaking San Pedro de Petra, the parish church of Petra, which was in a state of continuous disrepair. Serra's ancestors lived in Petra during the community's earlier years and therefore witnessed, and may have participated in, the hard work of building the convento. In 1577, Antonio Abram—Serra's great-great-grandfather—purchased a house in the Barracar.[11] In 1625, Serra's grandfather would inherit this house from his father, and by then the Convento de San Bernardino, located just up the block, was well established.

-*※*-

Serra's most visible ancestor in the early records of Petra is his paternal grandmother, Juana Serra y Abram.[12] She was the daughter of Antonio Abram and Juana Abram y Salom. Their surnames—Abram and Salom, derived from the lineage of their parents—suggest a complicated and layered history. The name Abram (Serra's paternal great-grandfather) is Hebrew for Abraham, and Salom (Serra's paternal great-grandmother) means "father" in Hebrew. Serra's grand-parents and parents were indisputably practicing Catholics, but the names Abram and Salom suggest that some of Serra's distant ancestors might have been Jews or conversos.[13]

In 1689, Juana Serra y Abram died a widow and was buried in the Convento de San Bernardino, as was typical.[14] She had lived out her final years of illness in the Barracar with the help of her adult daughters, Juana, Esperanza, and Sebastiana, with whom she shared her home. She was by no means wealthy but left a small gift—five *sueldos*—to the parish rector. She also asked that thirty Masses be said in her honor, ten at the parish church and the remaining twenty in the convento. Juana divided her possessions and property among her seven children, giving each of them small parcels of land that she and her husband, Miguel, had acquired during their lives.[15]

Juana's bequests to her children reveal the seigneurial relationships and financial obligations that structured economic and political life in Petra during Serra's life. To Juana Serra, her eldest child, and to Juan, her youngest child, she left half of her house and its small yard. But along with this inheritance came the responsibility of giving annually ten *sueldos* to the Reverendo Común. To her daughter Margarita, Juana left a small plot of land near the Moli Vell—the old mill—but Margarita was charged with paying each year four *barcillas* of wheat to the descendants of Don Gregorio Villalonga, one of the few families that owned substantial tracts of land in and around Petra; the family was likely one that had received land in the distribution just after the conquest.[16] Miguel, the oldest son, and sister Esperanza also inherited small pieces of land; each was required to make annual payments to descendants of the Villalongas. Sebastiana and Antonio, Serra's father, received half of a small plot along the road to Palma. Their annual payment: one *barcilla* and three *almudes* of wheat and five *sueldos* to the town. Juana divided a final piece of her land—a small field and vineyard in Son Maimó—into two sections, with one going to her daughters and the other to her sons. All of the children had the obligation to pay each year two *sueldos* and ten *dineros* to one Jaime Riutort, the notary who had drawn up the will. These inheritances may have marginally improved the lives of Juana's seven surviving children, but they also enmeshed them in a system of obligations that drained their wealth and made any sort of economic advancement difficult.

The marital histories of Juana's children also reveal the straitened circumstances of Serra's extended family. Of Juana and Miguel's seven adult children, three—Juana, Miguel, and Esperanza—and perhaps a fourth—Juan—never married.[17] This fact suggests that the family's resources were too limited for them to secure marriage partners.[18] And those who did marry married relatively late, only after it appeared that the couple could sustain themselves. Junípero's father, Antonio, did not marry until he was thirty-one years old and his bride, Margarita, was twenty-nine; by then, both of Antonio's parents were dead, and he could rely on his modest inheritance.[19]

When Antonio Nadal Serra married Margarita Rosa Ferrer in 1707, they took up residence with Margarita's ailing and widowed mother.[20] It was in that home, on the Calle Segona in the heart of the Barracar, that they passed their first dozen years together. In 1719, a mere four weeks after Margarita's mother died, the couple moved to the Serra family home in the Barracar, a move that was made possible by Miguel Serra's giving his brother Antonio his part ownership of the house.

Personal tragedies and the general deterioration of conditions in Mallorca in the early eighteenth century turned the early years of the marriage into ones of hardship. In the first decades of the eighteenth century, food shortages were felt especially keenly in Petra. The 1702 and 1703 harvests were meager. In 1710, late rain destroyed much of the crop of cereals, and grain had to be imported at great expense.[21] Bad harvests followed in 1711 and 1712, and the War of Spanish Succession brought many families to Mallorca from Sardinia, placing even more pressure on the island's limited food supply.

The agricultural crisis that threatened Mallorca in the early eighteenth century was a legacy of the island's social and economic structure. After James I's original land distribution in the thirteenth century, few people actually owned the land on which they lived.[22] Most was owned by a few rich families and worked by those who leased it or worked it as day laborers. There was little if any incentive for anyone to increase agricultural production. In a majority of years across the sixteenth, seventeenth, and eighteenth centuries the island did not produce enough food to feed its own population. For most people in the Mallorcan countryside hunger became the norm. While starvation was rare, hunger was common in the Barracar in the early eighteenth century, especially during the years when Antonio and Margarita were just getting settled.

Sixteen months after they exchanged marriage vows, Antonio and Margarita welcomed their first child into the world. Baptized on January 4, 1709, he was named Miquel Joseph Serre in honor of Saint Michael and Saint Joseph.[23] In Catholic belief Michael played many roles. He was esteemed as the heavenly leader of Christian forces against Satan and the powers of hell, as the angel who carries the souls of the dead to heaven for judgment, as the angel who actually weighs the souls of the dead, and finally, as the champion of Christian people and the patron of the Catholic Church. Given the importance of Saint Michael in Catholic tradition and belief, it is little wonder in the final decades of the eighteenth century that nearly one in five male heads of households in Petra was named Miquel.[24] Joseph, meanwhile, was the husband of Mary, who Catholics believe is the mother of Jesus Christ. In early modern Spain, Joseph was venerated as a good and just man.

Despite the hopeful names that Antonio and Margarita gave their firstborn, the infant Miquel Joseph died soon after baptism.[25] The baby's death may have been followed in the coming years by failed pregnancies, for it was not until three years later that Margarita gave birth to another child, a daughter, Juana Rosa María. Named in honor of John the Baptist—the prophetic itinerant preacher who foretold the coming of Christ and later baptized him—and the Virgin Mary, Juana Rosa María Serra also died in infancy.[26]

Antonio and Margarita must have despaired at the loss of their first two children.[27] They might have found consolation among family and friends who had also lost young ones, an all-too-common event in Petra during the early modern period. In a typical year in the seventeenth and eighteenth centuries, between 25 and 35 percent of all newborns in Petra died within their first twelve months of life. Surprisingly, from 1709 to 1711—when Miquel Joseph and Juana

Rosa María were born and died—nearly nine in ten newborns lived at least one year.[28] So, the couple's grief may have been sharpened by the apparent unusualness of their misfortune.

It was the couple's third child, born just after midnight on November 24, 1713, who would grow up to become the famous Franciscan missionary. At his birth the future Catholic icon and California pioneer was, like his brother, given the widely adopted names of Miquel and Joseph. The second Miquel Joseph Serre was baptized the same day as his birth, in the parish church, according to the custom in Petra.[29] A little more than three years later, Margarita gave birth to a daughter who, like her older brother, would survive to adulthood. She was named Juana María, essentially the same name as her deceased older sister. In 1720, at the age of forty-four, Margarita gave birth to a baby girl who died soon thereafter.[30]

In Petra, and in the Barracar, Serra was a very common family name.[31] Some of the Serras were related to Miquel Joseph, but others were not. Thus, to distinguish themselves from the other Petran Serras, Miquel Joseph's family had acquired two additional family names, Cifre and Delmau.[32] Most likely, when young Miquel Joseph played with the other children in the Barracar, he was referred to as Miquel Joseph Delmau, or perhaps simply as Delmau. Delmau was the first of two alternate names he would acquire in his life, and each would carry with it a very different identity.

Next to nothing is known about Serra's life as a child. But it is likely that his father was a strict disciplinarian who liberally doled out corporal punishment, not only because this would have put him in the mainstream of early modern Spanish parenting, but also because Serra's mature statements seemed to indicate that he had endured such an upbringing. The young Serra probably hewed to a narrow path because of his father's stern treatment of him and at the same time internalized the values that rendered such punishments socially acceptable. As an adult, he would preach in support of fathers punishing their sons with physical blows. Such behavior, Serra argued, when delivered in moderation—striking the right balance "between love and severity"—was beneficial to the child. An ideal father,

Serra believed, "because he loves him with fatherly love, he teaches him [his child] to obey; when he fails in anything, he scolds him and punishes him, so that the son corrects his deviations." Administered in this fashion, Serra came to believe, the punishments of a father are not like those of a tyrant or a king, but "rather they are acts of pure love."[33]

Serra's formal education began early and occurred outside the home, as his parents could neither read nor write. The Convento de San Bernardino, where Serra spent much of his youth, attracted boys not just from Petra but from many, if not all, of the surrounding communities. There Miquel Joseph began to study the Catholic doctrine that would guide his life and acquire the sharpness and clarity of mind through which he would excel. As a young boy, he learned the catechism and the basic prayers that all observant Catholics recited daily. Then he mastered Latin, became an accomplished singer, and learned to read and write both Mallorquí and Castilian with great skill—which, for a rural Mallorcan of the early eighteenth century, was rare indeed. Illiteracy was so common that even some municipal officials of Petra could neither read nor write; for instance, Miquel Homar, one of the regidores of Petra, could not sign his own name.[34]

Thus for the young and strikingly talented Miquel Joseph, studying at the Convento de San Bernardino meant not just a daily physical separation from his parents but the beginning of an emotional and intellectual separation. Every morning, when his father went to work in the fields, Miquel Joseph walked the short distance to the convento, taking a literal and figurative path far different from that of family members, who spent the majority of their time in the fields or their homes. And soon, Miquel Joseph's life would be one guided by the Franciscans and his own spiritual calling rather than by his own biological father and mother.

※

Befitting a town that functioned as a regional center, Petra had its surgeons, shoemakers, weavers of silk, wool, and linen, tailors, shoe repairmen, preparers of wool for weaving, potters and sellers of pottery, millers, merchants, carpenters, pipe makers, blacksmiths, butchers, pharmacists, and masons.[35] But nearly all Petrans made their living in the agricultural flatlands surrounding the town, working as hired hands in plots that they did not own or on land that they leased. Miquel Joseph's father was no exception. By the time Miquel Joseph was a toddler, his father had acquired numerous parcels of land,[36] but they did not make him wealthy, and in fact during hard times may have only become a burden. These plots of land were small and scattered through the countryside. Working them would have been inefficient; getting to and from these places could have eaten up much of his day and exhausted any animals he brought with him to work the land. Furthermore, every year Antonio had to pay taxes on the houses he owned and annual tribute payments to the land's original owners. In good years, he paid additional taxes and tithes on whatever he was able to harvest.

So Antonio Serra and his family essentially lived at the edge of poverty, as did most Petrans, and Miquel Joseph must have grown up in a home with few possessions and no luxuries. The house where he was born has been demolished, but the home to which Miquel Joseph moved when he was a young boy still stands. On the ground level was a small kitchen, an eating area, and space for the family wagon and mule. Above were two sleeping lofts, one for the children and another for the parents. The rooms were enclosed but provided imperfect protection from the elements, and many were shared by humans and animals alike. In the back of the house was a small garden with a few trees and most likely a pig, some chickens, and maybe a cow. Some houses in the Barracar had their own wells for water, but it appears that the Serras' did not.[37] Their water would have come from the cistern at the convent just up the street.

The Serra home was typical of the poorest communities on Mallorca. There were some 489 households in Petra when Bourbon officials inspected the village and determined the economic situation of its families in November 1729. Fully three-quarters of Petra's heads of households got by only through their wage labor.[38] Their families were exceptionally vulnerable to fluctuations in climate and economy that characterized Mallorca in the early modern period. They had no guarantees of steady work, had little or no savings, and lived in full awareness that a season's wages could be wiped out during crop failures and that they were just one stroke of bad luck away from destitution. It was into this kind of family that Serra was born.

If there was any luxury or aesthetic beauty to be found in Petra or in Miquel Joseph's life, it was down the street from his home in the Convento de San Bernardino. As the site of his early education, where his ancestors were buried and his family gathered to worship on Sundays and special feast days, the convento was a haven of sorts. That his parents were devoted to it is revealed by their regular donations to support one of its confraternities.[39] However small, donations such as theirs paid for the completion of the church's buildings in 1679 and for the gradual acquisition over the following decades of the liturgical art that adorned its interior.

The Convento de San Bernardino was important to the Serras not just as a source of water and education and as a place of worship but because its constantly tolling bells dictated the tone and the structure of their days and lives. During Miquel Joseph's childhood the main bell at the convent must have been a source of community pride, for it had been purchased quite recently, in 1708. This bell would have called the Serras to Mass every day. Its rapid tolling would have signified joyous occasions. Its slow tolling would have alerted all that someone in the Barracar had died. Furthermore, the bell would have regularly chimed the hours of each and every day. In the truest sense, then, Miquel Joseph grew up beneath the bell, its tolling setting and signaling the rhythms, moods, and rituals of his life.

The convento's church was a veritable tableau of those elements of Catholic belief to which Petran Franciscans hewed most closely during Miquel Joseph's childhood.[40] The gilded main altar was completed in the 1720s and constructed around a statue of the Most Pure Mary. The notion of the Immaculate Conception—that Mary herself, from the moment of her conception, had been preserved without the stain of original sin—did not become Catholic dogma until 1854, but long before then it was a central and distinguishing aspect of Franciscan belief, one to which Mallorcans were particularly devoted. Above Mary in the chapel stood the figure of Saint

Bernardine of Siena (1380–1444), the namesake of the convent. In the fifteenth century Saint Bernardine became famous as the "Apostle of Italy" for his extended travels and his popular missions in Italy, during which he preached for peace and reconciliation among feuding communities. The Franciscans considered him among their greatest orators; he was canonized six years after his death. Flanking Mary on the altar were two of Saint Bernardine's followers: Saint John of Capistrano (1386–1456) and Saint James of the Marches (1391–1476). Both were priests who traveled the European countryside on popular missions and were said to have brought untold numbers into Catholicism through their eloquent and powerful sermons. Saint John of Capistrano was canonized in 1724, and Saint James of the Marches was elevated to sainthood in 1726, when Miquel Joseph was studying at the convento.

The Franciscans at the Convento de San Bernardino tried to emulate their convent's namesake and the men they placed on their altar, and therefore they spent a good deal of time beyond Petra, preaching in the smaller communities of the region. Thus, from an early age Miquel Joseph understood the Franciscan life as one committed to building Catholic houses of worship and spreading the Gospel.

Because it highlighted the Immaculate Conception before this belief was Church dogma and surrounded Mary with two Franciscans who had only recently been canonized, the central altar of the church was evidence that the Franciscans of Petra were at the cutting edge of Franciscan and Catholic belief. By contrast, the remainder of the chapels in the convent were traditional; they were dedicated to Christ and his Crucifixion and leading Franciscans, such as Ramon Llull and Saint Francis of Assisi, Saint Bonaventure, Saint Anthony of Padua, Saint Clare, Saint Rose, and Saint Salvatore. All of these side chapels were at various points in their construction during Miquel Joseph's childhood. Thus, in a sense, Miquel Joseph came of age within an institution that itself was coming of age, and his years of day school at the convent must have been ones of excitement and energy. A good deal of this excitement originated in a Petran, the Franciscan Antonio Perelló Moragues, who was a leader of the convento in Palma and a prime mover behind the creation of the altar in Petra. He would become Serra's most important mentor.

-*%*-

While Miquel Joseph was studying at the convento, life in Petra entered a period of sharp decline. Bad harvests in 1710–1712 were followed by a fleeting and hopeless resistance to an invading Bourbon army in 1714–1715, the imposition of the Decrees of the Nova Planta in 1717–1718, and then an increase of taxes to support the occupying army and new levies on imports. In the 1720s there were wild fluctuations in climate between drought and wind and rain. In 1723 famine threatened, and wheat had to be distributed to the poor. In 1729 the town's leaders were forced to go to Palma in search of food.[41] Shortages of food pushed up the prices of wheat and flour, making them scarce among the poor. Moreover, the inclement weather and the crop failures of these years meant all Petrans spent more time indoors, a development that could only hasten the spread of disease. By the 1720s, Petra was in the throes of a full-blown demographic crisis, and its population declined by nearly 17 percent, from 2,500 to 2,082. The final years of the 1720s— Serra's teenage years—were nothing short of disastrous as Petrans buried nearly seven hundred of their own. Newborns, young children, and adults—all died in large numbers.[42] By 1729, Bourbon officials found that 64 of the town's 489 households were living on alms, and another 62—nearly all of whom were headed by widows and spinsters—were simply too poor to pay their taxes.[43]

These years of crisis forced Antonio and Margarita Serra into a hard decision. By 1729, Miquel Joseph was fifteen and Juana María thirteen, and their parents must have been thinking seriously about their children's future and their own economic survival. We know nothing about the family discussions and deliberations that culminated in Miquel Joseph's parents taking him to Palma to begin his formal training for the priesthood, but it seems likely that the hardships they faced were a cause. Clearly, Miquel Joseph could not have pursued a career in the Church unless he had excelled in his studies at the Convento de San Bernardino. By one account, at the convent he had learned Latin "perfectly," and he became so "skillful in plainchant" that he and the other students would sing with their professor in the choir on feast days.[44] It is easy to imagine the studious Miquel Joseph catching the attention of his teachers, some of whom probably returned to the Convento de San Francisco in Palma and brought the talented boy in Petra to their superiors' attention.

Miquel Joseph's move to Palma to study for the priesthood was a logical culmination of his education at the convent, but his entering the clergy also made good economic sense for the Serra family given its limited means and the declining conditions in Petra. Antonio and Margarita must have realized that Miquel Joseph's prospects for marriage, given their own lack of wealth, were poor. Half of Antonio's own siblings had not married, and they had come of age in much better economic times than his own children. At the earliest, Miquel Joseph probably would not have married—if he was typical of his era—until the early 1740s, when he would have been in his early thirties. Giving Miquel Joseph the economic means to do so some fifteen years down the road would have drained much of the family's resources and made it even more difficult for his sister Juana María to find a spouse. So perhaps Antonio and Margarita determined that for Miquel Joseph a life of celibacy in the Church was preferable to the one of permanent bachelorhood that he was likely to lead in Petra. A career as a Franciscan was an exalted vocation, and though challenging, it meant a structured and secure life. Giving a child to the Church was an honor, an indication of the parents' own devotion to Catholicism, and a very public statement of their values and virtue. For generations many of Petra's most talented boys had followed their teachers into the Franciscan order. In fact, hundreds of Petrans probably found careers in the Church in the centuries before Miquel Joseph was born. More important, though, between 1680 and 1730 more than forty Petrans—probably all of whom had been students at the convento—joined the Franciscan order. Another eleven became Dominicans, seven joined the Augustinians, and one became a Jesuit.[45]

If protecting their own daughter's marriage prospects by sending Miquel Joseph into the secure life of the clergy was Antonio and Margarita's plan, they succeeded brilliantly. Miquel Joseph, of course, went on to a storied career, and his sister married and had three children, one of whom—Fray Miquel de Petra—attended the convento in Petra, joined the Capuchin order, and achieved fame on the island as a leading mathematician, architect, and professor.[46]

When Miquel Joseph left the Barracar in 1729, he left behind a suffering family and community. The maladies of the 1720s had cut through the ranks of the Serra family, and nearly all of Miquel Joseph's aunts and uncles and cousins were dead. Other than his parents and sister, it is hard to see what would have tied him to Petra and the Barracar. For years he had been developing strong bonds with the Franciscans, with their world of literacy, denial, devotion, and evangelism. He would return periodically to Petra over the coming decades, but his loyalties and responsibilities and deepest and most enduring personal ties would be to the Church. His sister Juana María would remain in Petra, and she and her husband would look after Antonio and Margarita in their final years, just as Miquel Joseph's fellow Franciscans would always look after him.

THREE

Becoming Junípero

Miquel Joseph's parents likely brought him to Palma in the summer of 1730, when he was sixteen years old.[1] The Serras would have left the Barracar early in the morning so as not to get caught in the countryside at night, for fear of bandits. On their way out of Petra they would have passed by either the convent where young Miquel Joseph had been educated or the parish church where he and his family had been baptized. Almost certainly they would have passed by the small plot of land—the *cuartón de tierra*—that the Serras owned along the road to Palma. As they made their way west through rural Mallorca, they would have traveled through fields of wheat or barley, punctuated by an occasional windmill, and several small, Petra-sized towns. Here and there were manicured fields and clusters of *algarroba*, or carob, trees, whose fruit was often used to feed the island's pigs. The Serras would have seen Palma's fortified walls from some distance. The walls were built to keep foreign marauders at bay, but they now served primarily to protect the city from the occasional peasant uprising. Passing through the great city's gates, the Serras plunged into a crowded urban world of twisting stone streets and steep stairways—a long distance from Petra, in more ways than one.

Serra's parents must have realized the momentous nature of their trip to Palma. Surely they were proud of their boy. But when Miquel Joseph entered the Catholic Church, he was giving his life over to the institution, and from that day on he would follow his God's will—as he understood it—and the orders of his superior, not those of his own father and mother.[2] Having already lost three children, Antonio and Margarita might have pondered the fact that they were about to lose, in a different way, another. The separation between Miquel Joseph and his parents—one that began with his education at the convento in Petra—was soon to become a chasm. Once in Palma, Antonio and Margarita entrusted Miquel Joseph to "a devout priest, a canon of the cathedral." They did so, in the words of one observer, "lest" young Miquel Joseph "forget what he had been taught from childhood concerning doctrine and good morals."[3] How long Antonio and Margarita Serra stayed in Palma is not known. Most likely they commended their son to his new guardian, offered a prayer asking support for Miquel Joseph's new life, and said their warmest goodbyes to their son. In the years to come, he would see his parents again, but only infrequently and only after his entrance into the Church was complete.

Petra was a regional center to which the devout came from surrounding villages to pray at the Convento de San Bernardino; Palma, though, was at the heart of Catholic worship not just in Mallorca or the Baleares but in the western Mediterranean. Palma's importance in the Christendom of the western Mediterranean was evident in its cathedral, one of the glories of medieval Spanish architecture. Its origins are shrouded in myth, but it was probably initiated just after the conclusion of James I's conquest of the island in 1229, perhaps in fulfillment of a pledge the king had made during the difficult crossing from Spain to Mallorca. In size and grandeur, in Spain it is second only to the cathedral in Seville. Situated just inside the city's walls and overlooking the Mediterranean Sea, the cathedral dominated Palma's cityscape.

Palma's cathedral was largely completed by 1609, was rededicated in 1613, and underwent a series of renovations in the decades just before Miquel Joseph arrived in the city. Each of its more than one dozen interior chapels—one was dedicated to San Bernardino, others to Christ and various saints—was spectacularly adorned with statues, gilded framing, and fine oil paintings. Just to the side of the main altar were the tombs of the Mallorcan kings, the island's heroes.

Perhaps the most stunning aspect of the cathedral—at least to the modern eye—is its enormous rose window, still among the largest in the world. The cathedral was built on the ruins of a mosque, and so is physical evidence of the attempts by Spanish and Mallorcan Catholics to eradicate Islam. In Miquel Joseph's day, on the cathedral's altar stood treasures: the enormous *custodia* used to display the consecrated host and gigantic candelabrum of silver and gold. When filled to capacity, the cathedral could seat thousands, as many people as lived in Petra and all of its surrounding communities.

The central cathedral was but one of many Catholic places of worship in Palma. The city was divided into five parishes, each of which had its own church. There were at least forty-one other churches,[4] as well as numerous large convents and monasteries in the city. The monastery of Nuestra Señora de Carmen was home to 152 friars. The Dominican monastery had 100 friars, and the Franciscan Convento de San Francisco had 106 padres.[5] And there were other institutions of lesser size. Several nunneries collectively were home to some 400 women.[6]

Beyond the ubiquity in the city of Catholic priests, churches, monasteries, and nunneries, there were other, less obvious but no less important signs of Catholicism's imprint. Palman legend has it that one day in the seventeenth century, a man, most likely a Protestant who had come to the island on business and was "playing at Bowls in the Street," "happened to lose, upon which he blasphem'd in such a scandalous manner" that the priests from a nearby church rebuked him. Further enraged by the priests' words, the man apparently let loose with a tirade that included "some infamous Expressions against the Virgin." He then hurled the ball he had been playing with and struck a statue of the Virgin, which to everyone's amazement and horror "immediately shed Drops of Blood at the part where it was struck." In fear, the man fled to his ship, but the ship was struck by a lightning bolt and disappeared without a trace into the sea. The stone stained by the blood of the Virgin remained, serving as a reminder to those in Palma of the omnipresence and omnipotence of the Catholic God and the fate of those who insulted the Church.[7]

Nevertheless, Miquel Joseph would have encountered vestiges

of the other religions that had once played an important role in the city's culture. That Palma was once home to Muslims was apparent in the palace of the Almudaina opposite the cathedral; it had been constructed as a fort by Mallorca's Muslim rulers only to be later turned into a royal residence by Mallorca's Catholic kings. Yet there was—in a neighborhood known as the Call—a community of conversos. Miquel Joseph would have traversed the Call often. Its converso families still lived in the shadow of the persecutions of the late seventeenth century. The majority worked as merchants or in some aspect of the silver trade or the production of jewelry; they were not allowed to join any of the city's trade guilds other than that of the silver workers. They were the objects of ridicule and scorn, even though they had long professed their conversion to Catholicism. They had never been accepted by Palma's Catholic community; in Serra's day, canvas paintings of those convicted by the Inquisition in 1691 hung in the Convento de Santo Domingo in the heart of Palma. The accused were portrayed wearing the sanbenitos that signified their punishment: the reconciled wore a diagonal Saint Andrew's cross and held a green candle; those to be burned wore a hood and robe, with flames and demons painted on both. The names of all these families appeared in bold beneath the canvas.[8] As late as the early nineteenth century, the Church of Santo Domingo was filled on Sundays with families who came from across the island to stare at the images of the executed.[9] The Call and the scorning of the conversos revealed the dark underside of the legend of the stone stained with the Virgin's blood and the city's spectacular cathedral and churches.

The year Miquel Joseph arrived, Palma was home to roughly thirty-three thousand people.[10] Most of the male heads of household were artisans, craftsmen, laborers, or merchants. They may not have been wealthy, but they also were not locked into the seigneurial relationships that held back rural folk. Miquel Joseph's first home was likely in the Almudaina neighborhood, the site of the cathedral, Bishop's Palace, and important government offices.

To the west of the Almudaina and across an old river channel was the parish of Santa Cruz, where Palma's longshoremen, shipwrights, sailors, and fishermen, and a handful of merchants who worked in the Lonja, Palma's house of exchange, resided.[11]

By far the largest parish in Palma was Santa Eulalia, which, along with the neighboring parish of San Nicolás, was where the city's one thousand or so conversos lived. The parishes of Saint James, Santa Eulalia, and San Nicolás were also home to the majority of the town's artisans, merchants, weavers, bakers, tailors, shoemakers, hatters, and day laborers.

While the neighborhoods of Palma varied in character, they shared four problems: filth, disorder, disease, and hunger. The unpaved streets were rife with holes and other hazards dangerous to humans and animals alike. It was not until the beginning of the eighteenth century, after the promulgation of the Decrees of the Nova Planta, that the free circulation of pigs within the city's walls was prohibited. But this law was widely ignored. At night, moreover, criminals prowled the same streets; only in the early nineteenth century did the city install public oil lanterns. A center of international commerce, Palma attracted to its port not only foreign merchants but also, inevitably and unwittingly, disease. And while the city had small fields for emergency crops, food shortages were common, as they were across the island, especially among the city's poor. When disease and hunger were striking, it was not unknown for thousands of the city's residents to flee to the homes of relatives in the countryside, where they might escape contagious, fast-spreading disease and perhaps find some food.[12]

Miquel Joseph would have carved out an orderly life in this chaotic city through the daily ritual of Catholic observances. Before long, he also began to study philosophy at the Convento de San Francisco, situated just a short walk from the cathedral. He would have seen familiar faces, as doubtless some of the Franciscans there had taught him at the Convento de San Bernardino. And he saw other Petrans whom he had known since his youth and who had, like him, been brought to Palma to study for a career in the priesthood. But there would have been many more unfamiliar faces; the courses taught at the Convento de San Francisco were open to a wide variety of students from Palma and the other Balearic islands who were pursuing a basic education to prepare themselves for any of the literate professions.[13]

Soon after he began his studies at the convento, Miquel Joseph was presented to Father Antonio Perelló to request entry into the Franciscan order. If admitted, he would spend a probationary year as a novice, and then if that went well, he would officially join the order. Six more years of study for the priesthood would follow. Perelló, the native Petran who had been a guiding force in the creation of the altar at the convento in their hometown, had recently been reelected Franciscan provincial. In the small world of the Franciscans of Mallorca one imagines that Perelló had heard about Miquel Joseph and had met him before this meeting. Thus, Miquel Joseph and the canon had good reason to expect positive results from this interview. But Perelló did not grant Miquel Joseph's request. Believing that Miquel Joseph was too young, Perelló told him that he would have to wait before he could become a Franciscan. Technically, though, Miquel Joseph was not too young to join the order, and once Perelló received proof of Miquel Joseph's age from the parish archive in Petra, he admitted the boy into the order.[14]

Miquel Joseph donned the Franciscan habit on September 14, 1730, two months shy of his seventeenth birthday. He would spend the next year in relative seclusion as a Franciscan novice in the Convento de Santa María de los Angeles de Jesús just outside the city's walls. He was one of a score of boys who began their novitiate that year; they joined the ten Franciscans who were in charge of the convento.[15] It was a year in which Miquel Joseph would prove to the master of the novices that he had the intelligence, fortitude, and religious devotion for life as a Franciscan. While in theory all novices were free to leave at any point, it is hard to imagine how Miquel Joseph, from poor and illiterate parents in rural Mallorca, could have left the convent or where he would have gone had he come to the conclusion that the life of a religious was not for him. There seems, however, to have been no crisis of faith. Raised in the shadow of the Franciscan convent, Miquel Joseph, one could say, was to the Franciscans born.

Miquel Joseph spent much of his seventeenth year deepening his

ritual observances. Before entering the novitiate, he was an observant Catholic, perhaps even an enthusiastic believer. In Petra he had
attended Mass regularly and fulfilled his obligations to confess and
receive Communion. Now he doubled and then redoubled his ritual
observances, all under the direction of the master of novices. Miquel
Joseph learned to pray at regular hours day and night, perform basic
chores around the convent to reinforce his humility, and fast and
deny his body during what was intended to be a year of intense reflection on Christ's suffering. He would also begin to practice the
self-mortification that was characteristic of his life and of leading
Franciscans of the age. He wore a hair shirt during the day that
irritated the skin and at night lacerated his flesh with a rope or iron
lash. Over the course of the year, he not only tested his faith and
gained a solid knowledge in the justifications for nearly all the ritual
practices of Catholicism but also began to establish a reputation as a
particularly devout and dedicated Franciscan.

When Serra reflected back on his novitiate year, he used to say
that he was "almost always ill" and that his small stature limited
what he could do: he was unable to reach the lectern in church and
was not able to help his "fellow novices in the necessary chores of
the novitiate." At the suggestion of the master of novices he spent
every day as an altar boy would, assisting at Mass, something he had
probably done at the Convento de San Bernardino. A year of broken
sleep and meager rations punctuated by fasting and other bodily trials could not have helped his health.[16]

❖

An avid reader, Miquel Joseph immersed himself in the chronicles
of the order and became enthralled with the lives of leading Franciscans. Some of these chronicles were simply manuscript accounts of
Mallorcan Franciscans; others were polished and published narratives
of the lives of those deemed especially virtuous by the Church.
These narratives were anything but dry theological tracts; part of
their intent was to inspire young men to devote themselves to Franciscanism, and they were filled with drama and miraculous occur-
rences carried out by individuals who seemed superhuman.[17] For
Miquel Joseph, in addition to Saint Francis and his teachings, the

lives of three Spanish Franciscan missionaries—Fray Antonio Llinás, Saint Francis Solano, and Padre Antonio Margil de Jesús—proved especially inspirational. They had led lives of fervent devotion and sacrificed all for Christ. They dedicated themselves to spreading the Gospel and believed intensely not only in the need to bring pagans into Catholicism but also in the importance of increasing the religious fervor of those already within the faith.

As a boy in Petra, and no doubt during his novitiate, Miquel Joseph heard about the life and accomplishments of Fray Antonio Llinás. Llinás was born in 1635 in the village of Artá, located a mere fifteen miles from Palma. He rose through the ranks of the Franciscan clergy in the 1650s and early 1660s but grew frustrated when he did not win appointment to one of two vacant professorships at the university in Palma. These professorships were highly sought after but were exceptionally difficult to attain. In 1664, when two Franciscans came from Mexico searching for volunteers as lectors in New Spain, Llinás volunteered with alacrity. He sailed to Mexico and spent the next fifteen years teaching in various friaries in the region of Querétaro, north of Mexico City.[18]

In Querétaro during the late 1670s, Llinás experienced a career and identity crisis; he was unsure if he should devote his remaining years to work among the unconverted Indians of northern New Spain or the Catholic "faithful" in the heart of the colony whose religious fervor had waned. Already a respected lecturer and orator, he was sent back to Mallorca in 1679 to represent his province in Franciscan discussions and elections that were to be held in Madrid in 1682.[19] Llinás spent two years preaching "missions"—essentially revivals—first in Mallorca and then around Menorca and mainland Spain. At this time word was beginning to spread in Franciscan circles of the establishment in Portugal and Spain of two colleges where apostolic missionaries might go to learn how to further their work among the faithful.[20] This intrigued Llinás, steeped as he was in the earlier missionary goals of Ramon Llull.

As part of his duty representing the Franciscans of his province, Llinás met with Father José Ximénez Samaniego, the minister general of the Franciscan order. Samaniego was aware of these new colleges and a promoter of the belief that the Franciscans also were ordained by God to work among the unbaptized Indians in the far north of New Spain.[21] Llinás asked Samaniego for permission to recruit eleven missionaries for the Sierra Gorda region, situated in the mountains to the northeast of Querétaro. Samaniego replied that Llinás should do more and encouraged him to establish a college for these missionaries and those who might come after them for work among the Indians of the north. Llinás secured authorization to establish a missionary college in Querétaro, and in March 1683 he arrived in Veracruz with twenty-seven Spanish Franciscan recruits.[22] Soon thereafter, Llinás established the apostolic College of Santa Cruz in Querétaro, an institution that would shape the life of Serra and scores of other Franciscans.

Doubtless, Serra was inspired by most, if not all, of the Catholic saints, but the canonization in 1726—when he was a boy of thirteen—of Saint Francis Solano, the "Apostle of Peru," had a great effect on him then, and later when he read about him during his novitiate.[23] Solano was born in Spain in 1549, and after a successful career there he went to Peru in 1589. He was said to have converted thousands of Indians, miraculously cured the sick, predicted the future, and inspired to great devotion all who came in contact with him. After his death in 1610 his garments were said to have been the sources of miracles. His chronicler, Fray Diego de Córdova Salinas, wrote, "All his life, from the time God called him to the religion, was a continuous martyrdom of penance, self-mortification, fasts, and afflictions against his body."[24]

Solano believed intensely that to atone for his own sins and to emulate Christ, he needed to punish or mortify his own body. Most evenings he drew his own blood with rigorous beatings. When asked by another Franciscan how he might imitate this sort of punishment so as to inflict the most pain, Solano advised him to "beat himself in different parts" and to be certain that he removed his undergarments so that he whipped his bare skin. Just as he believed that he had been saved through the blood of Christ, Solano believed that through his own mortifications he would be made whole and healthy.[25] Not content just to scourge himself at night, Solano lacerated his body by running naked through fields of cacti.[26]

In the career of Fray Antonio Margil de Jesús, Miquel Joseph found a man who lived like Saint Francis Solano in the very region of New Spain that Llinás had opened for evangelization. Margil de Jesús was born in Valencia in 1657 and went to New Spain in 1683, having been recruited by none other than Llinás. Before he departed for Mexico, Margil in fact traveled throughout Mallorca; Serra's own teachers might have met him or heard him preach. As a missionary to Indians, Margil de Jesús worked intensively in Central America and New Spain, from Costa Rica to Louisiana. He was one of the first missionaries to Texas, where he missionized alongside several Mallorcans. Soon after his death in 1726—the year of Solano's canonization—numerous chronicles of his life began to circulate, and some would have made it back to Mallorca and into Miquel Joseph's hands.

Margil de Jesús's life conformed to a familiar pattern: he ate and slept little, left the professoriat for the New World, worked among Indians in New Spain, and believed intensely in self-mortification. Margil de Jesús disciplined his body by wearing a hair shirt and through excessive fasting and cultivated neglect. After more than a decade of continuous wearing and frequently mending his tunic, it all but fell off his body. He allowed his feet and face to become infected by insect bites. And, of course, he subjected himself to "cruel" punishments and bloody self-mortifications.[27] He whipped himself with an iron *disciplina*, perhaps in direct emulation of Llinás, who was known to scourge himself late at night when others were trying to sleep.[28] Margil de Jesús undertook "such penances," he insisted, to make the "brute" in his body realize who he was,[29] to protect his own "innocence," and to approach the purity of Christ's selfless devotion. It was after these devoted and often bloodied disciples of Saint Francis that Miquel Joseph modeled himself.

⊷✠⊶

Having completed his year of probation in the convento and satisfied his superiors that he was ready to irrevocably commit to a life as a Franciscan, Miquel Joseph prepared to make his profession to the order. But before he did so, he made a major decision: he chose to mark the transformation that had come over him during his novitiate by changing his given name, a custom followed by some but not all Mallorcan novices. He would no longer be one among countless other Miquel Josephs, even though his namesakes were pillars of the Church. Rather, he would take the name Junípero after the colorful and singular early companion of Saint Francis whom Serra admired as "the greatest exemplar of holy simplicity."[30]

Junípero was an unusual choice for a name, one that does not easily square with Miquel Joseph's own youth or the man he would become. Brother Juniper is a complicated figure and one entirely unlike Llinás, Solano, or Margil de Jesús, or any of the saints Miquel Joseph admired. He joined the order in 1210 as a lay brother, was never ordained, and was not learned. On the one hand, one can easily see what Miquel Joseph saw in this man. Brother Juniper seemed resistant to the temptations of the flesh; his "purity" was said to make the devil flee; and he was generous to a fault with the poor. He was capable of great self-awareness and never feared death. And he was of sufficient inner strength to spend six months in self-imposed silence. But on the other hand, Brother Juniper also carried on like a mad, irreverent fool, often to the embarrassment of the order. He was constantly giving away all of his clothes and appearing naked in public. When a close friend of his died, he shocked his brothers by professing a desire to dig up the body and make the man's skull into a drinking cup so as to more easily hold dear his memory. Simply to amuse and invite scorn upon himself, he played seesaw along a busy road so that all who saw him would think him insane. And when asked to cook for his fellow Franciscans in the convent, he decided to make not one meal but enough food for a fortnight. He gathered pots and kettles and threw into them fresh meat, unshelled eggs, and poultry, feathers and all. He worked feverishly on the meal and was proud of his efforts. But what he served was so disgusting that his chronicler remarked there was "no hog in the whole of Rome hungry enough to have eaten thereof."[31] For all these antics he was mocked by adults and children and scolded by his superiors.

Yet Brother Juniper paid little attention to critics. So certain was he of his own convictions that he had no trouble going against the wishes of none other than Francis himself. He poked fun at his father guardian and outwitted his superiors. Behind all of his follies and antics was a simple and irrefutable logic and virtue, and perhaps this is why Miquel Joseph so admired him. For example, one day when a sick brother asked for a pig's foot to eat, Brother Juniper immediately grabbed a knife, cut off the foot of a pig foraging in the forest, and gave the foot to the man. This act not only enraged the owner of the pig but brought embarrassment to the order. Brother Juniper insisted that he should be praised for this act of charity and that the pig belonged not to the man but to God. Ordered by Francis to make amends to the pig's owner, Brother Juniper tried instead to convince the man of the goodness of his deed. Eventually, the aggrieved man realized that the "simple" Juniper had severed the foot for "charity's sake." He then killed his pig, cooked it, and gave it to the Franciscans "out of compassion for the said wrong he had done them."[32] Upon learning of how the man had been so moved by Brother Juniper, Francis was said to have uttered the words that have been frequently used to explain why Miquel Joseph was so drawn to this man: "Would to God, my brethren, that I had a whole forest of such junipers."[33]

Miquel Joseph was a follower of Saint Francis, but there is nothing in his later life—or even in his youth—to suggest that he did so in a manner similar to that of Brother Juniper. Junípero Serra was never a simple, lighthearted jester, and he never invited criticism as a means of edifying others. So stern was the adult Junípero Serra that it is next to impossible to imagine him giving away all his clothes or setting himself up to be the butt of a joke. Serra was as serious and calculating as Brother Juniper was simple and impulsive. Miquel Joseph's selection of the name Junípero appears impulsive or aspirational. Perhaps the choice was an act of self-abnegation or simply the blunder of an impulsive and impressionable youth who could not yet imagine himself as the imposing and rigid man that he would become. Or maybe it was an indication of who had caught his fancy most recently and who he longed to be. In choosing the name Junípero, Miquel Joseph saddled a serious and mature leader with a curious moniker, one that he perhaps spent much of his adult life knowingly trying to overcome.

Fitting or not, it was as Junípero Serra that Miquel Joseph gave his life to the Franciscans on September 15, 1731. From that point

on his identity and goals would be those of his order. Kneeling before none other than Fray Antonio Perelló, he pledged to live in
"obedience, without property, and in chastity, in order to serve God
better and to save my soul." Perelló responded with a promise that
had first come from the lips of Saint Francis: "If you observe these
things, I, on the part of the Almighty God, promise you life ever-
lasting, in the name of the Father and of the Son and of the Holy
Ghost."[34] Perelló then led Junípero Serra and the newly minted
Franciscans in an oath to defend the belief in the Immaculate Conception. With his profession to the order complete, Junípero Serra
was now and forever a Franciscan. He would always look back upon
that day with affection and was fond of stating that "all good things
came to me with profession."[35] He firmly believed that because he
had given his life to the Franciscans, he was able to overcome his
illness and infirmities and "gained health and strength and grew to
medium stature."[36] In other ways too he would grow beyond "medium" stature.

FOUR

Priest and Professor

Having completed his novitiate, the young man formerly known as Miquel Joseph returned to Palma as Padre Junípero Serra. He took up residence in the centuries-old Convento de San Francisco, a place renowned in Mallorca and beyond as a center of Franciscan learning. Its large and elaborate church was adorned with enormous and magnificent paintings that told the story of the island and the Catholic Church, and the convento itself was decorated with liturgical art and portraits of famous Franciscans. Appropriately, the church was the final resting place of the bones of the greatest of all the Mallorcan Franciscans, Ramon Llull; his mandible was one of the most treasured relics at the convento, and Serra probably gazed upon it with awe. This hallowed ground would be Serra's home for nearly two decades. While the convento itself—with its art, history, tradition, and more than one hundred friars—must have been somewhat intimidating to Serra, many of the people there would have been familiar to him. Sixteen other young men had completed their novitiate and now joined the convento. Among them was another Petran, Guillermo Rosselló. Furthermore, many of the more senior Franciscans at the convent had known Serra since his childhood, when they had served at the Convento de San Bernardino in Petra. While Serra's profession meant he was a member of the order, it did not mean that he was an ordained priest. Not only was he still too young for ordination—twenty-four was the minimum canonical age—but he had six more years of study before him, and then his career began to open up in many directions, some of which were unanticipated and life-changing.

※

Serra began his formal studies in the fall of 1731, when he and thirty-two other students embarked on a three-year course in philosophy. Most were of quite similar background and upbringing, having come from small towns in Mallorca and Menorca; only one was from Palma.[1] The course in philosophy covered a range of topics: logic, dialectics, metaphysics, and cosmology. Three years later Serra turned to theology and such topics as "the tract as conscience," "habitual grace," and "angels."[2] Serra's Latin lecture notes from his final year of study suggest an assiduous mind and make plain his skills as a copyist and calligrapher. His notes reveal his pride in his new knowledge and in the preservation of it in written form. Upon concluding his notes for his courses, he was fond of writing his name in an attractive and artistic scroll. And when he thought it was all over, when he had recorded the last notes of his final course as a student in June 1737, Serra wrote in elegant script, "Today I finished my studies."[3]

The six years of study that Junípero Serra completed with honors inculcated in him ideas that Franciscans of the time took to be fundamental and indisputable. In the world of the convento, students mastered what their professors taught them in lecture, just as their professors had done as students a generation earlier. The beautifully recorded notes of lectures left by generations of students at the Convento de San Francisco, however, reveal the roteness—and, at the same time, the effectiveness—of the instruction. There is a startling similarity between the notes of Junípero Serra, who studied during the 1730s, and those of Francisco Noguera, one of his students in the late 1740s.[4] Much of what Serra learned came straight from the Middle Ages through the ideas of Ramon Llull and John Duns Scotus, leading lights of centuries past who believed that the universe was composed of concentric circles of heavenly bodies surrounding the earth. How Serra reconciled these teachings with the widely accepted teachings of Copernicus, Newton, and Galileo is not known.[5] Passion for the subject matter, the ability to commit much of it to memory, and devotion to revealed truths trumped creativity and new inquiry at every turn. Only the greatest Franciscan thinkers emerged as theological innovators; the overwhelming majority, Serra included, were imitators and emulators in their religious observances and understanding of the world. At the convent, Serra learned how Franciscans understood the world and human nature, and he had mastered subtle interpretation, problem solving, and logical reasoning, but all of this occurred within a system that put the highest value on intellectual conformity.

The best students won the chance to follow in the steps of their teachers and continue the transmission of inherited knowledge. Given his manifest talent and commitment, it is not surprising that Serra was one of seven students at the convento selected to be evaluated for a position as a professor of philosophy.[6] Serra did so well on the competitive examination in 1737 that just after his twenty-fourth birthday he was appointed lector of philosophy. The official document appointing him to this position was signed by two Petrans who were prominent at the Convento de San Francisco, Fathers Antonio Perelló and Juan Homar.[7] As of yet, however, there were no vacancies for professors. Serra would not begin teaching until the fall of 1740, when another three-year cycle of courses began.[8]

Even as he immersed himself in philosophy and theology, Serra was studying for the priesthood. In December 1731 he received "tonsure and minor orders" as a first step in this direction. As a surviving handwritten manual prepared by one of his Franciscan contemporaries in Palma suggests, Serra prepared for this moment by committing to memory not just when priests did certain things but why they did so and what happened to them if they did not live up to canonical requirements.[9] For example, before his novitiate Miquel Joseph had learned to help chant the canonical hours, but it was only in preparation for his tonsure exam that Serra had to learn how those hours of prayer were to commemorate different moments in the life of Jesus Christ. Serra was now expected not only to know the import of the canonical hours, but also the meaning of the sacraments and scores of other technical aspects of the priesthood. He was learning not how to minister to people but the requirements of the priesthood. Continuing his progress, Serra was ordained a subdeacon in 1734 and a deacon in 1736. Most likely, he was ordained a priest in December 1737, shortly after his twenty-fourth birthday.[10]

In 1738 he earned the right to preach, and in 1739 he was given the
authority to hear confessions.[11]

Serra spent the 1730s preparing for a life as both a priest and a professor, and in the following decade he began to fulfill his potential
in both of those vocations. He was not a parish priest, and so was
not assigned to a parish or a specific community, where his normal
duties would have included administering the sacraments. Nor did
he have pastoral responsibilities. Rather, as a Franciscan he was charged
with inspiring a stronger faith in others through an exemplary life of
devotion. And he was to support the work of parish priests by venturing beyond the convento into the small communities of Mallorca,
where he would offer inspirational sermons and hear confessions, all
in an attempt to bring Mallorcans closer to God and make their
salvation more likely.

Serra was to emulate the lives of Saint Francis and San Bernardino,
two men who owed their fame in part to their abilities as moving
orators. In February 1739, only one week after he was granted the
right to hear confessions, Serra began to preach around Palma and
the rest of the island.[12] He preached in the island's interior rural
communities of Alaró, Montuïri, and Felanitx and also returned
many times to Petra to preach in the Convento de San Bernardino.
He also gave sermons to the north in the mountains at Bunyola and
Selva and in Palma's parishes, convents, and nunneries. The themes
of his sermons were often tied to the liturgical calendar and saints'
days, and thus they varied in topic from the glories of the saints, to
specific prayers and commandments, to the need to contemplate the
Virgin and the body of Christ.[13] Serra developed a broad repertoire;
the library at the convento was full of printed volumes of sermons as
well as those in manuscript. Serra also had for his own use a copy of
a published set of sermons relating to Lent.[14] He used all of these
resources as he developed his own inspirational sermons, many of
which he may have committed to memory.

Not long after Serra became an ordained minister, he settled
into his position as a professor of theology at the Convento de San
Francisco. He had been officially appointed in January 1740 but did

not begin teaching until September. This appointment was a mark not just of intellectual accomplishment but of Serra's high moral standards and Catholic piety, for the Franciscans believed that morality and wisdom went hand in hand and that the acquisition of the former depended upon the latter. Serra made clear to his twenty-eight students on the first day of class that there was no separating the moral life from the intellectual life. "Wisdom will not enter into a malevolent soul nor into a body subject to sin," Serra lectured.[15] Philosophy was the study of "mental light," and Serra explained to his students that he would be taking them on a long journey through Lullian and Scotistic understandings of the "leader among mental disciplines and the science of sciences." Before concluding his opening lecture, he gave a testimonial to the virtues of the Immaculate Conception, and he urged his students to love the Virgin Mary as had Duns Scotus, a contemporary of Llull's and one of the great defenders and proponents during the Middle Ages of the belief that Mary was without the stain of original sin.[16] This must have had a great effect on his pupils, for one drew in his notebook a crude picture of five steps leading to a portal, beneath which he inscribed a saying common to Franciscans of the day:

> Nadie pase por este portal
> Sin que diga por su vida
> María ser Consebida
> Sin peccado Original[17]

Three years later, Serra drew the class to a close with great formality. Clearly, for all, the course had been hard work. "On looking back upon our labors," and to congratulate one another, Serra stated, "we can sing out the lines of Virgil in which the poet proclaimed to men suffering that Jove 'will not soon dispose to future good our past and present woes.'" Asking from his students only that they say a prayer for him upon learning of his death, Serra remarked, "I am no longer your professor but your most humble servant." He was met with applause. He had cast a spell over some of his students; two, Francisco Palou and Juan Crespí, would follow him for the rest of their lives.[18]

Serra's success with his first class led to additional teaching assignments and greater honors. Since the late fifteenth century Palma had been home to a university named in honor of Ramon Llull, the great intellectual and mystic of the Middle Ages. In 1692, the university had been reorganized and began to offer a wider range of courses. Pope Clement X gave it a formal title, the "Pontifical, Imperial, Royal, and Literary University of Mallorca," but it was simply known as the Lullian University. The offices of the university were in the heart of Palma, but the school had no real buildings of its own for classrooms and meetings; the faculty was composed of distinguished members of Palma's most outstanding convents. Since the university's reorganization, Franciscans had held the important professorships in Scotistic philosophy and theology.[19] When Juan Homar, a Franciscan and native of Petra, retired from his chair in Scotistic philosophy, Serra was appointed to the position.[20] He was to take over the chair on January 25, 1744, the day that the Church annually honored Ramon Llull.

At the time of his appointment Serra was barely thirty years old, and his rapid rise may have incited the jealousy of other professors affiliated with the university. Just three months into his new post, Serra appears to have been challenged in a university meeting by one Miquel Ramonell, who asserted that in some unspecified manner Serra was usurping his powers and privileges.[21] It is likely that Serra had assumed—correctly—that his chair meant he was Ramonell's superior. Ramonell seems to have lost this battle, as Serra's name appears above his from that date on in the records of meetings at the university.[22] There were no more public rebukes. Serra soon became a full and active leader in the education, examination, and graduation of students at the university. Over the next five years he would participate in the degrees of more than one hundred students.[23] Serra's responsibilities in these exams varied. Sometimes he listened. Other times he asked questions or posed an argument of his own. On a few occasions, he vested successful doctoral candidates with the robes befitting their academic accomplishments.

※

Serra did not spend his years as a professor-priest within the clois-
tered walls of the Convento de San Francisco. Legend has it that he
frequently walked the streets of Palma distributing small printed
devotional images of Brother Juniper that he had pressed on a wooden
block of his own carving. Moreover, Palma's cultures and customs
meant that the members of the convento, as in most corporate communities in early modern Europe, were often on public display.

Processions—in which members of the corporate community
paraded through streets and public spaces—could be small, involv-
ing only select members of a convento, or they could be large and
composed of the members of artisan guilds, secular clergy, religious
confraternities, elected officials, and representatives from all of the
city's convents and nunneries. These larger urban spectacles were
important moments, when the various spiritual, political, and arti-
sanal communities in Palma came together in celebration or prayer.[24]
Priests carried crosses, banners of their orders, and even sacred relics
from their churches; artisans displayed standards and symbols of
their professions; and ordinary people often dressed in outlandish
costumes and rode on horseback. These processions usually concluded with a Mass in the central cathedral or in one of the larger
parish or convent churches. Serra would have participated in scores
of processions during his years at the convento, on feast days, in
honor of a special occasion—such as the birth of a future monarch
or the canonization of a saint—or when fear or crisis gripped the
island. Surely, Serra, when he was a young boy, participated in processions in the Barracar, and some no doubt had passed by his house,
but those of Palma were much more dramatic and grand affairs.

One of the most spectacular processions in Palma during Serra's
years there occurred in the wake of the War of Spanish Succession.
The Ottoman Empire had taken from Spain the strategically important town of Oran, on the North African coast, southwest of Mallorca. In 1732, Spain organized an expedition to retake the fortified
city, and when the fleet of more than five hundred ships sailed from
Barcelona in June, Mallorcans prayed for its success. They wanted
the Turks, whom they considered infidels and responsible for much
piracy in the Mediterranean, defeated and punished. Serra and other
faculty of the Lullian University, along with many students, went to

the convento to pray for a Spanish victory. Weeks later, when word reached Mallorca that the expedition had taken Oran in just three days, wild celebrations erupted in Palma. A procession of men from the confraternity of Saint George rode horses through the city's streets, carrying torches.[25] The following evening Serra joined all members of the convento to sing prayers and parade the silver tabernacle of the Immaculate Conception. A number of days later, hundreds of artisans in costumes staged a reenactment of the enslavement of Turkish captives, the overthrow of the king of Oran, and what they saw as the defeat of Islam. It was a raucous celebration that mixed the holy and the profane, that brought together priests in their finery, nobles in outfits befitting their elite status, and artisans in their humble work clothes.[26] A week after it had begun, the celebration concluded with fireworks attended by thousands on the waterfront. By the 1740s, owing to his participation in these processions and celebrations and others like them, Serra would have been a well-recognized member of the community of San Francisco beyond the walls of the convento.

Because he involved himself in the life of the city, Serra heard of crime, violence, and scandal—and of how the Bourbon state administered punishment. For example, when a "Moor" confessed to murdering a priest, he was baptized and hanged. Then his right hand was cut off and placed on a city gate as a warning, and his body was burned.[27] In 1741, Palma was scandalized when a well-respected naval officer ran off with a nun from one of the city's convents.[28] Apparently, she had dressed in a man's clothing, and they had escaped on a French ship. The two were soon caught and brought back to Palma as criminals. The nun was stripped of her veil and sentenced by her order to a life of seclusion and silence. Her suitor was condemned to death. As he was marched through the streets of Palma to his execution, he cried for God's forgiveness, held high a crucifix, and furiously beat his chest.[29] Then, with the condemned man "kneeling with his neck on the block," the executioner cut a rope, causing a huge knife to fall on the officer's neck; his head was severed violently.[30]

-»※«-

Serra's maturation as a priest and professor during the 1740s occurred against a backdrop of deepening political, economic, and demographic crises in Mallorca. As the island suffered one calamity after another, the joyful processions of the 1730s gave way to doleful public prayers in the face of drought, cold, famine, disorder, and political repression. These crises were part of a larger, continental catastrophe, but Mallorcans suffered more than the rest of western Europe because of the island's inadequate agricultural production, the choices of its political leaders, and the imperial ambitions of the Bourbons. Mallorcans cheered the successful invasion of Oran, but they lamented other moments of Bourbon adventurism that seemed of no benefit to the island and a clear detriment to its inhabitants. The 1740s may well have been the most difficult years in Mallorca since the Black Death of the Middle Ages.

To a great degree, the terrible events that occurred in Mallorca in the 1740s resulted from a quick and temporary shift in the earth's climate and weather patterns.[31] Typically, winters in western Europe are moderated by cool ocean air. But in the 1740s dry and frigid arctic air settled over much of the continent, decimating agriculture across much of Europe. As a result, there was widespread unemployment in rural areas, and in cities industrial production came to a halt.[32] The unemployed huddled in chilled and crowded rooms, hastening the spread of epidemic disease. In Mallorca, a land with a chronically unreliable agriculture, an urban population that raised little of its own food, and a high percentage of rural people working land that was not their own, the 1740s proved nothing short of catastrophic.

Typical of the period were heavy snows that blanketed the island, even Palma.[33] In the slightly elevated agricultural plains, fig trees, olive trees, and fruit trees were destroyed. It was often so cold and windy that Mallorcan fishermen were unable to take to the sea. Food production on the island stalled, and baked goods other than bread—probably always a luxury—grew increasingly rare and expensive. Peasants who tried to get into Palma to sell food were arrested or turned away, suspected of being beggars or carriers of disease. Hunger stalked Palma and the rest of the island. These were hard years even within the convento, where food was rationed. And in

1744 an epidemic tore through the island, killing perhaps ten thousand people. Mallorcans tried everything to stave it off, but bleeding, purgatives, and an assortment of homemade concoctions all had no effect; most of the sick died within five days of showing first symptoms. Survivors faced unprecedented chaos. For instance, one piece of land and a vineyard in a rural community were said to have changed hands eight times in twenty days.[34]

As famine and illness settled over Palma, the government rationed wheat and outlawed large gatherings of people. By 1748 it was illegal to feed barley to cattle, for by law it had to be provided to bakers.[35] Soldiers were put in charge of the distribution of baked goods, and bakers who prepared unauthorized types of bread were subject to the death penalty. The bishop of Mallorca even went as far as declaring that Catholics could eat meat during Lent. In these years Serra was among the general procession imploring God to halt the strong winds that were preventing ships from sailing in search of provisions for the island. And he was among the Franciscans who marched through Palma in 1749 praying for rain and the end of the plague that continued to thin Palma's population. As one resident in Palma wrote of these years, "It was pitiable to see young women and mothers with three or four children asking for alms . . . No one had money; the craftsmen were unemployed. The rich could not collect their rents. Everyone was in the greatest misery. Greater were the number of homes that lived on one meal a day than those which enjoyed two and fortunate were the ones that could enjoy even one warm meal a day."[36]

Compounding the suffering was a government that seemed corrupt, callous, even cruel. Bourbon officials were deaf to Mallorcans' calls for aid. The imperial government even diverted wheat bound for Mallorca to feed its soldiers and enrich favored merchants. It also raised taxes throughout the 1740s, only further unsettling the island. But it was the Bourbons' impressments of Mallorcan men into their military that most enraged the island. When Ferdinand VI assumed the throne in 1746 and then promptly intervened in the War of Austrian Succession (1740–1748), he needed soldiers, and no volunteers could be found. In January 1747 some fourteen hundred men—young and old—were arrested in Palma and the countryside and sent to fight for Spain in Naples. The arrests continued through late spring. Apprentices were seized, and if there were none to be found, older artisans were taken. Teachers were forced to turn in lists of their students. Workshops closed, and soon only little children were found in schools. Even newlyweds and men training for the priesthood were caught up in these dragnets. As one contemporary chronicler wrote, this period was the "saddest" yet in Mallorca's troubled history.[37]

⤛⁕⤜

It was in the middle of this terrible period, in the winter of 1744, that Serra was invited to give a weeklong series of Lenten sermons in Palma's Convento de Santa Clara.[38] These sermons, copies of which have survived to this day, offer a sense of Serra's learnedness, the level of emotion he brought to his preaching, and the type of God he believed in. They show that Serra attempted to "convert" his listeners through personal appeals and familiar metaphors and demonstrate his conviction that everything, from the human body's design to what he saw as God's punishments, had a holy purpose. Each sermon encouraged the listener to climb one of what he believed were the "five steps of the ladder or staircase of divine softness."[39] (Unfortunately, the fifth and final sermon is missing. It likely dealt with penance and confession and what Serra took to be their curative effects on the soul and conscience.) Each of the sermons stands on its own, but together they are clearly a response to the troubles of the 1740s, one unified by Serra's belief in a just and loving God, one whose everything is "sweet and soft."

In the first sermon, given on his first night at the Convento de Santa Clara, Serra urged, cajoled, begged, coaxed, and pleaded with his listeners to "taste and see" the Lord.[40] He argued that the Lord has a good and benevolent disposition. He is "soft," and his sweetness is almost as addictive as a mother's milk. While a harsh temper rushes and upsets everything and "usually ruins it," a good disposition, by contrast, "arranges everything peacefully, softens everything, and attracts everyone with its love." Furthermore, the Lord, Serra suggested, talked to people through two voices: an interior voice, one that entered the heart; and an exterior voice, which entered through the ear and came from the minister. Serra urged his listeners to be attentive to the softness of both voices, reject all earthly things, and begin to ascend the spiritual staircase of glory.

On the following night, Serra moved to how "soft" and "light" are the "yoke"—by which he meant the burdens and constraints—of holy and divine law. "Today, Christians," Serra stated, "I wish to show you that the Law that the Lord has given is very soft and easy to keep."[41] Serra posed a question: "What is easier, to live a good life or a hard one?" He then argued that contrary to common belief, it was easier to live a life in accordance with the Lord's precepts than one in violation of them. What was thought to be harder by those who did not know the Lord was in fact easier for those who did.[42] The solution to this contradiction, Serra revealed, was that the way to a holy life was only called narrow because it seems to be, but in reality it was not. "Why," Serra then asked, "do you not try to taste the way of the Lord?" Quoting Saint Augustine, Serra offered his proof of his argument: "For those who live loving the Lord, the ways of the Lord" "are soft and light."[43] Serra then invited his listeners to discover the gentleness of the "yoke" of the Lord and the "softness" of his law. Why is it soft and sweet? Serra asked. Because it comes from God and because it is the road to eternal salvation.

On the third night, Serra turned to another seeming contradiction, one that would have been on the minds of Mallorcans in 1744: If the way of the Lord is soft and sweet, why does he send his children so many "sufferings" and "labors"? Serra opened with a wry acknowledgment of the increasingly oppressive policies of the Bourbons, and of Mallorcans' true monarch:

> The splendid and vibrant voice of a bugle should ring, today, in this temple, before I start my prayer because I come to make a public announcement, to publish a royal edict. Start congratulating yourselves, happy subjects of that monarch that always demonstrates even more his goodness toward us and the tender love with which he loves you. What I have to announce to you is the great price of a coin with which you all should become rich, today. And what is this coin of such high price? Well, Christians, this coin is constituted by the

sufferings and labors that the Lord sends us in this life, and its value is so great that with it one can buy heaven's glory.[44]

The miseries of daily life, Serra explained, were gifts from God. Just as a doctor bleeds a patient and a carpenter shapes wood with a knife, so too God lovingly helps and sculpts the human. This kind of vernacular analogy would have resonated with Palma's residents. Their tribulations, said Serra, were the most evident proof that God loves his people "infinitely." Gathering a head of steam, he continued: "Well, then, faithful Christians! When you find yourselves pursued by the tribulations of this life, do not imagine that the Lord forsakes you, do not consider yourselves unfortunate; rather, on the contrary, consider yourselves the happiest, because then one can see, clearer than ever, how much the Lord loves you. Oh, if you knew how to appreciate it! How you would bear them with the greatest love, patience, and conformity with the will of God!" According to Serra, accepting that trials sent by "the Lord" are "soft" and of "infinite value" is the "third step in the stairway to God."[45]

On the fourth night, Serra explained that the "sweetness" and "softness" of the Lord extended to his forgiveness and mercy. Serra invoked Psalm 144: the Lord's mercy was like light because no matter how great the darkness (or sin), "in the same moment that the sinner goes, remorseful, toward God, that light puts it aside immediately." God's mercy was also like a fountain: it flowed and purified always, from the beginning to the end of time. Thus, for Serra, understanding the extent of God's mercy was the fourth step of the "mystic stairway to Heaven." Taking a somewhat dim view of human nature—or perhaps just to be certain that no souls were left behind on this Lent—Serra argued that God's mercy was not to be used "as a means to commit more sin." He concluded the fourth sermon by juxtaposing civil law, which could be unforgiving, with God's mercy, which in Serra's words was "very different."[46] With repentance, Serra stated, came mercy. Most likely, the acts of repentance, contrition, and confession were the focus of the fifth, missing sermon; for Serra, the sacrament of confession was the final step on "the mystical staircase."

These sermons make clear that Serra by his mid-thirties was a skilled writer and gifted orator. After years of study and of listening to the sermons of others, he had a broad set of examples on which to draw. His Lenten sermons were not dry scriptural exegeses or narrow theological arguments that he might have presented during his courses, but rather were intended to speak to his listeners in a practical way. Of course, nearly every one of his sentences was grounded in the Bible or in the lives of the saints, which would have impressed his more learned listeners.[47] But his occasional use of plain language, and the frequency with which he punctuated his sermons with direct pleas—"Oh, Christians"—surely helped him forge a connection with any Mallorcan audience, learned or not. Moreover, his pleas to "taste the Lord," to walk on his road, and to wear the soft "yoke" of his ways would have appealed to Mallorcans weary of life during the troubled 1740s. Serra's irreverent suggestion that the monarch was going to enrich them all through gifts of coins must have struck a nerve among those who had grown tired of the Bourbons doing just the opposite. The burden of Serra's message, however, was still a conservative one: he counseled acceptance of the social, religious, economic, and political order and all the sufferings that came with it.

As Serra's reputation as a speaker grew, he began to make more trips outside Palma to preach in the small towns and villages of the island. In the village of Selva during Lent in 1747, he was heckled by a woman he believed was possessed by the devil. "Keep on yelling! Keep on yelling! But you will not finish this Lent!" cried the woman.[48] The next year, in the spring, he was in the town of Alaró for three days of prayer for charity for the poor.[49] And then, in 1749, he was invited to give Lenten sermons in Petra's parish church.[50] He arrived in the Barracar in early February, ten days before Lent,[51] and soon joined the padres from the Convento de San Bernardino and the leaders of the communities of Villafranca de Bonany and Ariany in a procession and public prayers for rain.[52] He probably gave variations of the same Lenten sermons that he had prepared for the Convento de Santa Clara five years earlier. In the two decades since he had left Petra, Serra had acquired a formal education, impressive

titles, and great distinction, but he was still known by Petrans as
Delmau, the first of his alternate names, one that conjured a pre-
cocious child, not a mature, serious, and respected preacher and
professor. When local officials recorded the events in the town in
1749, they noted that "Padre Lector Junípero Delmau" had preached
among them in that year.[53]

Yet to Serra's eyes, Petra could only have appeared as a shadow
of its former self. He visited with his parents, his sister and her family, and maybe a few distant relatives, but by then most of his own
extended family had succumbed to either old age or disease. The
people of the Barracar he had known in the 1720s were mostly gone.
The streets and houses were still the same, but many of the voices
and faces would have been unfamiliar. In every way, Petra—like
Palma—was a community in crisis. Its population had declined from
about twenty-five hundred in the early 1720s to twenty-two hundred in 1744, and then again to about eighteen hundred in 1749. In
a sure sign of the crisis in the community—and the decrease in resources and the dampening of optimism that came with it—there
were fewer marriages every year: in 1741 there were thirty-six in
Petra; in 1749, only ten.[54]

Doubtless, Petra's decline was troubling to Serra, even though
he believed and urged others to believe that hardships were evidence of God's love. But even as Serra preached in Petra about the
need to accept the difficulties of life, and as he visited with his parents and sister in the Barracar, his mind was elsewhere. He had begun to listen more intently to his own heart, to the "interior voice"
of God, and had set in motion a great change in his life, one that
would take him far away from his native village and the land of his
birth forever.

The Serra who returned to Petra in 1749 was a well-established and
respected member of the Franciscan community in Mallorca and a
celebrated teacher at the Lullian University in Palma. And he was
still young, only thirty-five years old. In Mallorca men of his caliber
went on to become Franciscan provincials and to assume great powers in the Franciscan hierarchy on the island and perhaps even on

the mainland. As a rising Franciscan from Petra, Serra had as a role model and mentor in Father Antonio Perelló, a native of Petra, who had gone from humble origins in the Barracar to the pinnacle of Mallorca's Franciscan world. It had been Perelló who had admitted Serra to the Franciscan novitiate, given him the habit a year later, and facilitated his move into the ranks of the professoriat. Perelló could have blocked Serra's steady advance, just as he had when he believed that the small boy was too young for the order in 1730. But Perelló had seen talent and devotion in Serra, perhaps when the young Miquel Joseph was still at the convento in Petra, and he had supported Serra at every important point in his career. Perelló became more than Serra's superior; he shaped how Serra thought about himself and how he envisioned his life's trajectory.

So it was to Serra's immense sadness that Perelló died in February 1748, at the age of seventy-five. At the time of his death Perelló had already retired from teaching at the Lullian University and the Convento de San Francisco. He had taught the same morning course in theology that Serra now taught, and he had served three times as provincial, as well as in even higher positions of authority in the Franciscan hierarchy and as an examiner for the Inquisition. As a native of Petra, and certainly as one of Perelló's most accomplished acolytes, Serra was picked along with Fray Guillermo Rosselló, also of Petra and a professor of theology at the university, to offer introductory remarks and comments for a printed version of the funeral sermon for Perelló, given by the current Franciscan provincial, Fray Pedro Antonio Riera.[55] In his comments Serra lamented that with Perelló's death he had lost his "dearest friend, most prudent counselor, and most powerful support."[56]

Serra also remarked on Perelló's decision to live his whole life on Mallorca. Riera had likened Perelló to the phoenix, the mythical bird who is born on an island and dies in the nest of its birth. While trumpeting the accomplishments of Perelló, Serra noted that he could have achieved even greater glory had he been able to imagine a life beyond the limits of Mallorca. Serra also likened Perelló to the "bird of the sun," and he lamented that Perelló "could readily have gained more significant honors . . . in other places . . . with greater opportunities for showing off" his abilities had he not chosen to die in his "obscure fatherland" of Mallorca.[57] Serra was not exactly criticizing Perelló; rather, he was pointing out that Perelló's desire to remain in Mallorca had naturally circumscribed his accomplishments and fame.

With the death of Perelló, Serra contemplated what glories and holy deeds he might be passing up if he followed in the path of his mentor. He was, moreover, free from Perelló's expectations for him. So he was receptive when an interior voice—one that he believed was the voice of God—called him "to employ his talents to convert the gentiles, who, for lack of one to teach them the road to heaven," could not achieve salvation.[58] Apparently, this interior voice "of the Lord" rekindled desires that Serra had first felt during his novitiate but that had "become deadened" after so many years of study. Serra, however, was uncertain if he had correctly understood this interior voice. For resolution, he prayed to Mary and to Saint Francis Solano—the "Apostle of Peru"—that another Franciscan in the convent would hear a similar calling. Serra did not want to go alone; he wanted another friar "to accompany him in the enterprise and such an extended journey" so far from home.[59]

We cannot know exactly when Serra began to ponder going to Mexico, or New Spain as the colony was called, but it might have been in the spring of 1748, only a few months after the death of Perelló. The Franciscan missionary colleges of Santa Cruz in Querétaro and San Fernando in Mexico City had commissaries in Spain recruiting missionaries, and in July of that year, while he was in Petra, Serra made the unusual choice of preaching about Saint Francis Solano. Evidently, just as he was coming home to Petra, he was seriously contemplating leaving Mallorca forever.[60] Or perhaps it was his thoughts of leaving Mallorca that led him back to Petra one final time.

While he was awaiting confirmation from God of his call to New Spain, Serra confided in no one. The topic of his sermon in Petra may have hinted at his plans, for Raphael Verger, one of his colleagues at the convento in Palma, somehow heard that a member of the community desired to go to New Spain. Verger approached his friend Francisco Palou, Serra's most dedicated student, to discuss the rumor. Neither Verger nor Palou figured out who this person might be, but as they discussed the matter further, both felt themselves called by God to go to New Spain as well. Verger was unable to leave the convento at the time because of his teaching duties, but Palou, who was not to begin teaching until the fall of 1749, could more easily follow his heart. He felt, however, that he could not make the decision to leave the convento without first talking to his teacher and mentor.[61]

Palou gathered his courage and revealed his heartfelt desires to Serra, who broke into tears of joy: he believed that his prayers had been answered. Serra then unburdened himself, telling Palou that he was "the one who" intended "to make this long journey" and that he would have been "sorrowful" to go without a companion.[62] Serra had apparently always believed that Palou would be interested in going to New Spain, and now he concluded that it was God's will that they go together. The two devoted another week of thought and prayer to their decision, and then they requested permission from the Franciscan commissary general to join the College of San Fernando in Mexico as apostolic missionaries. But as the college's quota was already filled, Serra and Palou were put on a waiting list. Thus, with their futures undecided, Serra had headed to Petra for Lent, and Palou had remained in Palma, hoping for a letter saying that they would soon be traveling to Mexico.

Why Serra and Palou kept secret their intent to become apostolic missionaries in New Spain is not clear, for their new calling was not unusual and in fact very highly regarded within the Franciscan world. Franciscans were by vocation evangelical; they sought to convert others to a more dedicated form of Catholicism. In the thirteenth, fourteenth, and fifteenth centuries Franciscans had traveled throughout Europe giving popular missions intended to stir Catholic devotion. Other Franciscans had carved out careers preaching to those they deemed infidels, namely Protestants, Jews, and Muslims in Europe and Africa. After the discovery of the New World, the Franciscans' missionary efforts shifted, and huge numbers left their convents in Spain and elsewhere to become missionaries to Indians. Other mendicant orders, such as the Dominicans and Augustinians, also sent legions of missionaries to the Americas. So, too, did the Jesuits. By the 1680s there were more than forty-four hundred Catholic missionaries in Spanish America, working in seventeen different missionary fields.[63] Most of these missionaries had come from Spain.

In the first half of the eighteenth century, as the Bourbons sought to control the frontiers of their American possessions at minimum expense, they turned to missionary orders to pacify Indians.[64] During that period, more than four hundred Spanish Franciscans left Spain for Guatemala, the Yucatán, Querétaro, Zacatecas, Jalisco, and Michoacán, as well as Peru, Paraguay, New Mexico, and Florida.[65] Many of these men came from Mallorca, which had had since the days of Ramon Llull a strong tradition of exporting missionaries. Franciscans from the island had been pioneers in north-central New Spain as far north as Texas. Some had gone as far afield as the Philippines.[66] Mallorcan Jesuits also went in considerable numbers to South America in the seventeenth century and the first half of the eighteenth century. More than one hundred went to the Río de la Plata region of Peru and Bolivia between 1607 and 1767. Serra may have known that as recently as March 1734, nine Mallorca Jesuits had sailed for Paraguay and that in July 1745 another twelve followed.[67] When the Jesuits were expelled from these missions in 1767 in a wave of Bourbon reforms, more than two dozen Mallorcans were still there.[68]

The accomplishments of Mallorcan missionaries in the Americas varied. Some, like Antonio Llinás, became famous among the Franciscans. Many were very young when they left the island and made hardly an imprint on the other side of the Atlantic. Like Guillermo Vicens, a native of Petra, most labored in obscurity, and the only word that reached Mallorca of their lives in distant colonies was a death notice. Others, such as Antonio Oliver, who was born in Palma in 1711, were like Serra members of that city's Franciscan community and educated professors and scholars who chose to give up a promising career on the island for a difficult life as a missionary across the Atlantic. Oliver devoted his final decades to establishing missions outside Lima; when he died in 1787, his brethren gave him a formal funeral and buried him in an elegant marble sepulchre.[69]

Thus, while Serra would open up new frontiers in New Spain, in leaving Mallorca as a missionary he broke no new ground.

The Franciscans who left Mallorca in Serra's day took special inspiration from the writings of a Spanish nun, María de Jesús de Agreda.[70] Serra was particularly taken with her assertion that she had had a revelation from the Virgin Mary and had gone a seemingly impossible number of times to the region that is now the American Southwest.[71] She claimed to have been carried to what is now present-day New Mexico on the wings of Saint Michael and Saint Francis and to have been protected there by angels. Through divine intervention María de Agreda preached the Gospel in the language of the Indians. Most of the time in the New World she was dressed in a Franciscan habit. Sometimes she would make three or four trips in a single twenty-four-hour period.[72] While no Spaniard had ever seen her in New Spain and she was said to have never left her convent—for she bilocated—her stunningly accurate descriptions of the Spaniards and Indians of New Mexico won over many skeptics and detractors. Etched in the minds of men like Serra were her statements about what she had learned during her revelations, namely that God had ordained that "the Indians, on merely seeing" the Franciscans, "would be converted."[73] To Serra her writings were not the fantasies of a crazed nun but evidence that God favored the Franciscans in the evangelization of the New World and was aiding them in miraculous ways.[74]

In part because of the popularity of the writings of María de Agreda, the recruiter from Mexico City's College of San Fernando, Father Pedro Pérez de Mezquía, had secured the thirty-three missionaries he was looking for by the time that Serra and Palou expressed their will to go to New Spain. But not all of the volunteers had the courage to travel to unknown lands. In fact five of the Franciscan volunteers, all of whom hailed from the mainland of Spain, chose not to venture across the world "for fear of the sea."[75] As soon as Pérez de Mezquía learned of this, he wrote to Serra and Palou and told them to make their way as soon as possible to Cádiz, the port city on mainland Spain from which the Spanish fleet and merchant ships departed for New Spain and where the other recruits were assembling. But Pérez de Mezquía's letter never reached Serra or Palou. So he sent another. But again his letter did not reach its intended recipients. According to Palou, who heard from "a certain reliable padre in the convent," Pérez de Mezquía's letters had been "lost" "somewhere between the friary portal" and the cells of Serra and Palou. Pérez de Mezquía was forced to write a third time, and this letter finally got through, reaching Palou in Palma on Palm Sunday, March 30, 1749. As soon as church services were concluded, Palou hastened to Petra to meet with Serra. Upon learning the news, Serra was happier "than if he had received a royal decree naming him to a bishopric."[76] But he kept the news to himself. He remained in Petra through early April so that he could complete his Lenten duties and perhaps spend time with his sister, nephew, and aged parents. Palou, at his request, headed to Palma and arranged travel for the two to Cádiz.

After almost two months away, Serra returned to his community in Palma on April 8 or 9. Within a few days he would be gone again, this time for good. On April 13 he bid a tearful goodbye to the canon who had taken him in when his parents had delivered him to Palma in 1730. He said goodbye to all at the convento and went so far as to kiss the feet of all of its members, from the most senior Franciscan to the youngest novice. Then he and Palou walked from the Convento de San Francisco to the wharf, passing the cathedral and the palace of the Almudaina on the way. In earlier years the waterfront would have been bustling with merchants and stevedores, but in the spring of 1749 it was probably relatively quiet. The two Franciscans boarded the small vessel that would take them on the first leg of their journey. Serra knew that he would never return to Mallorca, and so did the men of the convento. One of his students and friends, Francisco Noguera, recorded in his notebook that Serra and Palou had left for Mexico on that day and that he "did not expect to see them ever again."[77] Like the men he admired most, Serra intended to die in a distant land as an apostolic missionary, either as a martyr or simply when his body gave out.

As Serra and Palou sailed toward the horizon, they must have felt a rush of emotion. Neither had ever been off the island. The gentle rocking of the boat in the Mediterranean, the sea air, the gradual shrinking of the island behind them as they sailed north toward the Spanish mainland—all of these would have made real what they had read in Franciscan chronicles. If his own testimony is to be trusted, Serra felt neither sadness nor regret over all he was leaving behind—his parents, sister, and few remaining family relations in Petra and, in Palma, the brotherhood of the Convento de San Francisco, the crowded streets, lively neighborhoods, glorious cathedral, and his colleagues and students of the university. He never gave a second thought to his decision to leave all of it behind. There could be no doubts: he was enacting God's will, just as he had heard it through a voice in his heart. Hindsight was akin to doubting the perfection of God's plan. Even as he made his permanent break with Mallorca and ventured into new lands across the ocean, he would never leave behind what mattered most to him: his Catholic faith. And the teacher would have at his side his favorite and most devoted student and ardent follower, Francisco Palou, who would become a lifelong companion on this journey so far from home.

PART TWO

Central Mexico

FIVE

The Voyage So Far

Junípero Serra left Mallorca with a desire to convert Indians to Catholicism and a belief that greater challenges and eternal rewards awaited him in New Spain. But when he sailed, he was unprepared for the practical challenge of winning others over to his religion. In its Mallorcan context during Serra's day, the term "conversion" most commonly referred to the process through which Catholics took up a more serious form of religious practice.[1] And Serra had been good at encouraging his countrymen to do this. But the apostolic missionary attempting to convince non-Catholics to see Jesus Christ as their savior needed a different set of skills. Serra was accomplished, but he was also a specialist. As a priest, he was exceptionally knowledgeable about Catholic doctrine and ritual, and he was an eloquent and effective orator. But the esteem that he enjoyed was specific to the world in which he was raised. As a priest and professor, Serra worked among people who had already internalized Catholic beliefs; Mallorcan Catholics over the centuries had progressively stamped out other religions that had taken root on the island. Serra seemingly had had no contact with anyone who held beliefs fundamentally contrary to his own.

Converting Indians in New Spain, Serra would eventually learn, was not simply a matter of showing the cross, as some believed, or of arguing logically and presenting self-evident truths in the manner of Ramon Llull. Conversion involved forming a personal connection with people from very different backgrounds and belief systems, gaining their trust, building something new out of or on top of indigenous practices, and offering material benefits, not just abstract promises of potential salvation or threats of eternal damnation. A respected professor who had spent much of his life in study and in conversation with Franciscans and other Catholics, Junípero Serra nevertheless still had much to learn.

-❊-

Serra and Palou did not sail directly to New Spain. On the first leg of their journey—a two-week voyage to Málaga—they traveled on an English cargo ship bound for London.[2] The ship probably originated in Menorca, an island east of Mallorca that had been held by the English since the end of the War of Spanish Succession in 1713. And almost as soon as the ship left Palma for Málaga, Serra began clashing with the captain over matters of faith. This very well may have been Serra's first encounter with someone who held outspoken religious beliefs that were different from his.

The captain was an English Protestant who was well versed in the Bible and confident in his own understanding of Christianity and in what he saw as the errors of Catholicism. But Protestantism was not merely different to Serra and all devout Catholics of the time. Protestants were not Christian cousins who shared similar beliefs and spiritual ancestors but dangerous heretics who needed to be confronted. That the captain was English didn't help the necessarily tense relations between him and Serra; Spain and England were constantly at war, and their peoples viewed each other with at best suspicion. The captain spoke Portuguese, a language similar to Spanish, and it was in that tongue he and Serra debated. A ship captain pontificating about the truth of Protestantism was an absurdity to Serra, who probably thought it made as much sense for a ship's captain to interpret the Bible as it did for a Franciscan priest to pilot a ship. In Mallorca, highly educated priests translated the Bible from Latin and interpreted it for their parishioners. To the captain, Serra's mocking dismissal of his readings of the Bible was a violation of decorum and custom, for on his ship he was accustomed to a good measure of deference. When the captain cited a passage of the Bible, Serra responded with a learned and logical refutation that he believed carried the day but that served only to anger the captain.

Palou wrote, in a hagiography of Serra composed and published nearly four decades later, that Serra's skill had left the captain "discredited and shamed."[3] More likely is that Serra's rebuttals had left the captain furious, "obstinate," and, in Palou's words, not "amenable to reason." At one point the captain became so angry that he threatened to throw Serra and Palou overboard; later he "placed a dagger" at Serra's throat, apparently, Palou assumed, "with the intention of taking his life."[4] Finally, in a fit of uncontained rage "the captain threw himself upon his bed." After these antics, Serra and Palou dismissed the captain as a perverse, angry heretic. Serra believed that he had won the debate. But the episode reveals just how unaccustomed he was to having his own beliefs and authority challenged. There had been no dialogue, just an unproductive argument between two men playing their roles as representatives of their respective religions and nations.

After a tense fifteen days at sea with the English captain, Serra and Palou arrived in Málaga. For five days they lodged in a Franciscan friary, waiting for a ship to take them the short distance to Cádiz. The journey there was seemingly uneventful. Sailing west from Málaga along the southern coast of Spain, they passed through the Strait of Gibraltar, into the Atlantic, and then north to Cádiz, where they dropped anchor on May 7, 1749. In the eighteenth century, Cádiz was the point of departure for Spaniards heading to the New World, and thus it was often a layover for missionaries awaiting passage to Mexico. Serra and Palou themselves would spend four months in Cádiz in anticipation of their transatlantic voyage. But theirs was a short wait compared with that of other Franciscans in their group. Twelve had already been in Cádiz for six months when they arrived.[5] A second group of some thirteen Franciscans would sail several months after Serra, and in this group at least five spent well over a year waiting for their ship.[6]

The Franciscans Father Pedro Pérez de Mezquía had recruited, and whom Serra and Palou met in Cádiz, came from all over Spain. Five were Mallorcan. Only two—Serra and Palou—had held professorships. The rest, with one exception, had been ordained relatively recently; most were in their mid-twenties. Serra, at age thirty-five, was the second oldest of the recruits. Father Manuel Cardona of

Valencia, who was just a year younger than Serra, was appointed president of the group. But Serra stood out for his experience and erudition, and before long he emerged as one of the group's spiritual leaders. Palou wrote that the others came to see Serra as the most pious of the lot; this might be true, but without a doubt the younger Franciscans would have deferred from the outset to a man of Serra's age and immense learning, believing that the latter was a mark of great piety.[7]

Not until his baggage was on board the ship that would take him to Mexico did Serra write to Petra and inform his family that he had left them forever. To have written earlier might have been a mistake, given the uncertainty of his departure date and the possibility that his ship might never sail. By the time he had reached Cádiz, Serra's parents knew of his plans, but not from him. On August 20, 1749, he wrote a farewell letter to his family and friends in Petra, who he believed were in "great sorrow." He sent the letter to his fellow Franciscan in Petra, Father Francisco Serra at the Convento de San Bernardino.[8] Fray Francisco was to read the letter to Serra's illiterate parents and to his sister and her husband. Serra insisted that only they hear its contents. He asked Fray Francisco to console his family members as they struggled with the news that they would never see him again "in this life." Serra wrote of his hope that he would perhaps be "joined" again with his family, "forever in future glory," after their salvation. He encouraged his parents and sister to take comfort in the same belief.[9]

With the exception of Serra's sermons of 1744, we have known him to this point only indirectly, through his accomplishments, Palou's writings, the places and social contexts in which he lived, and the various institutions to which he devoted his life. This very personal letter—it is the oldest piece of correspondence in his hand extant—tells us much about who Serra was. By age thirty-five his Catholic upbringing, education, and vocation had shaped his every thought, action, and emotion. His letter reflects his priestly demeanor and outlook and the degree to which Catholic belief permeated his being. Serra comes across as a devoted son, but his devotion is expressed through his fervent Catholicism. Serra did not reminisce about his parents' love for him or their contributions to his upbringing. He made no statement of appreciation for what his parents had done for him, nor did he attempt to repay an emotional debt, settle an account, or acknowledge his affection for them. Rather, he was writing with an eye to eternity—with concern for his parents' spiritual welfare and for what lessons they might take from his decision to go to Mexico.

Serra instructed Fray Francisco to remind his mother and father that he had left them to be an apostolic preacher, "the highest vocation they could have wished me to follow"; that they had little time for grief when compared with eternity; that he had left them for the "love of God"; that they should accept that he had left and should "bend" themselves to God's will; that they should not "fret" over his departure but "prepare themselves for a happy death which of all things in life is the principal concern"; and that they should "rejoice" in their son who is a priest and "prays for them every day." Serra believed that if he succeeded in his new calling, his prayers would "become more efficacious, and they [his parents] in consequence [would] be the gainers."

Serra wrote from his heart but in a way that was meant to appeal to logic. If only his parents could see the joy that filled his heart as his date of departure approached, "then surely they would always encourage [him] to go forward and never to turn back."[10] He asked Fray Francisco to remind his father of his visit not long ago, when his father had been so ill that he had received extreme unction. Junípero had sat by the side of his father who, believing that he was soon to die, told his son, "My son, let me charge you to be a good religious of Saint Francis."[11] Junípero explained that it was to fulfill his own father's wishes that he had set out on this course. "So do not be disconsolate," Serra urged his father, "when I am carrying out your will, which is one with the will of God."

In language that echoed his 1744 Lenten sermons, Serra, ever the didactic preacher, told Fray Francisco to let his parents "attribute what they now lament to no one but God, our Lord." In doing so, Serra believed, "they will learn how sweet is his yoke, and that He [God] will change the sorrow they may now experience into great happiness." To his mother, Serra's advice was terse: "In all our troubles say always: 'Blessed be God, and His holy Will be done.'"

To his sister, who also had apparently only recently recovered from a grave illness, Serra was instructional. She should "give thanks to the Lord for whatever He does. Now, whatever He wills is always for our good." If Serra saw a lesson for his family in his departure for Mexico, he also saw in his sister's return to health evidence of a larger plan: "In all probability the Lord gave her complete recovery of health so that she might be a consolation for our good parents, against the time I had to leave them."[12]

And then, after imploring his family to "be conscientious in attending church, in going to confession and receiving Communion frequently, in making the Stations of the Cross, in a word, in striving in every way to be good Christians," Junípero Serra drew the letter to a close by breaking with them. "A Dios, mon para. Good-by my dear father! A Dios, mon mara. Farewell, dear mother of mine! Good-by my dear sister Juana! Good-by my beloved brother in law." He urged his sister to take care of her son, little Miquel, and "to see to it that he becomes a good Christian and a studious pupil and [that] the two little girls grow up [to be] good Christians!" "Trust to God," Serra instructed his nephew and nieces, "that your uncle may yet be of some service to you. Good-by and farewell!"[13] He sent his final regards to a cousin, an aunt, and a few distant relatives. Aware of the challenges that lay before him, Serra asked the father vicar of the Convento de San Bernardino to pray to Saint Francis Solano for his safe arrival in Mexico. Serra never wrote to his parents again. His father would die in 1753; his mother the year after. Serra would, however, write once more to Fray Francisco and on two occasions to his nephew, Miquel, who would grow up to become a priest and achieve fame on Mallorca. By the time that Serra's farewell reached Petra, he was in the middle of the Atlantic, thousands of miles from Petra and still thousands of miles from his destination.

Serra and Palou boarded the *Nuestra Señora de Guadalupe* on August 29, 1749, with eighteen other Franciscans and sailed the following day.[14] The final papers approving his travel to Mexico described him as "thirty-five years old, of medium height, dark complexion, scant beard, and dark eyes and dark hair." Palou was "twenty-six years old, of medium height, dark complexion, and dark eyes and dark hair."[15] Just after boarding—once it was clear that they would not be returning to the community at the Convento de San Francisco in Palma—Serra told Palou that they should "stop using all of those titles of respect and superiority in regard to each other." Serra, now considering Palou his equal "in every respect," told his student to cease calling him "Master" and "Your Reverence."[16] Palou would not follow his request.

By Serra's day, transatlantic voyages had become somewhat routine. They were protracted and tedious, and at times frightful, but the merchant ships that carried men and goods to Mexico and then treasure back to Spain were by and large sturdy and reliable. Their captains and pilots knew the seas and the winds and sailed with a confidence won during the more than two centuries that Spain had ruled the seas. Serra and Palou sailed on a merchant ship whose seasoned captain, Juan Manuel de Bonilla, was part owner of the vessel.[17] It was probably due to Bonilla's experience, the *Guadalupe*'s size—it was officially registered at 311 tons—and veteran crew, as well as Serra's own constitution that Serra could describe his voyage as far as the Caribbean as "a happy one" with "few bad experiences."[18] Palou cast the adventure in a different light, suggesting that it was full of "inconveniences" and "scares."[19]

On September 8, a week out of Cádiz, the *Guadalupe* reached the Canary Islands, off the coast of Africa. Rather than stop for provisions, Bonilla sailed on. Weather permitting, Serra and the other priests celebrated Mass daily and heard confessions in the evening. Slowed by light winds, the voyage dragged on and freshwater ran short. With the Caribbean nowhere in sight, Bonilla ordered the ship's water rationed; until the *Guadalupe* reached Puerto Rico two weeks later, Serra and Palou were each allotted only one small glass of water with each of their two meals. Serra became so thirsty that he confessed he would "not have hesitated to drink from the dirtiest puddle in the road." He apparently ate little and talked less so as not to "waste the saliva."[20] Yet Serra was among the lucky. From time to time, a Mallorcan sailor on ship slipped him an extra ration of water.

On October 18 the *Guadalupe* arrived in San Juan, Puerto

Rico.[21] The port city had been founded in the early sixteenth century and had evolved as a way station for ships coming from Spain; in 1749, it had about four thousand inhabitants. Serra and Palou went to a "hermitage" for lodging, then to the chapel, where Serra announced that the Franciscans would preach a popular mission.[22] The Franciscans' mission—essentially a public revival—lasted for eight days. By most measures it was a success, although it left Serra humbled. The gatherings were well attended, and Serra and the other Franciscans heard confessions from the earliest hours of the morning until midnight. Yet Serra noticed that when Father Cardona, the leader of the band of Franciscans, preached, "the audience was shaken with tears, lamentations and beatings of the breast and [after he was done] for a long time the church still resounded with their shouts and cries." Incredibly, the people were still weeping when they returned to their homes. But when it was Serra's turn, though he focused "on the most terrifying subjects" and used his "voice to its fullest extent," "not a sigh was heard" from the pews. In his own estimation, his preaching was "straw," that of Cardona and others, "gold." He scolded himself as "one utterly lacking in interior fervor, being unable to find the right words to move the hearts of my audience"; he prayed that God would enable him to "become more useful in this higher calling."[23] While some of Serra's professed self-loathing was a typical demonstration of Franciscan humility, it is clear that the skills that had won him admiration in Mallorca were not well suited to an American audience. Unlike in Mallorca, the people of San Juan were not well versed in Catholicism and represented a medley of ethnicities and classes, and so a broad variety of life experiences and beliefs.

Still, Serra's two weeks in Puerto Rico were a welcome respite from the rationing of freshwater on the *Guadalupe*, the monotony of Cádiz, and the want of Mallorca. As a measure of their gratitude for the padres' work, the residents of San Juan showered the Franciscans with "chocolate, pipe tobacco and snuff and lemonade." Moreover, two Mallorcan gentlemen in San Juan bestowed upon the Franciscans "fruits, preserves, money for buying meat, tallow for candles at night . . . and articles of every description."[24]

Once the *Guadalupe* had been reprovisioned, it set off for Veracruz. But the ship ran aground leaving San Juan, and departure was delayed until November 2. A month after that date, the *Guadalupe* was within sight of Veracruz when a north wind began to blow. It grew in intensity and finally forced the ship from the coast. "For days," Serra wrote, "in that fierce storm we were lost far from our destination." It was a hurricane, and Bonilla had no choice but to head to sea. With the ship taking on water, the mainmast weakening, the strong winds showing no sign of abating, and the crew staging a mutiny "against the captain and pilots, asking that the ship be run ashore so that some at least might be saved," the Franciscans on board feared for their lives and devised a plan to save themselves.[25] Each wrote the name of his favorite saint on a piece of paper. The names were placed in a bowl, and the padres prayed, "to know, by drawing lots," who would be their "special patron and protector from among the saints."[26] All agreed that if they survived, they would offer a special Mass and sermon to honor the saint whose name had been chosen. Serra wrote Saint Francis Solano on his slip of paper. The winner, though, was Saint Barbara, whose feast day was in fact that same day, December 4. In unison the padres cried, "Viva Santa Bárbara!" According to Palou, at that instant "the tempest ceased."[27]

Two days later—ninety-eight days after it had left Cádiz—the *Guadalupe* anchored in Veracruz.[28] The ship's arrival in Mexico's principal port had come not a day too soon. Its mainmast was gone and its hull full of holes. Serra believed that it was only through the intercession of Mary and Saint Barbara that they had not been lost at sea. Several days later, when the Franciscans gathered to honor Saint Barbara, Serra—despite his sense that he had failed as a preacher during the mission in Puerto Rico—was asked to give the sermon. Preaching to his brethren, he was at his oratorical best. Palou reported that on that occasion Serra "preached with such perfection and eloquence that all his listeners were astonished . . . for up to that moment not the least of his great talents had been known."[29]

With the debt to Saint Barbara honored and repaid, and secure of his place among the Franciscans in Veracruz, Serra wrote again to Petra, informing Fray Francisco of his safe arrival in Veracruz. "My health is perfect, with nothing at all worth mentioning," Serra wrote. "I must have been the only one of all the religious—Franciscans as well as Dominicans and their servants—who did not get seasick. While the others were deathly sick, I hardly knew I was at sea. And that is a fact."[30] Serra was brimming with confidence and eager for new challenges.

-*⊱⊰*-

When Serra disembarked from the *Guadalupe*, he stepped into a world that had endured many successive cataclysms since the arrival of conquering Spaniards more than two centuries before. After Tenochtitlán fell in 1521 to Hernán Cortés's forces and tens of thousands of his Indian allies, Spain established a claim over the lands and peoples of Mexico formerly ruled by the Aztec state. In so doing, Spain gained nominal control over more than a million and a half people in the Valley of Mexico and perhaps twenty million others who had been tributaries of the Aztec. In an orgy of greed and exploitation, Cortés and his followers plundered Tenochtitlán. Hardly had the ruins of the great city cooled before Cortés pressed on, looking for other regions to conquer and then rule. Over the following decades, Spanish conquistadores tried to extend Spanish dominion over a vast expanse of Central and North America, from the Yucatán Peninsula in the south to Florida in the east, and as far north as New Mexico. Other Spanish conquerors explored and invaded South America. In all of these regions, Spaniards made territorial claims, hunted for treasure, involved themselves in native polities, forced Indians to labor and provide tribute, and attempted to establish Catholicism as the exclusive faith.

There are a number of parallels between how Spaniards governed Mallorca after they defeated the Muslims in 1229 and how they ruled Mexico after first arriving in the 1520s. In both Mallorca and Mexico, conquering Spaniards appropriated large tracts of land, formally established the Catholic Church, and incorporated the region into larger imperial frameworks of governance and domination. For the Mallorcan Serra, these parallels were really ironies. After all, Mallorcans had long resented the various imperial powers that had dominated them. But Serra, given the strength of his faith and mission, was almost surely oblivious to the contradictions that came with his presence in New Spain and his purpose there.

New Spain, however, was no Mallorca. In Mallorca, Spaniards expelled the majority of Muslims, whereas in Mexico they sought to put the vastly more numerous Indians to work for them. Through a system known as the encomienda, conquistadores received the right to extract tribute from specific Indians in a certain area. In return, the encomenderos were to protect their Indian wards from enemies and provide for their religious education as Catholics. As exploitative as this system was in its design, it was often more so in practice, becoming merely a cover for coerced labor. In the 1540s, the Spanish Crown sought to rein in the increasingly independent and wealthy encomenderos by limiting the heritability of their grants. By the early seventeenth century their numbers had dwindled from nearly one thousand to about fifty.[31] And by then the Catholic Church had emerged as a staunch defender of the rights of Indians against the encomenderos, who clerics asserted had done little to bring religion to those under their authority. In another major difference between Mexico and Mallorca, Spaniards brought enormous numbers of enslaved Africans to New Spain to supplement the labor of Indians in silver mines and on sugar plantations.[32] By and large the colony of New Spain was culturally and racially mixed by the eighteenth century; Mallorca, by contrast, had become homogeneous.

Indians everywhere in Mexico had met Spanish initiatives with a range of responses from resistance to accommodation, but they could do nothing against the diseases the Spanish brought with them. Epidemics had been common in Mallorca, but Europe had never witnessed anything like the decimation of Mexico's native population by smallpox, measles, plague, and various other diseases. In a catastrophe without precedent, the population of the Valley of Mexico dropped from between 20 and 25 million in 1519 to below one million in 1630.[33] By 1742, the population of Mexico had recovered somewhat, to around 3.3 million, but by then that number included roughly 400,000 Spaniards.[34] Additionally, with Old World diseases came horses, pigs, cattle, and sheep, animals that often ran wild and trampled native crops, polluted streams, and contributed to deforestation and to the general decline in the Native population's health and ability to feed itself. Spain's response to the damage it was causing was to force the survivors into larger settlements, where they could be taxed and ostensibly evangelized.[35] The Native communities that Serra encountered in 1749 were but a faint reminder of the sprawling and vibrant civilizations of Cortés's day.

Spain's conquest of Mexico was made possible by more than military might, disease, and the introduction of foreign and destructive species. The crusading Catholic Church played a key role as well. Soon after the European discovery of the Americas, the Church was emboldened by its victory over the Muslims in the reconquest of the Iberian Peninsula; just as Franciscans had been among the first to come to Mallorca, they were among the first mendicants to work in Mexico after 1521. In 1524 twelve Franciscan apostolic missionaries came to Mexico, seeing themselves as the potential catalysts of mass conversions that might usher in a millenial age and hasten the end of the world. By 1559, the mendicant orders had made a lasting mark on New Spain. Although there were fewer than one thousand Franciscans, Dominicans, and Augustinians in the colony at the time, they had established some 160 convents in Mexico alone. Supported by the military, the mendicants baptized more than four million Indians in Mexico, many of whom had received little Catholic instruction.[36] In a land as vast and complex as Mexico, Indians responded in a number of ways to the alien but very insistent newcomers: some resisted; some focused on the similarities between their own beliefs and those of Catholics; others saw the missionaries as defending them against the encomenderos; still others found refuge from a newly chaotic and deadly world in the certainties of Catholic belief.[37]

By the middle of the sixteenth century Spanish authority in Mexico was entrenched. In 1528 the Crown established an *audiencia,* or royal court, in New Spain. In 1535 it initiated the Viceroyalty of New Spain, a large administrative unit governed by a viceroy, a Crown official who had great powers but could be restrained by the judges of the Audiencia. Under successive viceroys the Crown created an expansive administrative system that tied the colony to Spain. Eventually, the Viceroyalty of New Spain stretched from Central America to New Mexico, California, and even the Philippines, but each of these regions, as well as many others in between, was governed by a lesser Crown-appointed official, whose authority was limited by the viceroy and various deliberative advisory councils. Finally, through the Real Patronato, which gave the Crown control over ecclesiastical appointments, the Spanish monarchs had the ability to control elements of the Church within New Spain.

The Spanish Crown extracted enormous amounts of wealth from New Spain in the sixteenth century, mainly in the form of bullion, but a century before Serra arrived in Veracruz, New Spain had become less profitable for the mother country. The Crown had barred the colony from producing finished goods, requiring that colonists purchase them from Spain. Officials in Seville controlled all trade between Spain and the colony; products bound for the New World had to be shipped on Spanish vessels manned by Spanish crews. The Crown enforced stifling monopolies on mercury, gunpowder, salt, pulque, and tobacco, levied a tax on everything sold, and took up to 20 percent of all wealth generated from the mines. Church tithes also consumed much of the wealth generated in the colony. In the seventeenth century, when the mines of New Spain began to produce less, when there were severe labor shortages, and when Indians resisted Spanish authority, the colonial economy became less profitable for Spain, a development that had severe ramifications as far away as mainland Spain and Mallorca.[38] The Bourbon Reforms, Spain's attempt to return New Spain to profitability for the home country, began to go into effect in Mexico just after Serra's arrival. And just as the shift from the Hapsburgs to the more centralized rule of the Bourbon state was traumatic for Mallorca, great changes also accompanied this development in New Spain. Nevertheless, from the coastal region of Veracruz, where Serra disembarked, to the mountainous lands north of Mexico City, where he would live for many years, the signs of the Spanish imposition of power were visible and unmistakable, even though Native customs, religions, and languages persisted everywhere.

❖

The main virtue of Veracruz, the official port of entry into New Spain, was that it was defensible; it was situated in a narrow channel protected by a massive fort on a nearby island. Because it had only one purpose, the city remained small.[39] Surrounded by swamps and wetlands, it was a notoriously unhealthy place.[40] Like many cities in New Spain, it was home to a range of rival religious orders— Dominicans, Jesuits, Augustinians, and Franciscans—and the town's residents were diverse, products of the collision of worlds that was colonial Mexico. More than half of the town's fifty-seven hundred residents were Indians, Africans, mestizos, or mulattoes.[41] The Spaniards were for the most part soldiers, sailors, and those who provisioned them, or men of the cloth. The rest of the town's residents were poor people of color who worked as common laborers. Their languages, cuisines, dress, and religious beliefs were unlike any Serra had ever encountered.

Serra did not linger in Veracruz, nor did the other missionaries. Palou became "deathly ill" as soon as he disembarked, and the Franciscans immediately prepared for the 250-mile journey to Mexico City. As a general rule Franciscans were supposed to travel on foot, so as to avoid any appearance of luxury and pride and to better emulate the life of Jesus Christ and his humble follower Saint Francis. The rigors of the transatlantic crossing and the unfamiliarity of the roads between Veracruz and Mexico City, however, made it acceptable for the padres to ride horses or mules. The royal treasury, which covered the costs of padres' travels from Spain to their destinations, provided transportation by "horseback and with some comfort" from Veracruz to their convents in Mexico.[42] Serra, however, feeling in good health and wanting to show others that he intended to live by the Franciscan rule even across the sea, chose to walk to Mexico City. He did so along with one other Franciscan, an Andalusian whose name is not known. Palou and the other eighteen Franciscans rode to Mexico City.

Serra began his two-week trek in mid-December. The lightly traveled road wound through forests and over barren lands, across rivers and between mountains. There were towns here and there, but for most of the way food, water, and shelter were hard to come by, especially for men who did not speak the languages of the local Indians.[43] Nevertheless, the road was clearly marked, and Serra and his Andalusian companion had a general sense of where they would spend each night. They left Veracruz on foot and "without any other guide or provisions for the journey than their breviaries and their firm confidence in Divine Providence."[44]

During this journey, the less familiar the landscape and the more challenging the route, the more Serra encountered manifestations of his Catholic faith. Ultimately, therefore, Serra's walk to Mexico City became a means for him to affirm his Catholicism amid his strange new surroundings, and his experience demonstrates the degree to which he believed in a divine presence and that there was divine approval for his work in Mexico. One evening, just beyond Veracruz, after a long day on foot, Serra and his companion lost their way. Darkness set in, and the temperature dropped. The town where they hoped to spend the night was across a river swollen by rains, and the padres were uncertain how or where to cross. They prayed to Mary, and soon "on the opposite side of the river they saw an indistinct figure moving." Serra, not believing his own eyes, called out: "*Ave María Santísima!* Is there a Christian on the other side of the river?" The figure answered that there was and asked Serra how he could help. Serra explained that they needed to know where to ford the river. The figure then led them to a safe crossing. Once across, they came upon the figure: he was a well-dressed and courteous Spaniard of few words. Leading them to his house, he gave them dinner and beds to sleep in. The following morning, after the padres got back on the road, they found themselves walking over ice; they realized then that had the man not provided them with shelter, "they would have perished from the rigors of the inclement cold." Serra believed it was only through the beneficence of Mary that they had "found that man in that place at such an unlikely hour and on so dark a night."[45]

The next day, when the two padres were overcome by thirst, fatigue, altitude, and a blazing sun, the man reappeared, gave to each a pomegranate, and then rode off on horseback. The fruit—one that in the Old Testament symbolizes the bounty of the promised land—refreshed them, quenched their thirst, and gave them the strength to finish their day's march. Serra believed that this man was either Saint Joseph himself or a "man whose heart this Saint had touched to do these acts of charity towards them." The following day, just when Serra and his companion were again overcome with weariness and hunger, the man once again reappeared, offering each half a loaf of bread, which they found delicious and refreshing enough to allow them to continue.[46] As these events suggest, to be a Franciscan in Serra's day was to believe more in divine intercession than simple good fortune: it was to see God's hand in everything. Mysterious travelers were saints or their emissaries. They were signs of divine intervention for those who "walked in the Lord."

Serra and his companion trudged on, fortified by the bread, but soon Serra's feet began to swell, and that night, when they staggered into the hacienda where they were to sleep, Serra could no longer stand. Palou wrote that the inflammation "was attributed to mosquito bites because of the great itching he felt."[47] The coastal lowlands around Veracruz were infested with mosquitoes and a small bug known locally as a *nigua*, a sand flea or a chigger. One traveler who passed through Veracruz in 1769 noted that chiggers were very common and that "the Indians have their feet badly marked by them."[48] In an attempt to recover, Serra rested a full day at the hacienda, but while asleep he "unconsciously . . . rubbed the one leg too much . . . so that a wound resulted which . . . lasted during all his life."[49]

Neither Serra's sandals nor his habit provided much protection for his feet and legs, and it is no surprise that he suffered from insect bites soon after he left Veracruz. Emulating the lives of the saints, he did little if anything to protect himself. Serra knew that Father Margil de Jesús had done nothing to prevent mosquito bites because he believed that frightening them away deprived them of food and distracted him from prayer.[50] The inflammation and infection that predictably followed Serra's self-neglect brought him discomfort, perhaps even pain, on and off for the rest of his life. But for Serra this was a pleasurable sort of pain; it was perhaps one of the only kinds of pleasure a Franciscan like him was allowed to know. For Serra, there was no better way to travel "the way of the Lord" than with a physical infirmity, especially one that was visible to all. Through passivity, neglect, or self-mortification, men like Serra punished their bodies in the belief that doing so allowed them to achieve and express a closeness with Christ's passion and final hours. Serra's inflamed and ulcerated leg was a means for him to affirm and model his own religious beliefs, just as Christ's suffering on the cross was the central edifying moment in Catholicism. Thus, even after his injury, Serra never wore anything on his feet other than sandals, arguing that he traveled better with his feet and legs bare.[51]

As Serra and his companion ventured farther inland, toward the town of Xalapa, a regional trading center situated well above sea level, they passed through villages, cultivated fields, and a landscape that was increasingly dominated by the soaring volcanoes of central Mexico.[52] Roughly forty miles from the capital city, Serra caught his first glimpse of what the Spanish knew as the Pico de Orizaba, the highest volcano of Mexico, whose summit rises to 18,500 feet. On December 31, 1749, Serra and his companion spent the night at the sanctuary of the Virgin of Guadalupe just outside the City of Mexico. According to Catholic belief, it was on a nearby hill that in 1531 a dark-skinned Virgin Mary had appeared before the Indian Juan Diego, thereby cementing in the minds of Spaniards and a good number of Indians that Catholicism was destined to become the religion of Mexico. On the morning of January 1, 1750, Serra and his companion "said Masses of Thanksgiving" in the shrine of the village Tepeyac. They thanked the Virgin for the safety of their journey, and then they proceeded into the City of Mexico. Serra had traveled more than seven thousand miles from Mallorca. He arrived in Mexico City fully convinced that in the New World as in the land of his birth, the saints and the Virgin Mary were ever present and that Catholicism was the one true religion.

Mexico City, like Palma, was a religious, economic, and administrative center, only a much larger one. Its people, size, grandeur, and setting made it unlike any place Junípero Serra had known. Long before Spaniards had come to Mexico, Tenochtitlán was already one of the world's great cities. It had been founded in the distant past by warriors from the north, who went on to extend their dominion over much of Mexico. By 1519, Tenochtitlán was home to perhaps 250,000 people; another 150,000 lived in the immediate surrounding areas. It was in Mexico City that the rulers of the Aztec lived; it was from there that they oversaw the vast system of taxation and tribute that brought enormous wealth to them and their city; and it was there that for centuries the Aztec religious elite had overseen the various rites of worship that sustained their world.

Much of the city—especially its sacred sites and monumental buildings—was targeted for destruction by the Spaniards during the conquest. In an attempt to wipe out native beliefs and practices that they took to be barbarous and savage, Spaniards razed temples, palaces, and public buildings. Then they put the Indians to work building new palaces, churches, and government buildings often atop the conquered peoples' sacred sites (just as the Spaniards had done in Palma). By the middle of the sixteenth century, Mexico City was the seat of New Spain's political and religious leadership. It was the home of the viceroy, who governed the colony with his advisers, the archbishop, who oversaw the Catholic Church in Mexico, and the merchant class that dominated the economic life of the colony. In the decades after Tenochtitlán fell, Spaniards, using untold legions of forced Indian laborers, drained some of the wetlands in the city, converted many of its canals into roads, and rebuilt the town according to a grid pattern mandated by the king. But during the same era, the city's residents were dying off; disease, dislocation, and overwork took a very heavy toll.[53] By 1610 the Indian population of Mexico City had fallen to thirty thousand.[54]

In 1750, when Serra arrived, the city's population had started to grow once again and was roughly equal to that of Mallorca. Of the hundred thousand or so people in Mexico City, some fifty thousand were Spaniards, forty thousand were mestizos, mulattoes, or Africans, and the rest were Indian.[55] The city still sat on an island in the middle of a large lake; its inhabitants traversed the city via canals, causeways, and avenues. Unlike major European cities, Mexico City was not surrounded by a defensive wall. This made it easier for Indians from the countryside to enter the city to sell their wares and produce.

On his journey from the shrine at Guadalupe to the College of San Fernando, Serra traversed the whole city and experienced firsthand the sights and smells of the burgeoning capital as it awoke. He walked by or through the numerous outdoor markets that sustained the city; one contemporary of Serra's estimated that in 1750 the city's inhabitants each year consumed some 300,000 sheep, 15,500 cattle, 25,000 pigs, 2 million arrobas of flour, and 15,000 fanegas of corn, as well as innumerable quantities of fruits, beans, fowl, and fish.[56] After witnessing famine upon famine in Mallorca, Serra would have been struck by Mexico's bounteousness.

Serra walked across Mexico City that morning on streets that were for the most part wide and straight but "dirty, muddy, and poorly cobbled."[57] People thronged the streets, as did their animals, especially horses and dogs. Water carriers and porters were ubiquitous, and many would have already begun their day when Serra was making his way through town. The workshops of artisans, such as painters, carpenters, and leather workers, would have opened for business and spilled out into sidewalks and streets, and virtually everywhere, in stalls, porticoes, and street intersections, petty merchants would have been getting ready to sell candies, toys, serapes, tools, and hats; similarly, vendors would have been preparing atole, tamales, pastries, and hot chocolate. Had Serra come to town later in the day, he would have been captivated and perhaps alarmed by the performers—acrobats, tightrope walkers, and puppeteers—who worked in the streets and the great number of pulquerías, the small establishments that sold the alcoholic beverage favored by the people of Mexico as well as poor Spaniards and mestizos. In time, in the 1760s and 1770s, the Bourbons would try to crack down on what they saw as the licentious street culture of their most important colony, but when Serra arrived, Mexico City's streets were still in their full postconquest glory. Funeral processions were common, while lovers courted in the streets and plazas and, if so inclined, escaped to the darker corners of town, especially the sheltered porticoes of the religious convents, for trysts.

If the street culture bespoke the city's plebeian aspects, its grand avenues, paseos, and monumental buildings signaled to Serra that he was in an imperial center, not a colonial outpost. The Plaza Mayor in the center of town was grander than any town square in Mallorca. And while the cathedral was not the architectural masterpiece that was the cathedral of Palma, it was nevertheless enormous and elegant. Its interior was spectacularly adorned with paintings and sacred ornaments imported from Spain or made of gold and silver plundered from the Aztec or extracted from mines in the north. Across from the cathedral stood the imposing Palace of the Viceroy and the offices of the powerful men who ran the colony. Scattered about town were other impressive and notable buildings, including those of its university. The city, however, had been built upon the unstable ground of a lake bed,[58] and many of these buildings, including the cathedral, had begun to sink into the ground.

Mexico City also bore the unmistakable imprint of the Catholic Church. The city itself was divided into parishes—some inhabited by Indians, others by Spaniards—each with its own church and priests. And everywhere, as in Palma, there were additional churches devoted to specific saints and convents run by the religious orders. By 1750 there were at least eighty-four churches in Mexico City, and all the major orders had a strong presence; the Franciscans alone maintained ten convents. And as Serra headed across town, he would have been heartened by the regular and frequent tolling of church bells, announcing the time of day or the onset of religious observances.

Serra's ultimate destination that morning, the Franciscan convent at the College of San Fernando, was on the edge of town, beyond the Alameda—a great parklike walkway—and in the Spanish parish of Santa Veracruz.[59] A little after 9 a.m., he and his companion completed their trek. They rang the college's doorbell to signal their arrival, but the padres were still at morning prayer. Serra went straight into the church of the convent to offer prayers of thanksgiving for the conclusion of his journey. Soon after, he was given a warm welcome by Father José Ortés de Velasco, the guardian of the college, who himself had missionized among the Indians of New Spain, and by Father Diego de Alcántara, one of the founders of the college.[60] Fray Diego greeted Serra with familiar words of admiration: "Would that someone would bring us a forest of junipers." With the characteristic humility and self-abnegation that led him to sign his early letters "Junípero Serra, a most unworthy priest," Serra replied, "Reverend Father, our Seraphic Father did not ask for this kind, but for others very different."[61] To a remarkable degree, Junípero Serra was now back in a familiar world, the one that he had known since his days as a novice on the outskirts of Palma in the fall of 1730. A schedule of daily prayers, Franciscan brotherhood, and the companionship of Francisco Palou—these would again constitute the foundation of his daily life, as they had in Mallorca. The Protestant ship captain who had so frustrated him at the outset of his journey was now but a distant memory.

SIX

The Sierra Gorda

Serra arrived at the College of San Fernando in Mexico City on January 1, 1750. Ideally, new recruits spent two years at the college while their superiors determined their fitness for missionary life.[1] Unexpected developments would shorten Serra's stay to only five months. As in Cádiz, he spent his time in Mexico City in preparation for a new journey and for the work that would await him at the end of it. He integrated himself into his new Franciscan community, read widely, prayed deeply, and learned about Indian missions from veterans of the frontier at the college. He would soon head off to the Sierra Gorda, a region north of Mexico City, where he would bring focus to the century-old attempt to convert the Pames Indians to Catholicism and European methods of agriculture. Serra would seek not only to reorganize the Indians' lives but also to manage the Spanish soldiers and settlers in the region. It would be a period of new challenges and of success and disappointment in equal measure. He would leave the Sierra Gorda an experienced administrator who knew how to organize missions and win the support of the Spanish political authorities. Although he would surpass his predecessors in his achievements among the Pames, he would not make the lasting and positive impact on their lives that he intended—far from it. And he would not yet have the chance to work fully as an apostolic missionary, spreading the Gospel among the unbaptized to fulfill his God's calling. Even after a decade of work in the missions of New Spain, Junípero Serra's greatest challenges and accomplishments would still be years away.

-※-

When Serra arrived at the College of San Fernando in 1750, it was relatively new, having been founded in 1733. Its central mission was to send missionaries into frontier regions to convert Indians, but it was established in the capital in response to the official view that Mexico City's population and surrounding communities needed more religious oversight than its parish priests could provide.[2] The college's cornerstone had been laid in 1735, and its church would not be formally dedicated until 1755. In 1750 the rising, unfinished church was nevertheless impressive; upon its completion it became the second largest in Mexico City, after only the cathedral. Eventually, the interior of the church would be adorned with magnificent and outsized paintings, and its altar decorated with statues of Franciscan luminaries. Next to the church was the padres' quarters, and just beyond that were fields and orchards that marked the city limits.[3]

Serra, like all the other new arrivals, was assigned a confessor. His was Father Bernardo Pumeda, a Spaniard who also served as master of novices. Serra asked Pumeda for permission to live in one of the small cells of the novitiate rather than in the main convent; in preparation for his work in the field, he wanted to live as simply as possible and immerse himself in daily prayers and discipline as if he were dedicating himself to Catholicism for the first time. Pumeda granted Serra the right to pray in the novitiates' compound, but the college rules specified that professed Franciscans were not allowed to reside with the novices.[4]

Liberated from the professorial and priestly responsibilities that had demanded so much of his time in Palma, Serra embarked on a rigorous regimen of prayer and study.[5] The college library covered all the branches of learning that Serra was most interested in: history, philosophy, theology, and moral theology.[6] Serra read anew about the accomplishments of the Franciscans in Mexico, mined books on sermons, preaching, and catechesis, and turned to specialized manuals for missionaries to Indians, such as Alonso de la Peña Montenegro's *Itinerario para parochos de indios,* the most influential field manual for the administration of sacraments to Indians. Montenegro was also the Franciscans' most important authority on the conversion of Indians.[7]

In words that Serra must have expected yet still found daunting, Montenegro argued that faith would reach the Indians' hearts "through the ears." Serra, therefore, would have to learn the Indians' languages if he hoped to convert them.[8] Montenegro also asserted that the whip was essential for the Indians' "devotion, decency, and good order."[9] Montenegro's manual and its teachings would soon be as important to Serra as his own breviary and Bible; before long he had acquired a copy of the manual for his own use.[10]

Serra availed himself of the leaders of the college, such as José Ortés de Velasco, the college guardian who had spent years in Indian missions. Midway through his Mexican "novitiate" the remainder of the Franciscans recruited to the college arrived from Spain.[11] At the head of this second group was Father Pedro Pérez de Mezquía, who had evangelized among Indians in Texas alongside Margil de Jesús. Pérez de Mezquía had also been a central figure in the Fernandinos' establishment of missions in the Sierra Gorda. Ortés de Velasco and Pérez de Mezquía would have informed Serra that Indians were like children, mired in the superstitions of their ancestors and easily tempted by the devil. The Indians could be converted to Catholicism, but only if they took up agriculture, which would domesticate and regulate their lives. The influential and fervent Margil de Jesús met with great difficulty in his attempts to enact this transformation in the north, but Franciscans like Pérez de Mezquía and Ortés de Velasco held fast to their beliefs and sought to apply them to Indians wherever they worked. Their views shaped those of the newly arrived Junípero Serra.

Shortly after the arrival of the second group of missionaries, Ortés de Velasco approached Serra and the other Franciscans at the college with an offer: volunteer for immediate work in the Sierra Gorda—an isolated region north of the capital where the college already had five missions—and he would waive the customary two-year term of residence in the college. With the recent and sudden deaths of four missionaries in the Sierra Gorda, the college had been relying on missionaries from another college to staff its own missions.[12] Serra volunteered immediately. Quoting from Isaiah, he said to Ortés de

Velasco, "Here I am; send me."[13] Out of the group of thirty-three Franciscans who had recently arrived at the college, Ortés de Velasco chose eight, and among them were Serra and the Mallorcan friars who had followed him to Mexico, Francisco Palou and Juan Crespí.[14] The oldest of the group, Serra was named president of the Sierra Gorda missions by Ortés de Velasco but declined the position, arguing that he had no experience working with Indians.[15] Nevertheless, there is no indication that anyone other than Serra was the Franciscan in charge of Santiago de Jalpan, the head mission in the Sierra Gorda, or had authority over the padres who ran the other four missions. Serra was, in fact, if not in name, father president of the Sierra Gorda from the beginning of his years there. And by June 1751, Father Bernardo Pumeda, in a letter to José de Escandón, identified Serra as the father president of the missions.[16]

In early June 1750, Serra and Palou set out from Mexico City on a journey through the often arid and mountainous lands between the capital and Jalpan. At the time, Jalpan had been an outpost of Spanish settlement for more than two centuries. Its small population was made up of Spanish and mixed-race soldiers and settlers, Pames Indians, and more acculturated Tlascalan Indians who had long ago been relocated there. Jalpan had its own presidio, or military fort, and the town and mission were relatively secure from Indian attack. Jalpan's mission both ministered to Indians and served as the parish church for the soldiers and settlers in the region. Escorting the padres north were Indian interpreters and a soldier, who had come from Jalpan with horses and mules. Unsurprisingly, Serra still chose to walk. Despite aggravating his leg wound, he reached Jalpan on June 16, with Palou at his side.[17]

In the earliest years of the Spanish conquest the Sierra Gorda was part of Nueva Galicia, an expansive administrative unit of New Spain centered on the provincial city of Guadalajara that encompassed the frontier region stretching from some 150 miles to the north of Mexico City to both the Pacific and the Gulf of Mexico. The Sierra Gorda itself was topographically varied, characterized by arid flatland, lush canyons, high mountains, and wild rivers all at once. It was home to the Pames and the Jonace, peoples who hunted, gathered, raised crops, and lived in small villages throughout the region. The Jonace were the less populous of the two and lived in the region between Mexico City and the Sierra Gorda. The Pames lived farther north, in the narrow valleys and mountains of the Sierra Gorda range. Before the Spanish conquest, the groups had been tributaries to the Aztec. While there are no reliable population figures for the Pames at the time of their first contact with the Spaniards in the sixteenth century, they numbered in the tens of thousands.

The Spaniards considered the Pames and the Jonace to be distinct peoples but nonetheless part of a larger group of Indians that they referred to dismissively as Chichimecas. The word is of unknown origin, but a widely held Mexican folk belief traces it to a Nahuatl expression meaning "dirty sons of dogs."[18] The term's widespread acceptance by Indians and then Spaniards suggests the degree to which the sedentary peoples of central Mexico viewed the nations of the north with derision. Spaniards in Serra's day saw these Indians in a similar light, for the northerners had none of the characteristics that Spaniards considered the hallmarks of a civilized people: literacy, domestic agriculture, fine clothing, and permanent settlements. To the Spanish the people of the north were barbarians who lived a desperate daily existence.[19] The Pames did, however, practice their own form of agriculture and inhabit semipermanent villages,[20] but the Spaniards still believed that they needed to be rounded up, moved to fertile valleys, taught the basics of communal agriculture, and indoctrinated into Catholicism.

For more than two centuries, the Pames had fended off the most onerous aspects of Spanish colonization. Many learned to speak Spanish and even went by Spanish names, but by and large they lived in their own villages and followed their own economic rhythms and religious beliefs. To a large degree the nature of their society, even as it invited Spanish condemnation, allowed them to avoid incorporation into the expanding Spanish imperial realm.[21] In fact, what the Spanish took as signs of stupidity and backwardness were in many ways part of a strategy of survival; the Pames—living as they did in a virtual non-state existence and producing little surplus—were not only less desirable targets for incorporation into New Spain's economy but also less susceptible to it. The Spanish would never bring the Pames fully into the fold of their civilization, but of all who tried to do so, Serra and Palou came closest to succeeding.

Serra would become famous for extending the Spanish frontier into California, but the Sierra Gorda of his day had been a site of missionary work since the early decades of the conquest two centuries before. For many of those years, Augustinians, Dominicans, and Franciscans vied for supremacy over the Pames, each finding little success. Missions and padres came and went; they were, respectively, poorly staffed and greatly outnumbered by settlers and indigenous peoples. But at the dawn of the eighteenth century, the Franciscans began to acquire a reputation for establishing missions that appeared to have a chance of bringing lasting change to Indians of the north. The Franciscans' progress can be credited largely to Fray Antonio Llinás, the Mallorcan who in the late seventeenth century revolutionized Franciscan missionary work through his founding and leadership of the apostolic College of Santa Cruz in Querétaro. Some of the first Queretan missionaries trained in Llinás's college were sent into the Sierra Gorda, where they made modest inroads into Native society between 1683 and 1740.

Frustrated with the slow pacification of the Sierra Gorda, royal officials appointed José de Escandón the head military official of the region in 1742 and in December of that year ordered him to end the jurisdictional quarrels between missionaries and stamp out Indian raiding that the Crown believed had undermined the region's settlement and economic development. Escandón had been a leader in the local military since the 1730s and had put down a Jonace rebellion in 1735 and 1736.[22] Most important, he knew the Sierra Gorda, was familiar with its topography and Indian populations, and had won the trust of soldiers as well as Franciscans. Franciscans from Llinás's college had developed a sterling reputation for their missionary work in the north; Escandón's efforts would allow them to dominate the Sierra Gorda, if only for a generation.

In January 1743, intending to formulate a plan to bring the Pames under the control of the Church and the Crown, Escandón embarked on a *visita* of the region with some fifty soldiers on horseback and two Franciscans from the College of San Fernando, Fray José Ortés de Velasco and Fray José García. Typical of a man of his place in Spanish society, Escandón wrote that the Pames lived "more like *fieras* [wild animals] than men."[23] At the *cabecera* of Jalpan, where missionaries had worked on and off for more than 160 years, he found "not even one who could make the sign of the cross."[24] None of the Pames at the mission knew the basic Catholic prayers of the *doctrina*, the daily recitations typical of missions. The local Indians did grow corn at least. The area had abundant sources of water, fertile soil, and plentiful trees, which Escandón believed would allow for the construction of homes and a permanent society. Escandón concluded that the Indians at Jalpan would quickly become productive cultivators of the land once Spanish techniques were introduced.[25]

At nearby Tilaco, which was visited by an Augustinian friar only once a year, Escandón found the mission in ruins—the church was nothing more than a flimsy and dilapidated hut—and the Indians largely untrained in Catholic prayers.[26] Escandón also visited three other sites—Agua de Landa, Tancoyol, and Concá—where there were Indians but no previously established missions; he reported that Pames were asking for padres from the College of San Fernando. Though somewhat remote, these sites were by no means beyond the reach of Spanish colonization. At Landa, for instance, a military captain, Don Gaspar Fernández de la Rama, had a rancho of "ganado menor" (sheep and goats), and at Concá he owned a sugarcane hacienda worked by some forty-six families (215 people in all, 71 of whom were his slaves).[27] Escandón quickly called for the Fernandinos to establish new missions at Concá, Tancoyol, and Landa and to replace the Augustinians at Jalpan and Tilaco.

The mid-1740s were an interesting period for the establishment of missions in the Sierra Gorda, for it was a time—certainly among the last—when religious and military officials in Bourbon New Spain were still working together to organize mission districts in frontier regions. At the same time, however, Bourbon officials were curbing the power of the Church and the religious orders elsewhere by secularizing missions. In this process missionaries gave way to parish priests drawn from the secular clergy; these priests administered sacraments but had little say in how Indians lived outside the church. After secularization, Indians would pay tribute to the Church and the Crown, something that was increasingly important to Bourbon administrators. Indians would also enjoy more freedom in just about every aspect of their lives. Thus, to help justify the new missions, missionaries and Escandón argued that they would be secularized within a decade of their establishment, knowing that this end would likely not be realized.

Escandón returned to the Sierra Gorda in the spring of 1744 to carry out his proposals. He was accompanied by his customary escort along with Fathers Pérez de Mezquía and Fernández de la Rama and a local official, the caudillo Mathías de Saldívar. Escandón instituted a Spanish process known as *congregación*, although with only limited success. The goal of the policy was to count all the local Indians, record their names and family relations in a census, and then relocate them from their villages to a central mission, such as Jalpan. Escandón dutifully created a household census of the Indians he intended to congregate at Jalpan, beginning with the current Pames governor, Don Agustín Pérez de la Cruz.[28] Two centuries into the Spanish period in the Sierra Gorda, powerful Pames men like Pérez de la Cruz carried Spanish names and titles, yet they were still tied to their indigenous communities. Despite his efforts, Escandón was able to relocate only about 50 Pames to Jalpan. In the belief that they would move permanently to the mission, Escandón had them build new houses and jacales immediately adjacent to the mission church. This small group did so with "resignation" and, according to Escandón, left "the wilderness they had inhabited."[29] But another 1,445 Pames stayed in their villages, some of which were miles from Jalpan; they would come to the mission only periodically.[30]

Under Escandón's plan, each year in Jalpan leading Indians would continue a practice that had been initiated earlier but carried out inconsistently: they would gather to elect from among themselves the *oficiales de república*, the Indian men whom Spanish officials would turn to when they sought to control the larger Native community. In most cases this meant the election to municipal office of those who were already held in high esteem by their people. At Jalpan some six days after the registration of the Pames in the census, Don Balthazar Coronel was elected and took the office of governor, replacing the man whose name had appeared above his on the census, Don Agustín Pérez de la Cruz. Don Lorenzo Torres, who traced his ancestry to the original Indian settlers of the region, was chosen to be first alcalde. Also elected were another alcalde, two alguacils, a regidor, and a secretary. Escandón exhorted them to work with the soldiers and missionaries.[31] He then repeated this process—the congregation of Indians and the election of their officials—in San Miguel de Concá, Santa María del Agua de Landa, San Francisco del Valle de Tilaco, and Nuestra Señora de la Luz de Tancoyol. By early May he had established five missions at which he had secured lands, assigned Franciscans from the College of San Fernando, and registered more than four thousand Pames.[32]

By the summer of 1745, Indians were regularly attending religious instruction at the missions Escandón founded, except when they were needed in their villages to tend to their communities' harvests. To the Franciscans, the solution to the problem of the Pames returning to their villages was obvious: get them to adopt European modes of agriculture. Whereas the Pames practiced slash-and-burn agriculture, the padres dismissed it out of hand. They insisted that the Pames work large communal fields with oxen and plows, believing that this transition "would completely destroy the Indians' custom of *sembrar en rozas* [slash-and-burn agriculture], which is the reason," Pérez de Mezquía argued, "that until now they have lived like savages." To facilitate this change, the padres introduced oxen at all of the missions; Indians at Jalpan had in fact begun to use these animals to plant fields of corn. But Jalpan was the exception.[33]

Pérez de Mezquía, on the heels of his own *visita* to the missions a year after they were founded, compiled his own plan for the missions, creating a regime that was still in place when Serra and Palou arrived in the Sierra Gorda in 1750. Indians were to assemble at the church every morning for prayer. Then, after the adults had departed for their work at the mission or in their milpas, the padres were to give the children five years old and above the same lesson morning and afternoon. Adult Pames who were not yet baptized—very few of whom came to the missions—Pames who wanted to marry, and those who were preparing for their Easter confession were also to be present for instruction morning and afternoon. This instruction was to be in Castilian, not the language of the Pames. On feast days all Indians attached to the mission were to attend Mass, and once their names were called from the mission register, they were to come forward and kiss the padre's hand. Pérez de Mezquía believed that unless the Indians were provided with food from the mission, they would spend their days "wandering" the countryside in search of food and thus never come to catechism or Mass. Therefore he ordered the padres to devote their annual stipend of some two hundred pesos to the purchase of "tools and other things needed to carry out effectively the planting of crops" in mission fields. Furthermore, the padres were to acquire cattle, oxen, and other livestock, "so that from these sources the Indians could maintain themselves, living in community as was practiced at the beginning in the Church."[34] Pérez de Mezquía hoped, in essence, that the Indians would live in a manner similar to the first Christians.

In December 1746, Fray Ortés de Velasco reported that steady progress was being made in the missions. Notably, the padres had learned the Pames' language. According to the Pames' interpreters, the Franciscans spoke the language quite well.[35] As Pérez de Mezquía had envisioned, the Fernandinos had used their stipends to purchase livestock, and by then each mission had twenty oxen. Nevertheless, the mission fields still did not produce enough grains to feed the Indians, and the padres continued to give the Pames corn, beans, and any other food they had.[36] By the end of 1748, when Father Ortés de Velasco compiled another report on the status of the missions, it was clear that the missions would not soon be thriving communities rooted in communal agriculture.[37]

When Serra and Palou got to Jalpan, they found that some Pames had embraced the Fernandino plan, but most had not.[38] From August 1748 to September 1750 the padres at Jalpan baptized 130 Pames, but only one of these was an adult; over the same period, the missionaries gave Communion to only sixty-two Indians at the mission, a sure sign that they believed that the overwhelming majority of Indians at Jalpan did not fully understand the sacraments. Disease also played a role in the mission's struggles. In the first five years of Jalpan mission, for example, 746 Pames succumbed to various epidemics.[39] A similar story was unfolding at Concá, Landa, and Tilaco, where absenteeism and disease thinned the missions and where the Pames paid little attention to the religious instruction the padres offered. At Landa some Indians had apparently memorized the prayers taught by the Franciscans, but most recited them without understanding or belief.[40] At Concá the population had fallen from 439 to 248, at Landa from 640 to 401, and at Tilaco from 749 to 416.[41] Overall, the population of the five missions had declined from more than 4,000 in 1744 to 2,600.[42] For the padres, the situation was most bleak at Tancoyol, where one of the Franciscans had recently died in a fire that had consumed the mission itself. There, the small number of Pames who stayed at the mission, one padre reported, listened to Mass "without objection, but few believed it."[43]

The missions—but, more important, the Pames affiliated with them—were in crisis. Pames families had become smaller and fewer with the spread of disease and the dislocations resulting from the Spaniards' attempts to relocate them to the missions. In the two and a half years or so before Serra arrived at Jalpan, an astounding 90 children and 270 adults had died and been buried at the mission. By the fall of 1750, 40 percent of the local Pames families were childless, one-third had one child, and only about one in ten couples had more than one child living with them. The number of widows and widowers had increased from forty-one to fifty-seven, and, perhaps even more significantly, dispersed among the population were some thirty-one orphans.[44]

Similar developments undermined the Pames communities affiliated with the other missions, and the increased mortality in the missions profoundly affected the Pames' economic and social organization.[45] Many couples had no children to help them work their milpas, and many children had no parents to feed them. At Tilaco alone, about forty children were being raised by widowed parents. One wonders about the degree to which the Sierra Gorda missions under the Fernandinos had begun to function as day-care centers and orphanages. And though all this suffering must have troubled Serra and the other recently arrived Franciscans, they must have believed that the cracks in Pames society presented them with the opportunity to remake some, if not all, of it.

Traditionally, assessments of Serra's accomplishments in the Sierra Gorda have rested on the writings of Palou, who claimed that Serra baptized large numbers of adult Indians in the Sierra Gorda, left no Indians in the region unbaptized, and brought every one of them to a life "under the bell," meaning to one of the Franciscan missions. But these claims are impossible to corroborate. There is no evidence that Serra baptized large numbers of adult Indians in the Sierra Gorda. The work of missionaries in the region in the early decades of the eighteenth century, the 1744 head counts and congregations of Escandón, and the work of the Fernandinos from 1744 to 1750—combined, these left very few adult Pames unbaptized in 1750. Moreover, while hundreds of children were baptized in the Sierra Gorda in Serra's years (and we know that he baptized some of them himself), between 1744 and 1758 only 148 adults were baptized in all five of the missions, a very small number.[46] Serra spent most of his time at Jalpan, so it seems unlikely that he would have baptized many of these Indians. Moreover, a report on the state of the missions compiled in 1764 reveals that between October 1758 and sometime in 1764, the baptism of small numbers of adults in the Sierra Gorda missions continued, but at a very slow rate, evidence that not all the few remaining unbaptized adult Pames of the region were swayed by Serra and his colleagues.[47]

Likewise, there is little evidence to support Palou's claim that by the time Serra left the Sierra Gorda, all the Indians there had been "civilized" and were "living in towns under the bell."[48] The expressions "by the bell" and "under the bell" were how the Franciscans described Indians who lived at the mission and followed the sort of disciplined and regimented life the padres prescribed for them. If Indians lived "under the bell," they did not just live in earshot of the missions; they lived as Catholics according to the Fernandino plan. But what the padres called fugitivism—Indian flight from the missions—was a constant challenge, one that Serra could not resolve, even though doing so was one of his highest priorities. In fact, Serra had urged the soldiers posted at Jalpan to retrieve Indians who had little inclination to live at the missions.[49] This was tried, but the often brutal tactics employed by Spanish soldiers did little to thwart Indian fugitivism. In 1762, long after they had left the region, Serra and Palou both signed a report explaining that on many occasions soldiers went in search of Indians in the hills and mountains and had returned with numerous "lost sheep."[50] In 1755 soldiers had brought some 162 fugitive Indians back to the missions, in 1756 some 135 were brought back, and in 1757 around 100 were returned to the missions. The problem, though, did not end then, as in 1761 another 30 were brought back.[51]

Since most of the Pames in the Sierra Gorda had already been baptized by 1750, Serra's main tasks were to convince Indians to stay in the missions and practice Catholicism daily, improve the physical structure and interior of the mission churches, and manage Indian-settler relations. For a Franciscan whose main experience had been teaching theology and philosophy and delivering learned sermons, these were tall orders. What Serra lacked in knowledge of the Pames and their language, however, he made up for with optimism.[52] He also brought confidence, strong leadership, and excellent administrative skills to his work in the Sierra Gorda. Ultimately, Serra made his mark on the Sierra Gorda through his more intensive application of the Fernandino plan, his work to expand agriculture at the missions, and his role in the construction of new churches. All of this occurred during a period in which the population of the missions increased by nearly 35 percent, rising to thirty-five hundred from twenty-six hundred, on account of an increasing birthrate and an absence of disease. As a result, agricultural productivity rose during Serra's years. The missions began to store portions of the harvested corn and beans in granaries, allowing the padres to distribute daily rations to Indian families in an attempt to keep them at the mission year-round. When possible, if the padres could purchase items with surplus funds left over from their stipends, they distributed blankets, shoes, pants, hats, and wool.[53]

At the same time, Serra insisted that Indians in all the missions attend daily catechism as well as Mass on Sundays and Catholic days of obligation. Adults attended in the morning before work, and children in the morning and afternoon. At the center of this daily Catholic worship was the Corona de la Virgen Santísima, a rosary devoted to Mary. The missionaries also created bilingual confessionals and catechisms, and since all Pames spoke the same language, these were put to use across the region. Serra always maintained that he was terrible with Indian languages, so the bilingual confessionals and catechisms were probably created by Indian interpreters.

Serra's insistence that the Pames adopt European agriculture was not just about producing food but also about putting Indians to work and keeping them at the missions, and his program for the construction of churches had the same purpose. Serra wanted Indians to practice Catholicism in beautiful structures, but he also believed that building churches would "wean" the Pames "from the idleness in which they had been raised and had grown old."[54] Thus, as soon as the missions' agricultural program could sustain Indians at the missions year-round, Serra set out to build new churches. When he arrived, the physical state of the missions was as varied and uneven as the Indians' own embrace of Catholicism. For example, at Jalpan the church was too small to hold all the people at the mission on feast days. But by the time Serra left the region, new churches were nearing completion at every one of its missions. These churches not only represented a transformation of the built environment— they stand to this day—but, in the eyes of the padres, cemented the place of Roman Catholicism in regional village life and gave evidence of the successful conversion of the Pames.

Serra played a major role in the reorganization of Indian labor that the building of new churches required. In Jalpan, he "broached the subject of their building a church of stonework," and the Indians "agreed to it, offering themselves to haul the stone (which was at hand) and all the sand, to make the lime and the mortar, and to serve as helpers in carrying it to the masons."[55] In the same way that the tillers of fields at Jalpan received special gifts from the padres for their hard work, it seems very likely that the Indian men who carried the stone and sand for the masons were responding to economic incentives from the padres. Building the church at Jalpan occupied the Pames during the dry season that typically runs from October to May, when Indians had no work to perform in the mission fields and the padres had no way to keep them around. The padres feared that during these months the Pames would leave the missions and return to the countryside, where they would descend into idleness and vice. Thus, the construction of the church at Jalpan was not just about providing a suitable place of worship for a growing community; for the padres it was also about finding another way to structure the Indians' time and to control them.

Given the importance that Serra placed upon the cultivation of "industry" among the Pames, it is no surprise that he himself worked hard on the construction of the church at Jalpan. As a Franciscan he delighted in labor that taxed his strength and challenged his body. He carried stones, made mortars "with the boys as if he were one of them," helped carry the timbers required for the building, and worked with masons to complete the walls. His small stature did not prevent him from taking part in the heavy work necessary to build the churches. To compensate for being shorter than the Indian men he hauled materials with, he would often place a piece of his own mantle on his shoulders so that he could carry his share of a beam's weight.[56]

Serra was in many ways the general contractor overseeing the churches' construction. The completed church at Jalpan is impressive: it is more than 150 feet long and 30 feet wide, with a vaulted ceiling. A building of that size and complexity required skilled carpenters, blacksmiths, painters, and masons, many of whom were brought to the region from Mexico City. Serra paid their wages with alms, with a portion of the stipends the padres received from the Crown, and, after securing approval from the mission's Indian leaders, with money raised by selling off surplus corn.[57] The padres at the other four missions followed this same plan. Indians in effect apprenticed with the imported master craftsmen, and by the late 1750s each of the missions had its own stonemasons, carpenters, ironworkers, painters, and gilders.[58]

The design of churches served a pedagogical purpose for Serra, who had their facades and interiors present key Catholic figures and miraculous events. The facade at Jalpan, for example, was crowned with a statue of Saint James, one of the original apostles of Jesus, the patron saint of Spain, and the defender of Spain from the infidels. According to tradition, in the year 40 James was evangelizing in Spain with little to show for it, until the Virgin Mary appeared before him atop a pillar carried by angels; so a representation of Our Lady of the Pillar was installed below Saint James in the facade. Across from Saint James stood a statue of the Virgin of Guadalupe, who reportedly appeared before the Indian Juan Diego just outside Mexico City in 1531. To the padres these two apparitions of Mary signified the universality of the Catholic Church and the triumph of Catholicism in Spain and Mexico. Both statues of Mary were particularly meaningful to Serra, given his militant evangelism and his complete devotion to Mary and the Immaculate Conception. To the Pames, the sculpture of the Virgin of Guadalupe with her Indian headdress might have been moving, but they also might have been horrified by the Franciscan seal in relief above the church's main door showing the crossed arms of Jesus Christ and Saint Francis. Both arms are nailed to a cross, and the wounds on Christ's arms seem reminiscent of the blisters and scars of smallpox, a disease that frequently ravaged the Sierra Gorda.

Statues, paintings, altarpieces, and all of the items that the Franciscans needed to perform the Mass and observe the sacraments filled the interiors of the churches. At Tilaco and Jalpan the Fernandinos inherited mission churches that Augustinians had already decorated. But the missions of Landa, Concá, and Tancoyol were created by Escandón in 1744; for them, the royal treasury spent nearly four thousand pesos on liturgical art and materials necessary to administer the sacraments.[59] Over the next few years, under Serra's guidance, the College of San Fernando and the padres at Jalpan and Tilaco purchased more art and artifacts to adorn their interiors.

To Serra, the expansion of mission agriculture, the shift in the Pames' labor and residential patterns, and the construction and adornment of mission churches were proof of the advancement of Catholicism among the Pames.[60] He believed that in modifying the external world of the Pames and in creating impressive churches, he had remade their interior world. But time and again, events would prove Serra wrong about his impact on the Indians, here in the Sierra Gorda and later in regions that were even more remote.

❖

Perhaps the strongest proof that the Pames had not been remade under Serra's tutelage is that the Franciscans felt the need to punish Indians who went astray. Serra took special care to monitor all aspects of the Pames' lives, both public and private. When Indians created what the padres termed "sinful" and "public scandals"—usually meaning adultery or drunkenness—the Franciscans responded with whippings, what they termed "paternalistic rigor,"[61] a practice that was the norm in Spanish society but not among the Pames. That Serra approved of this form of corporal punishment is not in doubt, though there is no record that he personally administered it in the Sierra Gorda. Serra would later write, "That spiritual fathers should punish their sons, the Indians, with blows appears to be as old as the conquest of the Americas; so general in fact that the saints do not seem to be any exception to the rule."[62] Because Serra believed that Indians, if left on their own, would retreat from Catholicism and return to their native beliefs, he had every mission in the region take roll on Sunday after Mass. Those not present risked punishment.[63] Serra required Indians to get permission to leave the missions, and if they were going to miss Mass, they had to attend services elsewhere and return with written proof that they had done so.[64]

Still, Serra did not seek to remake every aspect of the Pames' lives, and the Indians showed little interest in doing so themselves, resisting the Spanish influence by continuing to practice important aspects of their culture. They held on to their own language and lived in their own homes, many of which were located some distance from the mission compound. Serra did not thwart their economic pursuits, provided that they did not interfere with the work at the mission or the Franciscan religious program. In fact he mostly encouraged Indians to work for themselves, as long as the mission fields did not need their labor. The missions under Serra were agricultural institutions, not centers of craft production. Indians worked in the fields but did not weave cloth, make shoes, or produce saddles or any household items. Thus, while Indians came to rely on the missions for a basic sustenance, everything beyond corn and beans they either had to grow themselves or acquire through trade. And this was apparently their preference.

The Pames' household economy had a relatively strict division of labor that supported the indigenous economy. Women harvested istle, the fibers from agave and other plants, and used it to produce ropes, blankets, and carpets. From palm leaves they made mats, as well as small brooms, mesh bags, nets, and pots. Some of what women made they used themselves, but they also produced for trade or sale. Their husbands, it seems, traded these goods for various household items, or they sold them for cotton, which the women then spun and wove into cloth for clothing.[65] Their participation in long-standing regional exchange networks often took Pames men far from the missions for days, perhaps even weeks.

Yet even as they held fast to many aspects of their culture, increasing numbers of Pames participated in the sacraments at the missions. At Tilaco, for example, where the padres had found few "believers" in 1750, some 280 adults confessed and around 100 took Communion during Lent in 1758. During the rest of the year, some adults confessed and took Communion as a part of their regular devotions; others died with last rites.[66] Similarly, at Landa in 1750, "few" of the adults were prepared to participate in the annual Lenten confession or Communion; by 1758, "many" did.[67] Serra saw these changes as evidence of the gradual triumph of Catholicism over the Pames' religion. In the fall of 1752, when he returned briefly to the College of San Fernando for administrative matters, he brought what he claimed was a trophy of their victory over the forces of "hell." It was the face of a woman carved out of white translucent alabaster. Apparently, the Pames referred to it as Cachum, whom they revered as the "Mother of the Sun."[68]

The item came into Serra's hands after Spanish soldiers had been sent into the distant parts of the Sierra Gorda to torch the homes of Pames who refused to move to the missions. In one of these places, on top of the highest point of a mountain range, soldiers encountered a structure built of grass and sticks. Unbeknownst to them, this was a temple where the Indians worshipped and where they kept the revered alabaster icon. Three or four times the soldiers tried to ignite the temple. Finally, when the sergeant ordered the men to set it afire in the name of "God and his Most Holy Mother," it erupted into flames. To the soldiers' horror, the temple gave off billowing, fetid smoke. But the idol had survived; the temple's guardian had retrieved it before the structure was burned and had hid it away. He continued to venerate it and show it to people who traveled a great distance to ask for its help. After the Indians were brought to the missions, the guardian hid the icon in a cave high up in the mountains. Eventually, it came into the hands of a Pames man who had converted to Catholicism, and he gave it to Serra after the priest had asked him about the incident. Serra deposited it for safe-keeping at the College of San Fernando in Mexico City, and there it resided as proof of the Fernandinos' victory over native religion.

Serra was not just in charge of the Indians affiliated with the Sierra Gorda missions and the padres resident in them; he also had to manage their relations with the soldiers and settlers of Jalpan. In September 1752, more than two years into his work in the region, Serra became convinced that some of the non-Indian settlers in Jalpan were prac-ticing "sorcery, witchcraft, and devil worship." That September, when he was in Mexico City, he wrote to the office of the Inquisition ac-cusing a married *mulata*, Melchora de los Reyes, of sorcery, based on accusations he and Palou had already gathered. Apparently, an-other woman, Cayetana, an acculturated Nahua who was married to a mulatto and had been placed under arrest in Jalpan, had confessed to these crimes. She had made a fantastic claim: a large number of the settlers of Jalpan had been "flying through the air at night," and presumably both Melchora and Cayetana were among this airborne group. In a world in which the Spanish nun María de Jesús de Agreda could bilocate and be in her Spanish convent and the American Southwest at the same time, so too could these women transform and fly. On these journeys Melchora and others met "in a cave on a hill," where, Serra believed, they would "worship and make sacrifice to the demons" who appeared "visibly there in the guise of young goats and various other things of that nature."[69] This was not a case of superstitions and folkways gone awry; these Catholics, Serra charged, had entered into a pact with "the devils."[70] And such a pact, in the eyes of the Inquisition, was a dire heresy and one that called for, at a minimum, formal investigation. Serra was especially concerned that these devil-worshipping, mixed-race settlers would interfere with the conversion of the Pames. And, in fact, he even claimed that Indians had begun to join in these gatherings. While Indians new to Catholicism could not be punished by the Inquisition, the settlers surrounding them certainly could, and Serra thought it imperative that their "evil" be put to an end.[71]

Typically, once the office of the Inquisition received these sorts of charges, it would call upon one of its field agents, a *comisario*, to carry out an initial investigation that the office would then use to decide whether the case merited formal charges and prosecution. But regions like the Sierra Gorda that did not have secular priests or long-established missions most often did not have a resident *comisario* either. Such was the case in Jalpan in 1752. The Inquisition therefore appointed Serra *comisario*. Serra received this appointment in Mexico City one day after the office of the Inquisition considered his letter, and a few days later he took his oath of office, which involved swearing himself to secrecy.[72] While the historical record gives no indication of what became of Serra's investigation into the activities of Cayetana and Melchora, he was not one to let matters drop, and if he did in fact have his way, the meetings in the cave would have ceased. What we do know for certain is that by the fall of 1752, Serra was a *comisario*, and thereafter wherever he went, he had the authority to act on behalf of the Inquisition to investigate witchcraft, sorcery, and heretical acts. To the extent that his commission was widely known, his presence would have prompted caution, if not fear, among non-Indians whose devotion to Catholicism might have been less than total or perhaps even unorthodox.

At about the same time that Serra was charging some of the residents of Jalpan with devil worship, he was involved in a major dispute with soldiers and settlers who lived in the valley of Tancama not far from Jalpan mission. The origins of the dispute can be traced to the mid-1740s, when the missions were established by Escandón. In 1743, Escandón relied heavily on Mathías de Saldívar, the "caudillo y cabo a guerra" in Jalpan,[73] for he knew the locations of Indian villages and the best places to situate missions. Saldívar was present when the Franciscans and Indians took possession of the missions and when their boundaries were measured and marked. Much of this work was done, in fact, at his own expense. Saldívar had his own house just outside Mission Jalpan's new boundaries. But it was just a home for his family, not a larger property where he could raise crops and livestock. Before the mission was established, the Saldívars grazed and pastured their animals on land near Jalpan. But Escandón brought this informal use of the land to an end in 1744 so that the mission would have the necessary resources to re-cruit and retain Indians. As a form of compensation, he granted Saldívar land in the adjacent valley of Tancama. Because the mission had now taken all of the arable land in and around Jalpan, he also gave the other soldiers and settlers of Jalpan permission to establish a new settlement in the same place, which they called the Villa Nues-tra Señora del Mar de Herrera.

Unrest ensued, for this land in the valley of Tancama had been home to many Pames before 1744, and they had gathered fruit from it long before the Fernandinos' arrival.[74] Following the creation of the villa, the Tancama valley became home to more than 30 soldiers and their families.[75] Altogether, the group numbered around 130. With their arrival came complaints from the Pames and the mission-aries of Jalpan to the viceroy about encroachments on Indian land.[76] Moreover, there were other signs that the padres' relations with the settlers had begun to sour. Through the mid- and late 1740s, Saldívar had been a local purchasing agent for the missionaries, and he was regularly compensated for goods he provided to Jalpan mission. In 1749, the year before Serra arrived in the Sierra Gorda, Saldívar re-ceived two hundred pesos, a significant sum, for the goods he pro-vided to Jalpan. But with Serra's arrival—and the controversy over land use in Tancama—Saldívar's work for the missions suddenly came to an end.[77]

By the early 1750s, the padres had themselves become inter-ested in the fertile Tancama valley, worrying that the lands adjacent to Jalpan were insufficient to support the mission population year-round. Moreover, Serra saw the settlers at Tancama as a hindrance to the advancement of his missionary program. The settlers, with only a few exceptions, were poor and of mixed ancestry, and Serra con-sidered them a corrupting influence and objected to their proximity to the mission.[78] Only the Saldívars had any wealth. On the rancho of San Juan—located in the Tancama valley—Juan de Saldívar, also an official in the military force at Jalpan, had some 100 cattle, 40 mares, 10 horses, and 16 mules. Juan's father, Mathías de Saldívar, at some point had moved his rancho to a place called Saucillo, in the next valley over, and there he kept 150 cattle, 60 horses, a mule train, and 4 oxen.[79] Despite the settlers' small numbers and limited livestock, by the early 1750s the Franciscans were charging that the settlers were encroaching on mission lands; soon the padres joined forces with the Indians at Jalpan and Landa to demand that Escandón relocate them to a more distant valley. During the heat of this controversy Serra was father president, and if he had not convinced the father guardian in Mexico City that the soldiers and their families had to be moved, the controversy would not have exploded or perhaps even arisen in the first place.

In December 1751, the viceroy, in response to complaints by both Indians and Franciscans at Jalpan, suspended the settlement at Tancama and ordered the Saldívars and others out of the valley upon penalty of one thousand pesos. The viceroy also decreed that alternate sites for the settlement be identified, and he allowed the Indians to again take fruit from the valley.[80] But as of 1753, the Saldívars had neither moved nor paid the fine. Faced with this intransigence and what must have been Serra's growing ire, the viceroy ordered Gaspar Fernández de la Rama to seize property from the Saldívars to cover the unpaid fines; he was also to evict the Saldívars and all settlers from the valley of Tancama. Fernández de la Rama seized from Mathías de Saldívar religious paintings, furniture, firearms, candles, a box of correspondence, clothes, and 150 cattle, 40 mares, 20 horses, 4 oxen, and a train of mules. Captain Juan de Saldívar's losses were similar. It is hard to fathom the Saldívars' continued resistance. Perhaps they were gambling that the Fernandinos, like the earlier missionaries, would eventually leave and that they, the entrenched soldiers and settlers, would prevail. Ultimately, the Saldívars would learn that to challenge the Crown, and a Franciscan like Serra, was to risk all.

In January 1754, the Crown ordered Don Vicente de Possada to Jalpan to initiate formal proceedings during which the new location of the settlement would be decided. On February 4, 1754, Possada read aloud the complaint in the presence of Serra and Palou; Pérez de Mezquía, who had come to the Sierra Gorda to see the controversy resolved; Juan de Saldívar and two dozen other soldiers and settlers of the villa; and the Indian officials of Jalpan. In front of the group, Serra, Palou, and Pérez de Mezquía affirmed that they wanted the settlement moved.[81] Possada then announced that this was the will of the viceroy, and the soldiers affirmed that they understood. The soldiers at first expressed their preference to move to the valley of Saucillo, as it had adequate water and land.[82] But days later Don Juan de Saldívar stated that he and the other soldiers opposed any such move and wished to stay at Tancama, for they believed it was the only proper place for a settlement.[83]

Despite the soldiers' opposition, the process of relocating the villa moved forward, and Serra was active at every stage. Over two weeks he accompanied Possada and Palou and Padre Molina of Landa on a firsthand inspection of various alternate sites for the villa and helped them choose Saucillo, located in a valley east of Jalpan. Apparently, Saucillo had land for planting and grazing, as well as springwater. Serra also probably had a hand in the sharp and lengthy letter that soon came from the College of San Fernando condemning the Saldívars and stating that they alone opposed this move and all the padres' efforts.[84] What is perhaps most striking about the process is the strong participation of the Indian community through its elected village officials. At Jalpan the Indian governor, Don Diego Francisco, and the first alcalde, Don Agustín Pérez de la Cruz, as well as the fiscal of the church and eight other alcaldes from the villages affiliated with the mission, signed and submitted a written statement offering their support for the padres' efforts to have the soldiers evicted from the Tancama valley. In their petition the Indian leaders contradicted the soldiers' repeated claims that the padres starved them and beat them "cruelly."[85]

When nearly another year passed without action, Serra and the Indian officials of Jalpan traveled to Tancama, where Don Juan de Saldívar and his brother Don Juan Antonio de Saldívar and all of the other soldiers and settlers were informed by Spanish officials that they had two months to leave. At this point the Saldívars and some twenty others agreed to do so but again refused to go to Saucillo. Rumors soon began to circulate that the Saldívars were intent on staying in the valley and that they were pressuring others to do the same. Serra then demanded the expulsion of the settlers and soldiers by force if they were not gone in two months.[86] This evidently did the trick, for when Serra returned to the site in late January, he found only abandoned homes and one old man, who claimed that he was moving to Saucillo but that his animals kept coming back to Tancama on their own, out of habit.[87]

In the end the Saldívars had not directly impeded the settlers' abandonment of Tancama, but the latter had still feared that if they settled permanently at Saucillo, the Saldívars—their appointed superiors, or *cabecillas*—would somehow exact revenge on them for their acquiescence to the missionaries and the Crown.[88] Seeing that the settlers could not satisfy both the viceroy and the Saldívars, the local judge in charge of the case ordered Capitán Juan de Saldívar and the caudillo Don Juan Antonio de Saldívar to appear before him and all the soldiers of the villa. Had Mathías de Saldívar not died shortly before the order, he too would have been summoned. At the hearing, the judge then rescinded the Saldívars' grants of land as well as their titles and offices and confiscated most of their remaining animals. In one bold stroke, he had ruined the Saldívars; in the words of the viceroy, the settlers would now understand "that the Saldívars were no longer an excuse not to settle at Saucillo."[89]

With the Saldívars broken, the new villa quickly emerged. Two weeks later, Serra watched as the settlers took possession of Saucillo and as the boundary between the new town and the missions of Jalpan and Landa was determined. Before long, the households at Saucillo numbered forty-four, a street grid was created, and tracts of land were assigned to the settlers. This was a total victory for Serra. His mission had secured its lands, and the settlers had been put in their place. The Saldívars had fallen so far that Don Ignacio Vicente de Rubio, the husband of Catharina Saldívar (the daughter of Mathías de Saldívar), was forced to petition to join the scruffy transplanted community at Saucillo.[90] The surviving Saldívars would not soon forget that Serra and his fellow missionaries brought them down. Years later they would have their measure of revenge.

❋

In 1758, in a sudden development, Serra and Palou were reassigned to San Sabá, Texas, where the Comanche had destroyed a mission and killed two Franciscans.[91] Because Serra and Palou seemed to have succeeded in the Sierra Gorda where other padres had failed, the transfer to Texas was in many ways an indication of the high regard in which they were held in Franciscan circles. But their departure from the Sierra Gorda proved premature, for Spanish officials eventually decided that reestablishing the mission at San Sabá was too dangerous. Yet Serra and Palou would not return to their missions in the Sierra Gorda. Instead, they would spend much of the next decade back at the College of San Fernando, awaiting their next assignment. Why this happened may have had something to do with the timing of the decision not to reestablish San Sabá, the competence of their replacements in the Sierra Gorda, Serra's new responsibilities at the College of San Fernando, and perhaps a scandal that broke out in the Sierra Gorda after Serra and Palou had already left the region.

In 1761 dark stories began to circulate about the nature of Franciscan rule in the mountain missions. These cast Serra's years in the Sierra Gorda in a negative light and promoted the idea that the Fernandinos should be removed from the Sierra Gorda and the missions secularized. Clearly, among some Indians and soldiers, discontent with the missions and missionaries had been brewing for some time. The backlash was led by two Indian men, Agustín Pérez de la Cruz and Lorenzo de la Cruz, whose authority had long been acknowledged by government officials. Agustín Pérez de la Cruz had been the Indian governor of Jalpan on and off for many years, but with the establishment of the Jalpan mission he had been temporarily pushed out of office. Lorenzo de la Cruz—no relation to Agustín—was the interpreter and fiscal at Concá. Also at the center of the movement was a soldier, Mariano Lobaton, and the brooding Saldívars.

These men, and dozens of others, had met secretly in 1761 in Jalpan and Concá as well as in the nearby mining town of Escanela. Rather than singling out individual missionaries, the Indians' com-

plaints were directed at the whole Fernandino system. Their method
of attack was typical of colonial Spanish America: they wrote letters
to high-ranking officials and sought to turn the colonial bureau-
cracy against the Franciscans. What Agustín Pérez de la Cruz and
Lorenzo de la Cruz worked hardest on in late 1761 was assembling
a group of men who would travel to Mexico City or Valladolid—
the seat of the bishop of Michoacán—to deliver their complaints
to colonial officials. They seem to have accomplished this objective but soon found themselves under arrest for challenging the
Franciscans.

Months later, in January 1762, most likely soon after their imprisonment, Agustín Pérez de la Cruz and Lorenzo de la Cruz, with
the assistance of Raphael Mariano de Lima, wrote an indictment of
Serra's missions.[92] They claimed they had known many missionaries
but that under the Fernandinos they experienced an "exorbitant
harshness, unbearable work, the cruelest of punishments, and treatment that was at odds with the gentleness, moderation, and affection" required by Spanish law and expected by the Crown.[93] Mission
Indians, they charged, had been awakened before the sun rose,
forced to leave their houses, and taken in carts to the mission fields
by one of the padres, an Indian governor (who the Indians charged
was appointed and not elected as required by law), and the mayor-
domo; mission Indians were not allowed to return to their homes
until seven or eight at night; the work they performed was so arduous and unrelenting that if they wanted to eat, they were forced to
hold a tortilla in one hand and work with the other; and if they
tired or could not work, they were taken prisoner, shackled,
whipped, and then put in the stocks, punishments that priests and
missionaries, they charged, were forbidden by law to administer.[94]

After this hard work (which the Indians and Raphael de Lima
believed was prohibited by law), the Indians were forced to walk
several miles or more back to the mission carrying what they had
harvested. And they complained that all they got from the missionaries was a "quartillo de maíz," an amount they claimed was not
enough "to maintain the poor Indian, his wife, and children," who
were therefore "forced to look during the day for whatever they can
find to help them feed and clothe themselves and meet their needs."

Whatever else they could raise, such as chickens or chilies, they were forced to use to purchase other necessities, like salt.

While the missionaries in Serra's day had suggested that they were open to letting the Indians leave the missions, Agustín and Lorenzo told a different story. To get permission to leave the mission, they wrote, Indians had to pay the padres with a cup of chili or some other item. And if they returned later than expected, they would be whipped. For all of these reasons, the Indians believed that they were treated like the most debased of slaves.[95] The letter concluded with a call to remove the Franciscans and replace them with secular priests. While this would require the Indians to pay some sort of tribute to the Crown, the Indians considered this sort of vassalage far less onerous than what the Fernandinos had imposed on them. Agustín and Lorenzo as well as ten Indians and some settlers had been jailed for speaking out against their unlawful treatment, and now they wanted their freedom.[96]

Serra's successor as the father president of the missions branded these claims "false." Nevertheless, the military was moved to formally investigate the charges. Over several weeks, Joaquín Alexo Rubio, the new teniente and *capitán* of the presidio in the valley of Tancama, interrogated numerous Indians in Jalpan and Concá, and they all told the same story: they had been encouraged by the "ringleaders" to believe that if the Franciscans were replaced by a secular priest, they would be allowed to return to their milpas in the hills and attend Mass only when they wanted to. In the words of the Indian Silbestre Coronel, the Pames would "live as they had in the past . . . and that would be a good life, not like the one now with the padres," who whipped them, made them work, and gave them only small amounts of corn.[97] One man, Francisco Alonzo, blamed the Saldívars for the movement against the padres.[98]

Despite the numerous voices raised against Franciscan rule in the Sierra Gorda, all momentum for its termination and mission secularization stalled when Indians at Jalpan presented Rubio with a petition approved by at least 10 current or former Indian officials as well as around 125 other Indian men. The petitioners claimed that Agustín and Lorenzo, along with Lobaton and others, had coerced them into supporting secularization and that they had never really wanted a parish priest. The Indian petitioners now wholly embraced the Franciscans' rhetoric; they claimed they were poor Indians, only recently relocated to the missions and unable to pay tribute, let alone provide for themselves. They did not dispute that some among them had been swept up in the conspiracy, but they now claimed that they had been wrong and that God was punishing them with another terrible epidemic from which more and more were dying each day. The Indians at Jalpan called not for the replacement of the Fernandinos but for the punishment of those who had demanded their ouster.[99] The Crown agreed, and Agustín Pérez de la Cruz was given a prison sentence, and Lorenzo de la Cruz, Lobaton, and another soldier were banished from the region.[100] The Saldívars, who had already lost everything, escaped further punishment.

While the movement toward secularization had been derailed, the Fernandinos' reputations—including Serra's—had been dealt a blow: either the Indians under their watch had made little progress and had grown entirely dependent on them, or they had been treated cruelly by the missionaries and had developed legitimate resentments. Tellingly, the Indians' petition did not repudiate any of the assertions made against the missionaries. About the padres' punishments, their forcing Indians to attend Mass, and the payments in food they demanded in return for granting permission to leave the missions, the petitioners wrote nothing that would have been comforting to the missionaries or supportive of their cause. In a sense the Indians in Jalpan and Concá had protected themselves and thrown Agustín Pérez de la Cruz and Lorenzo de la Cruz to the wolves. None of this was Serra's problem, as he was no longer in the Sierra Gorda when the controversy erupted, but it must have disappointed him. As a member of the College of San Fernando, a resident there, and a member of its ruling council, he knew about the Indians' complaints and the ensuing investigation. In fact, they might in part explain why a man of Serra's obvious talents never asked to return to the Sierra Gorda and why he was never encouraged to do so.[101]

※

During the 1760s, the Sierra Gorda missions declined in power and influence as Pames culture enjoyed a resurgence. Thus, Serra's efforts had brought only temporary changes to many Pames. After he left, the population of the missions dropped from about thirty-five hundred to fewer than three thousand in 1764, as Pames left the missions and as higher mortality rates returned.[102] Well aware that Indians in the Sierra Gorda had continued to resist many aspects of Fernandino rule, Fray José García, the guardian of the College of San Fernando, instituted a series of reforms in 1766. A lighter touch would now be implemented, one that Serra would have resisted. García bowed to the Pames' practice of coming and going from the missions as they pleased, as long as they did so peacefully. He decided that Indians who had left the Franciscan missions of the Sierra Gorda for ones administered by other orders would no longer be pursued and brought back by soldiers, as long as they lived peacefully at their new missions. To lighten the workload in the missions, and increase the Indians' share of the missions' harvest, all Indians would be given a daily ration of corn, and since all of the mission churches in the Sierra Gorda except Landa were now complete, mission-grown corn would be used to feed the Pames instead of being sold to raise funds for construction. Finally, García reaffirmed that the missions' surpluses of corn or beans could not be sold without the permission of the Indians' *gobernadores*, alcaldes, and fiscals.[103]

These policies loosened the Fernandinos' grip on the Pames, dismantled many aspects of Serra's work, and probably hastened the day in 1770 when the missions would be secularized and Franciscans would lose control of them. Within a year of secularization Indians whom Serra had no doubt evangelized returned to their hillside homes and villages and their traditional forms of agriculture and trade.[104] In the words of one particularly disappointed friar, the Fernandinos' work among the Pames had "come to nothing." The Indians had returned to their "dens," and the churches had become homes to "wild animals."[105] These churches survived, which was in itself important; they were and remain exemplars of frontier baroque design. But they were also symbols of the one brief period in the more than two hundred years of Spanish rule in the Sierra

Gorda that the Pames—largely as a result of Serra's efforts—were incorporated, however reluctantly, into the Spanish colonial order. Determined survivors in a hostile world, the Pames—with their de-centralized economy, far-flung settlements, and resilient culture—would continue to weather assaults by missionaries and agents representing the Spanish state.

SEVEN

Popular Missions and the Inquisition

Serra returned to central Mexico in September 1758, but with his transfer to San Sabá canceled he began to divide his time between the College of San Fernando and months-long journeys into the countryside. At the college, he became master of novices, and hence a model for young men seeking to live a life of intense Franciscan devotion. In the countryside, he for the first time emulated the life of San Bernardino de Siena: he walked from village to village, preaching to thousands upon thousands of Catholics, hoping to lead them to confession and Communion. But Serra's work in these years also at times included another duty. On more than one occasion, when he was on a popular mission, he was called on by the Mexican Inquisition to investigate people whose actions suggested that they were in league with the devil. Serra committed himself to both jobs—leader of popular missions and agent of the Inquisition—with characteristic intensity. Though each required distinct skills—one involved inspiring Catholics to stronger faith and the other involved ferreting out those who were the religion's ostensible enemies—Serra very likely saw no contradiction between them. Both were merely part of his duties to the Franciscan order and to his God. Yet each reveals a very different side of his character, and each would leave a vastly different legacy.

When he returned to the College of San Fernando in 1758, Serra was welcomed back into a community that accorded him tremendous respect. In the triennial elections for officers in 1758, he was among those receiving the most votes for office and was elected to a three-year term on the college's governing council.[1] Three years later, he finished third in the election for guardian and was chosen to serve as the master of novices for the college.[2] This was a post to which Serra, because of his rigorous devotion to daily prayers and his teaching experience in Mallorca, was exceptionally well suited.[3] As master of novices, Serra took charge of a small group of men who had been admitted into the order, overseeing their spiritual lives and ensuring they spent their waking hours at prayer and study.[4] And since the master was expected to root out those who did not meet the order's standards, he constantly scrutinized his new charges' lives.

In some ways Serra's work in the novitiate resembled his attempts to remake the Pames in the Sierra Gorda. But Serra found among the novices what he rarely if ever found among the Pames: absolute dedication to the Church and a willingness to spend endless hours in contemplative prayer. Serra modeled for the novices— just as he had done among the Pames—a life lived completely "under the bell" and fully devoted to Catholic observance.[5] A bell awakened Serra and the novices at midnight for an hour of communal prayer. Some of the other padres returned to sleep after midnight prayers, but Serra prayed continuously until 4:00 in the morning. He continued his prayers in his cell until 6:00 a.m. or morning Mass. He prayed communally until noon, when the padres gathered for lunch. At 2:00 p.m., he said vespers, taught a class for an hour, and then took a siesta. All of these stages in his daily routine were punctuated by the ringing bells. Communal prayer began again at 5:30 p.m. The padres dined at 6:00. Sometimes Serra helped serve food, even though that was not one of the master's responsibilities.[6] To further discipline his body, Serra ate little, and he typically pushed back from the table, left his food, and read aloud while others dined in silence. Most observant Catholics abstained from meat during Lent and on days of obligation, but Serra rarely ate meat at any time of year.

After dinner Serra performed acts of penance in the solitude of his cell until a final bell at 8:00 signaled the start of four hours set aside for silence and sleep. When he slept, he held his cross and

mumbled prayers from the daily recitation. But like Saint Francis
Solano, Antonio Llinás, and Antonio Margil de Jesús, he slept little,
frequently performing dramatic and bloody acts of penance instead.
Not content to punish his body with the usual routine of fasts and
vigils and hair shirts, Serra would steal away to the choir chamber to
lash himself furiously with blows that echoed through the otherwise silent college.[7] Serra's accommodations in the college were as
spare as his prayer ritual was intense. He lived by himself in a small
cell with little more than a bed, a desk, a chair, some books, and the
basics of Franciscan life: a crucifix; a *cilicio,* or hair shirt; a *disciplina*;
and an assortment of books, mainly devotional novenas and perhaps
dictionaries.[8]

This rigid schedule of prayer, teaching, and discipline, a regime
that was occasionally interrupted by administrative responsibilities
at the college, characterized about half of Serra's time in the decade
after he left the Sierra Gorda. The retreat into the missionary college,
an insular community of ardent and almost desperate believers, was
intended by Llinás and other leading Franciscans to steel the missionary's faith and prepare him to venture out into the world as a
model of spiritual dedication for lapsed or indifferent Catholics. So
Serra often left the college with a small group of fellow Franciscans,
traveling to distant provinces of New Spain to preach. In some ways
this brought him back to his days of itinerant revival preaching in
Mallorca. But there Serra knew the countryside like the back of his
hand and was rarely away from the Convento de San Francisco for
very long. In Mexico, he traveled far and wide for months at a time
and through unfamiliar territory.

The blueprint for Serra's popular missions in New Spain was
first created in the Middle Ages, when great numbers of Catholic
missionaries fanned out across France, Spain, and Italy.[9] These it-
inerants brought Catholic belief to men and women in villages and
the countryside who rarely if ever saw a parish priest, attended Mass,
gave a confession, or received Communion. The Catholic Church
feared that many of these people had lapsed into pagan practices or
heretical beliefs and that those who still adhered to Catholicism did
so without fervor or emotion. The first great Franciscan itinerant
preacher was none other than the namesake of Serra's training

ground in Petra, Saint Bernardino of Siena, who moved throughout Italy, spurring religious awakenings wherever he preached. Soon after, Ignatius of Loyola, the founder of the Society of Jesus, devoted his life to a similar kind of continual mission.

The missionary wave that more proximately influenced Serra emerged out of the Council of Trent (1545–1563), the Catholic Church's response to the Protestant Reformation. The council codified Church teachings and the administration of the sacraments and sponsored teams of itinerant missionaries.[10] These men were the shock troops of the Counter-Reformation; they traveled on foot from village to village throughout Europe, delivering moving and even frightening sermons intended to entice listeners into confession and repentance.[11] In Spain, they effectively launched a second *reconquista*. By the mid-seventeenth century, these popular missions had essentially been standardized across Europe. Typically, one missionary (though sometimes more) would preach doctrine, while the others in his group sought to motivate their audiences with sermons on sin, death, and hell.[12] Missionaries also took it upon themselves to help feuding communities and estranged family members reconcile.[13]

The missionaries whom Serra most admired were those who participated in lengthy and dramatic popular missions.[14] Saint Francis Solano's most famous mission took place in 1604, in Lima and the Peruvian countryside. He was reputed to have moved huge numbers of Catholics to confession, to abandon their sinful ways, and to unburden themselves of deep-seated resentments and enmities.[15] The popular missions of Margil de Jesús were no less fervent or notable. According to one observer, so eloquent and lively were his sermons that they were "like darts of fire that burned the heart."[16] His life, in fact, seems to have been one continuous popular mission. Best known for his missions across New Spain, he was also remembered to have preached and heard confessions on the ship that brought him to the New World and on the overland journey from Veracruz to Mexico City.

Fray Antonio Llinás undertook popular missions in Spain, the New World, and Mallorca, his homeland. In 1680 and 1681, one generation before Serra's birth, Llinás preached a popular mission in

Petra. This mission was said to have brought peace to the village and in particular to a man whose son had been murdered. The father was especially grief stricken because he had hoped that his son would care for him in his old age. When Llinás came to Petra, he noticed that the man avoided his sermons. Llinás went to his home, prayed for him, cried for him, and even kissed his feet as he begged him to let go of his bitterness, confess his sins, and thus avoid damnation. Ultimately, the man broke down, cried, and pardoned his son's killer.[17] Decades later, when Serra was growing up in Petra, Llinás's visit was very likely still part of the small village's communal memory. Serra, though he was born and came of age in the heyday of popular missions, only truly began to contribute to it after he had left the Sierra Gorda.

The College of San Fernando had been founded in 1733 in part to address the spiritual needs of the growing population in Mexico City. But beginning in 1749, as the Crown began to secularize large numbers of *doctrinas* (proto-parishes served by mendicant priests) throughout New Spain, there arose a great need for the Fernandinos to go on popular missions beyond the capital.[18] These secularizations—while intended to weaken the mendicant orders—placed impossible demands upon an overworked and inadequate number of parish priests. In the 1750s and 1760s many of the parishes of New Spain had no priests in residence; some had not seen a priest for years or decades. So bishops invited Franciscans into their dioceses to preach popular missions and administer sacraments. Though they typically granted the Franciscans permission to come into their dioceses for no more than six months, they hoped that the padres' impact would outlast their missions.[19]

Not long after his return to Mexico City, Serra began to preach to the city's residents. He preached in and around Mexico City on other occasions, most likely during the years 1760 and 1763. In 1763 he ventured south to Oaxaca on a mission that took him away from the college for nine months.[20] From Oaxaca he trekked through regions that priests had only infrequently visited. He spent between September 1765 and May 1766 on a mission north of the capital, venturing through remote parts of the Sierra Gorda and then northeast into the Huasteca. He also traveled for months along the Gulf of Mexico preaching a popular mission. On each of these missions Serra was part of a small contingent of Franciscans, and very likely their leader.

Popular missions were extended performances that the padres repeated in place after place with only minor variations. Before they left the college, the role of each of the padres was defined. Serra would have held meetings and decided which lectures, instructions, and sermons each of his companions would deliver. Some padres focused on the catechism, others on motivating listeners to confess. In preparation for the mission, Serra gathered his books, clothing, and the liturgical items he intended to bring with him, especially those that might arouse the passions of his audiences. When he went on a mission, Margil de Jesús brought only "his breviary, a skull, a crucifix, the Holy Bible, and some notebooks with outlines for his sermons."[21] In Serra's day the college mandated that the padres carry with them a painting of Mary as the Divine Shepherdess, since the goal was to return lost sheep to the Catholic flock.[22] The college forbade the missionaries to bring with them certain theatrical props for use during sermons, such as crucifixes with attachments and hinges that allowed the padre to make Christ's eyes open and close and his arms and legs move. Apparently, leaders at the college were concerned that some people would be fooled by these contraptions and believe that they had witnessed a miracle.[23]

Once he had bidden farewell to the college, Serra and his companions began walking. A mule or a horse might have carried his baggage, but since popular missions were very much theater, Serra always traveled on foot to demonstrate his humility. His ulcerated leg and the limp it may have left him with would only have added to the effect. Serra and his companions walked in a tight group, like brothers and friends.

Because the padres had to be invited by a bishop to undertake a mission, their arrival was generally known in advance to locals and often greatly anticipated. Sometimes, though, Serra and his group tried to catch a town's residents by surprise, to make the opening of their mission especially dramatic. In Antequera (Oaxaca City), Serra arranged to enter the town on the first of March, to restrain any raucous celebrations associated with carnival.[24] In silence, his group entered the city on the Sunday before Lent; they went about the streets in pairs. They raised a crucifix, sang hymns, and began to preach. Drawing a crowd, Serra and the other padres proceeded to the cathedral, where they invited all to return the following day.

More typically, after Serra and the other Franciscans arrived at their destination, they launched what they called their "spiritual assault." They sought out the town's secular leaders in the hope that their attendance at the mission would encourage others to participate as well. They began the mission that evening, with a lantern-lit procession during which they chanted popular hymns and formally announced their arrival. Once a crowd had gathered, Serra or one of the other padres stood on a table or chair above the throng and encouraged those gathered to attend the mission, to listen during sermons, and ultimately to confess. Doing so, Serra assured them, would win them indulgences, "special rewards" or extra consideration that would shorten the time that their soul might be confined to purgatory.[25] Then Serra or one of the padres would ring a bell three times and deliver a short sermon—a *fervorino*—no longer than thirty minutes. Ideally, this sermon was not threatening or menacing, as it was the opinion of the college leaders that "harsh and unrestrained words do not edify but rather exasperate and irritate."[26] In closing, the preacher explained that the mission would begin the next day.

The following afternoon, after Mass, one of the padres gave doctrinal instruction, and another presented an introductory sermon. Serra and the other padres were aware that this sermon could last no longer than an hour. A boring and tedious sermon, the college advised, would only drive people away and prove inconvenient for women who had children and husbands who expected them home. A shorter sermon that left the audience hungry for more was better than one that, as the college's leaders put it, "disgusted with the imprudent wordiness."[27]

An especially dramatic moment in the mission's opening act came at the close of the first day, when the padres performed an exorcism. Serra, as the leader of the mission, would have overseen this ceremony. In his loudest voice—and echoed softly, after every pause, by the other padres—Serra would have spoken words that had been carefully scripted by the Catholic Church to drive away any demons that might interfere with the mission. Upon conclusion of this rite, Serra reassured the community that the demons had now been banished, and he warned it that "bad Christians"—those opposed to the padres' work—could still "do what the devils would not, by impeding others or advising them not to attend the mission."[28] Actual confessions—the ultimate goal of the popular mission—began the following day. Those seeking to make a confession would have found Serra and the other padres waiting for them in the church, either in a confessional box or in a secluded alcove. Men and women lined up separately and in an orderly manner to confess their sins.

Serra and his band of missionaries were not always welcomed by all. In some rural parishes villagers fled at the sight of the padres' approach because they did not want a critical light shone on their actions and lifestyles.[29] Others attended the padres' sermons and gave confessions simply to win indulgences or because they feared the consequences of not doing so. And on at least one occasion, Serra believed a local person poisoned him. After performing the Mass and drinking the wine, Serra felt as if he had drunk lead. His skin changed color, he lost his speech, and he nearly fell to the ground. Only after removing his vestments, resting in the sacristy, and drinking curative oil did he revive.[30] If Serra had in fact been poisoned, this was an extreme kind of resistance to his popular missions; more often, people just stayed away.

Because the missions involved large gatherings, the attendees—as well as the padres—risked contracting contagious diseases. In 1765, Serra was leading a popular mission with two other padres in the village of Tamiahua, a small town on the Gulf of Mexico north of Veracruz. With Serra was a young Franciscan, thirty-seven-year-old Fray Antonio de Jesús y Ganancia, a favorite son of Mexico City.[31] The padres had reached Tamiahua after a grueling trek over more than twenty miles of sometimes barren territory. Within days the mission came to a halt when Jesús y Ganancia was "assaulted" by a terrible fever. He retired from the mission and took to bed. When it became clear that Jesús y Ganancia would not recover, Serra was devastated. And when it appeared that Jesús y Ganancia was near death, Serra did his best to comfort him, telling him that he and his brethren were desperately sad to see him die before their work was done. Jesús y Ganancia then said, "Oh, Señora, you alone are pretty and you alone are beautiful, and that which you showed us in Mexico is only a shadow [of your beauty]. Let us go!" Serra, hearing these words, thought that Jesús y Ganancia might be talking to Mary. "Where are you going, Fray Antonio?" asked Serra. "A la Gloria," responded Jesús y Ganancia with his last breath.[32] Thus, the final moments and death of Jesús y Ganancia only affirmed for Serra his belief in a divine presence.

To his popular missions, Serra brought immense learning, great emotion, unwavering commitment, and one quality that had not characterized his work in Mallorca: a practiced theatricality born of experience preaching to audiences moved by emotional sermons. He abided by the college's prohibition on artifices and trick crucifixes but nevertheless employed dramatic methods and the occasional prop, often to great effect. Serra mortified his flesh so severely while preaching about "enemies" or "tongues" that Palou thought he did his body lasting damage.[33] Serra was known to take out a chain, expose the skin of his back, exhort the assembled to repent, and then fiercely beat himself in an attempt to do penance for the sins of others. Once, in Mexico City, a man was so moved by this spectacle that he seized the chain from Serra and began to flog himself while crying that he, not Serra, was the true sinner. So "violent" were the strokes that the man fell to the floor and died, but not before he received last rites from the padres.[34] At the conclusion of his sermons, when he recited an act of contrition, Serra would raise his crucifix in his left hand and then, in emulation of Saint Jerome, grasp a large rock with his right hand and pound his chest with such force that many expected him to fall dead.[35] When he preached about death, judgment, hell, and eternity, Serra held aloft a broken skull or thrust a burning candle through one. He would also hold up a large candle with four braided wicks. When lit, the candle, Serra believed, gave the assembled a vision of the flames that awaited the damned in hell. To drive home this point, and to the horror and probably excitement of his audience, Serra would extinguish the candle against his chest, burning his own skin.[36] These theatrics were increasingly a part of the practice of Franciscan Catholicism out of doors in the eighteenth century, especially in non-European lands where people were unfamiliar with the subtleties of Catholic practice and belief yet captivated by the spectacle.

Serra believed that popular missions changed lives, and that if he did his work well, God might signal his favor. Palou saw such a sign during Serra's mission to Antequera in the spring of 1763. There, Serra met a woman who for fourteen years had been living with a rich and powerful married man. After attending Serra's mission, she confessed to Serra her desire to change her life. Apparently, when, at Serra's urging, the woman told the man that she would no longer live with him, the man threatened to take her life or his own. Serra then quickly found her a home elsewhere in the city. The woman's lover, however, made good on his threat. He took a halter, tied one end around his neck and fastened the other to the top of the iron gate of the house where the woman had taken refuge, and then he jumped. Palou recorded that just as the desperate and grieving man took his last breath, an earthquake shook the town. The next day, when the lifeless corpse was discovered dangling from the gate, the woman, overcome with remorse for what she now saw as her sinful life, cropped her hair and paraded through the city, wailing, asking pardon from all.[37] As horrible as this tale was, the Franciscans saw it as a triumph. Serra certainly did not approve of the man's suicide, but he had saved the woman from eternal damnation, and she was also now an inspiration for the city's spiritual reconciliation and rejuvenation.[38]

Events like these figured prominently in Palou's biography of Serra, published in Mexico in 1787; one was the subject of the only illustration in the volume. It is an image of Serra, not in Mallorca, or at the College of San Fernando, or even in a mission in California, but as he must have appeared on one of his popular missions in central Mexico. Serra holds a stone in his right hand and a crucifix in his left. At his feet are a broken skull and a chain and burning taper, his tools of self-mortification. Next to them stands a chalice of tainted wine that may be intended to recall Serra's probable poisoning. All around him are sinners—some are Indians, others are Spaniards or Creoles—being moved to repentance by his words. They clutch their hearts. They avert their eyes from Serra, who rises above them, his head in the clouds. He stares into eternity without emotion. He appears severe, a resolute, remote, and statuesque Franciscan who stands ready to punish his own body to atone for the sins of others. For his popular missions, Serra had reinvented himself; he was no longer the logician who had delivered learned and persuasive sermons in Mallorca. Nor was he the serene padre who had preached ineffectively in Puerto Rico upon his first arrival in America; he had since learned how to connect to New World audiences. During his popular missions in New Spain in the 1760s, he sent a blunt and dramatic message to the thousands of people who came to hear him speak: Return to Catholicism, confess, and repent, or face eternal damnation.

⋇

While striving to inspire the masses of New Spain, Serra worked—as a *comisario*, or field agent, for the Spanish Inquisition—to rein in and even prosecute people who held and practiced beliefs that the Church considered heretical and dangerous. Like the spread of popular missions in Europe after the Protestant Reformation, the Spanish Inquisition formally emerged in the wake of the Council of Trent's concern about sects and beliefs that ran counter to Roman Catholicism.[39] Years as a student and then as a professor had prepared Serra for this most confrontational aspect of his missionary life in New Spain.[40] Only two full records of his actions as a *comisario* have come to light, but it is unlikely that these reflect his full involvement with the Holy Office in New Spain, given the secrecy that always surrounded the Inquisition. In any event, these sources allow us to see Serra more clearly and from a new vantage. Clearly, he could be as inquisitorial as he was evangelical. He saw Satan as a present and powerful force and believed that supernatural events were common in New Spain. And he was a calculating and unrelenting interrogator of those he thought had committed crimes against the Church and were a threat to society.

Today, the Inquisition is rightly regarded as an institution that sowed terror wherever it extended its long reach. It was regarded similarly in Serra's day, but not by everyone. For a Franciscan like Serra, working for the Inquisition was a badge of honor; it was an indication of his piety, discretion, trustworthiness, and conformity to dogma. Most, if not all, of the leading missionaries of Serra's day worked for the Inquisition, just as his mentors in Palma had done. Because they were often the highest-ranking Catholic officials in frontier regions with no parish priests or bishops, acting as an agent of the Inquisition came naturally to leading Franciscan missionaries. Serra's associates Fathers Bernardo Pumeda and Francisco Palou also acted as *comisarios* for the Mexican Inquisition.[41] Serra had briefly worked for the Spanish Inquisition in Mallorca, where the Holy Office had a history of overturning lives and convulsing society, but the eighteenth-century Mexican Inquisition was far different. It had neither the resources nor the inclination to carry out such grand terror campaigns. Instead, it largely focused on prosecuting degenerate priests and removing prohibited books from circulation. In Mexico, there was always a wariness of Judaizers, witches, and heretics, but there were no autos-da-fé.[42]

In the winter of 1755–1756, three years after his appointment as *comisario* and his investigation of Cayetana and Melchora (the witches and devil worshippers in Jalpan), the Inquisition called on Serra to investigate Antonio Bonifacio de la Ramírez in the town of Río Verde, west of Jalpan.[43] Father Pumeda had been in Río Verde giving a mission when he was paid an unexpected visit by a barber named Joseph Manuel Ignacio Sánchez, who had heard from his brother-in-law, Alejandro Rodríguez, that a man named Antonio Bonifacio had signed a certificate (an *escritura* or *cédula*) renouncing his Christianity and forming a pact with the devil. Joseph Manuel, fearing retribution from Antonio Bonifacio, visited Pumeda and denounced Antonio Bonifacio in secret. Pumeda forwarded his denunciation to the office of the Inquisition in Mexico City and added that Antonio Bonifacio was a bad and dangerous man whose brethren, or "cofradia," had refused to participate in any way in the mission. Since Pumeda was on a popular mission and soon left Río Verde, Serra took over the case. Assisting him as an ecclesiastic judge was his fellow Mallorcan Juan Crespí.

Serra oversaw a preliminary investigation in which a notary recorded testimony from witnesses who might be summoned to collaborate on formal charges if they were indeed brought by the Inquisition.[44] Serra never called Antonio Bonifacio to testify for fear that he might lie or flee.[45] At the outset of the inquiry, Joseph Manuel and his brother-in-law gave the same account. Five months earlier, Alejandro Rodríguez was riding a mule alongside Antonio Bonifacio when Alejandro—an unskilled rider—fell from his mount. Antonio Bonifacio then told Alejandro that he could give him "a *remedio*" so that "no beast would make him fall" again."[46] Antonio Bonifacio confided that he was a good rider because he had an *escritura* signing his soul over to the devil and that the devil helped him to be a good "*vaquero, toreador*, lover, and other similar things."[47] Antonio Bonifacio said that there was a man in Río Verde who would make a similar certificate for Alejandro for only two pesos.[48] Alejandro did not recall if the *escritura* was in fact signed by Antonio Bonifacio, only that it was a "very small" piece of paper and "full of handwritten letters." Alejandro added that lots of *escrituras* like this were sold in Río Verde.[49]

Serra asked Alejandro who made these *escrituras*; the latter replied that he did not know. "In Reverence to God," Serra implored Alejandro to examine his memory and "to think if he perhaps had been wrong in anything he had said and if he had said the entire truth." But Alejandro had nothing to add. Frustrated, Serra stated that the Holy Office had information that years earlier another person had written a similar *escritura* turning his soul over to the devil. Again, and with more force, Serra said to Alejandro, "*Examine your memory and tell the truth*."[50] Alejandro would only say that he could not recall any similar thing but that when he was a boy he had heard it said, by whom he would not divulge, that one Anselmo Balderas sold herbs that were used for "bad things." Three days later, Alejandro reviewed his testimony and affirmed his willingness to repeat it verbatim in front of the judges of the Inquisition, even though he knew that it was prejudicial to Antonio Bonifacio.[51]

Notwithstanding Alejandro's willingness to testify before the Inquisition, Serra knew that his preliminary investigation had come up short. Because Alejandro's testimony was so "timid," out of a fear that Antonio Bonifacio might learn of it and attempt to kill him, he had been unable to build a stronger case. The officials of the Inquisition decided not to press the case. Since Antonio Bonifacio was the only person known to have had such an *escritura* and it was not even clear if he had signed it, the case seemed to be an isolated incident, not one that imperiled the larger community.[52]

❖

In a world in which women flew through the night and frustrated vaqueros forged pacts with the devil, Serra must have been a busy *comisario*. But the only other surviving record of his work for the Inquisition comes from a case he pursued more than ten years after his investigation of Antonio Bonifacio. In September 1765, Serra set off from Mexico City with Palou and two other padres on a popular mission. Their destination was far to the north, beyond the Sierra Gorda. They would be gone from the college for nine months; they would spend seven of those months preaching and hearing confessions in the province of Huasteca, in its capital, Villa de los Valles, and in remote northern towns and villages, such as Aquismón and Valle del Maíz, that had not been visited by missionaries in decades. In the spring of 1766, in Valle del Maíz, a woman named Dominga de Jesús had approached a local military official, Lieutenant Melchor de Media Villa y Ascona, with a troubling report. She had been ill for years and suspected that another woman, María Pasquala de Nava, had cast a spell on her. The lieutenant arrested María Pasquala, interrogated her, and elicited from her an incriminating declaration. Serra was put in charge of the case and soon began, under the auspices of the Mexican Inquisition, another investigation of witchcraft at the edge of the Spanish Empire.[53]

On April 14, 1766, Serra opened the inquiry by calling Dominga de Jesús to testify.[54] A thirty-five-year-old widow and *parda* (a woman of mixed Spanish, African, and Indian ancestry), Dominga de Jesús told a long and fascinating tale. She asserted that her troubles had begun three years earlier, when she developed a persistent cough, hoarseness, and unbearable tightness in her chest. Only with tremendous effort could she talk. Various medicines and remedies had given her no relief, and thus she came to believe that her illness was caused by an evil spell (*maleficio*). Her suspicions deepened when a free *mulata* named Agustina Vasquez told her that she

(Dominga de Jesús) was the victim of an evil spell and that because of the spell worms had lodged themselves in her neck. Dominga de Jesús then went to see María Pasquala, who had a reputation as a healer. Dominga de Jesús begged María Pasquala, "for the love of God," to cure her. But María Pasquala "looked at her [and while] smiling told her that she could not cure her." Dominga de Jesús repeated herself, begging again "for the sake of God." This time María Pasquala agreed but only on condition that Dominga de Jesús give her some cloth and come to her house for a cure. Dominga de Jesús gathered the cloth and went to María Pasquala's house. The latter removed an old bandage from her visitor's chest and applied an herbal remedy. María Pasquala also gave Dominga de Jesús a drink and told her that she had a sickness in her lungs.

Dominga de Jesús immediately began to experience terrible abdominal pains and tried to heave something out of her chest. María Pasquala smiled and assured her that she was cured. Dominga de Jesús's pain subsided. She was free from the cough for a week, and her hoarseness lessened. But her head hurt, and her fingers swelled. Weeks later María Pasquala gave her another drink, and as soon as she took it, the cough and the hoarseness returned with great force; she also started to feel pain throughout her body and thought she was going to die. Later, when Dominga de Jesús confronted María Pasquala, the supposed healer told her that she would die just like another woman she had poisoned. Dominga de Jesús then went to see the lieutenant, who arrested María Pasquala.

María Pasquala had at first denied that she was a witch, but then she confessed to the lieutenant that it was true: she had cast a spell, and the spell was contained in a doll in her house. The soldiers retrieved the doll and asked María Pasquala to explain. She said that the doll represented Dominga de Jesús and then removed from the doll two little pieces of stone that she had placed in its chest; when she did this, Dominga de Jesús felt relief in her chest, and when María Pasquala took a nail from the head of the doll, Dominga de Jesús felt as if a thorn or nail that had been tormenting her had been removed. María Pasquala untied two strings and a thread of white silk from the neck of the doll, confessing that with these she had hoped to kill Dominga de Jesús. While in jail María Pasquala agreed to cure Dominga de Jesús, and for several days she applied a balm to her throat but then declared that Dominga de Jesús could not be cured because there was another woman, Agustina Vasquez, who was still intent on doing her harm. Agustina, however, had fled the town and could not be found.

Serra listened intently to Dominga de Jesús's testimony, saying little and asking only a few questions.

Ten days later, Serra ordered María Pasquala brought before him.[55] As the accused, she had not yet been officially charged or informed that she was under suspicion. She had no counsel to advise her and probably very little understanding of the perilous situation she found herself in. In theory, this approach would lead to a full confession, not one that was limited to the charges leveled in a denunciation.

"Where are you from?" Serra began.

Accurately, but perhaps somewhat sarcastically, she replied with the location of her imprisonment: "The House of Lieutenant Don Manuel."[56]

"Why are you here?" Serra asked.

"Because I am under arrest."

"And who arrested you?"

"The lieutenant, the alguacil, and other officials."

"Where were you arrested?"

"In my house in Valle del Maíz."

"And how did you come to the Villa de los Valles?"

"After I was arrested, I was brought here by the lieutenant."

"And do you know why you were arrested and brought here?"

"Because of the woman named Dominga de Jesús, who made false accusations about me before the father guardian of Valle del Maíz and the lieutenant."

"What did Dominga de Jesús say?"

"That I gave her a cure that made worse the cough from which she was suffering."

Serra pushed her, just as he had done a decade before with Alejandro Rodríguez. The transcript records Serra saying: "That does not seem like an adequate reason for your arrest, and for you to be put in irons and held in prison, and therefore, in accordance with

God and your conscience, tell us: *Do you think there is another reason for your arrest?*" Serra was giving her the chance to confess or to elaborate on her claim that Dominga de Jesús had leveled false accusations.

María Pasquala told Serra, "The lieutenant went to my house and found some herbs and asked: 'What are all these herbs for?' And I said they were for cures. And the lieutenant said I was a '*bruja*, an *hechicera*,' and that the herbs were for 'witchcraft [*brujerías*].' And I said that was not true, and then the soldiers ransacked my house and found no more than a doll, which was a toy of my daughter's, and they began to say that it, too, was for witchcraft, and the cause of the misfortune of the woman Dominga, who was sick, and that I had killed two other people with herbs and witchcraft, to which I said I gave them *medicamentos* and had not hurt anyone."

Serra then asked the crucial question: "Have you made a pact with or had communication with the devil?" The word Serra used was important: *brujería*, the legal definition of which was "a pact with the devil." The prevailing belief was that the devil would not help someone without getting something in return, usually a person's soul after he or she died. Absent a pact with the devil, María Pasquala would have been guilty of a lesser crime: *hechicería*, or simple witchcraft or black magic. This was still a crime, but it was not in itself a heretical act or one that was deemed a grave threat to society.[57]

Perhaps aware of what was at stake in the question, María Pasquala stood her ground, responding, "No, but it is true that *el demonio* had appeared before me several times in the form of a Pames Indian, and other times in the form of a dog, and other times as a cat, and other times as an owl, or as an eagle, or as a small lizard, or like a snake, or in the form of a centurion on a black horse with an embroidered saddle."[58]

Serra asked, "Have you made any pact or concert with the same enemy?"

"No," she said.

"What was it that the devil said to you, and what did you ask him?"

"He asked for my soul, . . . and he said he would give me clothing and support . . . but I said no, that I did not want his clothing or support."

"Have you ever learned or carried out any *hechizos* or *brujerías*?"

"No," she said.

The following day, Serra called the corregidor of Villa de los Valles to testify. Serra held up two pages and asked the corregidor if he recognized them as the declaration that María Pasquala had given earlier in Valle del Maíz. The corregidor stated that the pages constituted the confession, but he could not convince Serra that these had actually been María Pasquala's words, since the pages were not signed. The earlier, self-incriminating declaration of María Pasquala therefore could thus not be evidence of a pact with the devil. At this point, Serra could not prove the case against María Pasquala, who naturally could not be punished for rebuffing the devil. She might have used black magic to cure or injure Dominga de Jesús, but her case did not warrant a referral to the judges of the Inquisition in Mexico City. Serra would have to try again.

Two days later, Serra summoned María Pasquala from jail and read aloud her testimony, word by word. She verified it all and added that as a Christian she never could have committed the acts she had been accused of, was not a witch, and had never wronged anyone. Serra then used to his advantage the fact that María Pasquala did not know the nature of the case being built against her. Holding the unsigned declaration María Pasquala had given weeks earlier to the lieutenant, Serra said, "Can you deny that on another occasion you gave a sworn declaration admitting to the crimes that you are now charged with by the Inquisition? Because if you deny having done so, you will then be guilty of perjury." Again insisting that she was a Christian, María Pasquala denied committing any crimes.[59] But she was cornered—by her own words, by Serra's careful interrogation, and by a process that was stacked against her.

Serra told María Pasquala to pay attention and to listen to him read the document he was holding. He directed her to try to remember if she had admitted to anything contained in it. He then read slowly from her earlier declaration:[60]

[María Pasquala] declared that she made a pact with *el demonio* a year ago, and that the devil had tricked her, and he had won her soul, and that she was content. She said this devil was known as the devil who carries the pall [*el Diablo que cargaba el Balleton*]. This devil used to go by her side, and he told her to gather herbs to do harm to the *cristianos*; and that she had killed with these herbs a man as the devil had commanded . . . and that the devil had commanded her to poison Dominga de Jesús because she was a good singer . . . and had told her to make a little doll of rags [*muñeca de trapos*] . . . and that she brought *el Balleton* meat and candies, . . . and that he got mad at her when she mentioned God, . . . and that when she went out she sometimes came upon him in the form of a Pames Indian, a coyote, a cat, or a skunk, . . . and that he embraced her when he was in the form of a Pames Indian, and that she slept with him and that they had carnal relations . . . and that at night the devil took her to where there were bats . . . and that in the form of bats some of their accomplices came to suck the blood of little children, and that she had sucked the blood of little ones who died without baptism, . . . and that some of the Pames Indians had brought peyote and that others had gathered at the mission of Valle del Maíz, all of them widows, and that they too came as bats, and that they too had their little devils and that they too sucked blood from little ones . . . and that *el Balleton* had told her to get a bone from a dead person in a cemetery so that they could have good luck in their gambling, . . . and that *el Balleton* had told her to stop praying the rosary and to not pay attention to the saints and that when she went to confess that she should not confess more than two sins, and that that was enough, and that when she took Communion she should take the Eucharist from her mouth, place it on her finger, and stick it to a beam beneath the *comulgatorio* . . . and that she should not pray . . . and that when she asked the devil where he went, he said he went to hell or to the caves and that he got mad at her for not wanting to go with him.[61]

Confronted with this damning and incriminating document, María Pasquala now said that she had done these things in the past but did not do them anymore.[62] Seeking further clarification, Serra read over the declaration once again, asking her after each sentence, "Did you declare that? Did you do that?" She denied only that she had had carnal relations with the devil and that she and bats had sucked blood from unbaptized infants. She explained that she had in fact taken the Eucharist from her mouth and stuck it on a beam but only because she felt the need to clear her throat. She added again that everything else was true, but that it was all in the past, and that now she did not do any of those things.[63] Her words fell on deaf ears.

Serra had elicited from María Pasquala a near-total confession, which eliminated the problems posed by her earlier and unsigned confession. Her crimes, her heresies, were now clear: she had entered into a pact with the devil, relinquished her soul, murdered, poisoned, and even desecrated a cemetery at the devil's request. Further, she had committed a sacrilege by smearing the consecrated host on a beam. To Serra, María Pasquala represented what could go wrong in a land where too many people had little or no understanding of or interest in Catholicism. Serra would have been especially wary of María Pasquala, simply because she was a woman and a widow; like most Spanish men of his time, he viewed all women as weak and vulnerable to temptation, particularly those without a husband. María Pasquala's mixed racial background also raised Serra's suspicions. She was variously described in the record of the case as a *mulata* and as *loba natural*. Part Indian and part African, she would have been seen by Serra and others as of weak temperament and highly aggressive.[64]

Serra was also concerned by María Pasquala's association with Pames who used peyote, a hallucinogenic. Mexican Church officials were horrified by the common Indian practice of associating the drug with the most important figures in Catholicism. For example, in 1617, in Mexico City, the drug was referred to as "Niño Jesús," or as the "Santísima Trinidad"; in Zacatecas between 1626 and 1665 it was known as "Nuestra Señora," and at many times in the first half of the eighteenth century it was referred to in the north as "Santa María."[65] Finally, Serra was very likely alarmed, if not scandalized, by María Pasquala's account of retrieving a bone from a cemetery. She claimed that she did so to bring her luck in gambling, but the Otomí of the Sierra Gorda used powdered bones in their fertility rites in the belief that semen was produced in bone marrow. Two women in the Mexican north in fact had been called before the Inquisition in the late seventeenth century to answer charges that they had used powdered human bones in their witchcraft.[66] Serra would not have been aware of this earlier trial, but he probably knew of the Indians' use of human bones in their ceremonies, and he must have suspected María Pasquala had not only aligned herself with the devil but also subscribed to some of what he saw as the most dangerous beliefs of Sierra Gorda Indians.

Having secured a confession and documented María Pasquala's depravity, Serra was just about done with the case. He was not responsible for issuing a verdict, however. He reviewed and sealed the documents of the inquiry and sent them to the office of the Inquisition in Mexico City so that officials there could determine the next step. Serra notified the inquisitors that if they wanted more information, he could speak with them in person after his return to Mexico City.[67] Upon his recommendation, María Pasquala was sent to Mexico City, where the judges in the office of the Inquisition would examine her more formally.

In the Villa de los Valles, in his interrogation of María Pasquala, Serra had uncovered what he saw as real evidence of the presence and temptations of the devil. In ways that are hard for the modern reader to fathom, Serra believed that evil could be anywhere. But what made his world livable was the fact that God was everywhere. As Serra learned, one day you could meet an agent of the devil, and the next you could be hosted by Jesus himself. On his return to Mexico City after his investigation of María Pasquala, Serra found himself once again in the immediate presence of the Lord, just as he had many years earlier on the road between Veracruz and Mexico City. One night, on their monthlong journey back to the capital, Palou and Serra were unsure where they would sleep. While contemplating sleeping in a field under the stars, they saw a house a short distance away. When they entered the house, a man with his wife and a child offered them shelter and "with unusual neatness and kindness" served them supper. The next morning, on the road, Serra and Palou met some muleteers. Surprised to see the two padres out so early and so far from any accommodations, the muleteers asked them where they had passed the night. In a house just up the road, the Franciscans explained. Hearing this, the muleteers incredulously responded that there was not a house or ranch for many miles in the direction they had come from. Serra then understood that it had been Divine Providence that had granted them shelter and hospitality and that—undoubtedly—their hosts had been Jesus, Mary, and Joseph.[68]

As Serra and Palou were ambling back to Mexico City riding a spiritual high, María Pasquala was traveling the same road in chains and under military guard. Once in Mexico City, she would spend five and a half months below the headquarters of the office of the Inquisition, imprisoned in what was known as the *pulguero*, a dark, damp, flea-infested dungeon.[69]

Serra and Palou arrived back at the College of San Fernando in late June 1766. Serra promptly wrote to the Inquisition suggesting that Fray Joseph Miguel Pereli, a priest and *comisario* in residence at Tampamolón, take over any further investigations in the María Pasquala case; his request was promptly approved. In the fall, Pereli interviewed Dominga de Jesús and interrogated dozens of Indians and mestizos who knew María Pasquala, and most said the same thing: "She is a witch and everyone knows it." Pereli went to the church where María Pasquala had been observed taking the Holy Sacrament from her mouth and smearing it on a beam. Pereli inspected the beam with great care and found no evidence of the Eucharist, "but because this was such a public sacrilege committed by María Pasquala de Nava," he "ordered that the beam be removed, burned, and replaced immediately."[70]

In mid-October, Pereli forwarded sixty additional pages of testimony to the office of the Inquisition. On December 10, the charges against María Pasquala were summarized in Mexico City. A day later she was declared to be a "true witch who had made a pact with the devil."[71] Later that same evening, she was found sprawled on the ground outside her cell, mortally wounded, as a result of an unspecified and "grave accident." A doctor was called, as was a priest, who conditionally granted her extreme unction. María Pasquala lingered and then died at 12:45 a.m. Wrapped in a blanket, she was buried the next day without ceremony in an unmarked grave.[72] Had María Pasquala lived, as one found guilty of forming a pact with the devil and witchcraft, she would have been whipped, banished from her home village, and sent to a place where her reputation was not known and presumably where she would not have any opportunity to cause harm.[73]

María Pasquala's fate was tragic, and Serra as an agent of the Inquisition played a major role in it. Given his upbringing in Mallorca and his nearly twenty years in Palma, a city shaped by the Inquisition, and his many years in Mexico, Serra knew that María Pasquala would most likely be punished severely when he sent her to Mexico City. But he saw her as a witch and could not have done otherwise. Nothing in the historical record suggests that Serra knew of her death. Yet he would not have been surprised to learn that one who had gone so far astray had suffered such a gruesome end. Serra was known by the officials who oversaw the Inquisition in Mexico City, and word must have traveled to him about her death.

We know nothing of Serra's contact with the Inquisition in his later years, or if he even had any. He never resigned his post as *comisario*, and his appointment was not for a set period of time or a certain region. Most likely, though, his career as a *comisario* ended with the case of María Pasquala.[74] Part of his job as a leading Franciscan had been to work for the Inquisition, and it is a sign of his orthodox beliefs and diverse talents that he brought the same rigor and acumen to that responsibility as he had to his evangelism in the Sierra Gorda and to his popular missions throughout New Spain.

PART THREE

California

EIGHT

"A Work So Holy"

It was in 1767, nearly two decades after he left Mallorca for New Spain, that Serra began to fulfill the desire that had propelled him across the Atlantic Ocean. In Palma twenty years earlier, Serra had eulogized his mentor, Fray Antonio Perelló, as a great man whose greatness was nonetheless circumscribed by the fact that he never left his small island homeland. On this count he had broken from Perelló's example, bidding farewell to Mallorca to fulfill God's calling as an apostolic missionary to Indians. But in the Sierra Gorda he had ministered to few Indians who had not already been exposed to Catholicism, and at the College of San Fernando in Mexico City, on popular missions throughout Mexico, and as a *comisario* of the Inquisition, his duties were not altogether different from those of his Franciscan colleagues in Spain. Surely, Serra found his work in New Spain challenging and satisfying, and he distinguished himself among his fellow Franciscans in his piety and commitment. But none of his accomplishments had equaled, let alone surpassed, those of the island-bound Perelló. Had Serra died in 1767, when he was in his early fifties, he would have been little remembered beyond Petra or the Sierra Gorda. But he had many more, and eventful, years ahead of him. In 1767 and 1768, the Spanish Crown unexpectedly gave him the opportunities he had craved since his novitiate. Serra seized these with his usual energy and determination. He secured and then reorganized one mission field for the Fernandinos and then finally pioneered a major new one, earning both lasting fame and enduring notoriety in the process.

※

Serra's chance for glory arose because of a change in the Bourbons' governance of New Spain, which, in the mid-eighteenth century, was becoming less profitable and more unruly with each passing decade. Influenced by Enlightenment thinking, the empire began to take a more rational, scientific approach to the administration of its American colony. Kings Felipe V (1700–1746) and Ferdinand (1746–1759) integrated Spain's disparate regions into a more coherent political entity (to the frustration of many independent-minded regions, such as Mallorca, which were increasingly subjugated to centralized Bourbon authority). In the 1760s, Carlos III (1759–1788) attempted to do the same with New Spain, especially after the Seven Years' War saw his empire lose ground in North America to England.[1]

In the Treaty of Paris that concluded the war between England and France, Spain, as an ally of defeated France, lost Florida to England, though it gained Louisiana west of the Mississippi. Spain's missions in Florida had been destroyed by the English in the early eighteenth century. But across the northern frontier, all the way from Baja California to East Texas, Spain still relied on missions and presidios to secure its territory and create a buffer to protect the productive silver mines that lay between the northern frontier and central Mexico. Non-Indians were few in number across the far northern frontier, except in the communities of El Paso (2,635), Santa Fe (2,324), and San Antonio (about 1,000). All told, New Mexico's population was under 3,000, Sonora's was around 8,000, Texas had about 2,500 Spaniards, and Baja California had far fewer than one thousand.[2]

To oversee the reorganization of New Spain, Carlos III sent a *visitador general*, José de Gálvez, to the colony, granting him extraordinary powers that in some areas superseded the viceroy's.[3] Gálvez arrived in New Spain in August 1765 and began a comprehensive overhaul of the colony's administration. He especially emphasized reforming its northern frontier, where, as he saw it, the presidios were a drain on royal coffers and the missionaries were too slow to bring Indians into the Spanish fold as taxpaying citizens. But his vision was not just about strengthening existing Spanish

Spanish troops conquering Mallorca's capital in 1229. Detail of the altarpiece painted by Father Pedro Niçard between 1468 and 1470. (Museu Diocesà de Mallorca)

A man working the land outside the village of Petra, Serra's birthplace. Serra would encourage Indians in Mexico and California to adopt similar forms of agriculture. On the left is the San Pedro parish church, where Serra was baptized. On the right is the Convento de San Bernardino. Detail of a map created by Cardinal Antonio Despuig y Dameto in 1785. (Museu de Mallorca. Photograph by Patrick Tregenza)

Serra's childhood home in Petra's Barracar. (Photograph by Patrick Tregenza)

Petra's Convento de San Bernardino, where Serra was educated and his grandparents and parents were buried. (Photograph by Patrick Tregenza)

Saint Francis of Assisi founded the Franciscan Order in 1209 and devoted his life to spreading the Gospel. He was widely emulated in early modern Europe for his vows of poverty, his life of devotion, and his receipt of the stigmata in 1224. (*I Fioretti*, Venice [Christophorus de Pensis], Dec. 15, 1490. This item is reproduced by permission of the Huntington Library, San Marino, California)

Father Antonio Perelló Moragues was born and raised in Petra, and was Serra's most important mentor. He died in 1748. The following year, Serra left for New Spain, never to return to Mallorca. (Attributed to Fray Francesco Caimari, 1775. Convento de San Bernardino, Petra. Photograph by Jaume Gual)

In Serra's day, Palma (the Ciutat de Mallorca) was a walled city of narrow, winding streets. Its port was a nexus of trade between western Europe, the Mediterranean, and North Africa. Catholic churches, convents, and monasteries dominated the cityscape. (Antonio Garau, 1644. Biblioteca de la Fundación Bartolomé March, Palma)

Palma's Gothic cathedral is among the largest in the world. It is more than 120 yards long and 55 yards wide and holds the tombs of the Mallorcan kings James II and James III. (Photograph by Patrick Tregenza)

Ramon Llull was a leading Mallorcan religious thinker, writer, and missionary. Most likely he died in Mallorca in 1315 and was buried in the Convento de San Francisco the following year. This painting, executed c. 1620 by Miquel Bestard, shows his burial procession leading into the Convento's church. (Ajuntament de Palma de Mallorca)

Saint Francis Solano was canonized in 1726, just as Serra's interest in missionary work was deepening. When Serra was unsure if he should devote his life to being an apostolic missionary in New Spain, he prayed for guidance to the "Apostle of Peru." (Reproduced from Lino Gómez Canedo's edition of Fray Diego de Córdova Salinas's *Crónica franciscana de las provincias del Perú* [1957] with permission from the American Academy of Franciscan History)

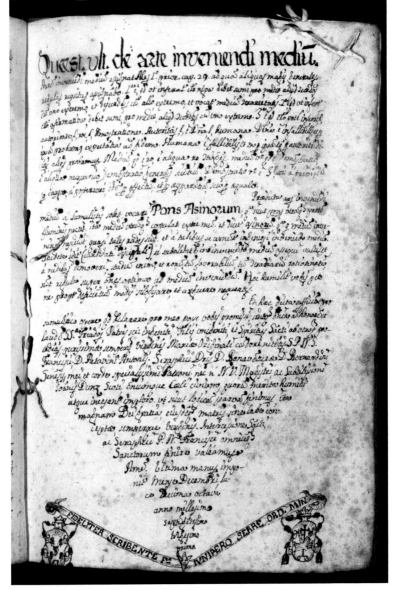

Serra's handwriting was clear and beautiful. He concluded his notes from a course in philosophy in the 1730s with FIDELITER SCRIBENTE FR. IUNIPERO SERRE ORD. MIN.: "Written Faithfully by Fr. Junípero Serre, Order of Friars Minor." (Archivo del Estado, Mallorca Public Library, Manuscript 882, Palma. Photograph by Patrick Tregenza)

In his work among Indians and in his commitment to an ascetic life, Serra emulated Fray Antonio Margil de Jesús, a Spanish missionary who was among the first Franciscans to establish missions in Texas and other regions of New Spain. (Isidro Félix de Espinosa, *El peregrino septentrional atlante*, 1737. This item is reproduced by permission of the Huntington Library, San Marino, California)

Serra was a devoted reader of the seventeenth-century nun Sor María de Jesús de Agreda. She inspired him to believe that Indians in remote places like California would be converted to Catholicism upon first sight of the Franciscans. (Anon., eighteenth century. Reproduction authorized by Museo Nacional del Virreinato, INAH-CONACULTA)

Serra arrived at the College of San Fernando in Mexico City on January 1, 1750. For the rest of his life he would be affiliated with the college. (Photograph by Patrick Tregenza)

At the college, Serra distinguished himself by acts of humility as shown here, where, over the objections of a servant boy, he performs domestic chores. (*Episode from the Life of Fray Junípero Serra*. Anon., c. 1787. Tucson Museum of Art, Tucson, Arizona)

As father president of the Sierra Gorda missions, Serra oversaw the construction of this stone church in Jalpan, with its elaborate facade illustrating the key moments and figures in the history of Catholicism and the Franciscan Order. (Photograph by Patrick Tregenza)

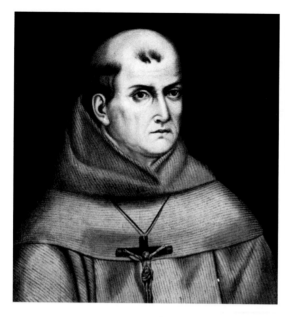

Serra was in his
mid-thirties when
he began his work
in Mexico, and this
portrait seeks to
capture his likeness
during those years.

(Copy made in late nineteenth
century of a now lost original.

Santa Bárbara Mission
Archive-Library)

In 1758 Serra left the Sierra Gorda intending to replace one of two Franciscans killed at Mission San Sabá in Texas. This painting narrates the deaths of the Franciscans at the mission. The most likely artist is José de Páez, a leading painter from whom Serra would later commission art for the California missions. (Museo Nacional de Arte, Mexico. Reproduction authorized by the Instituto Nacional de Bellas Artes y Literatura, 2013)

Because Spanish authorities deemed San Sabá too dangerous, Serra stayed in Mexico and divided his time between the College of San Fernando and the countryside, where he led religious revivals. On "popular missions," Serra would pound his chest with a rock and hold the crucifix high as he implored all in earshot to repent their sins and move closer to his God.

(Frontispiece engraving of Junípero Serra in Francisco Palou's *Relación histórica de la vida y apostólicas tareas del venerable padre fray Junípero Serra*. 1787, Mexico City. This item is reproduced by permission of the Huntington Library, San Marino, California)

After the expulsion of the Jesuits from Baja California in 1767, Serra led the Franciscans into the peninsula. This idealized view of mission life—painted by the Jesuit Ignaz Tirsch—represents what the Jesuits had hoped to build at Mission San José del Cabo. (Czech National Library, Ignaz Tirsch, Codex Pictoricus Mexicanus, Plate 8. Mission San José del Cabo)

The Rumsen of the Monterey region, where Serra established Mission San Carlos, covered themselves with woven skirts and fur capes. They made exceptionally fine baskets, as shown here in a drawing by José Cardero, an artist on the Malaspina expedition, which visited Monterey in 1791. (José Cardero, *India y Indio de Monterey*, 1791. Courtesy of Museo Naval, Madrid)

Concerned that the missions of Alta California were not on solid footing, Serra returned to Mexico City in 1773 to propose a reorganization of the provisioning and governance of the province. He met the viceroy in the viceroy's palace in the city's Plaza Mayor, depicted here by Fernando Brambila, an artist on the Malaspina expedition. (Fernando Brambila, *La Plaza Mayor de Mexico*, c. 1790. Courtesy of Museo Naval, Madrid)

Viceroy Antonio María de Bucareli y Ursúa (1771–1779). Bucareli approved nearly all Serra's proposals for the California missions and remained a staunch supporter of Serra's vision for Alta California. (Anon., *Antonio María de Bucareli y Ursúa*, eighteenth century. Reproduction authorized by Museo Nacional del Virreinato, INAH-CONACULTA)

Soldiers in California, armed with lances and leather shields, policed the countryside and usually escorted the Franciscans when they traveled from mission to mission. Serra never advocated forced conversions, but Spanish military force—though often stretched thin—was a constant presence in Alta California throughout the colonial period. (Tomás de Suria, *Modo de pelear de los indios de California*, 1791. Courtesy of Museo Naval, Madrid)

Indians at the missions often wore clothing provided by the Franciscans, for the padres considered the Indians' customary attire insufficient and emblematic of backwardness. Indians in the missions, when not performing assigned tasks or attending religious instruction, pursued their own diversions. (Louis Choris, *Voyage pittoresque autour du monde*, 1822. This item is reproduced by permission of the Huntington Library, San Marino, California)

Music and dance were central to California Indian culture, and they continued under the supervision of the Franciscans, as shown here at Mission San Francisco. (Louis Choris, *Voyage pittoresque autour du monde*, 1822. This item is reproduced by permission of the Huntington Library, San Marino, California)

Serra baptized three recently born Indians in December 1783 at Mission San Luis Obispo. In California the padres recorded in an orderly fashion every sacrament they administered. (Record of Baptisms, Mission San Luis Obispo, Dec. 1, 1783. This item is reproduced by permission of the Huntington Library, San Marino, California)

Soon after Serra died in August 1784, Francisco Palou suggested and Rafael Verger commissioned this painting. The ailing Serra is surrounded by Indians and soldiers as he receives the sacrament of final Communion from Palou. (Mariano Guerrero, *Fray Junípero Serra recibe el viático*, 1785. Reproduction authorized by Museo Nacional de Historia, INAH-CONACULTA)

When Serra died, Mission San Carlos was a work in progress and consisted of adobe buildings with thatch roofs. Most of the several hundred Indians affiliated with the mission lived in their own village just beyond the mission's buildings. (José Cardero, 1791. Courtesy of Museo Naval, Madrid)

In 1931, a statue of a heroic Serra by the sculptor Ettore Cadorin was installed in Statuary Hall in the U.S. Capitol. Serra holds a plain cross and a miniature model of Mission San Carlos. In 1963, on the 250th anniversary of Serra's birth, the U.S. Mint issued a commemorative medal inspired in part by the statue, but Serra's leg was now visible through his habit, calling attention to his physical infirmities.

(Photograph by Patrick Tregenza)

holdings. Soon after his arrival in New Spain, it would involve extending Spanish dominion much farther north. In Serra, he would find a partner for his grand ambitions.

Educated for a life in the priesthood before choosing a career in law,[4] Gálvez held the missions in greater esteem than most Spanish officials did but still shared the Crown's suspicion of certain religious orders. Reformers charged that missionaries contributed little to society while draining resources that could be put to more efficient use by parish priests. The Jesuits, as the wealthiest, most independent, and most international of the regular orders, were singled out as a particularly large obstacle to the new plans. Portugal had expelled its Jesuits in 1759, and France had done the same in 1764.[5] In late June 1767, with no advance warning to the Jesuits or the communities they served, Carlos III followed suit, expelling twenty-eight hundred Jesuit priests from Spain and twenty-two hundred from the Americas.[6] Many of those forced into exile were Mallorcans; for centuries Palma had been home to a large and active Jesuit community that regularly sent missionaries to the Americas. At the time of their expulsion, the Jesuits oversaw some 220 missions and around 300,000 Indians in Spanish America in missions. More than 100 of those missions were on the frontier of New Spain between the Sierra Madre Occidental and Baja California, but 78 were in the viceroyalty of Peru in lands that would later become Paraguay, Bolivia, and Chile, and others were in the upper Amazon and present-day Colombia and Venezuela.[7] Some of these were turned over to parish priests; others, especially missions on the remote northern frontier, were transferred to the mendicant orders— the Franciscans, Augustinians, and Dominicans—whom the Crown considered more pliable and less of a threat to its reform agenda. For example, the Franciscans at the College of San Fernando saw the missionary field of Baja California opened to them.

Baja California had been discovered in 1533 by Fortún Jiménez, one of Hernán Cortés's treasure-seeking pilots, but it was not until 1697 that Spain tried to settle the region, which then was home to some forty-eight thousand Indians.[8] Between 1697 and 1767 the

Jesuits established seventeen missions from San José del Cabo on the southern tip of the peninsula to San Francisco de Borja in the north, about three hundred miles from the current U.S.-Mexican border.[9] But they struggled to create viable agricultural settlements at these missions; Baja California was not only an arid, inhospitable environment but also one where the Natives spoke many different languages, and thus it was difficult for the missionaries to engage and govern them in a systematic manner. And in their efforts to build up their missions, the Jesuits nearly destroyed Indian life on the peninsula.

What happened to the Pericú Indians in southern Baja California demonstrates the destruction the Jesuits inadvertently wrought. By the mid-1730s the Pericú were seething with resentment at the missionaries' intrusion into their lives, and in 1734 they rebelled, destroying four missions and killing two padres and two servants, as well as several settlers, at Mission Santiago el Apóstol.[10] Within a few months the rebellion was put down by recruits from Sonora and the Cochimí Indians from the north; eight suspected Pericú ringleaders were arrested and shot. But the Pericú maintained control of the region. The following year, in January 1735, when a galleon from Spanish Manila dropped anchor in San Bernabé seeking provisions, Pericú warriors ambushed its landing party, killing all thirteen of its members. More than the slaying of the padres, this attack caught the attention of Crown officials, who sent men and arms to capture and exile the Indian leaders.[11]

A détente eventually set in in which the Pericú did not make war on the missions, but they did not go along with the Jesuits' plans for them either. They avoided the missions except when sporadically attacking them and their cattle. Epidemics of smallpox and measles brought to the region by Spaniards added to the Indians' woes. But by the end of the 1740s, when the populations of rival Indian groups had dwindled as a result of disease, the Spanish decided to relocate the Pericú to reconstitute a number of struggling missions. The main thrust of this *congregación* occurred in 1748, only a few years after the start of a similar effort in the Sierra Gorda that had sought to unify the Indian communities that Serra would oversee.[12] This was only partially successful, as many relocated Indians remained at the missions only part-time and others came to the missions only for Mass.

One thing that clearly differentiated some of the Jesuits in Baja California from Serra was their seeming disregard for the calamities that befell Indians under Spanish rule. After serving seventeen years in southern Baja California, the Jesuit Johann Baegert could write dispassionately of the devastation of the Indians from disease and other factors:

> They decrease annually. The world misses little thereby and loses nothing of its splendor . . . As a general rule, it may be said that the [Baja] California Indians are stupid, awkward, rude, unclean, insolent, ungrateful, mendacious, thievish, abominably lazy, great talkers to their end, and naïve and childlike so far as intelligence and actions are concerned.[13]

With attitudes like this it is little wonder that the Jesuits' efforts in Baja California bore "little fruit." By the 1760s, from the Spanish perspective, the missions of Baja California were failures. By 1768, the population of Baja California had fallen from 48,000 to around 7,149.[14]

Immediately after announcing the Jesuits' expulsion from Baja California on June 25, 1767, José de Gálvez and Viceroy Carlos Francisco de Croix (the Marqués de Croix) turned several of the missions over to secular administrators and called upon the College of San Fernando to provide missionaries for the twelve that remained. Fray José García, the college's guardian, chose Serra to lead the Fernandinos into Baja California and to serve as their father president, recalling him from a popular mission in Mezquital, about sixty miles from Mexico City. Serra, for his part, was eager to return to this challenging and important work; it had been almost a decade since he had headed the Indian missions in the Sierra Gorda. By July 12, he was back at the college; on July 14, Serra, Palou, and a band of Franciscans said their tearful goodbyes to their fellows and headed off for Baja California.[15] Serra and his traveling party rode more than five hundred miles by mule to the town of Tepic in western Sonora, arriving on August 21.[16]

-※-

Setbacks, both minor and serious, threatened Serra's movement into Baja California. The Fernandinos had planned to continue straight on to the capital of Baja California, Loreto, on the other side of the Gulf of California. But their ships were not ready, so Serra, as he had in Cádiz in 1749 while awaiting transit to New Spain, and then again in Puerto Rico while awaiting passage to Veracruz, found himself with time on his hands. And as he had both instances before, he organized a popular mission.[17] Over the next seven months, Serra and other Franciscans gave a mission in Tepic; other Fernandinos did so in the port city of San Blas and its adjacent communities.[18] More frustrating to Serra than the delay was the news he received in October that the viceroy had reassigned the Fernandinos to the Pimería of northern Sonora, where Jesuits had also been forced to relinquish their missions, and given Baja California to a group of missionaries from Jalisco; the viceroy was convinced, apparently by the Jaliscans, that the Fernandinos were obstructionist and better suited to Sonora, where they could work alongside Franciscans from their sister college of Querétaro. While it was not uncommon for rival orders to compete for new mission fields, the Fernandinos seem to have been caught completely off guard by the Jaliscans. In a letter to his superiors at the college, Serra made plain his despair: "The cold facts staring us in the face are—we are out of California, without infidels to convert, and maybe without any missions whatever." In Baja California, Serra imagined "thousands of infidels who are waiting . . . on the threshold of Holy Baptism," and he regretted that "such a field of evangelization does not exist in Sonora . . . They tell us that there [in Sonora] you have to walk many leagues through unpopulated lands to meet one infidel."[19] For Serra, the assignment to the Pimería was akin to a return to the Sierra Gorda, where there had been little opportunity for evangelism among the unbaptized.

Serra was fiercely obedient to his superiors, but he was less pliant to commands from military or civil authorities, especially those contrary to his own goals. Characteristically, he wasted little time trying to get the new orders rescinded, imploring the college to "search out every means possible, conformable with our religious profession."[20] He prepared a brief asserting that the Fernandinos should be sent to Baja California; rather than send it by post to Mexico City, Serra had Palou and another padre take it to Gálvez's temporary quarters in Guadalajara. Persuaded, Gálvez directed Palou to Mexico City to meet with Viceroy de Croix and even handed him a letter supporting the original policy. After meeting with Palou, the viceroy rescinded his order and sent the Fernandinos to Baja California and the Jaliscans to Sonora. Palou was back in Tepic on December 31, 1767, with the good news.[21]

Two and a half months later, Serra and fifteen Fernandinos sailed for Baja California.[22] They arrived in Loreto auspiciously, on Good Friday, April 1, 1768, and were met by the new governor of Baja California, Gaspar de Portolá—who had carried out the expulsion—and Father Manuel Zuzuárregui, the Jaliscan father president. Father Zuzuárregui and his colleagues would now depart for Sonora, and the Fernandinos would settle in.

This new phase of Serra's life and work marked a departure in scale and scope. After leaving the Sierra Gorda, Serra had devoted a decade to working with a small number of novices at the college and then the men and women he encountered on his popular missions. But now, once again as the father president of a mission field, Serra would make decisions for an enormous number of people, often affecting them adversely. In the Sierra Gorda, he had overseen five missions, all of which were within 25 miles or so of Jalpan and about 215 miles from Mexico City. Now he would reorganize and oversee fifteen missions of Baja California in a remote land over nearly 800 miles of thinly inhabited territory.[23] It was an expanse more than ten times larger than the Sierra Gorda or Mallorca.

By viceregal order, at first the Fernandinos had no real control over their new Indian charges: they were not to evangelize, recruit new converts to the missions, or interfere in the Indians' working lives. They were to administer sacraments and nothing more. The secular administrators whom Governor Portolá had appointed immediately after the expulsion of the Jesuits would continue to manage the mission Indians.

During his first few months in the region, Serra remained in Mission Nuestra Señora de Loreto, one of the smallest of the Baja

California missions, with just under one hundred residents when he arrived.[24] He assigned Palou to nearby Mission San Francisco Xavier and Juan Crespí, another fellow Mallorcan and a former student, to a nearby mission, La Purísima Concepción. The three Mallorcans would remain close and work together over the next decade and a half, first in Baja California and then farther north in Alta California.

A week after Serra arrived in Baja California, José de Gálvez set out from Mexico City for an inspection of the peninsula. En route he received news via a letter from the viceroy informing him of decisions made in Spain that would redirect his work in Baja California and change Serra's life. The Marqués de Grimaldi, the Spanish minister of state and a patron of Gálvez, had at the behest of the king ordered the preemption of a rumored Russian encroachment upon Spanish territory. Russia had been expanding down the Pacific coast in the hopes of extending its fur-trading enterprises, but the Russian-American Company had not yet reached California. Nevertheless, Grimaldi worried that Russia could soon threaten Spain's silver mines north of Mexico City. Gálvez, upon receipt of the order from Grimaldi, decided it was now imperative for Spain to claim and occupy Alta California to block a feared Russian advance.[25]

Spain's movement into Alta California was a long time coming. Not long after Jiménez's discovery of Baja California, Spaniards had pressed north from the peninsula. In June 1542, Juan Rodríguez Cabrillo, a commander in Cortés's assault on Mexico City, led three small ships out of a port north of Acapulco. Cabrillo's ships sailed into San Diego Bay and Monterey Bay but did little to quicken Spanish interest in Alta California. The wish to establish a Spanish outpost and way station on the Pacific coast took on strategic import after 1565 when Spanish vessels returning from the Philippines routinely began to approach the coast. And then it deepened after the English pirates Francis Drake and Thomas Cavendish ventured up the Pacific coast in the late 1570s and the 1580s.[26] Eventually, the viceroy, the Conde de Monterrey, chose Sebastián Vizcaíno, a veteran of several Pacific voyages, to explore the coast. In May 1602 he sailed for California, but encountering contrary winds, he did not reach Monterey until December, after a harrowing voyage. Vizcaíno explored the bay and named it for the viceroy. And there, beneath an ancient oak, the friars and men of the expedition held a Mass. Father Antonio de la Ascención, one of three Carmelite friars on the expedition, described Monterey in glowing terms, giving every indication that the harbor would make an ideal way station for Spanish ships. Yet Vizcaíno's voyage had cost forty-two of his men their lives. Furthermore, the Conde de Monterrey's immediate successor—the Conde de Montesclaros—discouraged further explorations when the threat privateers posed to the Manila galleons faded and improvements in ship design and construction made a California way station less necessary.[27] Thus, for more than 160 years the Spanish Crown did nothing to shore up its claim to the Pacific coast north of Baja California. But as soon as Gálvez heard from Grimaldi, he consulted Ascención's account of his journey and conferred with a naval engineer and pilot, among others, and together they devised a plan to send expeditions by land and sea to San Diego and Monterey, ports long known to Spanish pilots.

With his intention to plant the Spanish flag in Alta California firm in his mind, Gálvez arrived in Baja California on July 5. Alerted to Gálvez's plans to occupy Monterey, and perhaps forgetting his very recent anguish over the temporary reassignment of Baja California to the Jaliscans, Serra sang a celebratory Mass and ordered the bells rung in Loreto. Then he excitedly offered "himself as the first to go in person to raise the sacred standard of the Cross at Monte-Rey."[28] Gálvez accepted the offer, and he and Serra would soon begin to assemble the necessary men and materials to settle Alta California. But first they attempted to stabilize the missions in Baja California in the wake of decades of disease and failed Jesuit attempts at management.

Serra's solution to the problems facing the Baja California missions was the same that the Jesuits had tried to implement: convince the Indians to adopt Spanish forms of agriculture in the belief that they would live at the mission permanently and soon become Christians. Palou, who would take over for Serra in Baja California once Serra left to go north, represented the conventional thinking of the Franciscans when he wrote that too many Baja California

Indians lived "as they formerly did, in the hills like deer, supporting themselves with wild fruits" and avoiding the religious indoctrination that was the Franciscans' goal.[29] Neither Serra nor Palou could see that in a land as arid as Baja California hunter-gatherers had little choice but to move from place to place as they eked out a living by profiting from various ecological niches. To Serra and Gálvez, the one way forward was clear: "All Indians should live in settlements, so that they might be instructed and civilized."[30] This was the standard Spanish solution to what the Spanish saw as the waywardness of the Indians, one that Serra had applied unsuccessfully in the Sierra Gorda and that failed spectacularly in Baja California.

In late August 1768, Gálvez granted the Franciscans full power over the missions they had inherited, and he and Serra began to dramatically reorganize the missions, primarily by redistributing their Indian populations, just as the Jesuits had done.[31] This did not mollify Indian suffering; on the contrary, these policies only deepened it. Soon after Indians were relocated in September and October, fever and measles swept across the peninsula. Many of those who had been relocated died, and it seems almost certain that the relocation accelerated the spread of disease and hindered the care of the sick. The relocated Indians at Todos Santos—the Guicuros from Los Dolores and San Luis—complained to the governor of their poor treatment by Fray Juan Ramos de Lora, accusing him of "killing them by starvation, and ke[eping] them naked."[32] While the governor ultimately dismissed this charge as false, he became convinced that the Fernandinos did not respect his authority. Palou believed that other Baja California Indians, seeing this rift between the governor and the Franciscans, "lost respect for their father missionaries, failed to come to prayers and catechism, and stole anything they could, crops as well as cattle, resulting in the great deterioration of all the missions." Rumors spread among mission Indians that the padres could only preach, confess, and say Mass; the Franciscans, for their part, worried that they "could not correct or punish anyone" without provoking a full-scale Indian rebellion. They "were obliged to let" Indians "live as they wished, in order to avoid greater harm."[33] Deprived of the power to coerce Indians, the Fernandinos—just like the Jesuits—faltered in their plans.

In February 1772, Palou noted that in the little more than three years of Fernandino oversight, the mission Indian population of 7,149 had fallen by 2,055, a decline of nearly 30 percent due mostly to disease. He uncharacteristically sounded an alarm: "If it goes on at this rate in a short time Old California will come to an end." But, revealing the cultural blindness of the Franciscans, Palou also reported that the Indians, who now had more clothing and food than in previous years, were "content."[34]

Confronted with a deteriorating situation that in its broad outlines was not unlike the one they faced in the Sierra Gorda in the 1760s, the Franciscans soon wanted out of Baja California. Palou led the rush to exit (Serra had been in the north for years by this point), imagining that "a great harvest of" gentile baptisms awaited them "in the heathendom of Monterey." He looked longingly to the north, contrasting it with Baja California, where "there is not a town in which the Faith can be newly propagated." Moreover, Baja California's lands were too poor "to yield enough to enable the natives to support themselves or a priest, [and therefore] it could never be turned over to a Bishop." Seeking to protect—or to preempt— the order's reputation, Palou wrote to the guardian of his college insisting "it may not be said that the missions have been ruined by the missionaries of this apostolic college.[35] In several years, once they had a foothold in Alta California, the Fernandinos eagerly would turn Baja California over to the Dominicans.

In late October 1768, soon after the disastrous reorganization of the Baja California missions began, Serra and Gálvez turned to preparations for the settlement of Alta California. Serra traveled from Loreto to southern Baja California, where he and Gálvez had "long conversations" over the provisioning of the new missions and additional reorganization of the peninsula in the wake of the imperative to settle and provision Alta California.[36] After his meeting with Gálvez, Serra chose the Franciscans who would accompany the land and sea expeditions to Alta California. To free up additional Franciscans and church items for Alta California, he proposed closing two more of the formerly Jesuit missions and elevating another two more to parishes. Serra wanted each of the new missions, unlike those in Baja California, to be staffed by two resident missionaries. Otherwise, Serra believed, the missions would simply be too remote, and the Franciscans stationed there too lonely and too overwhelmed to carry out their responsibilities. Much to Serra's glee, Gálvez was impressed with the Fernandinos' work in the Sierra Gorda—the unfolding failure in Baja California had not yet become apparent—and he wanted the new missions of Alta California to be based on Spanish agricultural methods and strong Franciscan control. Hence, "he ordered that there should be packed and shipped all kinds of articles for use in dwelling quarters and field, with necessary implements of iron for working the land and planting, and every type of seed from both Spain and New Spain."[37]

All of this would come from Baja California, as did so much else that went into building the Alta California missions. From November 1768 through late March 1769, Serra traveled the peninsula, going from mission to mission in a search for extra chalices, vestments, baptismal fonts, thuribles, cassocks, surplices, cruets, crosses, bake irons, and liturgical and devotional paintings and statues that could be sent to Alta California. This task seems to have demanded his full attention.[38] Meanwhile, the presidio captain Fernando de Rivera y Moncada gathered animals and provisions.[39] Further drawing upon the resources of Baja California, the Franciscans planned to bring some of the most acculturated Indians from the peninsula with them, to help build the missions, introduce Spanish crops to the land, and demonstrate by their very existence the possibility of Catholic conversion to the Natives of Alta California. Serra's and Rivera y Moncada's efforts ensured that the first Alta California missions would have what the padres needed to perform the Mass, indoctrinate Indians, and plant crops. However, the preparations clearly weakened the missions in Baja California.

-»※«-

To secure Alta California for Spain, Gálvez envisioned three new missions and two military garrisons in support of them: a mission and a presidio in San Diego, a mission honoring Carlos III along with a presidio in Monterey, and a third mission somewhere on the coast between Monterey and San Diego to be named for the great Franciscan chronicler San Buenaventura. Gálvez planned for one overland expedition divided into two parties that would meet in San Diego. The larger party would blaze a trail into the unexplored lands between northern Baja California and San Diego and bring cattle and horses necessary for the new missions' agriculture. The smaller party would follow, with more men and provisions. Two ships, the *San Carlos* and the *San Antonio*, would meet the overland expedition in San Diego, and together they would claim the port for Spain and begin construction of the mission and the fort. A small party led by Portolá would then venture north in search of Monterey. A third ship—the *San José*—was to follow soon thereafter with more supplies for San Diego and Monterey.

Gálvez saw Serra as integral to the creation of missions in Alta California but worried that his physical condition might limit his involvement. Evidently, in his trip from Mexico City to Baja California—and his subsequent travel around the peninsula—Serra had exacerbated his leg injury. But Gálvez was so impressed by Serra's spirit and administrative skill that he decided to let him go north. The visitor general stated that he would "see to it that some provisions shall be anticipated which will facilitate the journey in so far as it is possible." He would "never consent" to Serra "going by sea," for it was the overland expeditions that would encounter Indians, many of whom may have had no experience with Spaniards or their religion.[40]

With men and provisions in order, on January 9, 1769, in the port of La Paz, Serra blessed the *San Carlos*, the first of the ships to sail for San Diego. After a Mass, Gálvez gave an encouraging speech, and the ship sailed on January 10.[41] Serra quickly departed for Loreto to continue his own preparations. Five weeks later, on February 15, the second ship, the *San Antonio*, sailed from Cabo San Lucas piloted by the Mallorcan Don Juan Pérez.[42] On June 16, the third ship, the *San José*, sailed from Loreto. The first overland party, headed by Rivera y Moncada and composed of Fray Juan Crespí, three muleteers, twenty-five soldiers, and a group of Indians, departed from the northernmost mission in Baja California on March 24.[43] On March 9, Governor Portolá, leading the second overland party, had left Loreto for the northernmost mission, and from there he followed Rivera y Moncada's route.[44] Serra would begin his own journey to the north a few weeks later and soon join the second overland expedition.

-※-

With two soldiers, a servant, one loaf of bread, and a piece of cheese, Serra headed north from Loreto early on March 28, 1769, to complete his move from central Mexico, where he had lived and worked among Catholics, to Alta California, a land of his dreams peopled by Indians unincorporated into Christendom. He traveled in a small mule train on what would be a seven-hundred-mile journey overland to San Diego.[45] Though he likely preferred to walk, in Baja California the distances between missions were great, and the land was arid and rocky, not to mention that there were few people to witness the theater of him on foot. Thus, a saddle, not sandals, carried Serra from Loreto to San Diego. During this transformative and arduous trip, Serra, at the request of his superiors, recorded his experiences in a diary, which reveals his assumptions about the Indians of the north and the depth and intimacy of relationships he had developed over the years with fellow Franciscans, in spite of the great distances that often separated them.

Serra was extremely close to many of the Fernandinos with whom he served. First in Mallorca, then during the Sierra Gorda years, and more recently in the College of San Fernando and on popular missions through central Mexico, Serra had forged robust friendships with many padres; though all were eventually assigned to new posts distant from one another, the camaraderie endured seemingly undiminished. His fellow Franciscans had come to admire Serra and value his companionship, and they looked forward to visiting with him when he rested at their missions on his journey north. These Franciscans treated him with great respect and affection. They greeted Serra in their finest vestments and feted him with "Indian dances and all the pomp and ceremony that is possible in such places."[46] And from many of the padres he gathered additional provisions for the journey north. Perhaps aware that if all went well, he might not see his companions for years, or perhaps ever again, Serra thoroughly enjoyed each visit on his way to Alta California.

As he headed to Alta California, Serra sojourned at five missions before rendezvousing with Portolá in the northernmost mission of Santa María.[47] Typically, Serra and his escorts would get on the road before sunrise and travel about four hours, until the sun became too hot for both men and animals. Sometimes their travel for the day would be completed by 9:00 in the morning.[48] When necessary, they would sleep under the stars.

Serra arrived weary and no doubt hungry at his first stopover, Mission San Xavier, where he was greeted warmly by Palou. They reminisced and talked business as well; Palou would be assuming the father presidency of the Baja California missions once Serra left, so they had a number of matters to discuss. Palou was alarmed by Serra's physical condition. His swollen left leg brought Palou to tears as he wondered how his former teacher—who was now fifty-five years old— would fare on the long road still ahead of him. Palou even told Serra that he "should not go with the poor health and little strength he possessed," and he warned him that he might slow the expedition or even cause it to "come to a disastrous end." But Serra refused to discuss his injury and told Palou that he had confidence that God would allow him "to reach not only San Diego, to raise and plant the standard of the Holy Cross in that port, but also Monterey." When Serra left Mission San Xavier on April 1 after three days of rest, "it took two men to lift him and to seat him comfortably in the saddle."[49]

Perhaps it was Serra's physical condition that prompted Palou to provide a surfeit of supplies—food, clothing, and "traveling conveniences"—for the journey to San Diego. Serra left the mission with "two sets of leather harnesses furnished with everything; two leather bags, and a liquor case with six flasks."[50] However, Palou's generosity—and his growing concern for Serra's physical comfort— left Serra uncomfortable. In his diary, he chastised himself for not refusing the gifts: "Sinner that I am, I am still attached to what suits me well."[51]

At Mission Guadalupe, the resident padre, Fray Juan Sancho, whom Serra had known since Sancho's student days in Mallorca, "gave" to Serra for his use a servant boy from the mission, who had been attending to Sancho.[52] For his journey with Serra, Sancho had the boy outfitted with new clothes, a leather jacket, boots, a horseman's complete outfit, and a mule. Serra did not record the boy's name in his diary, describing him as "a little page," "an acculturated little Indian of fifteen years of age who knew how to help at Mass, read, and do any kind of service." According to Serra, the boy was thrilled and his parents were proud that he was heading north with Serra.[53] Serra did not seem to have second thoughts about removing this boy from his family and bringing him to Alta California, a country still unknown to the Spaniards as well as the boy.

With his new page Serra set out on a two-day march to Mission San Ignacio. The first night they spent out in the open, but their hardship was eased by Padre Juan Medinaveytia at San Ignacio, who sent them dinner. Early the next morning, Padre Medinaveytia rode out to meet Serra, visited with him, then hurried back to his mission to prepare for Serra's arrival. When Serra got there at about 9:00 in the morning, Medinaveytia greeted him at the door of the church, in his vestments, surrounded by the mission's Indians. The following day, Sunday, April 16, Serra rested at the mission and renewed his own profession to the order, as did all Franciscans on that day. The next day they got a late start, withered in the scorching heat, and were forced to take refuge in a cave. In the evening, Serra's little group pushed on and slept once again under the stars.[54]

At Mission Santa Gertrudis, young Indians danced for Serra and performed special ceremonies. During the five days Serra spent at the mission, he visited with Father Dionisio Basterra, with whom he had gone on a long popular mission in Oaxaca a few years earlier, and he attempted to convince more than two hundred Indian families to relocate to the mission of La Purísima Concepción, where Serra and Gálvez believed they would be assured three meals a day and more suitable clothing.[55] Serra proposed to the Indians that they move, listened to their responses, and made the case again and again when they hesitated.

By April 28, Serra was at Mission San Francisco de Borja, where he visited with Father Fermín Francisco de Lasuén, who had served in the Sierra Gorda from 1762 to 1767. On May 5, six weeks and three hundred miles out of Loreto, Serra finally arrived at the northernmost mission of Santa María, where Portolá was encamped. For four days more provisions for the expedition arrived from a small bay in the Sea of Cortés. Meanwhile, Serra and Portolá inspected the mission and decided that—unlike Santa Gertrudis—it should not be relocated. When the new provisions were packed on the mules, Serra took a "kit" of items from Mission Santa María that he would need to perform Mass "en el camino," beyond the northernmost mission.[56] In the kit, Serra packed a frontal and chalice veil, an alb of fine linen, an amice, a striped cincture, a silver chalice with its paten and small spoon, six purificators, a consecrated altar stone, altar cloths of fine linen with lace, a pair of glass cruets, two more white cloths, a cloth for wrapping, and "a tin-plated host box full of altar breads."[57]

※

Now beyond the borders of Christendom, Serra started to assiduously evaluate the land for its ability to support a new mission. Was there a river that could be dammed for irrigation? Were there trees for shade and timber? Plants and animals for food? And most important: Were there Indians to recruit and perhaps one day baptize? He had waited two decades to meet such Indians, and so, only one day out of Santa María, he was crestfallen by the sight of empty villages, believing that the Indians had fled and "killed" his chance to "see them, speak to them, and embrace them."[58] However, just a few days later he would get another opportunity.

On May 13, after a full day's march, Serra, Portolá, and a light escort made it to a place the Cochimí Indians called Velicatá, which had been the northernmost staging ground for the expeditionary force led by Rivera y Moncada. Rivera y Moncada had arrived there in late December, his camp growing as more soldiers and animals destined for Alta California arrived. Eventually, his men constructed small huts for themselves and warehouses for the goods they eventually loaded onto the mule trains headed north.[59]

Serra and others concluded that Velicatá, with its good soil and its water, pasturage, and Indians, was an ideal place to found a mission.[60] Thus, it was in northern Baja California that Junípero Serra, on May 14, 1769, established his first mission, San Fernando de Velicatá. In a crude hut adorned with bells and a cross that served as a chapel, Serra, dressed in an alb and cope, said Mass with the items in his traveling kit.[61] The Mass was by necessity an improvised affair: the smoke of gunpowder had to stand in for incense, the hut was illuminated only by two small candles, and in the place of musical instruments the soldiers fired volley after volley from their muskets. After the Mass, Serra led the assembled soldiers and expedition Indians in the hymn "Veni creator spiritus."[62] He then raised the standard of the holy cross and inspected the area. But there were no gentiles in sight. Disappointed, Serra speculated that the celebratory gunfire had scared them off.[63]

The following day, May 15, 1769, was one of "great joy" for Serra, for he finally met Indians, who, at least in his eyes, had had little or no contact with Spaniards. Surely, though, these Cochimí had long been aware of the Spanish missions to the south, and Spaniards had lived in their midst since Rivera y Moncada's arrival in December 1768; they must have known of the dislocations and disease that had accompanied the establishments of missions farther to the south. But they still remained interested in the Spanish; they may have been desirous of trading with them.

That day, in Velicatá, upon learning that unbaptized Indians were approaching the Spaniards' camp, Serra was so overcome with joy that he praised God and kissed the ground, "giving thanks to His majesty that after so many years of desiring them He now permitted me to be among them in their land."[64] Dashing out of his hut, Serra came face-to-face with twelve Cochimí; ten were adult men, one was about sixteen years old, and another was a boy of ten. Serra marveled at the group: "They go entirely naked, like Adam in Paradise before the Fall." More incredible still to Serra was the Indians' lack of shame: "Even though they saw us completely clothed, never did they show the least sign of shame with their own lack of dress." To Serra, these Natives lived up to the Spanish depictions of uncorrupted Indians. One after another, the Cochimí allowed Serra to put his hands on their heads. Serra then gave them dried figs; Padre Miguel de la Concepción Campa y Cos (who had served under Serra in the Sierra Gorda and would run the mission after Serra departed) gave them raisins. Portolá gave them tobacco, and the soldiers gave them more food. The Indians gave the Spanish fish in return. So taken was Serra by the Indians that, Palou tells us, "during the three days he remained at Velicatá," he "did not suffer any pain" in his afflicted and ulcerous leg; "the joy and distraction over the foundation [of the mission] made him forget about his pain."[65]

As soon as the mission had been founded and gifts had been exchanged, Serra's work with the Indians began. With the assistance of an interpreter Serra told the assembled Cochimí how things were to be for them and their people from then on:

> In that very spot, a father would stay with them; . . . that his name was Father Miguel; that they should come to him, they and their friends, and visit him; that they should tell the others not to have any fear or timidity; that the Father would be their best friend; and these gentlemen, the soldiers, who are to stay with the Father, would do them much good and no harm; that they, in return, must not steal the cattle that grazed the fields, but when in need they should call on the Father and ask him for what they wanted; and he would always give them what he could.

Serra believed that the Indians did in fact comprehend his speech "fairly well, and gave evidence that they agreed to it all." But since Serra communicated either by signs or through an interpreter—and he had in mind a near-total transformation of their lives—this seems unlikely. Serra, however, was thrilled and believed that "before long, they would be caught in the apostolic and evangelical net."[66]

The new mission would be run by a Franciscan, but the Crown wanted its secular authority represented as well, and thus Portolá, in a moment of great cultural ignorance and arrogance—one that had occurred countless times before and would continue to occur for years to come—told a man whom he took to be the Indians' captain that while until "then he had been such merely by the wish and whim of his people, from now on he appointed him by the authority and in the name of our Lord the King." To provide for Father Campa y Cos and to attract Indians to the mission, Portolá turned over to Campa y Cos the supplies that Gálvez had set aside for the mission: a large number of cattle, forty fanegas of corn, and tercios of flour, hardtack, chocolate, figs, and raisins. And to protect Father Campa y Cos from Indians should they turn against the mission, Portolá left with him a detachment of soldiers.[67]

Having established the mission's religious and secular authority according to Spanish protocol and explained its rules to the Indians all in a single day, Serra and Portolá moved on from Velicatá. A few days later Serra learned by letter that forty-four Cochimí had come to the new mission and begun instruction in the basic rites and beliefs of Catholicism. He congratulated Father Campa y Cos and asked him that the first Indian baptized at the mission receive the name Francisco, in honor of Saint Francis.[68] For Serra the Indians' seeming interest in Catholicism was proof of the bilocating María de Agreda's assertion that at the mere sight of the Franciscans the "gentiles" would be converted to "the holy Catholic faith." Of the Cochimí "captain" at Velicatá who had presented himself and his people at the mission and given food to Serra and Portolá, Serra wrote: "May God make him a saint."[69]

During the first leg of the march north from Velicatá, over a mere ten miles, Serra's leg became so inflamed that some feared it had become cancerous. The next morning, after another march, the party reached a place with good water and pasturage. Serra and Portolá rested for five days while all of the men heading north in the second group finally rendezvoused. On the first rest day Serra was able to say Mass, but he had trouble standing on his feet, and the inflammation in his leg left him unable to sleep. He was so debilitated that he spent the next few days on his back in a makeshift bed.

When Portolá saw that Serra was bedridden a mere twenty miles into the frontier, he confronted him, telling him that he was incapable of accompanying the expedition. But Serra would not turn back. He once again responded that God would allow him to continue all the way to San Diego, and if that was not to be, he would "die on the road."[70] Portolá, realizing that Serra was determined to carry on, even though he was unable to either ride or walk, ordered the construction of a litter so that the Indians who had come along as servants could carry Serra to San Diego.

Serra had tolerated his leg injury—indeed he probably took some satisfaction in how the source of his discomfort was so visible to others—but he became alarmed when he realized that it might compromise the expedition. Unsettled by the burden he was now placing upon the expedition and its Indian helpers, he prayed that

God would somehow improve his condition. Confident that his prayers were soon to be answered, Serra approached Juan Antonio Coronel, one of the muleteers in the camp. "Son," Serra inquired, "do you know how to prepare a remedy for the wound of my foot and leg?" Baffled by the request, the muleteer said that the only sores he had healed were those of an animal. "Well then, son, just imagine me to be an animal," Serra replied, "and . . . make me the same remedy which you apply to an animal." Coronel did as Serra asked. He obtained some tallow, crushed it between two stones, mixed it with herbs he found in the camp, cooked all of these ingredients, and applied the resulting concoction to Serra's leg and foot in the form of a plaster. That night Serra slept soundly. When he awoke the next day, he stood up, recited his prayers, said Mass, and, much to the surprise of Portolá, was able to ride for six weeks over several hundred miles to San Diego without any assistance.[71]

Along the way, as the party passed through the territories of the Kilwa, Paipai, and Tipai,[72] Serra continued to scout for places to establish missions and to lament the flight of Indians before the advancing mule train. Ten days out of Velicatá, Serra and the others spotted two Indians watching them from afar. At Portolá's urging, the Indians on the expedition captured one of them after a violent struggle. Tied up, the injured and frightened man was placed at Serra's knees. It was in this manner—as a representative of a military force—that Serra had his first physical contact with an Indian north of Velicatá. Serra would describe the captive as a young man, about twenty years of age, who went by the name Axajui. He placed his hands on the man's head, recited the Gospel of Saint John, blessed him with the sign of the cross, and then had him untied.[73] Axajui was then taken to the governor's tent and questioned. Using signs, he revealed that he had been sent to spy on the party and that up ahead, where the trail narrowed, four villages were waiting in ambush to kill Serra and the rest of the men. Hoping to reassure the Indians of their good intentions, Serra and Portolá gave Axajui gifts and set him free.

The Indian attack never materialized, but the soldiers and Serra remained on edge. Even though the first group under Rivera y Moncada's command had cleared the way and scouted out campsites and watering holes, the makeshift road to San Diego, which wound over steep trails and across arid expanses, was difficult and at times harrowing. Increasingly, the Indians who had come north with the expedition began to desert. The three final Indians from Mission San Francisco de Borja fled on June 18.[74]

The next day, tempers flared. One of the governor's cooks, furious that another man's mule had blocked his path, "proved the strength of his sword's steel by running it through the buttocks of the burro," Serra recorded, "leaving it dead at his feet." For his crime the man was fired, fined, deprived of his own mount, and forced to follow the expedition on foot. That same day a mule was born, but since it was not able to keep up with the group, it was turned over to the Indians, who immediately slaughtered and roasted it.[75]

The expedition hugged the Pacific coast as it neared San Diego and began to encounter larger groups of Indians. Serra felt the "greatest pity" for them and lamented that so many of these "poor sheep" had no padre.[76] Some Indians generously gave the Spaniards food; others proved that they were, in Serra's estimation, not fools ("bobos") but keen traders. Rivera y Moncada's group had apparently been generous in giving out beads, ribbons, and various trifles, and now the Indians evidently expected the same, if not more, from Portolá and Serra. One Indian tricked Serra into lending him his glasses and then, to Serra's alarm, ran off. Serra finally got them back but not until they had passed through the hands of "the women and everyone who wanted them."[77] Finally, on June 29, after another five-hour march and months on the trail, Serra arrived at the port of San Diego, where he was pleased to see the *San Antonio* and the *San Carlos* anchored. Serra wrote to Palou that "the whole trip was a very happy one without mishap or change in my health."[78] He had been lucky. The first overland party had been plagued by desertions and hardship. But the real suffering had been on the *San Carlos* and *San Antonio*, and presumably the *San José*.

The sea expeditions had been a disaster.[79] The *San Carlos* had sailed on January 9, 1769; the *San Antonio* followed five weeks later. Buffeted by heavy seas and slowed by contrary winds, the *San Antonio*, piloted by the Mallorcan Don Juan Pérez, reached San Diego Bay first on April 11, 55 days after its departure.[80] Nearly all on board were weakened by the voyage, but no lives had been lost, and soon Pérez announced his readiness to sail on to Monterey. Two and a half weeks later the *San Carlos* dropped anchor in San Diego Bay, 111 days out of La Paz, and its arrival threatened to end the whole enterprise.

Soon after the *San Carlos* left La Paz, its water barrels sprang leaks, and the crew soon enough found itself with less than one barrel of fresh water. Vicente Vila, the ship's captain, headed for land and refilled his casks, but the water he did so with was contaminated, and much of the crew became direly ill. Compounding their woes, Vila then overshot San Diego and had trouble finding it when he doubled back. Then scurvy struck. In all, twenty-four men on board perished; only Vila, one sailor, the cook, and the Franciscan Fernando Parrón made it to San Diego.[81] When they arrived, they were helpless and near death. The crew of the *San Antonio* came to their aid, but then it sickened too, and eight more men died. The *San José* had sailed from Loreto on June 16, but it was nowhere to be seen and would soon be given up as lost. Gálvez's plan had failed. Portolá would need to improvise if he hoped to plant the Spanish flag at both San Diego and Monterey. He decided that the *San Antonio* would sail back to San Blas to reinforce its crew and find a new one for the *San Carlos*. Once the *San Antonio* had sailed, Portolá and all remaining healthy men would head north overland in search of Monterey; the hope was that the reprovisioned *San Antonio* would link up with Portolá either in Monterey or somewhere along the coast between Monterey and San Diego.

Making it as far as San Diego had been costly: dozens of men had died, many more had suffered greatly, and the already weak missions of Baja California had been stripped of men and supplies. Perhaps only Serra could then have seen the dire situation as a happy and hopeful one. In a jubilant letter written just two days after he arrived in San Diego, he told Palou that Alta California "was beautiful to behold," a "good country," one "quite different from Old California." There was not only fertile soil and sources of freshwater but also an "immense population" of unbaptized Indians awaiting conversion. For Serra, California appeared to be a promised land, untainted by prior waves of Spanish colonization, and a veritable blank slate. Here, he must have believed, there would be no royal officials attempting to secularize his missions, no querulous Indians to slander his missionaries, no entrenched settlers and soldiers like the Saldívars to oppose him at every step, no obstinate Indians whom soldiers would have to drag back to missions, and no witches like Cayetana, Melchora, or María Pasquala de Nava to spread paganism and fear. Instead, Alta California promised only "poor" and "naked" peoples who could be remade according to Catholic teachings.

Serra sincerely believed that the Fernandinos' experience in Alta California would be completely unlike their work elsewhere in New Spain—that they could, for the first time, win converts "without much difficulty," as he put it in a letter to his superior at the College of San Fernando. In their innocent state, the California Indians would be converted "at the mere sight" of the Franciscans, as María de Agreda had suggested. All that was needed were more padres to establish and run missions. Yes, Serra reminded his superiors, their work in upper California would require "many and dire sacrifices," but the road would not be hard for those with faith in the Lord. In a fascinating echo of the 1744 Lenten sermons that he gave in Palma, Serra reminded his father guardian that "to a willing heart all is sweet."[82]

Not all missionaries shared Serra's willingness to sacrifice himself (and indeed others) in distant lands. Before he even made it to San Diego, Serra learned that at least three of the padres assigned to missions in Baja California now wanted to return to the college. The isolation of the frontier was too much, they said. The odds of converting Indians were too low, and the personal sacrifice too great. Yet Serra, in a land even more remote than Baja California, was exactly where he wanted to be. To get there, he had, in his own words, walked "where no Christian foot had trod before," and now with pride and anticipation he found himself in a land of unbaptized Indians. As if to remind the father guardian and others at the college of where he was and what it meant to him, Serra closed one of his early letters from San Diego with a flourish that was at once dramatic, triumphant, and hopeful: "From this port, among the infidels, and destined Mission of San Diego, in California, July 3, 1769."[83]

-»%«-

The "infidels" whom Serra was now among were the Kumeyaay, the southernmost group of Indians in what is now the state of California. These people had trading relationships with those in Baja California, and they were part of a human mosaic that made California one of the most densely settled regions in all North America. Some 310,000 Indians lived within the boundaries of the present state in 1769. Approximately 60,000 lived in the coastal region between San Diego and San Francisco where Serra hoped to establish a series of missions.[84] The Luiseño and then the Acjachemen resided to the immediate north of the Kumeyaay. The Gabrielino occupied the coastal plain of Los Angeles, the Chumash inhabited an expanse from Malibu to San Luis Obispo, the Yokuts lived in the Central Valley, and the Salinan and Ohlone settled the central coast between Santa Barbara and the Golden Gate. The Pomo, Coast Miwok, Wappo, Patwin, and Eastern Miwok lived in the regions immediately north and east of the San Francisco Bay Area.[85] Although Alta California successfully supported a large human population, it was hardly disease-free. Even before the Spaniards arrived, a wide variety of infections were common, all of which led to high mortality among adults, especially those who lived in dense settlements.[86]

Every California Indian group has its own creation story. Most share a belief that the world originated in a union between earth and sky and that human beings, in one way or another, originated after a flood or out of some other chaotic situation in which birds or a creator made them out of earth or clay.[87] Less poetically, academic scholars have devised their own accounts, namely that the descendants of big-game hunters who came across the Bering Strait some thirteen thousand years ago first settled California ten thousand years before the present. More recent scholarship suggests that California was first populated thirteen thousand years ago by maritime peoples who were lured down the Pacific coast by curiosity and necessity as they harvested fish, seals, and walrus and some of the 750 other animals that teemed in the kelp forests up and down the coast.[88]

In Serra's day, and to a large extent still, California's topography, climate, geology, and flora and fauna were incredibly diverse and variable. Coastal California enjoys a Mediterranean climate of dry and cool summers and wet but mild winters. Farther inland summers are hotter and winters colder, especially at higher elevations. This varied land supported more species of plants and animals than any other region of its size in North America. Twenty-five percent of all the plant species in North America north of Mexico are found in California.[89] And in many ways, the diversity of California itself was mirrored in—and produced by—the wide range of peoples who lived there. In California, Indians spoke between eighty and one hundred languages, or one in five languages in North America.[90] With the exception of the Chumash, who had communities of more than 500 individuals, most California Indians lived in small settlements of between 75 and 250 individuals. Trade, marriage, and ritual connected many neighboring communities, and even ones distant, but most villages steadfastly maintained autonomy and protected their areas against encroachment.[91] These autonomous villages supported their own elites and religious and political leaders, as well as a range of folk who specialized in various crafts. One reflection of this tremendous diversity was the fact that California Indians had a basket for nearly everything. They made baskets for transporting goods of all weights and sizes, for winnowing seeds, storing and serving water and food, cradling and carrying infants, and covering their heads, as well as extraordinarily beautiful ones for presenting sacred and valuable items during exchanges and ritual observances.

As hunter-gatherers, California Indians built no large structures, made no pottery or metalworks, and, most important, did not practice agriculture. Thus, to Spaniards like Serra, they were exceptionally primitive, hopelessly backward, and perhaps even more wanting than he had imagined. But over many thousands of years, California Indians had developed their own political, religious, and economic systems, and those systems served them well. Adroit as they were, California Indians lived just about everywhere. They were skilled at moving their encampments to take advantage of seasonal variations in weather and food sources. And while they did not practice the domestication of wild plants that Serra intended them to, they were anything but passive recipients of the bounty of their land. In fact, they carefully and intentionally managed it to maximize their resources.[92]

Many California Indian groups did rely on one or two staple foods, such as salmon and acorns, but staples always fail, and the maintenance of a large and diverse precontact population in California was possible only because Indians used fire to manage their environments in ways that made them even more diverse, productive, and dependable. Every year, in late summer or early fall, and sometimes in late spring, California Indians set fire to thousands and thousands of square miles of their land.[93] On what was probably a ten-year rotation, they lit small fires that burned over the land but did not destroy trees. These fires enhanced the growth and diversity of plant and animal resources; they stimulated the germination and growth of grasses, fruits, greens, nuts, and seeds; they promoted the growth of sprouts and branches that they used to build baskets; and they increased the food supply for small and large game, especially deer and rabbits.

California Indians were not a preagricultural people who, given enough time, would have developed agriculture. Nor were they like the Pames, who rejected agriculture as a way of fending off Spanish dominion, or like the Indians of Baja California, who saw the futility of agriculture in their barren and arid lands. California Indians were on a completely different course, one that afforded them many advantages over domesticated agriculture. Their diet was far more diverse than the one that the Spaniards would introduce. And their means of making a living required far less labor and far less organization and coercion than what the Spaniards proposed for them. Small groups of California Indians managed their lands with great results through minimal labor. Thus, the nature of California Indian society—village communities that were relatively autonomous, egalitarian, and willing to move seasonally to maximize food production—was a direct outgrowth of fire ecology and made the Indians appear primitive—naked, hungry, idle, and rootless—to men like Serra. If only the people Serra considered "poor" and lowly "infidels" could be taught to work the plow, plant wheat, barley, and corn, and live in one place, Serra reasoned, then they would be on the road to salvation.

·※·

Serra's first months "among the infidels" were exceptionally busy and ultimately very disappointing for him. The *San Antonio* sailed on July 9 for San Blas;[94] on July 14, Portolá set out for Monterey with sixty-six men. Left behind in San Diego were those too sick to travel, and only a sergeant, Don José Francisco de Ortega, in command of eight able-bodied soldiers, remained to protect the settlement from the Kumeyaay, who had become tired of the Spaniards' presence, frustrated that the newcomers had nothing to give, and emboldened by the Spaniards' thinning ranks and obvious weakness.[95]

Two days after Portolá's group departed, Serra established Mission San Diego. Just as he had done at Velicatá, he said Mass and led the assembled group in songs and chants. Then, if any Kumeyaay were present, he would have told them that the padres had come to live with them, to help them, to feed and clothe them, and to lead them to salvation.[96]

With the mission established, Serra and Padre Parrón began constructing primitive shelters. In a hut dedicated as a temporary church, they placed devotional paintings and religious objects from Baja California. Not only trying to re-create the chapels they had left behind, the Franciscans hoped that the beauty of these objects might attract Indians to Catholicism. Serra and Parrón also tried to entice local Kumeyaay with gifts of food, but the Kumeyaay were more interested in the Spaniards' clothing and cloth. Some went as far as trying to cut pieces from the ship's sails. Even though they failed in this attempt, their actions forced the Spanish to post a two-man guard on the *San Carlos*, further weakening their position on land. The guard at the fledgling mission was from time to time reduced further—to four soldiers—when two guards accompanied Serra or Parrón for Mass on the ship.[97]

The Kumeyaay keenly observed the movements of the soldiers, and then they began to steal whatever they could get from the

Spanish settlement. On August 12 and 13, the soldiers had to drive off the locals with force. But that was just the beginning. On August 15, the Kumeyaay watched as two soldiers escorted Parrón to the *San Carlos* for Mass. Then, just after Serra had completed Mass at the mission, a group of twenty or more armed with bows and arrows and war clubs attacked. By then, Spaniards had been at San Diego for four months, and they had grown weaker. The Kumeyaay plundered and set the mission afire, stripped the clothing from the bodies of the convalescing soldiers, and even took the sheets from their beds.[98]

The corporal of the guard sounded the alarm, and the Spanish soldiers donned their protective leather jackets, readied their lances, and prepared their firearms. Seeing this, the Kumeyaay let fly a volley of arrows and retreated. The four soldiers, the carpenter, and the blacksmith opened fire. The blacksmith, running between the flimsy huts of the settlement, launched into a tirade that suggested the way many of the Spaniards who came north felt about the Kumeyaay: "Long live the Faith of Jesus Christ, and may these dogs, its enemies, die!"[99]

During the skirmish Serra and Father Juan González Vizcaíno took cover in one of the recently constructed huts. When Vizcaíno raised a curtain to peer out, an arrow pierced his hand. Serra, meanwhile, held in one hand a picture of Mary, and in the other he clutched his crucifix. Serra believed that with Mary's intervention he would not die or, "great sinner that he was," that "he would die well."[100] Serra's prayers were interrupted when his servant boy, Joseph María, burst into the hut and collapsed, mortally wounded, an arrow in his throat. As blood gushed from his mouth and temples, he asked Serra for absolution; he died fifteen minutes later, leaving Serra surrounded by a "sea of blood."[101] Soon the Kumeyaay retreated with their dead and wounded. At least three had been killed. For days the weeping of women over the dead could be heard at the mission.[102]

There were four casualties on the Spanish side: in addition to Father Vizcaíno, the blacksmith, an Indian from Baja California, and a soldier were wounded. All recovered quickly. Serra feared additional attacks in the coming days and even wrote a farewell letter to Palou and the College of San Fernando, but the mission "gradually quieted down."[103] A few days after the attack, the Kumeyaay asked for peace and for the Spanish surgeon to treat some of their wounded. The Spanish agreed to both; apparently, the Kumeyaay who were treated soon recovered. Perhaps fearing the Spaniards' guns, the Kumeyaay no longer even tried to steal from the soldiers. For their part, the soldiers built a wooden stockade around the mission.[104] In this tense atmosphere, the Franciscans made no progress in their attempts to evangelize the Kumeyaay.

Serra, however, employed all his skill in trying to sway a fifteen-year-old boy who seemed a possible convert. Serra gave him gifts, taught him some Spanish words, and convinced him to encourage others to bring their small children to the mission for baptism. Serra told the boy that the baptized would receive clothing at the mission and so dress as the Spanish soldiers. Within a few days of hearing this, a Kumeyaay man approached Serra with a young child. Serra came to believe in their interaction that the man wanted the child baptized. Serra gave the child Spanish clothes and gathered the soldiers and Franciscans to witness the first baptism at Mission San Diego. The corporal of the guard stood ready to serve as the godparent. Serra began the ceremony, but just as he was about to pour water on the child's head, the assembled Kumeyaay seized the child and took him back to their village. Evidently, the child's parents had wanted the clothing and nothing more. Serra was despondent and remained sullen for days; he saw his failure to baptize the child as a punishment for his own sins. For years, whenever he talked about this incident, his eyes would well up with tears.[105]

Portolá's overland expedition returned to a dispirited San Diego in late January 1770, "having [themselves] suffered, eaten [their] mules, and not having found Monterey."[106] In mid-December, Portolá's party had been in the vicinity of Monterey but had incorrectly concluded that the port had been hidden or destroyed by the passage of time. Before they began their long, painful trek back to San Diego, however, the men had raised a large cross so that if the *San José* or *San Antonio* appeared, its crew would know that Spaniards had been there.

Back in San Diego, Portolá saw that the settlement's stores of food were running low and that complete failure was a real possibility. All Spanish eyes scanned the ocean horizon for any sign of the *San Antonio*; without its provisions the expedition was surely doomed. They would eventually learn that the *San Antonio* had sailed from San Blas with a full load, but on orders from Gálvez it had sailed directly for Monterey. As day after day passed without any sight of the ship, Portolá finally declared that if the *San Antonio* did not arrive by March 19, the Spaniards would abandon San Diego and return to Loreto. To delay further would be to risk starvation on the road to Baja California.

Serra, well aware of Portolá's deadline, declared that he and Crespí would remain in San Diego "to the limit" of their endurances.[107] Serra did not want to leave a people he repeatedly described as "poor" and "naked" before they had been baptized, fed, and clothed. Moreover, he and the captain of the *San Carlos*, Vicente Vila, believed that Portolá had unknowingly found the harbor of Monterey and that the expedition's goals were within reach. Serra and Vila did not confront Portolá, but rather met in secret to discuss a contingency plan that did not involve forsaking Alta California. If the *San Antonio* did not appear and Portolá chose to retreat from San Diego, Serra and Crespí would await the arrival of the *San Antonio* on board the *San Carlos* and then sail with both ships for Monterey.[108]

The beginning of March saw Portolá's men packing for the journey to Baja California and Serra praying fervently to Saint Joseph, the patron saint of the expedition.

March 19 dawned with the *San Antonio* nowhere to be seen. Serra conducted a High Mass and gave a sermon, all in honor of Saint Joseph. Remarkably, that very afternoon the *San Antonio* was descried on the horizon, and the relinquishment of the colony was put on hold. When the *San Antonio* finally entered the harbor four days later, the colony was saved. The soldiers considered the sighting of the ship to be nothing short of a miracle.[109] Serra and Palou believed that Saint Joseph had interceded on their behalf, and until the last month of his life Serra would sing a High Mass on the nineteenth of each month in gratitude. Reprovisioned, the expedition could head north again in search of the elusive port of Monterey.[110]

Serra would sail on the *San Antonio*. Portolá would go by land. Two padres and a handful of soldiers would stay in San Diego.[111]

Portolá moved rapidly through territory that was now familiar to him and on May 27 reached the place where he and his men had raised a cross so many months earlier. Days later, on May 31, 1770, the *San Antonio* saw signal fires lit by Portolá's men and dropped anchor in what was clearly the harbor of Monterey. The voyage from San Diego had been relatively short but "trying" and "tedious," prolonged by contrary winds.[112] Serra was finally in Monterey, where he intended to establish his own mission "among the gentiles."

He and Portolá wasted no time. The *San Antonio* had arrived on Thursday evening. On Friday, Serra rejoiced with Crespí and Portolá over their success and proposed that on Sunday, the Feast of Pentecost, they celebrate a High Mass, raise a cross, and formally take possession of Alta California as José de Gálvez had instructed them to do. A small chapel and altar were set up under what they believed was the very oak under which Vizcaíno had said Mass some 166 years earlier. The ceremony opened with a reenactment of their arrival in Monterey, with Serra leading a procession from the water's edge and Portolá leading another on land; they converged in the makeshift chapel. Serra, in his vestments, knelt before the altar, which was adorned with a painting of the Virgin that Gálvez had sent with them for the ceremony. Serra sang the "Veni creator spiritus." The men then raised the large cross and set it in the ground. Serra sprinkled holy water all around, the standards of the Church and the Crown were unfurled, and "the men shouted at the top" of their voices, "Long live the Faith! Long live the King!" Bells were rung, rifles and cannon fired.[113] Then the Spaniards buried at the foot of the cross a sailor who had died on the *San Antonio* the day before.[114] Serra sang a Mass punctuated by cannon fire. And Portolá took formal possession of Alta California for Spain by "waving once more the royal flag, pulling grass, moving stones and other formalities according to law—all accompanied with cheers, ringing of bells, cannonades, etc."[115] That same day they established the presidio of

Monterey and the Mission of San Carlos.[116] As in San Diego, the mission and the presidio would be at the same site with soldiers and padres living in adjacent quarters yet pursuing very different goals. Before long, the dual-purpose mission-presidio would prove incongruous.

❧❦

For weeks after his arrival in Monterey, however, Serra was buoyant. Though constitutionally incapable of boasting, Serra, in a letter to Juan Andrés, his superior at the college, came as close as he ever had, and ever would. He congratulated not himself but Andrés that during the latter's administration the three missions of Velicatá, San Diego, and San Carlos had been founded and brought under the college's oversight. Serra told Andrés that if he had "helped in some measure" to create those missions—missions that everyone knew he had established nearly on his own, of course—he wanted no credit. He had merely been doing his duty for Andrés and the College of San Fernando.[117] Just as he had done in San Diego almost a year earlier, Serra asked Andrés to send yet more Franciscans so that he could establish yet more missions in his name. In this request, Serra's own pride poked through once again. He told Andrés that he should use caution in deciding just whom to send to Alta California, explaining that padres who chose to sacrifice themselves to "a work so holy" would face great challenges. He offered his own experience as an example, stating that while he had not experienced his work on this distant frontier as presenting hardships, such would not be the case for someone who did "not want to be deprived of anything." He insisted that Andrés not send him the kinds of men who "put on a glum face whenever there is work to be done, and are scarcely here before they become dissatisfied and anxious to return to the College." As if to underscore the implication that he could not be more different, Serra assured Andrés "that [on] the least order from Your Reverence I will go with promptness and pleasure— whether it be to move further or nearer, or to remain stationary here [in Monterey] as long as life lasts."[118]

Serra would indeed work in or for the missions of Alta California as long as his life lasted. He would die in Mission Carmel fourteen years later, near the mission-presidio he established in Monterey in June 1770. To his own growing satisfaction, unlike his mentor, Fray Antonio Perelló, he would leave his mark far from Mallorca, among "poor naked people" who he believed hungered for the faith and salvation only he could give them.

NINE

Securing Alta California

Serra was euphoric after arriving in Monterey, but he faced enormous challenges. Certainly he had foreseen the immense efforts it would take to turn the idea of Mission San Carlos into a reality and to convert the local Indians to Catholicism. But he had perhaps been less prepared to depend on soldiers who did not always share his priorities and unaware at first of just how difficult it would be to incorporate newly established missions in Alta California into the already overextended supply networks of northern New Spain. Serra's early years in Monterey, therefore, would demand his total commitment—but that was never in question. On top of that, though, they would require the application of diverse skills and experiences and immense confidence, and these he had acquired through his teaching in Mallorca, his service in the Sierra Gorda and Baja California, and his dealings with the viceroy and the *visitador general*. Serra, now approaching sixty, was at his greatest power, dreaming big as always but eventually grounding his vision in a pragmatic understanding of the difficulties of life on the frontier and the challenges inherent in establishing and sustaining missions in a land so remote that it could only be provisioned by sea. He was now not only more than four hundred miles north of San Diego and more than a thousand beyond Loreto but nearly two thousand miles and months away from Mexico City, the true seat of power in colonial Mexico. As a Franciscan engaging with a vast new population of Indians, and a long way from Church and political oversight and assistance, he would soon grow impatient with those who stood in his way and take unprecedented measures to protect his vision of Alta California. In short, his commitment to Alta California and his apostolic work there came to define the region and his very existence.

-※-

During the weeks after the establishment of the mission-presidio in Monterey, Serra occupied himself by logging the provisions being unloaded from the *San Antonio*, catching up on his correspondence with colleagues in Mexico, and trying to re-create on the frontier the forms of Catholic observance that had always structured his life. In 1770, the Feast of Corpus Christi would fall on June 14, and Serra wanted this important day—when for the first time in Monterey he was to carry the consecrated host in procession—celebrated with all possible pageantry. In a rare moment of self-doubt, he wondered if a procession would simply be too difficult to organize on such short notice; in particular, he worried that he had no means of properly illuminating the host so that all could see that "His Divine presence shone in this newly Christianized land." He fretted until the eve of the celebration, when, as if by "dew from heaven," as he put it, sailors discovered two cases of glass lanterns in the *San Antonio*'s hold.[1] With the lanterns illuminating the monstrance, Serra led the Corpus Christi celebration in Monterey as he had intended. Bells tolled and gunfire cracked, and religious men and soldiers alike joined in hymns and sacred songs. In a letter to Gálvez, Serra rejoiced that the procession came off with such "splendor that it might have been gazed upon with delight even in Mexico," which was no modest claim.[2] Completely absent from the celebration, however, were any Indians of the Monterey region.

Though Serra was energized by the Corpus Christi celebration, he had begun to view most of the soldiers as obstructionist, perhaps taking after their commander, Pedro Fages (Portolá had returned to Baja California). Fages had come close to spoiling the Corpus Christi celebration for Serra by insisting that the fortuitously located lanterns belonged to the ship; Serra was offended that he would only lend them to the padres and believed that Fages wanted to deny him the men and supplies he needed to build missions and convert Indians. For his part, Fages saw this as evidence that Serra wanted to take for his missions everything that the Spaniards had brought north. The general distrust between the two deepened over the following months. Serra's frustration with Fages stemmed from his dissatisfaction with the pace of the Franciscans' progress in Alta California. Serra wanted to establish more missions immediately, but he needed soldiers to guard them, and for that he was dependent upon Fages. In the summer of 1770 there was little Serra could do in Monterey other than fume, especially since he did not as yet have missionaries to assign to new missions. He was also eager to baptize the Rumsen, who lived near Monterey, but so far they had expressed little interest in the Spaniards or their religion. As Serra would learn years later, they believed that the Spaniards "had come out from under the ground" and "were the spirits of the old gentiles from the surrounding areas, who have come back in that form."[3] They had sent a few gifts to the padres and had promised to leave their children at the mission for instruction. But neither Serra nor his student and fellow Mallorcan Juan Crespí had any understanding of their language, and they had few presents to give them. By the padres' own admission, they could not engage the local Indians in a serious way. Serra pleaded with his superiors in Mexico to send blankets and clothes to Monterey "because people more naked [than these Indians] do not exist in the world."[4] Without more soldiers, missionaries, trade goods, and facility with the Indians' language, they would, at least in Serra's estimation, remain so.

The *San Antonio* sailed from Monterey in July 1770. The year that followed was a hard one for Serra; he found himself so isolated that he referred to it as another "year of novitiate."[5] Until the *San Antonio* returned in May 1771, Serra had little if any news from the outside world. And his partner in the Monterey endeavor was no Palou. Serra and Crespí had a lifetime of experiences in common—both had grown up in Mallorca, studied and lived at the Convento de San Francisco in Palma, and worked in the Sierra Gorda (Crespí had followed Serra to the New World)—but they did not always share a strong bond of affection. Crespí considered Serra a tad overbearing, and Serra thought that Crespí was fussy and hard to please. When Serra suggested to him that he trim the "minutiae" from his narrative of his journey north from Baja California, Crespí frowned and retorted, "Then you do not want me to tell things just as they are, or as I saw them?"[6] During their first few months together in Monterey, Crespí claimed that he could not live there on account of the "extreme cold, fogs, and bad weather," and he asked Serra to transfer him to another mission as soon as possible.[7]

As Crespí discovered to his dislike, winters in Monterey were cool and wet, and during summer days, even though it rarely rained, dense fog often covered the coast. But this region and its variable climate suited the Rumsen and Esselen peoples who had lived there for at least five hundred generations. They numbered between twenty-five hundred and three thousand in 1770.[8] The Rumsen and the Esselen spoke mutually unintelligible languages and had their own extensive and separate beliefs and rituals, ones Serra and most Franciscans dismissed as superstition.[9] Two of the Rumsen villages, Achasta and Tucutnut, were not far from Monterey, but three others, Ichxenta, Socorronda, and Echilat, were located some fifteen or twenty miles away, up more distant river valleys. The Esselen were farther to the south and a greater distance from San Carlos.[10]

The varied topography of the Monterey region supported a range of plants and animals, and the Rumsen and the Esselen used hundreds of them. These people lived in stable communities for much of the year, but they also maintained smaller satellite work stations where they produced and stored surplus foods—meats and acorns—for use over the winter. Their homes were constructed of wooden frames and covered by brush roofing. Like other California Indians, they crafted an enormous variety of fiber baskets for use in gathering, preparing, and storing food. Their clothing, however, was basic and utilitarian. Women wore skirts; men went naked or wore little clothing, occasionally covering themselves in skins or mud. In the colder months, they donned blankets of rabbit, otter, or deerskin. Women collected and processed acorns, seeds, roots, and berries, and they wove baskets, clothes, and household articles. Men fished and hunted game, birds, and sea mammals and made tools and weapons.[11] Like Indians elsewhere in California, they used burning, irrigation, and pruning to maximize food production and carried on elaborate trade with their neighbors to supplement the local economy.[12] Their skillful use of their environment and the stability of their belief systems initially allowed some to maintain a degree of distance from the Spaniards and their ideas.

In that first year in Monterey, Serra and Crespí made only small headway with the Rumsen. No adults were ready or willing to be baptized, but a number allowed their offspring to be christened, and between December 1770 and May 1771, Serra baptized thirteen Rumsen children at the mission-presidio; Crespí baptized another seven. Serra's first baptism was of a young boy from the village of Achasta. Serra named him Bernardino de Jesús, perhaps in partial remembrance of the Convento de San Bernardino in Petra.[13] Before long, four young Rumsen boys—Buenaventura, Francisco, Fernando, and Diego—were beginning to pick up the padres' Castilian.[14] Serra saw them not just as additions to his flock but as potential interpreters, and so he hoped to send two of the boys on the boat to Mexico so that during the voyage they would learn Spanish more rapidly.[15] In May, at the end of his Monterey "novitiate," Serra once again led a Corpus Christi celebration. This time it was made a much grander affair, he reported to Viceroy de Croix, through "the presence of quite a number" of "new little Christians," who participated as acolytes and altar boys.[16]

Despite the presence of some Indians at Corpus Christi, Mission San Carlos remained of little immediate consequence in the lives of most Rumsen. Serra and Crespí had come to Monterey with bags of seeds and the tools—hoes, plows, shovels, and picks—necessary for European agriculture, imagining that they would realize in Alta California the same vision they had brought to the Sierra Gorda and Baja California. But in Monterey the padres themselves had little success with their initial crops, and in their minds this further explained why no adult Rumsen joined the mission in the early going. Serra and Crespí planted a variety of seeds in a little enclosed garden. But the crops failed as the land was on occasion washed over by salt water from the estuary and so was "fit for nothing but reeds and nettles."[17] Unsurprisingly, the Rumsen remained wedded to their annual round of subsistence for years after the Spaniards arrived.[18] For the most part they stayed in their villages, seeing little point in interacting with men who had no material goods to offer. Had they joined the mission and then depended upon it for food, they would have starved.

Though Serra's progress with the Rumsen was halting at first, he wasted little time trying to expand his missionary field to encompass all of Alta California. Serra and Gálvez had originally planned for only three missions: San Diego, San Buenaventura, and San Carlos. Having brought San Diego and San Carlos into existence, Serra turned to the establishment of San Buenaventura as well as two additional missions, San Antonio and San Gabriel; this was now possible, in his mind, because the *San Antonio* returned in May 1771 with supplies and ten more padres.[19] But he believed that many more missions were needed even on top of these. Serra wrote letters to his superiors in Mexico proposing three more between San Luis Obispo and San Buenaventura; two between San Buenaventura and San Gabriel; and one between San Gabriel and San Diego. He emphasized that this would allow Franciscans to come to Alta California by land and to "sleep at least every third day in a mission belonging to the College." Serra's grand ambitions were most apparent in his exhortation to his superiors to seize the day, for they had before them the opportunity to make the College of San Fernando the "crown of the colleges." Not to mention that Alta California might even emerge as its own Franciscan province one day.[20]

The grandiosity inherent in Serra's plans—this was perhaps the first time in his life that he went way beyond his marching orders—set him apart from his fellow Franciscans and, at the same time, annoyed important officials from Monterey to Mexico City. His friend and fellow Franciscan Raphael Verger, who had been inspired by Serra to come to New Spain and was now the father guardian at the college and hence Serra's superior, warned him that he was moving too fast and told him, pointedly, that his direct communication with the viceroy and José de Gálvez had been improper. Around the same time, Verger wrote a letter to a Spanish official in which he praised Serra's apostolic zeal but added that he would have to be restrained.[21] By the summer of 1771, Serra had become pessimistic about support from the Crown and entrusted Verger with his views. "The usual procedure is this: the Colleges attempt to establish missions, and the King's ministers do their best through counterarguments to make it difficult," Serra told him. He added that he would accede to the wishes of his secular superiors but lamented that "they will see if I go beyond the dictates of obedience even by a hair's breadth."[22]

The military and civil leaders of Alta California similarly wished that Serra would leave the political governance of the region and its Indians to them. So deep had Serra's rift with Pedro Fages become that Serra intended to move the mission to a new location a few miles from the presidio. For a year Serra and Fages had quarreled over whether or not soldiers would work at the mission. And then the two had begun to argue about everything else. Fages did not approve of the way Serra and Crespí were building and furnishing the church or where they had buried a soldier in the cemetery. Serra, meanwhile, did not like that the soldiers kept the keys to the padres' quarters at the mission-presidio to monitor their comings and goings. None of this really surprised Serra; his years in the Sierra Gorda had convinced him that soldiers, though needed to protect the missions, often got in the way. But Fages had gone further by directly interfering with Serra's missionizing, refusing to allow Serra and Crespí to punish Indians without his permission.[23] This threatened Serra's ability to correct his "spiritual" children, and thus the entire enterprise. Fages only compounded Serra's frustration by refusing to give him more soldiers for new missions.

-※-

In the summer of 1771, with authorization from the viceroy and Gálvez, Serra initiated the relocation of Mission San Carlos to a spot on the Carmel River closer to the Rumsen and with greater access to arable land, directing a few workmen there to begin cutting down trees. Serra also apportioned the ten recently arrived padres under his watch throughout California. He assigned the two Mallorcans, Francisco Dumetz and Luís Jayme, to Mission San Diego. The two Antonios—Paterna and Cruzado—would go to San Buenaventura when it was established, and Pedro Benito Cambón and Angel Somera would be posted at San Gabriel as soon as it was founded. On July 7, these six padres sailed back to San Diego on the *San Antonio*. Also on ship was Fages, who had been promoted to captain after Rivera y Moncada's return to Baja California.[24] Remaining in Monterey for the time being with Serra were two more Mallorcan padres, Miguel Pieras and Buenaventura Sitjar, as well as the Catalonians Domingo Juncosa and Joseph Cavaller.

On July 8, with Fathers Pieras and Sitjar, Serra left Monterey to establish Mission San Antonio de Padua in the Santa Lucia Mountains to the south. Serra traveled the eighty-five miles on a mule, accompanied by an escort of seven soldiers, three sailors, and a handful of Indians from Baja California.[25] After five days they arrived in a verdant valley. Serra ordered the mules unloaded and the new mission bell suspended from a tree. In an action that surprised even his fellow Franciscan Pieras, Serra immediately began to ring the bell with abandon. He then cried out, "Come, you pagans, come, come to the Holy Church; come, come to receive the Faith of Jesus Christ." Confused by this spectacle, Father Pieras asked, "Why do you tire yourself here if this is not to be the spot where the church is to be built?" Pieras then pointed out what Serra must have known: "There was not a single pagan anywhere abouts." Pieras added that it was a "waste of time to ring the bell." Taken aback, Serra replied that his outburst was an expression of his overflowing heart and that he wanted the bell to be heard "throughout the world," just as María de Agreda had wanted the Gospel to be heard by gentiles everywhere.[26]

As they had in San Diego and Monterey, the Spaniards constructed a large cross, built a shelter, set up an altar, and inaugurated the new mission. One Salinan man from the region attended Mass, to Serra's great pleasure. Serra took this man's presence as a sign that the mission would in time grow to "become a great town of many Christians." As soon as the Mass ended, Serra gave this lone Indian many gifts, hoping to attract others to the mission. Later that day other Salinan did indeed approach. They gave seeds to the padres, and in return Serra gave them strings of shells and glass beads along with some corn and beans.[27] After a house was erected for the padres and their Indian "servants"—the Indians from Baja California—Serra left San Antonio on July 28 and returned to Monterey in a jubilant mood.[28]

Despite Serra's optimism, Mission San Antonio, like Missions

San Diego and San Carlos, was slow to develop into a "town of many Christians." Over the summer of 1771, the padres there baptized only four Indians, all of whom were young boys. Moreover, all were sick when they were brought to the mission, and three had their names entered into the burial register not long after they were baptized. Nearly all of the first sixty-one baptisms at the mission were of children, many of them likewise ill.[29] Not until May 1773 would the padres at the mission begin to baptize adult Indians.

Still, the Franciscans seemingly never lost hope that they would win over the Salinan at Mission San Antonio. They were encouraged by events that they saw as portentous, if not miraculous. For example, they found great meaning in an elderly woman, believed to be more than one hundred years old, who came to the mission for baptism. When the padres asked her why she wanted the sacrament, she explained that her parents long ago had told her that men had come to their land dressed as the padres were. These men, she had been told, "did not walk through the land, but flew." Apparently, one of these men had "told them the same things the missionaries were now preaching." The padres at first gave little credence to the tales of this old woman, until they learned that her beliefs were common among the Indians of the region. Palou and Serra believed that this woman, who went by the name Agueda, was proof of what María de Agreda had written generations earlier: that Saint Francis himself had sent two padres to the north, men who, "having effected many conversions, suffered martyrdom."[30]

Once back in Monterey, Serra devoted his efforts to the relocation of Mission San Carlos, since Fages had not yet returned from San Diego with soldiers necessary to found another mission.[31] Just as he had done in the Sierra Gorda two decades earlier, Serra pitched in as workers—four soldiers, three sailors, and a muleteer—constructed a palisade and various mission buildings. Again Serra drew inspiration and direction from María de Agreda, who had also written that this sort of manual labor was "noble" and "most pleasing to God" when it was performed in the pursuit of the conversion of Indians.[32]

Serra had gone to Carmel—the new site of Mission San Carlos—without a Franciscan companion. He had purposely left Crespí,

Juncosa, and Cavaller at the Monterey presidio, where they could attend to the spiritual needs of the soldiers. Away from the presidio and the other padres, Serra began to lead what Palou described as "a hermit's life." He lived in a makeshift cabin that barely protected him from the elements. This was in a sense another self-imposed "novitiate" for Serra, during which he seems to have returned to the Franciscan basics: daily prayers, physical labor, and a rigorous denial of all bodily comforts. Next to his temporary abode, Serra raised a large cross that became the object of his veneration morning, day, and night. When Rumsen children came to Carmel, Serra taught them to venerate the wooden cross and gave them glass beads or food he had prepared. Now living closer to the Rumsen, Serra tried to pick up bits of their language, but with little success. It was not until December 24, 1771, when the chapel and padres' quarters were complete, that Serra called for Crespí to join him at Carmel.[33]

To Serra the establishment of San Antonio and the relocation of San Carlos provided more evidence that the spiritual conquest of Alta California was well under way, if not preordained. But when he learned of the sad events at Mission San Gabriel to the south, he became convinced that all of his work in and for Alta California could come to nothing if some Spanish soldiers had their way. Mission San Gabriel was founded in September 1771 by Fathers Cambón and Somera while Serra was living in his hut at Carmel. The mission was situated among the Gabrielino, who at the time had a population that probably numbered around five thousand. They lived in more than fifty communities ranging in size between 50 and 150 individuals across what is now the Los Angeles Basin.[34] On August 6, the two Franciscans, escorted by fourteen soldiers and four muleteers, headed north from San Diego as part of a pack train loaded with supplies. In mid-August, when the padres were searching for a place to establish the mission, a group of belligerent Gabrielino had come upon them. Apparently, in response, one of the padres unveiled a painting of Our Lady of Sorrows, and Spanish legend has it that the painting so "captivated" the Gabrielino that they put down their arms and reached out in friendship to the

Spaniards. Less than a month later—in a location a few miles south-east of where the mission stands today—Cambón and Somera offi-cially established the mission. Soon large numbers of Gabrielino began to frequent it.

When Fages visited San Gabriel, he became alarmed about its lack of security and insisted that no more than five Indians enter the mission at one time.[35] This restriction infuriated the Gabrielino, who, with the encouragement of Cambón and Somera, had become accustomed to coming and going at will. They demanded the right to enter, most likely to trade and because their children regularly received gifts from the padres. Just as he was leaving San Gabriel to return to Monterey, Fages further tightened restrictions, ordering that not a single unbaptized Indian be allowed in the mission. Ex-actly what happened next is unclear, but according to Serra, "a sol-dier, who, with others, went out to round up cattle, or to defend it, or get himself a woman (as it was said after and seems the more likely), killed the principal chief of the gentiles, cut off his head, and brought it to the mission in triumph." Making matters even worse, the son of the chief was at the mission in the care of the padres. Serra was horrified by the soldiers' violence and upset that the need to increase the guard at Mission San Gabriel further delayed the establishment of Mission San Buenaventura. He thought Fages's policies could be devastating if widely applied. "If we are not al-lowed to be in touch with the gentiles," Serra lamented, "what busi-ness have we . . . in such a place?"[36]

As Serra reported to the viceroy, "the misfortunes" of Mission San Gabriel continued. The soldiers there, Serra charged, refused to work, quarreled among themselves, and "acted shamefully towards the Fathers." Some mornings, Serra stated, six or more would set out from the mission and terrorize the Gabrielino. "The soldiers, clever as they are at lassoing cows and mules, would catch an Indian woman with their lassos to become prey to their unbridled lust." Indian men who defended their wives were "shot down with bul-lets."[37] To Serra's horror, Fages had not put a stop to these outrages. Serra believed that the situation improved only when his God ar-ranged that the worst soldiers were sent to Monterey and a new corporal was assigned to Mission San Gabriel. Amid these setbacks

Cambón and Somera continued their evangelical work, but, as else-where, their first baptisms were all of children, and not until late 1773—almost two years after San Gabriel was established—did the padres at San Gabriel baptize an adult.[38] And it would be another year before they baptized a second.[39]

⋙⋘

The *San Antonio* had saved San Diego from being abandoned in 1770 and in 1771 had brought precious supplies and additional Franciscans to Monterey. In the early months of 1772, the *San Antonio*'s veteran Mallorcan captain, Don Juan Pérez, once again sailed for California with a ship laden with provisions desperately needed in Monterey and San Diego. Serra and Fages eagerly anticipated the ship's arrival. But Pérez was unable to locate the harbor of Monterey and was forced to drop anchor much farther south, near the Channel Islands. Flummoxed, he returned to San Diego. Similarly, at roughly the same time, the *San Carlos* had apparently sailed as far north as Monterey, but it too was unable to find the port and had returned to San Diego.

The continued absence of the ships led to famine in Monterey, at least for the Spaniards.[40] Had the Spanish had more mules in Alta California, the goods destined for Monterey could have been carried overland from San Diego, but with so few this was an impossibility. Fages, in an act of desperation, sent some of his men from the Monterey presidio south to hunt bear and purchase food from the Chumash.[41] In the meantime, at Carmel, Serra subsisted on milk from the mission's cows, the few vegetables from the mission's garden, and the charity of the local Rumsen and the Salinan now affiliated with Mission San Antonio, which sent provisions to San Carlos.[42] Recruitment of Indians to San Carlos and San Antonio dried up with the food supply. Serra nevertheless continued to believe in what María de Agreda had said: that "the gentiles, at the mere sight of his sons, will be converted to our holy Catholic faith." He insisted that if only the padres could secure more food and gain a command of the Indians' languages, all the Indians of Monterey would convert.[43]

Faced with famine, Serra and Fages decided to venture south to

San Diego in search of a way to get the food stores from San Diego to Monterey. Having arrived in Monterey in 1770 by sea, Serra had not yet visited the regions south of San Antonio and north of San Diego. So the journey to San Diego overland afforded him his first experience of a region and the many peoples that he believed were under his spiritual care. Serra also hoped to meet Palou in San Diego—it had been years since they had been together, and Serra sorely missed his company—and intended to establish Mission San Luis Obispo on his way.

On August 24, 1772, one year to the day after he had moved and reestablished Mission San Carlos in Carmel, Serra headed out with Fages, a group of soldiers, and a ten-year-old Rumsen boy, Juan Evangelista, whom Serra had baptized in March 1771 and who was now his servant.[44] Serra was leaving behind a San Carlos that was still in its infancy. There was a church constructed of timbers with a leaky earthen roof, a dwelling for the padres, and a small house for the soldiers, all inside a stockade. A larger church of logs and planks was under construction.[45] Few if any Rumsen had relocated to the mission, and the twenty-six who had accepted baptism were all children.

Moving quickly, the pack train arrived at Mission San Antonio on August 27. Four days later Serra was in the valley of San Luis Obispo. And on September 1 he raised a cross and founded Alta California's fifth mission, this one among the Northern Chumash. Serra left Father Cavaller, a corporal, four soldiers, and two Indians from Baja California at the mission. They had only a small amount of wheat and flour, and to subsist they traded with the Chumash and exchanged sugar and glass beads for meat and seeds.[46] As was the case at all the missions in Alta California, the earliest baptisms at San Luis Obispo were of children.[47]

Reaching San Gabriel ten days later, Serra was alarmed by the shortages faced by the padres there, given the supplies for the mission that were in San Diego. Not only did they have limited amounts of food, but they had too few candles and too little wine to say Mass regularly. Once in San Diego in mid-September, Serra and Fages resumed the disputes that had characterized their official interactions in Monterey. They disagreed over the size of the military escort needed for the planned Mission San Buenaventura, the distribution and storage of provisions for soldiers at the missions, the allocation of mules between the missions and the presidios, and the division of power between soldiers and missionaries in California, especially in matters concerning Indians.

After years of conflict each man was convinced that the other was not entirely forthcoming and was disrespectful of his power and authority. To some extent this tension was normal in every Spanish colony, where church and state contested for supremacy. Fages believed that Serra was cavalier in his approach to the safety of padres, and, if left to his own devices, would punish Indians arbitrarily and put soldiers in harm's way; Serra had no doubt that Fages was dragging his feet and damaging the prospects of new missions and conversions in California. Palou charged that Fages wanted to restrict the padres' interactions with the Indians to saying Mass—on this point, at least, he was correct—considered his own authority "absolute," and had become an "unbearable character."[48]

Serra was alarmed by Fages's methods, but he was even more concerned that the Catalan commander might have found an ally in the new viceroy, Antonio María de Bucareli y Ursúa, who had taken over from Carlos Francisco de Croix in September 1771. Croix had been a strong supporter of Serra and the missions and had even sent various items to the missions at his own expense. Faced with a local commander whom they viewed as obstructionist and a new viceroy who they feared might not be supportive of the Franciscans' work in California, Serra and the other missionaries at San Diego assembled to discuss their options. They were of one mind: Serra should travel to Mexico City as soon as possible and present to the viceroy his grievances against Fages and his plan for the administration and supply of Alta California. Serra's decision to go to Mexico City was an extraordinarily assertive move and one without parallel in the history of the Californias, if not all the Spanish borderlands. Father presidents of the northern missions did not leave their provinces to plead a case before the viceroy. When he was in the Sierra Gorda, Serra had concerns about the military's treatment of Indians and the missions, but he had no direct correspondence with the viceroy. All of his concerns were channeled through his superiors in the college.

Serra did not ask Verger, his superior at the college, for permission to return to Mexico. Given the infrequent delivery of mail in California, dependent as it was upon the annual arrival of the *San Carlos* or the *San Antonio*, Serra might have wisely concluded that writing to the college leadership for permission to travel to Mexico City would have led to years of delays. He might also have sensed that Verger, given his earlier rebuke of Serra for his direct correspondence with the viceroy and Gálvez, could insist that Serra stay in California and that he would work things out with the viceroy in his stead.

That Serra persevered with the original plan was a sign that he had become even more confident and more assertive after many years in New Spain.[49] Serra's experience in Baja California, where he worked directly with Gálvez to reorganize the peninsula, also probably convinced him of the need to go to Mexico City. With the support of his colleagues in San Diego, Serra boarded the *San Antonio* on October 17, 1772, accompanied by Juan Evangelista, living proof of what he believed was possible in California.[50]

Seventeen years earlier Serra had defeated the Saldívars, but the stakes were higher now. Fledgling missions could not survive without provisions. The Franciscans' authority over Indians in California had been challenged, perhaps even undermined. Serra's reputation, in this life and the next, hung in the balance. Moreover, Serra believed he had to ensure the conversion of untold numbers of Indians, whose salvation now seemed at risk. Fages must have been surprised, if not shocked, when he learned that Serra was headed back to Mexico City. In fact he tried to bar him from going.[51] But Serra did not heed his order. Fages may have been relieved that Serra would be gone for some time and might never return to California. If these thoughts crossed his mind, though, he would have underestimated Serra. The padre from Mallorca was too confident, too zealous, too committed, and too cunning and logical to be trusted with the viceroy and his ministers in a one-sided argument.

❋

Aided by smooth seas and favorable winds, the voyage to San Blas took a mere two weeks. In San Blas, Serra notified Verger of his arrival in Mexico and sent him the summary of his plan for saving the missions, one that he hoped to present to Viceroy Bucareli.[52] After a three-day mule ride Serra and Juan Evangelista arrived in Tepic in early November. There Serra received surprising news that surely lifted his spirits: the Fernandinos had chosen to relinquish the missions of Baja California and turn them over to the Dominicans. Not only would this allow the Fernandinos to wash themselves of Baja California, but it would free up more missionaries for Alta California. From Tepic, Serra wrote to Palou, asking him to reassign eight padres from Baja California to Alta California. By then Verger had already reassigned four Franciscans to the northern missions, and Palou had apparently written to Serra wanting to know if more were needed. Slightly wary of undermining Verger's authority, but supremely confident in his knowledge of what was best for the missions of Alta California, Serra told Palou to send eight padres north if Verger's letter could be interpreted as supporting such an increase. If Verger had specified that fewer than eight should be sent, then Palou should obey his order, and they would have to trust that God would put the matter right. No matter how many padres were sent, Serra hoped that Palou would be among their number so that the two could "live and die there together" in Alta California, something that Serra believed would be a "great consolation."[53]

Soon after Serra finished his correspondence, he and Juan Evangelista left Tepic and continued by mule to Guadalajara. By the time of their arrival around the twentieth of November, they had both fallen deathly ill. Serra was "burning with fever," and both received last rites. Juan Evangelista, like Serra, received Final Communion,[54] which was unusual for a California Indian;[55] the Franciscans typically deemed recently baptized Indians insufficiently knowledgeable of Catholicism to warrant the sacrament. Juan Evangelista's receipt of the final sacrament was an indication that Serra believed he had truly converted, as well as of his concern that if Juan Evangelista died, the conversion of the Rumsen Indians would be further delayed. Serra was convinced that his "relatives and countrymen would never believe his death was due to natural causes." Concerned that he himself might not make it to Mexico City, Serra sent Verger another letter, in which he restated all that he wanted from the viceroy.[56]

But both Serra and Juan Evangelista recovered and resumed

their journey. However, in Querétaro, at the College of Santa Cruz, Serra's fever returned. Serra went to the college infirmary and upon the advice of a doctor prepared again to receive last rites. Yet later that day, another doctor checked Serra's pulse and declared that if Serra needed last rites, then so did he. He told Serra, "You are all right; nothing is wrong with you." Serra took to the road again and arrived at the College of San Fernando on February 6, 1773, looking "very tired, worn, and thin."[57]

By the winter of 1773, Bucareli was well aware that discord between Fages and Serra was jeopardizing the Crown's enormous investment in Alta California. To Fages, Bucareli had written that he understood that in Alta California "only the spirit of discord and disunion" reigns, and that just as Fages complained about the comportment of the padres, so too did the padres "complain about yours." Bucareli considered the situation deplorable and lamented that the inflexibility of both parties threatened to bring about the "ruin of the new conversions."[58] As the complaints piled up on his desk, Bucareli found it difficult to reconcile the contrasting views of the situation and was unsure how to solve the problem that was Alta California.

Although weak and tired and with little appetite, Serra gathered his energies and, with the blessing of Verger, went to the grand palace of the viceroy in the center of Mexico City for his hearing with Bucareli.[59] As a Franciscan, Serra would not have been impressed by the sumptuousness of the offices of the highest-ranking minister in New Spain, but he knew power when he saw it. Serra had in mind nothing less than a thorough administrative reorganization of Alta California, and he told Bucareli as much. Bucareli must have listened intently—and as a devout Catholic he lent Serra a sympathetic ear—but it was too much to consider in one sitting.[60] He needed to see Serra's proposals in writing, and then it all would have to be studied and deliberated by his advisers. Before the meeting ended, however, Serra implored Bucareli to resupply Monterey, and Bucareli responded by ordering emergency shipments sent to the settlement. But these too would fail to reach their destination; the *San Carlos* suffered a broken rudder and made it no farther than Loreto. Palou, who had arrived in Monterey from Baja California during

Serra's absence, recalled that in that time cow's milk "was the manna that fed all."[61]

Two of the great ironies of Serra's life are that his most important contribution to California history was engineered outside the province and that his most influential piece of writing had nothing to do with theology and moral philosophy, the subjects he had excelled at as a student and professor in Palma. Serra was raised in and trained by the Catholic Church and the Franciscan order. That he was capable of composing sermons and theological treatises laden with scriptural citations and biblical allusions was evident during his time as a member of the professoriat and during his popular missions. But what set him apart from his Franciscan brethren and many Spanish officials of his era in New Spain was mastery of the art of composing dry, lengthy, logical, and persuasive memoranda. It was with this skill that he won over royal officials and essentially drove government action. When the missions of Baja California were reorganized, Serra was in effect the junior partner of José de Gálvez. Plans for the reorganization of Alta California, however, sprang from Serra's lively, logical, and focused mind.

Serra's follow-up memorandum to his meeting with Bucareli ran to more than eight thousand words. More than a litany of complaints, it contained thirty-two specific suggestions. Given the sweep of his proposals, Serra was wise to begin with his credentials. He was, he wrote, president of the missions of Alta California. In that capacity, he stated—with the immodesty the context required—he had been a part of "all that had happened in the new settlements from the exact day and hour they had begun" and had seen or investigated "all that had happened there."[62]

Serra's thirty-two suggestions addressed four general areas of concern: problems with the provisioning and supply of Alta California; shortages of skilled labor at the missions; the division of authority between soldiers and missionaries; and the soldiers' leadership and conduct, or what Serra saw as the problems therein. To alleviate the famine that gripped Alta California, Serra called for the *San Carlos* to sail immediately for Monterey and to be followed as soon as possible by a large ship under construction, the *Santiago*. All goods transported to the mission should be clearly marked, invoiced, and separated from those destined for the soldiers. Items for the soldiers should be warehoused separately and priced according to a new regulation. The scales at San Blas and each mission should be regulated; spoiled goods should not be shipped from San Blas; and more meat should be sent north. Additionally, mules should be transferred to the missions to allow for the movement of goods across the region, and cattle from the royal herd should be turned over to the padres. Furthermore, some of the missions needed bells, vestments, and sacred items the padres required to administer the sacraments and perform Mass.

To address the shortage of both skilled and manual labor, Serra asked that each mission receive four to six field hands from San Blas to till the land and raise crops and a group of married Indians from Baja California, to demonstrate to the local Indians the condition they should aspire to attain. Moreover, Mission San Diego had a forge but no blacksmith; Mission San Carlos needed a forge and a blacksmith; both missions lacked iron; Missions San Carlos and San Gabriel needed carpenters; and the whole region required a surgeon to replace the one who had gone insane and been removed from the province.

About Fages and the soldiers under his command, Serra was direct. To prevent desertions by soldiers, delays in establishing new missions, and general disorder in the ranks, Fages had to be removed or forced to retire. In Serra's words, "the harsh treatment and unbearable manners" of Fages had brought the province to the point of ruin. Serra hoped that he would be "discharged honorably, and without any humiliation whatsoever."[63] Moreover, in support of the troops whom he saw as oppressed by Fages, Serra requested that eight soldiers be allowed to retire and that others who had deserted be granted pardon once a new officer had taken charge. Leaving nothing to chance, Serra wanted Fages replaced by Don José Francisco de Ortega, a man whom Serra described as courageous, religious, and experienced. Serra also proposed specific numbers of troops for each mission guard and requested that soldiers who marry Indians be given a monetary reward. He also asked that in the future the soldiers facilitate rather than impede or tamper with the padres' letters to and from Mexico.

For Serra, though, it was not enough that Fages be replaced and the soldiers brought under tighter supervision. Rather, Serra wanted the viceroy to clarify the extent of the padres' authority over Indians. Thus, Serra—in the most important point of his memorandum—asked Bucareli not for new powers but for formal acknowledgment of the powers that Serra presumed the Franciscans already held. Specifically, he asked Bucareli to affirm and notify Fages or his replacement and the soldiers under his command "that the training, governance, punishment, and upbringing of the baptized Indians, and those who will be baptized, pertain exclusively to the missionary fathers, the only exception being for crimes of violence." Therefore, the padres could punish Indians as they saw fit, but soldiers could not "punish or mistreat" Indians without the padres' permission. As Serra told the viceroy, such policy had been the custom in New Spain since its "conquest," and it was "in uniformity with the law of nature concerning the upbringing of children, and an essential condition for the proper education of the poor neophytes."[64] Finally, to further solidify the Franciscans' control over the missions, Serra asked that at each mission the padres be able to select one soldier to serve as the mission foreman and that they be able to remove from the mission any soldier who they believed behaved scandalously. In sum, he sought to secure for the Franciscans near-complete control over the Indians and to check the power of the military. If approved, the net result would be more power for the Franciscans and less for the military, which would run counter to the general trend in New Spain during the era of Bourbon reform.

Two days after he had completed his memorandum, Serra traveled back to the palace of the viceroy and placed it in Bucareli's hands. But Serra was not finished. Soon thereafter, he heard that a plan was afoot to abandon San Blas and supply Alta California solely overland by mules from Loreto. To Serra this was folly, and using his pen as a rapier, he savaged the proposal. Serra conjured an annual pack train of more than eleven hundred mules winding its way north. Given that there were hardly any mules in Baja California, he wondered where the eleven hundred mules and some four hundred replacements would come from. Even if they could be found and taken to Baja California, they would soon die there without water and pasturage. And the presence of the muleteers necessary to direct this number of animals would cause chaos in California. Serra opined that never in his life would he see such a poorly conceived idea executed.[65] He was right. His arguments carried the day, and San Blas and its ships were saved.

Serra's lengthy memorandum had to be duly considered by Bucareli's advisers, and that took time. On May 6 the viceroy met with his counsel, and a week later Serra learned of their decision. To his "great joy" Serra had been granted nearly everything he had asked for. The padres' control over the Indians was confirmed and near total. Fages would soon be recalled. Soldiers would henceforth be removed from the missions at the padres' command. Manual laborers, blacksmiths, carpenters, and a surgeon would all be sent north. The padres' mail was now safe and would be carried free of charge to and from California. Prices would be regulated, and goods—food and clothes for Indians—would be marked and sent in large quantities. Deserting soldiers would be pardoned. There were still details to be worked out—such as the exact number of soldiers at each mission—but Serra had won his most important bureaucratic and administrative victory.[66]

With his work in the capital successfully completed, but unable as yet to return to Monterey, Serra found himself with more free time than he had had in years. There were no crosses to be raised, and no witches to interrogate, and no soldiers to rebuke. During this lull, he wrote a long-overdue letter to his nephew. Miquel was now a Capuchin friar and evidently had written to Serra recently for advice. Miquel's letter had reached Serra in Monterey, and the father president seemed a tad put-upon that his nephew expected him to write back. In his response, Serra reminded his nephew that he had written him a long letter in 1758 (fifteen years before), in which he had explained what he was doing and offered him spiritual advice. He now felt that Miquel should seek out the counsel of the fathers he lived with, not that of a distant uncle.

It was an unsentimental letter similar to the farewell he had written to his parents from Cádiz in 1749, though Serra did express his love for Miquel and noted that he commended him and his mother to God every single time he said Mass. But Serra explained that when he had left his beloved Mallorca, he had intended the break with those in his homeland to be permanent. He had, in his own words, decided to "leave not merely in body alone." Thus, he had seen no point "in keeping before his mind what he had left behind." As for his family and friends on the island, he hoped to see them again in eternity; he did not expect to see them again in this life. Serra told Miquel that his life was now in Monterey, among a "poor" people. California was where he hoped to die. He expressed to Miquel his desire to return to Monterey, where, with God's help, the Franciscans would "harvest in plentiful measures" the fruits of their labor. Serra allowed that he might write to Miquel once he was back in Monterey, just to let him know he had completed the journey, but he did not invite Miquel to write again. It is doubtful that Serra ever wrote again to Miquel, or to anyone else in Mallorca for that matter. His family and friends, he told Miquel, should take consolation that when he died they would learn of his death through the Franciscans at the Convento de San Francisco in Palma.[67]

In early September 1773, Serra prepared to leave the College of San Fernando for the last time. He was nearly sixty years old. Just as he had done in Palma nearly a quarter of a century before, he kissed the feet of his fellow Franciscans, asked them for forgiveness, and bade them a tearful farewell. He was again in poor health, so weak that he was almost unable to stand.[68] Many of the padres at the college believed that Serra was in fact too old and diminished to make the trip back to Monterey. Evidently, Verger, the guardian at the College of San Fernando, had similar concerns, for he sent Serra, Juan Evangelista, and Father Pablo de Mugártegui to Guadalajara by coach.[69] In Guadalajara, Serra recruited craftsmen—carpenters and blacksmiths and their families—as well as common laborers for Alta California.[70] He had so many applicants that he claimed he could have filled a whole ship with them. One point that had remained unresolved in the new dispensation was the matter of mules for the missions, and Serra wrote to the viceroy from Guadalajara, urging him to press the issue. He believed that without Bucareli's intervention, "even if it rained mules in Monterey, the missions would still be without any."[71]

By early January, the trio was in Tepic awaiting a ship. Finally, in the early morning hours of January 15, Serra sailed from San Blas on the *Santiago*. It was the ship's maiden voyage, and some on board feared that it was not seaworthy. Nevertheless, in addition to a huge cargo of supplies for California, the ship carried some ninety-eight people, among them a physician, three blacksmiths, two carpenters, and one Juan Conrado from the Sierra Gorda, who was assigned to Serra as his servant.[72] As usual, Serra had an easy passage, but Father Mugártegui, the pilot Juan Pérez, Juan Evangelista, and many others became sick with chills and fevers. A young man, Joseph Francisco Ramírez, whom Serra had recruited as a common laborer, died a week out of San Blas. When the man's body was thrown overboard, it was the first time that Serra, in all his travels, had ever seen someone buried at sea.

Pérez had been under orders to sail directly to Monterey, but with an ailing crew, unfavorable winds, and a largely untested ship he dropped anchor in San Diego on March 13, 1774. Three weeks later, Serra headed out overland to Monterey. On his way north he would inspect Missions San Gabriel, San Luis Obispo, and San Antonio. He promised the padres stationed at these missions that soon they would be richly provisioned.

During the final leg of his slow journey back to Monterey, Serra, with an eye toward recruiting more Indians to San Carlos upon his return, began to instruct Juan Evangelista on how he might describe all that he had seen in Mexico. They had been traveling together now for a long time, and Serra asked Juan Evangelista if he had ever imagined that there were entire countries with people who wore clothes and were Christian. The boy said no, that the Rumsen believed that the whole world was like their country; he assured Serra that he would now tell his countrymen that all such beliefs and the notion that the Spaniards had come from an underworld were "trickery." Serra also asked how the Rumsen had understood the large wooden crosses that the Spaniards had raised in Monterey a few years earlier. Juan Evangelista said that they had been afraid of them because "the sorcerers and dancers who roam through the night" saw one cross, "every night, ascend to the heavens, not as dark material like wood but glittering with light, and beautiful."[73] It is a measure of Serra's desire to understand and convert the Rumsen that he asked these questions of Juan Evangelista, but the fact that he did not pose them years earlier suggests the limits of Serra's genuine interest in California Indian understandings of the world.

Serra and Juan Evangelista finally arrived in Monterey on May 11, two days after the *Santiago*. Serra had been gone from San Carlos for twenty-two and a half months, and during that period the padres at the mission and the soldiers at the presidio had endured famine conditions. Most of the Rumsen who had joined the mission during Serra's absence had since left. But with the arrival of the *Santiago*, there was now food in abundance. The presidio warehouse was overflowing with grains, and the soldiers ended up dumping 200 fanegas of corn in the middle of the presidio. To clothe the Indians at the mission, San Carlos had received over one hundred blankets and nearly one thousand yards of cloth. To feed the Indians, the mission now had 900 fanegas of corn, 250 fanegas of beans, and large quantities of ham and meat. The padres once again enjoyed a supply of chocolate. And to attract Indians to the mission, the padres had received more than four hundred strings of beads in every color.[74] In Serra's estimation the mood of the province had changed dramatically nearly overnight: "The whole extent of the territory which, but recently, was weighed down with melancholy and suffering, is filled with happiness."[75] A month after his return, Serra rhapsodized that San Carlos had more than two hundred Indians who "three times a day eat from our hands" and who "pray, sing, and work." He fervently believed that the Franciscans in Alta California would now be able "to increase the numbers of Christians almost at will."[76]

TEN

Building a "Ladder" of Missions

Back in Monterey again and having passed his sixtieth birthday, Serra at first was unfailingly optimistic about the existing missions, even though he was often alarmed by the behavior of Indians and soldiers in them. He soon clashed with Fernando de Rivera y Moncada, Pedro Fages's replacement, and then with his successor, Felipe de Neve, about the establishment of new missions and the one issue that Serra was certain he had resolved, the padres' oversight and correction of Indians in the missions. Serra's trip to Mexico had indeed solved the most pressing logistical problems that had held back the new missions but not the entrenched ones, namely the contest between the Church and the military over control of the Indians and resources. No matter what Viceroy Bucareli had decreed, this struggle was an unavoidable aspect of Spain's colonial enterprise. However, during Serra's later years in Alta California, this tug-of-war was intensified by the governors' growing sense of their own powers and Serra's own realization, in the wake of new administrative reforms and the death of Bucareli, that he no longer had the support of the highest-ranking government officials in New Spain. At Mission San Carlos, Serra continued to realize his apostolic ambitions one sacrament at a time, but with each passing year—as he aged, as the Kumeyaay at Mission San Diego rose in rebellion, and as Governor Neve exercised the powers of his office—Serra's ability to shape the region of Alta California and mark it with the Franciscan imprint grew increasingly tenuous.

-✳⊱-

After his return from Mexico, Serra initially saw progress at the missions. All had cultivated young Indian interpreters and with them had gained a foothold in surrounding Indian communities. Moreover, with the arrival of more Franciscans in California, the missions were now unusually well staffed. Whereas under Jesuit administration each Baja California mission had had only one padre, San Carlos now had six, and San Antonio, San Gabriel, San Luis Obispo, and San Diego had three each. More interpreters, more Franciscans, more food, more beads, and more clothing—all led to more baptisms. By December 1773, when Serra was still in Mexico, the missions had administered 491 baptisms and counted 462 residents. At the end of the next year, after Serra had returned, the figures had nearly doubled, to 833 baptisms and 761 Indian residents. The missions had also performed 124 marriages of Indians, a sign that more adult Indians were affiliating with them.[1]

The developments at Mission San Carlos were striking and suggestive of what was taking place at the other missions too. With Serra's return, and the arrival of more food and gift items, such as beads and cloth, large numbers of Indians came to Mission San Carlos. In the last five months of 1774, some ninety-two accepted baptism, eighty-eight of whom were children. Moreover, by December roughly one hundred adults were under religious instruction; nearly seventy would be baptized in the first months of 1775. The mission compound also was beginning to take on an air of permanence. With the assistance of soldiers and the padres, Rumsen laborers had constructed of adobe a large roofed granary some thirty yards in length. They also completed an office for the padres, accommodations for the surgeon and the blacksmith and their families who had come from Mexico with Serra, and living quarters for two servants and the corporal stationed at the mission. The padres had overseen the building of adobe ovens in a kitchen at the mission for the Rumsen. Through Serra's efforts, the mission had also acquired a large collection of liturgical art that the padres would use to instruct the Indians about the mysteries of Catholic faith and belief. Notably, the mission church now also had a confessional, constructed out of local redwood. There was even an alarm clock so that the padres could keep track of their daily schedule of prayers and the morning and afternoon instruction of catechumens. The mission corrals held sixty-one cows, thirty-two pigs, fourteen horses, fourteen mules, and one donkey. Since Indians who had accepted baptism were to live permanently at Mission San Carlos, the padres placed great emphasis, as they had in the Sierra Gorda and across New Spain, on the cultivation of subsistence crops. The mission fields at San Carlos in 1774 had yielded almost three hundred bushels of wheat and corn.[2]

Believing that California Indians had the mental faculties of children, the Fernandinos taught willing ones the most basic Catholic prayers and concepts—the Our Father, the Ave Maria, the Ten Commandments—and a simplified children's catechism. Children below age nine they baptized without hesitation, but Indians nine and older had to demonstrate a basic comprehension of Catholicism beforehand. Typically, pre-baptismal instruction took months, if not years. In later decades, once Serra was gone, it would last only weeks. The Franciscans used devotional paintings or engravings of heaven and hell, the Catholic saints, and the final days of Christ as educational tools. Serra took a special interest in this art, ordering portraits of each mission's patron saint, and not only dictated the content of the paintings but also selected the painter, José de Páez, a noted mid-eighteenth-century artist popular in Mexico City.[3] The padres also taught Indian children and adults Catholic hymns and songs and chose the most talented for the mission choir. Others they taught to play stringed instruments; many eventually joined mission bands that performed a wide range of complex devotional music. California Indians had their own musical traditions, and many of those continued in the missions under the guise of Franciscan instruction.[4]

As the California missions attracted more adults, the padres found themselves devoting much of their time to managing the behavior of the newcomers, even though Indians at places like San Carlos continued to live in their own villages outside the mission stockade. At every mission it would be decades until the Indians actually lived in adobe structures. Nevertheless, the padres insisted that baptized Indians not leave the mission's village without their permission. Baptized Indians were to attend religious instruction daily and Mass on Sundays and on special days of obligation. They were to perform the tasks the padres assigned them, subject themselves to the padres' discipline and correction, and without exception follow Catholic rules regarding marriage and sexuality. Few Spaniards, other than the most dedicated priests, could live in full accordance with such a prescribed lifestyle. And the mission Indians, most of whom had previously condoned premarital sex and divorce, and in some cases polygamy, routinely ran afoul of the Franciscans' strictures and what they experienced as an alien and alienating code of personal behavior.

The padres answered violations of their moral strictures with warnings and then beatings. But when the Franciscans subjected adult Indians to corporal punishment or summoned soldiers at the mission to administer a flogging, conflicts followed. Corporal punishment was the norm in Spain in the early modern period but not among the Natives of California. In Serra's world, good fathers punished their children with blows. In this regard he and the Franciscans were not innovators; Serra once declared that the idea was as old as Spain's colonization of the Americas. As the self-appointed spiritual fathers of the Indians, the Franciscans in California saw it as their responsibility to beat their "children." Such had been the policy of the Fernandinos in the Sierra Gorda, and Viceroy Bucareli in his approval of Serra's memorandum had sanctioned its institution on the California frontier, even though the Crown earlier had sought to limit when and where priests in central Mexico could flog Indians.[5]

Time and again, the Franciscans found that curbing Indian sexuality was one of the biggest challenges they faced, and their frustration was likely compounded by the involvement of soldiers in various incidents. Serra heard of a soldier at San Luis Obispo who was caught having illicit sex with an Indian woman.[6] In January 1775, Simon Carpio, a muleteer from San Antonio, was caught in the act with an Indian woman at Mission Carmel. Serra had the woman locked up at the mission and hoped that the soldiers at the presidio would imprison and punish Carpio if they caught up with him.[7] As it turned out, they did, and he was placed in the stocks.

Indians in the missions were also punished for a wide range of activities, from simply ignoring the padres' commands to stealing livestock. In 1792, the governor criminalized the Indians' practice of burning the countryside, a strategy that had long been the foundation of their subsistence economy.[8]

Indians who chafed under the padres' oversight—or simply wanted to return to their villages and customary practices—often fled the missions. Just as he had done in the Sierra Gorda, Serra asked soldiers at the missions to bring the Indians back. In Alta California, the soldiers were known to refuse him, as they did in July 1775, when Serra asked for help in tracking down eight or ten "fugitive" Indians.[9] Serra ended up sending a party composed of Father Dumetz, the Baja California Indian Cypriano Rieva, and eleven adult Rumsen men after these persons. Nine of Serra's "lost sheep" were returned to the mission, bound and under arrest. Serra sent four of the men—Carlos, Geronimo, Cristobal, and Ildefonso—to the presidio for punishment. He kept their wives at the mission, probably under lock and key. Three of the men Serra sent to the presidio had previously left San Carlos in defiance of the Franciscans' commands and had been punished for it. This time, Serra wanted all of them locked up at the presidio and to receive "two or three portions of whippings on separate days." Serra believed that these punishments would serve "as a warning" and "may be of spiritual benefit to all."[10] The governor acknowledged Serra's request and carried it out.[11] Years later, when the forms of punishment carried out at the missions were called into question by a new governor, Serra replied that no less a figure than Saint Francis Solano, in his mission in Peru, had his assistants flog Indians who did not follow his commands. Serra did not doubt that from time to time there had been excesses and inconsistencies in the whipping of Indians in the California missions. Nevertheless, he insisted that corporal punishment was essential to the Fernandinos' effectiveness and averred that "everyone knows that the padres love the Indians."[12]

The steady growth of the existing missions in the mid-1770s was not enough for the ambitious Serra. Moreover, Franciscans who were working as supernumeraries at each mission were pressuring him to establish new missions so that they could strike out on their own.[13] In 1775, he had enough padres to establish four new missions and was eager to do so but again had trouble securing the support of California's military authorities. Serra had clashed with Fages over the latter's unwillingness to assign soldiers to new missions, and after Fages's removal Serra found himself battling his replacement, Fernando de Rivera y Moncada, over the same matter. Rivera y Moncada was a career soldier. He had joined the military in 1742 and risen to captain of the presidio in Loreto, a position that amounted to being the military governor of Baja California. He had not sought the military governorship of Alta California; after his service with Portolá in 1769 and 1770, he had retired with his family to a farm outside Guadalajara. Serra had wanted Don José Francisco de Ortega to replace Fages, but the viceroy had chosen Rivera y Moncada instead. No doubt aware of the challenges that Rivera y Moncada would face working along-side Serra, Bucareli ordered him to keep a diary and to periodically send him a copy of it. To Serra's frustration, Rivera y Moncada often reminded him that their dealings went into the journal, and so to the viceroy.

By July 1775, a mere two months after Rivera y Moncada had arrived in Monterey, Serra saw that he might pose a problem.[14] Rivera y Moncada had already rebuffed Serra's proposal that soldiers from San Diego and San Carlos be assigned to the still unfounded San Buenaventura. Writing to Bucareli, Serra declared in regard to the governor's refusal, "Evils that are not remedied in the beginning customarily are cured later only with more difficulty."[15] Serra viewed Rivera y Moncada as too cautious and believed that if a hundred more soldiers came to Alta California, the governor would still resist new missions.[16] Serra maintained that with the Indians at San Diego and San Carlos ever peaceful the guards at these missions or the nearby presidios could be reduced. He did not understand why Rivera y Moncada had twenty soldiers at the San Diego presidio. "What are all those people [soldiers] doing there on that little hill in San Diego?" he wondered in a letter to the father guardian at the College of San Fernando. "They have a nice view from there, and could be useful if by chance they are needed but it would be better if they were occupied in the advancement of the spiritual conquest," Serra believed.[17] For a year the two went back and forth on this issue and many other familiar ones: mules, the soldiers' relations with Indians, and so on. Their correspondence between the presidio in Monterey and the mission in Carmel became heated; at one point, Serra and Rivera y Moncada even resolved to meet in person in the hopes that etiquette might prevent them from saying what they had no problem writing.

In August 1775, their dispute over whether or not there were enough soldiers to establish a new mission in Alta California boiled over. Earlier in the summer Serra had received a copy of a letter from Bucareli to Rivera y Moncada that he understood as calling for the establishment of two missions in the San Francisco area, each with a guard of thirteen men from an anticipated contingent from Sonora under the command of Captain Juan Bautista de Anza. But when Anza was slow to appear in California, Serra pressed Rivera y Moncada to make soldiers available for at least one of the missions. On August 10, Serra received a letter from Bucareli regarding new missions; evidently, so too had Rivera y Moncada, for he traveled to Mission Carmel to talk to Serra about the news. Rivera y Moncada told Serra that founding a new mission would be very difficult, if not impossible, right now. They argued, and the meeting ended with Rivera y Moncada promising to mull it over.[18] The next day, however, when Serra had not heard from the governor, he made up his mind to go to the presidio at Monterey.

The meeting began warmly, with banter and lighthearted talk. Serra, however, misread Rivera y Moncada's pleasantries and assumed that the officer had agreed to establish a mission, probably San Buenaventura. Growing serious, Rivera y Moncada asked Serra just how many soldiers he needed for one new mission. Serra then repeated an earlier proposal: he would give up four guards from existing missions (two each from San Diego and San Carlos) and told Rivera y Moncada "it was now necessary for him to express those that he could give from the presidios."[19] In response, though, Rivera y Moncada suggested that they bring the whole matter to the viceroy. Serra said that doing so was not necessary, that they could make the

decision and the viceroy would be "satisfied."[20] Rivera y Moncada
then stated that he could not supply more than six men, which led
Serra to believe that with the four he himself was offering, he would
have ten in total. Serra then pushed Rivera y Moncada, asking for
two more soldiers, so that with an escort of twelve men San Buenaventura could finally be founded among the very numerous Chumash. "It cannot exceed six," responded Rivera y Moncada, meaning
that he would allow no more than six soldiers to protect a new mission. Taken aback, Serra asked why; Rivera y Moncada explained
that all the missions had been founded with six men. Serra uncom-
prehendingly asked about the ten men he thought they had just
agreed to.

"Six in total," responded Rivera y Moncada.

"Then it follows that the presidios are only contributing two
men?" Serra asked, his voice rising.

"Yes, Father. Yes, Father," answered Rivera y Moncada.[21] Rivera
y Moncada then explained that he had a letter from Bucareli ordering him not to exceed six men per mission. Serra replied that he had
a similar letter authorizing up to thirteen men for an escort. "My
orders are for six men," insisted Rivera y Moncada.[22] Uncharacteristically, Serra then exploded in anger.

"There is no such order!" thundered Serra as he banged on the
table.

"There is," said Rivera y Moncada in a restrained tone.

"There is not!" shouted Serra.

And so they continued until Serra came to his senses and said
that "such an exchange could keep up all night."[23] Indignant, Rivera y Moncada rose to his feet and lectured Serra, saying that in his
thirty years of service to the king he had always behaved with honor
and had never suffered any reprimands from superiors, and now,
here, a "father president, a spiritual and learned man, was taking
away from him his honor." When Rivera y Moncada was done, Serra
apologized and explained that he had meant no offense. Reflexively
logical, Serra pointed out that since he had come to ask for favors,
he could not possibly have intended to insult. Then Rivera y Moncada
produced two letters from the viceroy, both of which said "six men,"
not thirteen.[24] Serra had been wrong; he had misread Bucareli's often
illegible script.

The next morning after Mass, and when their tempers had cooled, Serra and Rivera y Moncada reached an agreement: Mission San Juan Capistrano would be established between San Diego and San Gabriel. Rivera y Moncada would provide four soldiers from the presidios instead of two, and Missions San Diego and San Carlos would each provide one.

But the discord between the two would continue, largely because of Serra's actions. There was a surplus of padres at San Carlos, and Father Lasuén had been given the temporary assignment of serving as chaplain at the Monterey presidio, a post that all the other padres had found loathsome. Lasuén, however, found it amenable and became close with Rivera y Moncada and the soldiers under his command. Because lodging was limited, he and Rivera y Moncada slept in the same room. Serra, however, was never fully comfortable with Lasuén living at the presidio, was wary of his budding friendship with Rivera y Moncada, and resented the fact that the soldiers expected the missionaries to say Mass at the presidio without compensation. Thus, he assigned Lasuén to found Mission San Juan Capistrano, even though he could have sent another padre from San Carlos. Rivera y Moncada valued having Lasuén as his own personal chaplain and appealed to Serra to leave Lasuén at the presidio. But Serra would not budge.

Lasuén began to say his goodbyes, and the women, men, and children of the presidio grew distraught, appealing to Rivera y Moncada to reverse the decision. But the governor was at his wit's end.[25] A delegation went to the mission and appealed directly to Serra, but the father president told them that his decision was final and that anyway, Lasuén was happy with his new appointment. In reality, Lasuén—in a manner typical of the Franciscans of Serra's day—was only content to go to San Juan Capistrano because it allowed him to show his submission to his superior. As Lasuén put it in a letter to Raphael Verger, the father guardian at the College of San Fernando, "It is in every respect the place for which I have felt the least attraction; and thanks be to God for that reason I find the greatest satisfaction in going there."[26] When Lasuén went to talk to Serra and relayed the sentiments of the women at the presidio, Serra brushed aside their concerns. Later that day, an exasperated Rivera y Moncada wrote of Serra in his diary, "Buena mollera de Padre!"— "That pig-headed Father!"[27]

Accompanied by Father Gregorio Amurrió, four soldiers, and four Baja California Indians, Lasuén left Monterey on August 21 for San Diego, where he would pick up two more soldiers as well as an additional contingent before heading north again to found San Juan Capistrano. He carried with him four bundles of glass beads to encourage the Acjachemen to frequent the new mission.

Rivera y Moncada never forgave Serra for how he had treated him in his quarters at the presidio, and the transfer of Lasuén only deepened his dislike of the father president. Once Lasuén had departed for the south, Serra expressed surprise at Rivera y Moncada's anguish and told the commander that he now regretted that Lasuén had left, as if he could not be recalled.[28] For Rivera y Moncada, the transfer of Lasuén was the final straw. He told Serra that he would never again set foot in Mission San Carlos,[29] and this stung the old Franciscan.

In October, amid a nasty exchange of letters with Serra about salaries and rations for workers at the missions, Rivera y Moncada began actively petitioning to be removed from Alta California. Serra, somewhat surprisingly, found his potential retirement problematic. As difficult as he found Rivera y Moncada, Serra shrewdly understood that it was preferable to go up against a man who had grown weary of battle than someone who was fresh to the job and full of energy.[30]

Meanwhile, on October 19, the commander of the San Diego presidio, Serra's favorite, José Francisco de Ortega, left his presidio with a dozen soldiers and Father Lasuén to establish San Juan Capistrano. Mission San Diego was left temporarily with a guard of only four soldiers. The day after Ortega's group arrived at its destination, Lasuén said Mass. He and the soldiers then constructed and raised a large cross, and they built a primitive shelter for a church. Over the next week, Lasuén used his stock of glass beads to entice local Indians to help cut wood, construct a corral, and stake out the boundaries of his new living quarters. With everything going according to plan, Father Amurrió left Mission San Gabriel with supplies and cattle for the new mission. But on the day Amurrió arrived, all were forced to abandon San Juan Capistrano. A messenger had brought news that just after midnight on November 5, the Kumeyaay had at-

tacked the lightly defended Mission San Diego.[31] They burned the
mission to the ground, killing Father Luís Jayme and a blacksmith
and mortally wounding the mission's carpenter. Serra's zeal for another mission had overridden his logic; he of all people should have
been aware of the danger inherent in reducing the mission guard at
San Diego, since he had been there at the previous attack in 1769,
when Portolá's departure for Monterey had left just him and a few
convalescing soldiers to face the fury of the "poor naked people."

Serra did not learn of the destruction of the San Diego mission
until the night of December 13, when a breathless Rivera y Moncada
broke his promise to himself and rode to Mission Carmel with the
news. Stunned, Serra initially responded by citing Scripture and
Franciscan belief—that Father Jayme's martyr's blood would fertil-
ize the spiritual ground of San Diego and lead to mass conversions
of Indians at Mission San Diego.[32] Serra and Rivera y Moncada met
again the following day, and the latter declared his intention to go
immediately to San Diego. Serra inquired if he might accompany
him, but Rivera y Moncada said that he would be traveling too fast
and perhaps even riding through the night. When Serra asked if an
escort might be provided for him to follow later, Rivera y Moncada
once again rebuffed the father president, telling him he had no soldiers to spare.

    Serra was stuck in San Carlos, though Father Juan Fuster of
Mission San Diego, who had survived the attack, had written to
him and recounted its harrowing details.[33] Six hundred Kumeyaay
had surrounded the mission, pillaged the church, and then torched
the mission's buildings, some of which had been completed only the
day before. Fuster and two soldiers had taken cover in a kitchen and
barricaded themselves behind several large bales of cloth that the
padres had set aside to clothe the Indians. With Fuster clutching the
mission's bag of gunpowder and shielding it from falling firebrands,
the soldiers fired their weapons, killing and injuring some of the at-
tackers. In the melee, Fuster was hit by a large stone in the shoulder
and blocked an arrow headed straight for his head with a pillow. At
dawn the Kumeyaay attacked in one final charge, but the soldiers

drove them off. The soldiers posted at the nearby presidio had apparently slept through the night and were unaware of the attack.

As soon as the Indians retreated, Fuster asked two Baja California Indians what had happened to Father Jayme. A search ensued. Before long, Jayme's body was found in a nearby arroyo, riddled with arrows and puncture wounds, his face a bloody pulp. "The only way my eyes could recognize him," Fuster told Serra, "was from the whiteness of his skin and the tonsure of his head." The soldiers assembled five stretchers: two for the dead—Jayme and the mission blacksmith—and two for the severely injured soldiers, and another for the master carpenter, who was mortally wounded and would die five days later. Everyone then retreated to the presidio.[34]

In the wake of the destruction, Serra felt that he was living in a "valley of tears."[35] With the abandonment of San Juan Capistrano and the destruction of San Diego, Serra had lost in a single blow two steps in the ladder (*escala*) that he hoped to construct on the road between Baja California and Monterey.[36] Moreover, this was not just a strategic setback but a personal blow. Serra had recruited two of the dead—the blacksmith Joseph Manuel Arroyo and the carpenter Joseph Ursulino—and brought them from Mexico in 1774 on board the *Santiago*. Father Jayme, meanwhile, was one of Serra's own, a fellow Mallorcan.

Yet these men and the two missions were not the only casualties. Serra's judgment would no longer command the same respect. Fuster, while certainly not pointing a finger at Serra, had concluded that the Indians had attacked "when they saw there were only four escort soldiers at the Mission, and that the soldiers who were necessary for the founding of Mission San Juan Capistrano had been withdrawn from the presidio."[37] In his correspondence with Rivera y Moncada, Serra had argued that the Kumeyaay at San Diego were docile. Rivera y Moncada was more wary of the Indians and had urged greater caution, though in the end, of course, he had approved the plan and agreed to lessen the guards at the mission and presidio.

Once word of the attack reached Mexico City, the father guardian instructed Serra that he was no longer to press for the establishment of new missions.[38] Serra complied with the letter of this directive but not its spirit. While he never again insisted on new missions for Alta

California, he did not hesitate to tell anyone who would listen that he "*desired*" them.[39] Somehow, he managed to find a measure of vindication in the destruction of the mission, for he had—he said—been insisting all along that soldiers should be in the missions, not in presidios.[40] This argument, however, rang hollow in Mexico City.

Serra never stated that the attack on San Diego had altered his view of California as a place destined to embrace Catholicism. To his dying days, he continued to believe that God was working in his own ways to bring about the conversion of California's Indians. But allusions to María de Agreda's writings—and her claim that Saint Francis himself had told her that the Indians of the north would be converted merely upon seeing the Franciscans—now disappeared from his correspondence.

With no way of investigating the attack or punishing its leaders—Serra could not get a letter to Mission San Diego to advise the men there, much less travel there himself without an escort of soldiers—Serra was forced to, in his own words, leave "the whole matter in the hands of God." But he wrote to Bucareli asking for the murderers not to be punished too harshly if they were caught, and that they then be pardoned—and "so saved, which is the very purpose of our coming here, and the reason which justifies it." Fearing a repeat of what had happened in 1758 when the military, after the destruction of the mission at San Sabá, had decided not to allow missionaries back into that part of Texas, Serra believed it was imperative that Mission San Diego be rebuilt as soon as possible.

In the spring of 1776, the aftermath of the San Diego attack was not the only challenge Serra faced as father president. In February 1775, his superiors at the College of San Fernando had written him a rather stern rebuke regarding what they saw as his mistakes and excesses. Serra did not receive the letter until more than a year after it was sent. The father guardian and governing counsel had issued an edict that Serra was not to transfer missionaries among missions without their approval; that he was to distribute goods equally between the missions; that the padres were to treat the soldiers with

"all consideration and prudence"; and that he was not to communi-
cate directly with the viceroy or other high officials, but instead
should direct all correspondence to the college. Not only was this a
serious critique of his leadership in California, but it came in the
form of a circular letter, which meant that Serra had to sign the rep-
rimand and forward it on to all the other missionaries in California
for their signatures too. Reading the letter, Serra was "ashamed."
But he signed the letter, passed it on, and then rebutted nearly all of
the charges against him, though he admitted that he had written to
the viceroy and the visitor general directly and said that he would
try not to do so in the future.[41] Later Serra would interpret the college as directing him not to write any "reports" to the viceroy, which
left open the possibility of sending letters.[42] Serra continued to cor-
respond with the viceroy, and eventually the college seems to have
dropped the matter. Serra, given his long and distinguished career
as a missionary and considerable accomplishments, had in some
ways become untouchable.

Serra desperately wanted to go to San Diego to reestablish the mission there and to revive the short-lived experiment at San Juan Capistrano, but without a soldiers' escort his only avenue south was by
sea. In late June 1776, when the *San Antonio* sailed from Monterey,
Serra was on board, arriving in San Diego on July 11. His sudden
appearance prompted considerable fear in Rivera y Moncada, who
believed that Serra's final destination might be Mexico City, just as
it had been in 1772, when Serra and Fages were locked in dispute.[43]

    Work began in earnest on the reconstruction of the San Diego
mission in late July and progressed rapidly and seemingly without
opposition from the Kumeyaay. Serra sent to the College of San
Fernando some seventeen pounds of silver that had been retrieved
from the ruins of the mission church.[44] With San Diego rising from
the ashes, and with news that additional soldiers were soon to arrive
in the region from Baja California, and with letters in hand urging
the reestablishment of San Juan Capistrano, Rivera y Moncada gave
his assent. Serra went to San Juan Capistrano in late October with a
military escort and reestablished the mission on November 1, 1776.

Then he headed north, passing through Missions San Gabriel, San Luis Obispo, and San Antonio on the way. He was back at Mission San Carlos on January 15, 1777.

In the six months that Serra was away, the northernmost part of Alta California had witnessed many important developments. In mid-September a large party of colonists under the direction of Joseph Joaquín Moraga established the presidio of San Francisco. Three weeks later Fathers Palou and Cambón established Mission San Francisco, and in January 1777 Father Tomás de la Peña founded Mission Santa Clara on the southern edge of the San Francisco Bay. There were now eight missions in Alta California. Serra had selected the padres for these two new missions, but he did not participate in their founding.

Upon his return to Monterey, Serra began preparing for another change in the region's military leadership. While Fages and Rivera y Moncada had been the highest-ranking military officers in Alta California during their tenures, the full governor of the Californias, Felipe de Barri, had remained in Loreto with little say in the governance of Alta California.[45] In 1777, in an acknowledgment of the increasing importance of Alta California, the seat of the governor of the Californias was moved to Monterey. Felipe de Neve, the new governor of the Californias, arrived in February. Neve had played an important role in the expulsion of the Jesuits and had spent many years administering Jesuit assets seized by the Crown.[46] Rivera y Moncada left Monterey a month after Neve arrived. His destination was Loreto, where he took over the daily administration of Baja California.

Neve and Serra enjoyed a brief period of good relations. Serra met with him at least three times soon after his arrival, and he came away impressed. Serra saw in Neve a decisive man of education with whom he believed he could "live in peace." After his struggles with Fages and Rivera y Moncada, Serra now resolved that he would work in harmony with the governor. But it was not to be. In Felipe de Neve, Serra encountered exactly the kind of man he feared when he heard that Rivera y Moncada was angling to get out of Monterey: Neve was fourteen years younger than Serra, skilled, innovative, energetic, and for the most part, uncompromising. He would eventually do for the presidios what Serra had done for the missions: streamline their finances and organization and make them sustainable. He would also try to reclaim from the missionaries some of the powers Serra had secured when he pleaded his case before Bucareli in Mexico in 1773.

Serra and Neve represented different understandings of the role of missions in late-eighteenth-century New Spain. Neve was the first governor to bring Enlightenment ideals and the Bourbon Reforms to California; his disputes with the old Franciscan arose out of the sea change in Spanish thinking about the role of the Catholic Church and missionaries. In the middle and late eighteenth century, men like Neve saw Catholic missions as anachronistic holdovers from a bygone era, as institutions dominated by authoritarian padres who held Indians in a state of servitude and delayed their entry into Spanish society. Neve would write that Franciscans' control over the Indians was excessive and oppressive and that it rendered "the Indians' fate worse than that of slaves." Furthermore, he found it troublesome that by all appearances the padres wanted exclusive control over Indians and their property and would not recognize any "other authority than that of their own religious superiors."[47]

The ideas and style of governing that Neve brought to California had been in circulation for some time. During Serra's years in the Sierra Gorda, José de Escandón had allowed the Fernandinos to have full control over Indians' lives, but in the region north and east of the Sierra Gorda known as Nuevo Santander, Escandón had experimented with another kind of colonial order, one that relied on parish priests, not mendicant missionaries. Neve effectively brought these ideas, which came to be known as the New Method, to Monterey.[48]

During his many years as a missionary to Indians, Serra had grown increasingly hostile to all interference, believing that it was only under Franciscan tutelage that Indians could become civilized. He would fight with Neve over many of the seemingly mundane issues that had undermined his relations with Fages and Rivera y Moncada, but he now had to confront new challenges as well. In a sense, Neve turned the tables on Serra: whereas Serra had fought with Fages and Rivera y Moncada over the role of the military in Alta California, now he would struggle with Neve over the role of missionaries in the region. Nevertheless, Serra would exasperate

Neve, just as he had Neve's less capable predecessors. Neve would come to believe that the padres, in particular Serra, used their "wiliness" to discredit and evade his orders and that "the [only] way to get along with them is to give in to their will."[49]

By April 1778, Serra and Neve were at odds. Serra believed that Neve was about to go back on his word and order Indians at Mission San Diego to work at the presidio, something that Serra opposed and believed was contrary to law. Serra counseled Lasuén, who was now at Mission San Diego, to simply refuse to give Neve Indian laborers, and if the governor continued to insist on the workers, Lasuén was to find a way to have the military set its sights on those Indians who were likely out of reach, namely those who came rarely if ever to the mission. Neve and Serra also clashed over whether padres had to hand over to the governor annual reports on the mission's inventories and population, information that they regularly prepared. Serra said that if the governor wanted the reports, he could get them from the father guardian. Moreover, he curiously stated that he did not have enough paper to provide Neve with copies of the reports. Through logic, stamina, and cunning, Serra prevailed in these and many other small disputes with Neve, just as he ultimately prevailed in a major one: Neve's plan to institute municipal governance by elected officials in the missions.

Neve ordered the Franciscans in December 1778 to allow Indians in the oldest missions to begin electing their own municipal officials, just as they had in the Sierra Gorda. This request came at a difficult time for Serra. He had learned in June that California was no longer under the authority of Viceroy Bucareli but, like the other northern provinces, was now under the jurisdiction of a separate unit, the Comandancia General of the Interior Provinces of New Spain. The goal behind this element of the Bourbon Reforms was to streamline the political administration of the northern frontier and somehow render it profitable, or at least less expensive to protect.[50] It is quite likely that Neve's decision to force elections in the missions was in fact an outgrowth of these new administrative designs. To head the new unit, Carlos III had appointed Don Teodoro de Croix, the nephew of the former viceroy, as commander general. Bucareli, the viceroy who had given Serra such great authority over the missions in 1773, was no longer someone Serra could count on to support his vision or appeal to in his growing dispute with Neve. Serra wrote Croix a generous letter in August, but the correspondence between the two was never warm, and Croix was always in Neve's corner. Serra sent his final letter to Bucareli in October 1778; Bucareli would die in April 1779. When Serra learned of Bucareli's death, he grieved, for he believed that—even with the administrative changes—Bucareli could have been of some service to the missions and missionaries.[51] Now the Franciscans would have to fend off Neve's initiative on their own.

The padres already recognized that Indian villages had their own leaders, but what Neve wanted them to do was replicate in the missions the town councils that characterized Spanish civil government. He was attempting to implement the imperial policy of assimilating Indians into the Spanish political system.[52] Indeed, Serra and his fellow Franciscans in the Sierra Gorda had seen this policy in action, but it had been instituted before their arrival, and the Indians who served as officials were generally much further along in their assimilation into Spanish society. For the Indians of Alta California, Neve believed that this civics lesson would be at least as valuable as the Franciscans' catechism. Indians at Missions San Diego and San Carlos were to proceed with the election of two alcaldes and two regidores; baptized Indians at smaller, more recently founded missions, such as San Antonio, San Gabriel, and San Luis Obispo, were to elect one alcalde and one regidor.[53] Upon being elected, each official was to report to the nearest military garrison, where the commander would install him in office in the name of the king. The Indian official would receive from the presidial commander a certificate he needed to exercise his powers; alcaldes also were to receive a large wooden staff that would symbolize their authority.[54]

Despite the presence of Indian officials in missions elsewhere in New Spain, and the fact that Serra had worked alongside them in the Sierra Gorda, where elections were the norm, the Fernandinos bitterly opposed Neve's elections. Serra wanted absolute control over the missions and the Indians who lived in them—which he believed he had secured in 1773—and thought that Indians so recently subjugated could not possibly be ready for a measure of self-governance, no matter how rudimentary. He feared that Indian officials would use their political power to pursue their own goals; that, in fact, had been his experience with the more "civilized" Indians in the Sierra Gorda. He also did not want Indians to learn that the Spanish governor, not the Franciscans, had ultimate civil and judicial authority over them.

But to Serra even more was at stake in this dispute than the Franciscans' claim on mission Indians: the definition and purpose of California's Franciscan missions suddenly seemed to be open to debate. In August 1778, Neve had drawn Serra's ire by insisting that there were no missions, only *doctrinas*, in Alta California.[55] *Doctrinas* were in essence secularized missions, self-supporting parishes that fell under the jurisdiction of a bishop, not a religious order. Missions had always been envisioned by the Crown and missionaries who staffed them as temporary establishments that were necessary to introduce Catholicism to the Indians. By the time Spain began establishing missions in Alta California, nearly all the missions of New Spain had been converted to *doctrinas* or parishes. In the Bourbon era, the conversion of missions to *doctrinas* was also a way to reduce the power of independent religious orders and to centralize Bourbon political authority.[56] Thus, by insisting that the missions were in fact *doctrinas* and that elections of Indian officials be held in conformity with Spanish laws and supervised by the *curas* (local priests), Neve was in effect challenging and even undermining the Fernandinos' understanding of the Franciscan enterprise in California.[57] When Serra heard Neve lay out these arguments, he was, as he put it, tempted to wonder if his "whole past life had been but a dream."[58] Predictably, Serra responded that the Fernandinos were apostolic missionaries, not parish priests, and that the laws cited by Neve in his insistence on the elections therefore did not apply.[59] At San Diego in 1779, Neve's insistence on elections prompted the Franciscans to threaten resignation, lest their acquiescence be interpreted as an admission that they were in fact parish priests.[60]

This conflict between Serra and Neve came to a climax just before Mass on Palm Sunday 1779, when the two exchanged bitter words at the Monterey presidio chapel. Neve had said something to

Serra that provoked the latter to shout back, "Nobody has ever said that to me because they could not say it to me!" The two trained logicians then descended into an absurd exchange.

After Mass and back at the mission, Serra felt wretched about his argument with Neve. He spent the better part of the evening arguing with himself and unable to focus his thoughts. He began to write a letter to Neve but could not complete it. Later that evening, overcome with agitation and fearing that he would be of no use the following day, Serra cried out: "¿Qué es esto, Señor?" ("What is the meaning of it, Lord?") As he would later write, just then a voice from within him repeated one of Christ's admonitions to the apostles: "Be prudent as serpents and simple as doves."[61] Reassured, he was finally able to sleep, at least for the few hours until morning prayers. And he decided to follow the governor's orders, but only in ways that would not "cause the least change among the Indians or in the mode of governing" established by Franciscans.[62] Serra believed that with God's assistance he could combine the simplicity of the dove and the cunning of the serpent to outmaneuver the governor and prevent the elections from diminishing Franciscan authority.[63]

As Serra directed, the Franciscans exercised their influence over the elections—especially in their second year—primarily by convincing Neve that only with the padres' guidance would both Indians and Spaniards profit from the elections. At several of the missions, according to Serra, the first elected Indian officials had committed crimes or behaved arrogantly, as if they were "gentlemen."[64] By January 1780, when the second annual elections were to take place, several had abandoned their missions, while others had been laid low by disease and were too ill to vote.[65] Consistent with Spanish law, Neve specified that only former Indian officials could act as electors, so he expanded the missionaries' role in the elections, telling them to supply "direction" when necessary.[66]

Meanwhile, Serra tried to prevent Indian officials from learning that Franciscan authority was not total. He instructed Lasuén to speak to the presidio officer whose responsibility it was to confirm the Indians elected to office: "Ask him to carry out this function so that, without failing in the slightest degree in his duty toward his superior officer, the Indians may not be given a less exalted opinion of the fathers than they have had until now." Furthermore, Serra preferred that the Indian officials remain ignorant of the responsibilities the military vouchsafed them. "The document that is used in conferring these offices on them," Serra advised Lasuén, "may be as powerful as they wish, provided Your Reverences are the only ones to receive it and read it."[67]

Such was the Franciscans' oversight that at many missions only Indians they trusted won election. But on top of this, Serra wanted to ensure that these few could also be subjected to corporal punishment, just like any other mission Indian, if they committed an offense or crime. Serra claimed, for instance, that once in office, and believing that he was exempt from correction by the fathers, Baltazar, the first alcalde of Mission San Carlos, "began to do just as he pleased." According to Serra, Baltazar "had a son by one of his relatives, and had a [Baja] California Indian flogged because he carried out an order from the Father missionary . . . And now . . . [he is] a deserter [and] adulterer, inciting the people here, meeting personally those who leave here with permission, and thereby trying to swell the numbers of his band from the mountains by new desertions of the Natives of this mission." In the Sierra Gorda, Indian officials—be they governors, alcaldes, or fiscals—enjoyed no exemption from punishment. Evidently, with Serra's approval, "they were flogged, or put into the stocks, according to the gravity of their offense." And as a result, Serra noted, "they took particular pains to carry out their respective duties."[68] Serra was backed on this count by most of his padres; in 1780, six of the eight California missions were led by Franciscans who had served in the Sierra Gorda, most under Serra's supervision.

Even after Serra had found a way for the padres to control the elections, he boldly opposed Neve at every turn, counseling Lasuén, his subordinate in San Diego, to upend the governor's annual election schedule by, in essence, equivocating: "Pretend that you do not understand—with the pretext that a year had not been completed [since the last elections] and that you are still awaiting a response from the letter you sent him by means of the Lieutenant."[69] In the face of Serra's intransigence, Neve realized, much as his predecessors had, that "there is no mischief these religious will not attempt if exasperated, such is their boundless unbelievable pride." He complained that his "politeness and moderation over more than four years have not been enough to turn them from the hostility with which they engage in surreptitious conspiracies against the government and its laws." Neve finally concluded of the padres: "There is no means whatsoever they would scorn." His judgment of Serra was severe but accurate: "He knows how to feign compliance in matters put before him, as well as how to avoid it."[70] About Neve, Serra would later write: "Common sense, laws and precedents mean nothing to him."[71]

Serra for decades had been an obedient servant of the Church and a key player in the expansion of Bourbon power, but he had done the latter to serve the Church and further his own apostolic dreams. Now, in his late sixties, he was becoming not just a prickly irritant to Neve and his Franciscan superiors in Mexico City but an anachronism. In the face of the energetic Neve, who intended to instill the power of the Bourbon state in California and its missions, and his own diminishing stamina, Serra was losing the ability to shape Alta California and its missions as he saw fit. His vision of missions dominated by his Franciscans was increasingly hard to realize. He still held immense power over the Franciscans in California and the Indians in the missions, but the aging Junípero Serra would increasingly devote his remaining time and energy to completing his own personal apostolic mission.

ELEVEN

Twilight

The Alta California of the early 1780s was far different from the one Serra had helped inaugurate in 1769. In his final years in Alta California, significant and dramatic events roiled the region: the Yuma destroyed a new Spanish settlement along the Colorado River and then killed its missionaries and settlers (1781); settlers (under the directive of Neve) established civilian pueblos in San Jose (1777) and Los Angeles (1781); and Dominicans or secular priests seemed poised to replace the Fernandinos in California.[1] There would also be significant milestones: the establishment of Mission San Buenaventura (1782), for instance. But Serra did not play an indispensable role in any of these events or their aftermath. By the late 1770s and early 1780s, Governor Felipe de Neve had become the driving force for change in the region. From the moment he began his appointment to the post of governor of the Californias in 1777, Neve had been encouraged by Commander General Croix to craft a new regulation that would restructure the province whose missions and presidios had been run along the lines hammered out by Serra and Viceroy Bucareli in 1773. Neve completed his work in the summer of 1779, but it was not until January 1781 that his new regulation for Alta California became law.

Neve's *reglamento* increased the pay of soldiers, called for more civilian settlement in California, and essentially took aim at Serra's vision for Alta California and his control of the missions. The number of Franciscans at each mission was to be reduced to one—something that Serra had bitterly opposed since his days in Baja California—so that padres could be assigned to a new set of missions to be opened farther inland. These missions were to be founded according to the New Method: padres were to focus on religious instruction and not interfere in the Indians' economic or political lives. The missions would have churches and padres' quarters, but they would not be provided with any of the tools necessary for animal husbandry or domesticated agriculture. Facing the potential loss of the fundamentals of their mission regime, Serra led all the missionaries in California in opposition to Neve's plans, and he was supported in full by the College of San Fernando. The Franciscans prevailed in that they protected their established missions in California, but Serra was being pushed aside, and founding missions in his chosen manner would now prove problematic.[2]

Moreover, as the presidios and the pueblos took root, and their affiliated communities of soldiers and settlers grew in numbers and influence, Serra and his missions were no longer synonymous with Spanish California. The land and sea expeditions of 1769 had brought fewer than 100 soldiers to the region, but later reinforcements increased the number in the province to about 170 by 1774. In January 1776, Captain Juan Bautista de Anza escorted more than 200 settlers to the region. A second group of 230 more colonists arrived in 1781.[3] Serra never took an active interest in the spiritual well-being of these settlers unless they came to the missions for Mass and the sacraments. He never ventured among them to offer a popular mission as he had done so many times in Mexico, and neither did he investigate any of them in his capacity as a *comisario*. His work and his concerns remained with Indians. With each passing year Junípero Serra exerted less influence on the overall shape of the colony itself. In the final years of his life, above all else, the baptisms and the confirmations he could provide to California Indians gave his life direction and motivation.

As father president in the Sierra Gorda, Baja California, and Alta California, Serra had ascended to the heights of his profession but had never lost sight of his chief purpose in New Spain: serving as an apostolic missionary. In the 1770s he began to lament that he was spending half of his time writing letters to contest initiatives put forward by the region's governors,[4] and he decided that he would invest more of the energy he still possessed in the baptism and confirmation of Indians at Mission San Carlos and across Alta California. He made this decision not only to save Indians but also because he thought it would save the missions of California. Furthermore, he believed that his dogged pursuit of baptisms and confirmations could not but help improve his own chances for salvation. More than anything, his missionary work would help him prepare himself to "die well," a final act that, as he put it, "of all things in life is our principal concern. For if we attain that, it matters little if we lose all the rest. And if we do not attain it, all the rest is of no value."[5]

All told, during his years in Alta California Serra baptized at least 530 Indians at Mission San Carlos, many of whom were christened as infants or young children.[6] Serra pursued the baptism of adults with special vigor. In the words of Palou, once Serra returned from Mexico City and was free from the troubles of negotiating with the viceroy, he "cast the net among the pagans, inviting them to the mission." During the day Serra would often be surrounded by Indian catechumens whom, with the assistance of an interpreter, he taught the central Catholic prayers. And "as they became sufficiently instructed," Serra "baptized them." Gathering this "spiritual fruit" was a great consolation to Serra during the periods when the establishment of new missions proved difficult.[7] Typically, at San Carlos, Serra would baptize adults in groups ranging in size from two to six. One day he baptized fifteen. On another occasion, he traveled thirty miles from the mission to baptize Pach-hepas, a village leader of the Excelen, a group situated some fifteen miles south of Mission San Carlos.[8]

For Serra, baptizing Indians was a defining act. It affirmed his own identity as an apostolic missionary and, he believed, increased the population of Christendom. Through the recitation of Catholic prayers, participation in the life of the mission, and adherence to a strict code of behavior, Indians under his tutelage could now be saved. But Serra did not think that the sacrament of baptism converted Indians to Catholicism, nor did he only baptize Indians who he believed had already converted to Catholicism. To Serra, baptism was the most important early step in a process that he hoped would culminate in the Indians' conversion. He knew that the Rumsen and others at first came to the mission—and accepted baptism—for food, clothing, and trade goods and to be near family who had already done so. He prized the sacrament because it brought Indians into the Church and because he believed it demonstrated their decision to live "under the bell" in accordance with the padres' rules and wishes. For all Indians, children and adults, daily religious instruction was to follow their christening in the form of a regular recitation of the catechism and the most important prayers. All adult Indians were to continue to have their beliefs refined through an annual confession during Lent when the padres probed their beliefs and encouraged them to amend their ways.[9]

When it came to formally bringing adult gentiles into Catholicism at Mission San Carlos, Serra took the lead. He baptized almost every one of the adult gentiles who received the sacrament at San Carlos when he was in residence.[10] When Serra had joined the Franciscan order, he had taken a new name for himself, to signal his new identity. For a similar reason, when he baptized Indians, he gave them Spanish names. He did so with great care and originality. Remarkably, he hardly ever bestowed the same name twice. For the 530 Indians he baptized at San Carlos, he used nearly 500 different names, of saints and other heroic figures in Catholic history and belief. Most, if not all, of the references were lost on the Indians, and they continued to use their original names; some Indians were even unaware of the name Serra had given them.

Though Serra's involvement in the instruction of Indians at San Carlos is not known, it is likely that it was significant. Serra probably had the final say over whether an adult Indian was adequately prepared to receive baptism. In general, he delegated few missionary tasks to his subordinates, even as he carried out the administrative responsibilities of the father president. To his death, he never took a relaxed, distant role in baptisms. On June 3, 1784, he baptized a thirty-year-old man from the village of Kalendaruc and named him Millan Deogracias in honor of the one thousandth baptism at the mission.[11] Serra would baptize another four adults within a week, the last on June 12, just two months before his death.[12]

Serra's deep commitment to personally administering baptism to adult Indians at Mission San Carlos in the last decade of his life is one reason he was so revered by his fellow Franciscans. It is also, perhaps, the quality that Serra's adversaries—and most likely even his close Franciscan colleagues—found so problematic: his desire for absolute control. One wonders what it was like to be a missionary serving under Serra at San Carlos. Fathers Juan Crespí, Miguel Pieras, Francisco Dumetz, Francisco Palou, José Murguía, Tomás de la Peña, Matías de Santa Catalina Noriega, and Diego Noboa—no doubt these men were fired by many of the same dreams that animated Serra, but working in the great man's shadow, they baptized very few adult Indians. Dumetz baptized sixty-eight, and not one of the other missionaries baptized more than fifty adult Indians at San Carlos during Serra's years in Alta California. The baptisms of adults padres performed took place only when Serra was on an extended trip away from the mission. These missionaries, like Serra, had ventured across the Atlantic and then to the far north to convert Indians to Catholicism. (Crespí, Pieras, Dumetz, and Palou had come from Mallorca.) As Franciscans, they had sworn obedience to their superiors. And they saw themselves as fortunate to have worked in the presence of an eminence such as Serra. But many of them nevertheless made clear their intent to found missions of their own.

Confirmation, unlike baptism and other sacraments, was typically administered only by a bishop. It was a sacrament intended to signify and strengthen the recipient's faith in Catholicism. When a frontier region had not yet been assigned to a bishop, though, missionaries could petition the Vatican for approval to administer the sacrament, but this authority was granted only under certain circumstances and for a limited period of time. When Serra took over as father president of the missions of Baja California in 1768, he noted that the outgoing Jesuit father president had performed confirmations with the Vatican's approval. Serra wanted to secure the same privilege, even though doing so was a long, complicated process that involved overlapping authorities and possible dissenters and was slowed by the great distances between Mexico City, Madrid, Rome, and Monterey.[13] His petition was not even sent by the College of San Fernando until 1774. Both the pope and the Council of the Indies signed off on it in 1774, but it was not approved by the viceroy until 1776. Serra did not get a copy of the formal patent authorizing him to administer the sacrament in Alta California until June 20, 1778. However, once he had the approval in hand, he committed himself to confirming as many Indians as possible before he died or by July 16, 1784, when the patent would expire.[14] It was not clear which would come first.

As soon as Serra received the patent, he set about making up for lost time. On June 29 he confirmed ninety-one children at San Carlos, and over the coming weeks and months he would confirm more children and some adults as well. With adults, Serra was at first cautious, only confirming those who could demonstrate to him an adequate understanding of Catholic beliefs and practices. Thus, as of late August, he had confirmed only 181 Indians at San Carlos, roughly one-third of the mission's Indian community.

Wishing to confirm Indians in the southern missions but now feeling too frail to travel to San Diego and back overland, Serra decided to go south by sea. He boarded the *Santiago* on August 24 and was in San Diego by September 15.[15] At the missions of San Diego, San Juan Capistrano, San Gabriel, San Luis Obispo, and San Antonio, Serra confirmed just about every baptized Indian. Evidently believing that he might not pass through these missions again, he had adopted a far lower standard for confirmations. At San Diego, Serra took particular satisfaction in confirming three of the five Indians who had killed Father Jayme; he also confirmed Carlos and Francisco, two of the leaders of that attack, for whom Serra had secured a lenient punishment. All told, at the five southern missions, Serra confirmed 1,716 people, nearly all of whom were Indians. He returned to San Carlos, arriving on December 23.[16] The rigors of this journey, however, had predictably aggravated his chronic leg injury, and he "suffered a great deal from the habitual disease of his foot."[17]

When Serra arrived back at San Carlos, he was exhausted. His leg now painfully inflamed, he did not go to the presidio even once during the summer of 1779.[18] During this time, moreover, Neve had received an order from the king that had made him concerned about Serra's permission to perform confirmations. It was not clear that the

Crown—in conformity with the Real Patronato—had actually agreed that Serra was the person designated to confirm in California. Furthermore, because Serra had petitioned to confirm before the Comandancia General of the Interior Provinces had been created, the patent had been approved by the viceroy rather than Croix. When Neve asked to see Serra's patent, Serra refused to show it to him, asserting that his college would not have told him he could confirm unless proper approval had been secured. The tension between the two increased when Serra asked for a military escort to accompany him to Santa Clara and San Francisco so he could confirm Indians at the two missions. Neve rebuffed the request, even though Serra begged him for the assistance. "To go, broken as I am in health, without anyone to accompany me—even though I wished to do it—is something I cannot do."[19] Both of Serra's legs were now causing him great discomfort. He had trouble standing long enough to say Mass. Resting and sleeping had become difficult.[20] Neve explained that he did not want his soldiers helping Serra break the king's laws, but if Serra would assure him that he would perform no confirmations in Santa Clara or San Francisco, he would have his escort. Serra agreed, and he was soon headed north.

Serra left Mission San Carlos and somehow walked the seventy miles between his mission and Santa Clara in only two days.[21] Palou, not realizing that Serra had already set out, had left Mission San Francisco with two naval officers and a surgeon in the hopes of ministering to the ailing Serra in Monterey and of then traveling with him back to San Francisco. By chance, Palou and Serra arrived at Santa Clara at the same time. The father president was hardly able to stand; the surgeon offered to attend to his leg, but Serra declined, believing that the treatment might make it impossible for him to make it to San Francisco.[22] Serra's pain evidently went away when he baptized several Indians at Santa Clara. On October 15 the group arrived at Mission San Francisco, and there Serra broke his pledge to Neve by administering 189 confirmations. Most were of Indians at the mission, but 39 were of sailors from the Spanish ships in the harbor, and 49 were of presidial soldiers and their families.[23] Serra justified his actions on the grounds that those in San Francisco had expected him to provide the sacrament. They had heard he was coming, and he did not want to leave them disappointed. Further, to not confirm, Serra had reasoned, would have given rise to suspicions and scandalous talk. People might wonder, had Serra done something that led the king to deny him this privilege? Had those in San Francisco done something that led Serra to deny them the sacrament? Confident that he had made the correct decision and protected his honor and that of the king, Serra left San Francisco and, on his return to Carmel, administered more confirmations at Santa Clara.

Neve was furious when he learned that Serra had gone back on his word, and he pursued the matter with his superiors. In mid-April 1780, Croix ordered Neve to seize Serra's patent and to forbid him to administer the sacrament until further notice came from Mexico City. As if he needed further evidence, Serra now knew that Croix was no Bucareli. Serra refused to turn the papers over, asserting that he had sent them back to Mexico City already for review by his superiors. Serra also pledged, on July 20, 1780, that he would stop administering the sacrament until he had approval from Croix.

The controversy dragged on until August 16, 1781, when Serra learned from Neve that the college had indeed secured the proper authorization and that he could begin once again to administer the sacrament. But in fact he had never stopped confirming; he had granted the sacrament on five different occasions at San Carlos during the interval. Once again, Serra had applied his logician's mind to the problem, arguing that the prohibition was against only public confirmations of large gatherings of Indians, not individual, private ones.

With the dispute resolved and able once again to confirm without risking conflict with the governor, Serra returned to the road, but his health and stamina continued to be a problem. With Crespí he went to Mission San Antonio in September 1781 for a few days of confirmations. The two then returned to San Carlos and in October ventured to Mission San Francisco, where the Mallorcans Serra, Palou, and Crespí were briefly united again.[24] Serra and Crespí then left for Santa Clara to attend the laying of the cornerstone for the mission's new church. But on their way back to San Carlos, Serra was thrown from his mule. His ribs were bruised and one of his hands injured. Serra was covered with blankets where he had fallen, and a doctor was summoned from San Jose. After being treated, and in pain, Serra rode back to San Carlos.[25]

There, to Serra's great surprise, Crespí soon fell ill. All remedies failed, and Crespí took to his bed for the last time. On the first day of 1782, in Serra's words, Crespí "gave up his soul to the Creator."[26] Serra and Crespí had known each other for decades, ever since Crespí had been Serra's student in Palma in the 1740s. They had worked together in the Sierra Gorda and Baja California, and for most of the time from 1770 to 1782, Crespí had been Serra's assistant at San Carlos. Understandably, Serra was shaken by Crespí's death. He soon complained that he no longer had the stamina to carry on lengthy correspondence.[27] And he asked the father guardian to send two new padres to San Carlos, ones who "are capable of learning the language and of taking charge of everything" because he himself was now "good for very little or nothing."[28] Clearly, he was thinking about who would succeed him, not only at San Carlos, but also as father president. He now relied on and confided deeply in Father Lasuén, who still was posted at Mission San Diego. Palou, whom Serra had always looked to as his most trusted assistant and replacement, was now also ill and had for several years requested permission to return to Mexico City. He only stayed in Alta California because Serra begged him to remain in the province.[29]

Ever since José de Gálvez had outlined his plan to settle Alta California in 1769, there had been the expectation of a mission along the Santa Barbara Channel amid the Chumash. Early published accounts of the expeditions of 1769 had even reported that Mission San Buenaventura had already been founded in the channel. But a persistent shortage of soldiers meant that new missions were established in areas with smaller Indian populations, and thus Mission San Buenaventura had been continually postponed. Serra was disappointed that his mission *escala* was missing this important rung between San Gabriel and San Luis Obispo. In 1779, though, he had been encouraged when he received news that the Crown now wanted three missions along the channel. They would be called San

Buenaventura, Santa Barbara, and La Purísima Concepción. But the foundation of these missions could not go forward until additional soldiers had been recruited from Sonora and until Governor Neve had completed the establishment of the pueblo of Los Angeles, a project that consumed him for most of 1781.

Finally, however, in February 1782, Neve requested two padres from Serra, one each for Santa Barbara and San Buenaventura. Undoubtedly suspicious of Neve's request for just one Franciscan for each mission, the ailing Serra elected to travel to San Gabriel to administer confirmations at missions along the way and then meet Neve and figure out the details of the new missions. On March 26, he set out from San Gabriel with a group that included Father Cambón and eighty soldiers and their families, most of whom were to settle at Santa Barbara, where a mission-presidio was to be established.[30] On Easter Sunday of that year Serra established Mission San Buenaventura, Alta California's ninth mission. The Spaniards raised a cross, recited familiar prayers, and gave the Chumash gifts to encourage them to help construct a church. Soon thereafter, in an optimistic mood, Serra wrote that the mission would before long be "second to none among those founded" in Alta California.[31]

When Neve arrived from Mission San Gabriel, most of the group headed north up the coast from San Buenaventura. In an indication of his own declining influence and of things to come, Serra was not consulted about the location of the second establishment, and when he spoke up against the spot chosen by Neve, the governor dismissed the father president's objections. On April 21, at Santa Barbara, Serra said Mass and inaugurated what be believed was a shared mission-presidio complex, just as he had done at San Diego in 1769 and at Monterey in 1770.[32] He dutifully inscribed the usual words in his new baptism register: "This new Mission and Royal Presidio of Santa Barbara."[33] But it was not to be.

Serra had not known that Neve intended to follow the New Method in Santa Barbara. Soldiers there would take the lead in dealing with local Indians, and the one padre would have no role in nonreligious matters. He would confine his activities to the administration of the sacraments, as if he were a parish priest.

Neve evidently explained none of this to Serra in advance, saying only that he would not establish a mission in Santa Barbara until after the presidio had been completed.[34] After three weeks of waiting, Serra gave up and headed north. In his estimation, the establishment at Santa Barbara could only fail. Its site was poorly chosen, and without two Franciscans it simply could not go forward. Indians would need the protection of the Franciscans in their dealings with the soldiers, Serra believed. But most of all he was disturbed that Neve had reduced the role of the padres to bystanders. "The Governor was acting as missionary," Serra scoffed. "He says that we don't have the gift for it, and he promised to give Father Cambón the formula for it."[35] Now in his late sixties, with decades of experience in the missions of northern New Spain, Serra was in no mood to rethink his life's work. He had no patience for the New Method or for Neve.

Serra had been expecting to find six new padres from Mexico City waiting for him when he returned to Monterey. What he got instead was a letter from the College of San Fernando explaining that the six Fernandinos who had been designated for Alta California had refused to go north once they had learned that the government had decided to follow the New Method for new missions. The padres reached this conclusion when they learned that the materials necessary to oversee the Indians' development of agriculture and trades were not to be sent north. Realizing that their control over the Indians would be limited and alarmed that they would be posted alone at isolated missions, the six Fernandinos who had volunteered to come to California had chosen to stay at the College of San Fernando.

Serra got even more discouraging news that fall. Croix had been promoted to lieutenant general of the royal army.[36] Yet his post as commander general of the Interior Provinces was to be filled by Neve, and the governorship of California had gone to none other than Pedro Fages, the Catalan whom Serra had all but run out of Monterey in 1773. Serra now had a foe in the office of the commander general and a governor with whom he had a bad history and who he now believed listened to Neve as if he were an "oracle" and was willing to carry out all of Neve's plans just to keep his job.[37] Serra saw no point in congratulating Neve on his promotion or asking him to support the development of the missions, for that would only have, in Serra's words, put Neve in the awkward spot of being "inconsistent with himself."[38] Recognizing that the New Method was still in favor among some officials in Mexico, Serra considered ordering the abandonment of San Buenaventura but hoped that because it had already been established, the Fernandinos' approach would take root. To staff the mission, Serra sent two Franciscans from Mission San Carlos, leaving only himself and Fray Mathías de Noriega to attend to the mission and the Monterey presidio. Without a third missionary at San Carlos, Serra was tethered to Carmel until the following summer. He devoted his time to baptizing and confirming Indians at the mission.

In the summer of 1783, just when Serra's health took another turn for the worse, the Franciscans Juan Antonio Riobó and Diego Noboa arrived separately by ship from Mexico. Serra had informed the college that Mission San Buenaventura had indeed been founded according to the Fernandinos' traditional method and that there was now not a single padre to spare in California. In response, the college had sent Riobó and Noboa. Upon their arrival at San Carlos Serra made plans to travel on a final round of visitations and confirmations in the southern missions. This was a trip he had long wanted to make, but now his health had given his fellow Franciscans pause. Serra was suffering from chest pains; evidently, he had experienced discomfort since his days at the College of San Fernando. Some attributed his condition to his self-mortifications while on popular missions in the 1750s and 1760s.[39] Serra's chest pains grew worse over the summer of 1783, but he could not be dissuaded from traveling to the southern missions. He was worried not about the trip to San Diego by boat but about the long overland journey back to Monterey. So ill did he feel that before sailing, he wrote Palou a farewell stating that his "return may only be a death notice."[40]

Serra left Noboa at San Carlos and with Riobó sailed south. After a brief layover in Santa Barbara they arrived in San Diego on September 7. Serra spent a month at San Diego convalescing and confirming and then ventured forth, endeavoring, in Palou's words, "to leave not a single Christian unconfirmed."[41] He confirmed at San Juan Capistrano for ten days and then went to San Gabriel, where he arrived on October 17.[42] By then, he was very weak. His chest pains were aggravated to the point that the padres expected him to die in their mission.[43] Serra could still say Mass and administer confirmations, but even Indians believed that the "Old Father," as they had come to call Serra, would die soon. Serra made no secret of his failing health and his own belief that his days were few.

While he was resting at San Gabriel, girding himself for the remainder of the journey back to San Carlos, he received a letter from Father Juan Sancho, a fellow Mallorcan, who had recently been elected guardian of the college. Serra replied immediately and with great tenderness; the letter suggests much of what was on his mind during his final year. For a man who had earlier insisted that he had left Mallorca and never looked back, it is notable how much Mallorca continued to shape his thinking about California and its missions. Serra hoped that Sancho might be able to revive the "primitive zeal" that Antonio Llinás had brought to the apostolic colleges in the previous century, and he confided how much he had hoped that Alta California might be made to resemble their homeland. Serra was especially troubled that he now expected to die before a second and third mission could be established in the Santa Barbara Channel. Those missions, Serra held, would have made eleven Franciscan foundations in Alta California. Mallorca was "a province made up of eleven friaries," and "in a flight of imagination" Serra had hoped to see in Alta California "a tiny replica among these gentiles with the same number of houses, with two friars in each of them." In failing health, with only tepid support from the government, and with no padres arriving from Mexico, Serra could only ask Sancho, "Who pays attention to such foolishness?"[44] Serra now was far removed from his earlier enthusiasm that the California missions might allow the College of San Fernando to become the crown of all the apostolic colleges.

Sancho's letter also indirectly reminded Serra of his mortality, informing him of the deaths and illnesses of so many of his fellow Mallorcans and Franciscans. As his body declined and his friends and colleagues died off, Serra could not help but begin to feel "the nearness" of his own death and that he was "falling apart." The trip to San Gabriel had left him "very fatigued" and afraid of the 350 miles that now separated him from Carmel, this from a man who had always taken to the road with gusto. Health permitting and

God willing, Serra told Sancho he would press on all the way to San Francisco, but he believed that this would be his "last pilgrimage."[45]

Serra in fact wrote to Sancho again before he left San Gabriel, to apologize for not offering condolences on the death of the guardian's mother, but that appears to have been a pretext to tie up loose ends and set the record straight. Serra thanked Sancho for reappointing him father president, even though it was impossible that he would serve for the full three-year term. "Though I do not know when I am going to die, I yet am convinced that I am not far distant from it," Serra told his fellow Mallorcan. "Above all," he wrote, "I know that from here onwards I am quite useless for *peregrinaciones*."[46] Serra then launched one of his final critiques of the soldiers and officers of California and their superiors, but with an uncharacteristic sarcasm and bluntness. He wanted Sancho to know that he had finally put an end to the padres' practice of providing spiritual care for the soldiers at the presidios. He wrote that the officers at the presidios took the padres for granted and seemed to "know our obligation better than we ourselves." The final straw for Serra was when one told the padres to bring their own wine when they came to the presidio to say Mass. Serra's reply had been unusually terse. "The custom of saying Mass [at the presidio] has lasted up until now," he stated flatly. As for a letter from Croix, the outgoing commander general, that informed Serra of the new punishments Fages was to impose on Indians who killed Spanish livestock, Serra told Sancho that his only reply to Croix would be to ask if the "new program directs them [the soldiers] to castrate the gentiles, hang the gentiles, disembowel the gentiles, and butcher the gentiles indiscriminately," as Serra now charged had occurred under Fages's watch.[47] Perhaps as much out of fatigue as restraint, Serra never sent such a letter. He continued to put his energies into the challenges in front of him. He finished confirming Indians at San Gabriel and got back on the road. He finally arrived at Mission San Carlos on December 15, having confirmed Indians at every mission along the way.

Serra stayed at Carmel through Easter. He recuperated, baptized, and confirmed. When he received from Lasuén a list of San Diego mission Indians who had not been confirmed, his heart sunk. He wrote to Lasuén that he was crestfallen he did not know how to fly.[48]

In late April, Serra made up his mind to travel north to bless the new church at Santa Clara and to administer confirmations at Missions Santa Clara and San Francisco. Palou greeted him at San Francisco on May 4, some nine months after Serra had written him a farewell letter. Two days later, Palou received jarring news: Father Murguía of Mission Santa Clara, with whom Serra and Palou had served in the Sierra Gorda and Baja California, was now near death. Palou rode off to be with Murguía, but Serra, growing weaker by the day and now afflicted with fever, remained at San Francisco performing confirmations.[49] On May 15 he did make it to Mission Santa Clara; there he confirmed and participated in the dedication of the new church the following day.

Palou intended to return to his mission, but Serra asked him to stay at Santa Clara to help him prepare for death. For he was now "worn out, and he could not possibly live very long." Serra spent several days with Palou in prayer, and his health improved a bit. He performed some baptisms and even traveled to an Indian village near the mission to confirm several Ohlone. When it was evident that Serra was not going to die, both shed tears and returned to their separate missions. They believed that they would not see each other again, and so not achieve what they both "desired, namely, to die together, or at least that the last to die would be able to assist at the death of the one to go first."[50]

By late May, Serra was at Mission San Carlos, having finally completed his lifetime of peregrinations. Again, he began baptizing at the mission, and he continued with confirmations until July 6. On that day Serra completed one of the goals that had given purpose to his final years: the confirmation of every Indian at Mission San Carlos. And he could also say that he had confirmed just about every Indian in the California missions who was eligible for the sacrament. He could truly claim that he had led and largely enacted what he took to be the "spiritual conquest" of California. To those in Mexico City who thought that either secular priests or another religious order might do a better job in Alta California, Serra reminded Sancho, in one of his last letters, that the Fernandinos had done their work alone "in a land where the name of Jesus had never been heard." He added that "the number of confirmations administered in these same territories by one friar from San Fernando is, at the present time, five thousand, three hundred and seven—5,307."[51] "If, after work such as this," Serra told his father guardian, "the Fernandinos deserved to be deprived of the possibility of missionizing among the infidels," the college would have to bear that news with patience. Serra believed that in confirming, he had worked for the salvation not only of the Indians but of his college as well. When his patent to confirm expired on July 16, Serra was said to have proclaimed what "the Apostle of the Nations wrote to the Gentiles": 'I have finished the course. I have kept the faith.' "[52]

On that very same day a ship from San Blas dropped anchor at San Francisco carrying news that essentially drew to a close Serra's life as a missionary and father president.[53] The ship carried a letter from Father Guardian Sancho to Serra, explaining that for the time being he would not be sending additional missionaries to California. He had no men to spare at the college. A number had died recently, others had returned to Spain, and there had been no new recruits from Spain to replace them. With no chance of more confirmations to perform and no possibility of new missions during the short time he had left, Serra had only one final goal. It was the goal that had in a sense directed his every waking moment since his recognition as a novitiate in Mallorca of the depthless well of faith within him: he wanted to die a proper Catholic death.

⊰✳⊱

For a missionary like Serra, who did not die a martyr, the end of life was often carefully scripted and staged. Serra studied how men like Margil de Jesús and Saint Francis Solano lived, and he knew how they died: surrounded by admirers and attendants who administered to them the last rites and helped them recite prayers intended to ease their final hours. Those closest to them were certain that the departed missionaries had gone straight to heaven.[54] Realizing that he would soon die, Serra tried to gather Franciscans who could help him die in the manner of Margil de Jesús and Saint Francis Solano. He wrote to the padres at San Luis Obispo and San Antonio and urged that one from each mission come to visit with him. From Mission San Francisco, Serra asked for Palou.

Palou arrived at San Carlos on August 18 and found Serra weak and mentally drifting away, or, in his words, "interiorly recollected." A few days later, a newly arrived royal surgeon attempted to treat the ailing Serra, but to little effect. Serra, however, was not yet bedridden and in his final days distributed cloth to Indians so that they could "cover their nakedness."[55] He wondered aloud why the padres from the other missions had not arrived, and when Palou investigated, he discovered that the letters had been overlooked by the presidio and had not been sent out. Palou then sent them by special courier.

By August 26, Serra was feeling so weak that he gave his confession to Palou. Then, on the following day, he asked for Final Communion, a sacrament that the sick almost always received on their deathbeds. Serra, however, was still able to walk the distance from his room to the mission church, and there he received Communion from Palou, in front of assembled soldiers and Indians. For most people who would soon die, Final Communion was a private act, but for Serra it was one last public demonstration of faith and piety. Later that day the presidio carpenter came at Serra's request to measure him for a coffin.

Serra felt worse as the evening wore on and asked Palou for extreme unction. He then passed his final night in prayer, in his room, on his knees, with his chest pressed against the boards of his bed in the belief that this posture relieved the pressure within. When that position gave him no relief, Serra sat on the floor or reclined in the laps of Indians from the mission who had come to care for him or to watch him die.[56]

The following morning several naval officers paid Serra a visit. Serra greeted them and to their surprise thanked them for having "come from so far off to this port to throw a little earth" on his coffin. Serra then told Palou to bury him in the church near Crespí.[57] Later that morning Serra was overcome by a fear that was eased only when Palou and those by his side read to him the Commendation for a Departing Soul. Serra briefly ventured outside his room, returned to his cell and prayed, sipped a cup of broth, and then lay down in his bed, holding his crucifix. He died in the early afternoon on August 28,

1784, three months shy of his seventy-first birthday. He had died as he had wished, with Palou by his side and having received all the final sacraments. Palou believed that Serra had gone to "sleep in the Lord" and "went to receive in heaven the reward of his apostolic labors."[58]

As the bells of San Carlos tolled, the people of the mission, Indians and soldiers alike, gathered to see the dead father president, who was now nestled in his coffin and surrounded by candles. He lay in state in his room until midnight, when his body was carried to the church. His funeral and burial took place the next day. A week later Palou led a requiem for Serra.

News of Serra's death reached the College of San Fernando in Mexico City in late November. On November 25, Juan Sancho wrote to his fellow Mallorcans that their "beloved countryman, the Reverend Father Lector, Junípero Serra," was dead. Of Serra's thirty-four years as a missionary in New Spain, Sancho reported that "all men said openly that that man was a saint and that his actions were those of an apostle."[59] Sancho's letters reached the Convento de San Bernardino in Petra and the Convento de San Francisco in Palma in early April 1785. At the latter, Franciscans said 225 Masses in Serra's honor and for Serra's soul.[60] In Petra, at the Convento de San Bernardino, where the young Miquel Joseph had been educated and where the accomplished priest had been preaching in 1749 when he learned that he was soon to depart for New Spain, the Franciscans said 30 Masses.[61] Serra's sister, Juana María, had died in October 1783, but doubtless some in Petra still remembered and therefore mourned the death of the man they had known as Padre Lector Junípero Delmau.[62]

Epilogue

After his death, Serra's renown only grew, much like the reputations of the men he had modeled his life after, such that today his name is recognized far beyond the places—Mallorca, the Sierra Gorda, Baja California, and what the Spanish then called Alta California—where he lived and carried out his work a missionary. Palou's biography of Serra, published in 1787, remained for generations the official record of his life, and it painted Serra as a saint in everything but name—hagiography in the literal meaning of the term. Palou's account is nevertheless proof of at least one historical fact: as few people have done, Serra mastered both his life and, for a time, his legacy. But neither Serra nor Palou could control how later generations would understand him and his life's work. For what Serra helped to initiate in California—colonization via an extensive "ladder" of Catholic missions, where tens of thousands of Indian lives were monitored, modified, and frequently shortened—was by every measure far more complex and destructive than he could have imagined.

When Serra died in 1784, most of the California missions were in their infancy: they had relatively few Indians in them, and their churches were far smaller and more rudimentary than those visited today by parishioners and tourists. Around six thousand Indians had been baptized at the nine missions established by Serra or under his auspices. These missions, by and large, were healthy settlements. And thus in 1784, in his final report on them, Serra was upbeat and optimistic. The previous year, he wrote, had been the best yet at Mission San Carlos. Indians in greater numbers were accepting baptism. They were marrying, confessing, and sustaining themselves with crops harvested from the mission's irrigated fields.[1] What Serra saw at the end of his life was the beginning of a major cultural transformation he had helped initiate in which California Indians would assimilate aspects of Spanish culture: religion, language, dress, music, literacy, art, animal husbandry, and domesticated agriculture. The California missions in his day thus formed a shaky bridge for Indians between the world of their ancestors and that of Spaniards. What Serra did not live to see and understand was that later, for many Indians, this bridge led to a graveyard.

In the years after Serra's death the missions' populations rose and then began a sharp decline. As their populations increased, disease cut a swath through them, leading to high mortality rates among all Indian infants, children, and adults. As Spanish diseases and livestock invaded the countryside and destroyed old ways of subsistence, Indians were unwillingly driven into the missions—not by Spanish soldiers, but by, very simply, hunger and the collapse of their villages.[2] Thus, in a morbid irony, the concentration of Indians in the missions—the first and necessary step in Serra's plan—allowed for the wide and ready transmission of disease that only accelerated new baptisms and expanded death's work. This became the missions' undoing and Serra's albatross.

Across the California missions one in three infants did not live to see a first birthday. Four in ten Indian children who survived their first year perished before their fifth. Between 10 and 20 percent of adults died each year, with women of reproductive age suffering the most because of the dangers associated with childbearing and introduced venereal diseases. These figures, while horrific, are consistent with disease-ridden early modern communities, like Serra's Petra, before the age of antibiotics. But the California missions were different in that the high mortality rates were unrelenting, year after year for decades. Ultimately, high mortality combined with the low fertility of women to render mission populations unviable.[3] Violence, natural disasters, and dangers associated with farm animals, as well as work- and transportation-related mishaps, compounded this tragedy.[4] In the decades after Serra's death, only the arrival of new recruits from greater distances maintained the missions' populations.

Had Serra lived to see this calamity, he might have thought he was back in Mallorca, the Sierra Gorda, or Baja California during their darkest days; he would have reminded Indians that their suffering was proof of God's love. Of those who survived at the missions, some would become practicing Catholics. Some would not. Some would flee what they saw as an oppressive institution. A number would violently rebel, just as the Kumeyaay had done in San Diego in 1775. A few would achieve power and influence either by association with the Franciscans or by election as alcaldes. Most went along with the missions because they appeared to represent the best of a few terrible options, to try to sustain their families, their culture, and their heritage in the bleakest of times.[5]

Serra had seen the toll of disease and colonization during his years in the Sierra Gorda and Baja California, but his unshakable faith that God was working for the conversion of California's Indians prevented him from understanding that California Indians might suffer the same fate. And the inevitable came but after his death. Father Mariano Payeras, who hailed from Mallorca and served as father president long after Serra, wrote in 1820 that the Franciscans in California found themselves "with a people miserable and sick, [and] with rapid depopulation of rancherías [villages] which with profound horror fills the cemeteries." Healthy Indians, once baptized and resident at the missions, became feeble, lost weight, sickened, and died. Mission San Carlos was exemplary to Payeras. In Serra's last full year there the mission population reached 614. It rose to 835 in 1796, but then disease took hold and the local supply of recruits dried up; the population plummeted, dropping below 400 in 1818. Neighboring Mission Soledad, meanwhile, was reduced to "a skeleton."[6]

In 1821, a year after Payeras wrote his lament, Mexico threw off Spanish rule, and California became part of the new independent nation. By then more than 65,000 Indians had been baptized in twenty Franciscan missions, but Indians living in them numbered only 21,750. The total reflected the recruitment of many thousands from distant valleys.[7] By the time the missions were secularized in the early 1830s, more than 80,000 Indians had been baptized between San Diego and north of San Francisco, but almost 60,000 had been buried, nearly 25,000 of whom were children under the age of ten.[8]

With secularization most Indians left the ex-missions for the countryside, the pueblos of San Jose, Los Angeles, and Monterey, or the expanding ranchos. Tragically, many of these people would die in California's 1844 smallpox epidemic. Nothing, however, could prepare the California Indians who remained for the brutality of the Anglo-Americans who descended on the region in the 1840s and 1850s. By 1855, after the gold rush and the establishment of American rule in California, the Indian population of the state stood at around 50,000, reduced from the 310,000 who lived in California in 1769 and a mere vestige of what Serra had seen when he came north from Baja California.[9]

Today, the legacy of the California missions and Junípero Serra cannot be separated from these terrible events. This has only been acknowledged relatively recently. Serra's legacy is more contested now than it was in 1787, when Palou's biography appeared, of course, but also more than it was in 1931, when the statue of Serra was installed in the U.S. Capitol. By and large, Serra is now remembered in not one way but three: as a pioneer, as a religious icon, and as a colonial imperialist. To many, Serra is the man who brought agriculture to the Golden State and who laid the foundation for California's future greatness. To some Catholics—some of whom descend from the mission populations—he remains a heroic and saintly embodiment of the religion's timeless virtues. Pope John Paul II accepted Serra's cause for canonization in 1985 and declared him venerable, the first of the three steps to sainthood. In 1988, the pope beatified Serra. To others, however, Serra's life embodies the evils inherent in a colonial system that promoted cultural genocide, sanctioned corporal punishment, and brought about the devastation of California's native peoples. Serra's staunchest detractors have turned him into California's Christopher Columbus, a man whose life story is overshadowed by the contests over his legacy. Three centuries after his birth, Serra's missionary endeavors—just like his own identity and that of the region he helped to settle—resist easy categorization, prompting debate and reinterpretation.

One thing that is clear is that the Serra honored in 1931 by the state of California with a statue in the U.S. Capitol is not the flesh-and-blood Serra of the eighteenth century. The bronze Serra is a stereotypical priest disconnected from his age. Serra's statue holds in its right hand a cross, not a crucifix, the primary object of Serra's devotion and the symbol of humanity's potential redemption through the physical suffering and death of God's only son. Similarly, the statue's left hand holds a California mission building, not the pounding stone that he used to strike his chest during his fiery sermons. This same imagined Serra appears on a medal minted in 1963 for the celebration of the 250th anniversary of Serra's birth. Here, at least, we can see that Serra's left leg shows through his heavy wool tunic, a reminder of the injury that dogged him for nearly thirty-five years as he traveled on foot throughout much of central Mexico and then Baja California and Alta California. Behind Serra is a Spanish ship that evokes Serra the pioneer, the man who brought civilization to an uncharted region. Serra stands alone on the shores of a bay, his weight on his good right leg, a vanguard in a virgin land. Yet the bay, the coast, and the mountains—all are devoid of people and their handiwork. It is a simple and simplifying image—just like the 1931 statue. Perhaps it was only as a pioneer, as a Lewis-and-Clark-like figure in a tunic, as a generic Christian, that Serra could have made it into Statuary Hall and the curriculum of every fourth-grade history class in California. But this bowdlerization came with a price. Catholicism and Indians—and the purpose of Spain's advance into California—were erased. And we do not see Serra as he was or how different his world was from our own.

What makes Serra such a necessary figure to get right is that he embodied a history of Indian-missionary relations nearly hemispheric in its scope. Serra, although he stands out as exceptional among his Franciscan peers, in his practice of Catholicism was typical of the thousands of Catholic missionaries who came to the Americas during the early modern period. His dismissive assumptions about Indians' religious practices and his belief that Indians had to be saved from their own barbarousness were likewise standard. It is hard to imagine that any other group played a larger role in shaping the early period of Indian-European relations than these men, who were called to these shores by their own religious desires and by a Spanish state looking to expand and secure its American territories. Millions of Indians, from the southern tip of South America to the northern hinterlands of Canada, and from the shores of the Chesapeake to the coves of Monterey Bay, were introduced to a central part of European culture and society by men in black or gray or brown robes who preached the Gospel of Jesus Christ and who attempted to reorganize their ways of life.

Father Junípero Serra, no matter how emblematic he was, though, was also replete with tensions and ironies, even paradoxes. He stated that he was always obedient to his superiors, but as he grew in stature and seniority, he did largely as he pleased, with few checks on his own authority and actions beyond the narrow confines of his own order and mission. He believed in the nearly absolute powers of the Church yet lived at a time when the Bourbon state was consolidating its authority over that institution. He had a domineering personality but was bereft of an individual self: he was opinionated, strong-willed, determined, and passionately devoted to his life's work but was typical of his age in that he had no real identity of his own beyond his order. As a deeply religious Catholic of the eighteenth century, he fervently distrusted his own intuition or inner voice, and he chose to follow his God's will as best he could discern it. Finally, and paradoxically, Serra lived a life in opposition to what California would become: a dynamic region defined by its diversity and integration into a global economy that transcends national boundaries. Serra's mission was to secure souls for the Church and territory for the Crown. To him, those who practiced faiths other than Catholicism were pitiful people, to be converted or removed.

There is thus a growing incongruity between the historical Serra—who devoted himself to the universalism of Catholicism, the suppression of individualism, and the renunciation of materialism— and the modern place to which his legacy is now bound: a state that in the American popular imagination has come to represent idiosyncratic individualism and the glorification of physical beauty; conspicuous consumption; racial, ethnic, and religious diversity; and technological progress. Serra, California's founding father, therefore, stands as an awkward symbol of California today. But perhaps for that very reason, he is a more potent reminder than ever of the firm beliefs, intense faith, and multifaceted lives of many of the men who were at the center of the successive upheavals that inescapably characterized, and followed, colonial enterprises across North America and elsewhere during the era of European expansion.

Notes

1. MALLORCA

1. On the prehistory of the island, see William H. Waldren, *Balearic Prehistoric Ecology and Culture: The Excavations and Study of Certain Caves, Rock Shelters and Settlements*, Part ii, BAR (British Archaeological Reports), International Series 149(ii) 192, 455–60; Waldren, *Beaker Ware from the Balearic Island of Mallorca: Ceramic Evidence from Four Beaker Contexts: Radiocarbon 14 Survey of Materials* (Deya de Mallorca, Spain: Deya Archaeological Museum, 1970); Manuel Fernández Miranda, *Secuencia cultural de la prehistoria de Mallorca* (Madrid: Instituo Español de Prehistoria, 1978); Pepa Gasull, Vicente Llull, María Encarna Sanahuja, *Son Fornés, la Fase Talayótica: Ensayo de reconstrucción socio-económica de una comunidad prehistórica de la isla de Mallorca* (Oxford: BAR, 1984); Victor Guerrero Ayusa, *Arquitectura y poder en la prehistoria de Mallorca* (Palma: El Tall, 1999); and Gabriel Pons i Homar, *Anàlisi espacial del poblament al pretalaiòtic final i al talaiòtic I de Mallorca* (Palma: Consell de Mallorca, Cultura i Patrimoni, 1999). See also Pere Xamena Fiol, *Història de Mallorca* (Palma: Moll, 1991); and volume 1 of Jaume Alzina et al., *Història de Mallorca*, 2nd ed. (Palma: Moll, 1989 and 1994).
2. Lorenzo Galmés Más, *Fray Junípero Serra: Apostól de California* (Madrid: Biblioteca de Autores Cristianos de la Editorial Católica, 1988), 22; and Alzina et al., *Història de Mallorca*, 1:127–33.
3. See Guillermo Rosselló Bordoy, *Mallorca musulmana* (Palma: J. Mascaró Pasarius, 1973); and Guillermo Rosselló Bordoy, *El Islam en las Islas Baleares: Mallorca musulmana según la Remembrança—de Nunyo Sanç y el Repartiment—de Mallorca* (Palma: Universitat de les Illes Balears, 2007).
4. The following discussion of the economy and commerce of Mallorca during the Middle Ages relies heavily on David Abulafia, *A Mediterranean Emporium: The Catalan Kingdom of Majorca* (Cambridge: Cambridge University Press, 1994).
5. Palma is the Roman name for the city. Muslims knew the town as Medina Mayurqa, but after the conquest of James I it was known as Ciutat de Mallorca until the Bourbon period, when the city reverted to its Roman name.
6. Galmés Más, *Fray Junípero Serra*, 22.

7. Pere Xamena Fiol, *Història de l'església a Mallorca* (Palma: Moll, 1986), 90.

8. Josep Juan Vidal, "El comercio de trigo entre Mallorca y Africa del Norte en los siglos XVI y XVII," *Mayurqa* 15 (1976): 73–92.

9. Abulafia, *Mediterranean Emporium*, 15.

10. On Ramon Llull, see Anthony Bonner, *Doctor Illuminatus: A Ramon Llull Reader* (Princeton, N.J.: Princeton University Press, 1985): and J. N. Hillgarth, *Ramon Llull and Llullism in Fourteenth-Century France* (Oxford: Clarendon, 1971).

11. Bonner, *Doctor Illuminatus*, 13.

12. Abulafia, *Mediterranean Emporium*, 14; J. N. Hillgarth, *The Spanish Kingdoms, 1250–1516 Volume II, 1410–1516, Castilian Hegemony* (Oxford: Clarendon, 1978), 123. Buenaventura Bonnet Reverón, "Las expediciones a las Canarias en el siglo XIV (continuación)," *Revista de Indias*, no. 19 (1945): 7–31; Buenaventura Bonnet Reverón, "Las expediciones a las Canarias en el siglo XIV (continuación)," *Revista de Indias*, no. 20 (1945): 189–221. In 1351 a bishopric was founded on Grand Canary, and the missionaries at that time were Mallorcan hermits aided by Canary Islanders who lived in Mallorca and had already been baptized.

13. Josep Amengual i Batle, "L'hèrencia lul-liana i la missió mallorquina a Canàries: La missió sense espasa," *Randa* 61 (2008): 73–91.

14. In 1448 Llull's remains were moved to an ornate tomb in the church. Bonner, *Doctor Illuminatus*, 43–44.

15. Abulafia, *Mediterranean Emporium*, 15–17. J. N. Hillgarth, *The Spanish Kingdoms, 1250–1516, Volume I, 1250–1410, Precarious Balance* (Oxford: Clarendon), 357. Barcelona merchants put up about 50 percent of the financial resources necessary for the conquest as the trade in Mallorca was considerable—about half the size of Barcelona trade and a huge lost market.

16. Moreover, in advance of his landing an invading force, the Aragonese rulers of the island had moved the people of the countryside into Palma and the interior city of Inca, fearing that James III would find among them allies. James III would die in battle in Llucmajor in 1349. Peter IV ordered the body of James III taken to Valencia for burial to prevent the fallen king from becoming a Mallorcan martyr. Peter IV also imprisoned the children of James III. The defeat of James III and the imprisonment of his family spelled the end of the brief period of Mallorcan independence between 1229 and 1343.

17. The Crown of Aragon was in essence a confederation of various kingdoms and principalities: Aragon, Catalonia, Valencia, and Mallorca. See Thomas Bisson's *Medieval Crown of Aragon* (Oxford: Clarendon, 1986).

18. Hillgarth, *Precarious Balance*, 229.

19. Hillgarth, *Castilian Hegemony*, 12.

20. Cloth and wool had been exported from Mallorca as early as the 1320s, but exports increased in the late fourteenth century. And in these years, according to one historian, "the cloth industry acquired a moral value in the eyes of contemporaries." Ibid., 8.

21. Neighboring Sardinia remained a major supplier of cereals to Mallorca. And in 1365 to 1374, desperate Mallorcans seized Sardinian ships headed for Valencia laden with grains. Ibid., 7.

22. José María Quadrado, *La judería de Mallorca en 1391*, ed. Eduardo Pascual Ramos (Palma: Lleonard Muntaner, 2008), 16–17; Baltasar Porcel, *Los Chuetas mallorquines: Quince siglos de racismo* (Palma: Miquel Font, 1991), 22–24; Antoni Picazo, *Els xuetes de Mallorca: Grups de poder i criptojudaisme al segle XVII* (Palma: El Tall, 2006). There was another attack on the city's Jews in October by a smaller but still large mob of four thousand. The leaders of this pogrom were peasants and city workers who seem to have taken out their economic frustrations on the Jews. See Hillgarth, *Castilian Hegemony*, 142. In 1435 a series of royal orders issued in Barcelona restricted contact between Jews and Christians in the kingdom of Aragon and deprived Jews of pursuing livelihoods in all but a few lines of work. See Porcel, *Los Chuetas mallorquines*, 32–33. The pressure on Jews in Mallorca to convert to Christianity was unrelenting, and in October 1391 most surviving Jews were baptized. But the degree to which conversos renounced their Judaism is unclear. What is clear, though, is that the ostracism of the conversos from Catholic society in Palma continued even as they sought to remake their world within the Catholic Church. In the early fifteenth century one group of conversos came together to essentially re-create their associational organization that had provided them with important social services. Converso leaders in Palma formed the New Confraternity of Saint Miquel in 1404, essentially bringing their own remaining social networks under the umbrella of the Catholic Church and winning official sanction for their own meetinghouse in Palma. See Natalie Oeltjen, "A Converso Confraternity in Majorca: La Novella Confraria de Sant Miquel," *Jewish History* 24 (2010): 53–85.

23. Hillgarth, *Castilian Hegemony*, 18. The Spanish Inquisition began in 1478, and on Mallorca it was instituted in 1488.

24. Ibid.

25. Ibid., 153. Unrest in Mallorca was expressed not just in terms of religious anxiety but also in terms of class as revealed in the peasant rebellion that shook the island from 1450 to 1453. This rebellion pitted Palma against much of the countryside and seems to have been stirred up by priests who did not want to pay a royal subsidy and "who exalted the biblical state of peasants compared to corrupt citizens." Ibid., 80. Rebels besieged the city but were crushed by troops; many of the defeated fled to Sardinia.

26. In these years Mallorca remained mired in economic depression, and population growth was stagnant. The population on the island expanded between 1459 and 1517 as measured by the number of households, but growth in these years was slowed by factors that had plagued the island for centuries: epidemic disease and agricultural shortfalls. See Josep Juan Vidal, *Mallorca en tiempos del descubrimiento de América* (Palma: El Tall, 1991), 11. This general situation was made worse by a rebellion in Mallorca known as "Las Germanías" against corruption. See Josep Juan Vidal, *Els agermanats* (Palma: Ayuntamiento de Palma, 1985). By 1573 the island's population had increased to more than 72,000, with about 16,000 living in Palma. Fiol, *Història de Mallorca*, 217.

27. A slight drop in temperature of just one degree is the equivalent of increasing altitude by some five hundred feet, and thus changes in climate dra-

matically reduced agricultural yields in Mallorca and elsewhere in much of the late Middle Ages. Andrew Appleby, "Epidemics and Famine in the Little Ice Age," *Journal of Interdisciplinary History* 10, no. 4 (Spring 1980): 643–63. There is no agreement about the dates of the Little Ice Age, with some scholars asserting that it began as early as the late thirteenth century.

28. Vidal, *Mallorca en tiempos del descubrimiento de América*, 27. In very good years the island also exported soap, cheese, capers, saffron, textiles, cloth, and blankets but nearly always in too small a quantity to affect the island's finances. This external trade—the importation of foodstuffs and the exportation of oil and other goods—was undermined by pirates who preyed upon the shipping lanes of the Mediterranean. Ubaldo de Casanova i Todolí, "El déficit alimenticio del reino de Mallorca a lo largo del siglo XVII y sus problemas de abastecimiento," *Mayurqa* 21 (1985–1987): 217–32.

29. Vidal, *Mallorca en tiempos del descubrimiento de América*, 46.

30. Juan Bautista Dameto, *The Ancient and Modern History of the Balearick Islands or of the Kingdom of Majorca: Which Comprehends the Islands of Majorca, Minorca, Yviça, Formentera, and Others. With Their Natural and Geographical Description*, 2nd ed. Translated from the original Spanish (William and John Innys, London, 1719: 8).

31. Julián García de la Torre, "Repurcusiones en el reino de Mallorca, de la expulsión de los moriscos," *Mayurqa* 21 (1985–1987): 191–95.

32. Plague devastated Spain between 1596 and 1602, killing some 600,000 to 700,000 people. Another equally brutal epidemic further devastated the country in 1647–1652.

33. Stanley G. Payne, *A History of Spain and Portugal* (Madison: University of Wisconsin Press, 1973), 290.

34. Alzina et al., *Història de Mallorca*, 2:45.

35. Fiol, *Història de Mallorca*, 228.

36. Ibid., 232–33.

37. Vidal, *Mallorca en tiempos del descubrimiento de América*, 60.

38. Fiol, *Història de l'església*, 218–19. It was not until 1768 that the Crown ordered the catechism taught in Castilian.

39. Ibid., 234.

40. In the middle of the sixteenth and seventeenth centuries, Jesuit missionaries were among the most active on the island. And in the eighteenth century, the Fathers of Saint Vincent de Paul made some 330 missions on the island.

41. Fiol, *Història de l'església*, 218.

42. Ubaldo de Casanova i Todolí, "Los alojamientos de soldados en el reino de Mallorca a lo largo del siglo XVII," *Mayurqa* 22 (1989): 733–44. Between 1610 and 1647, there were some thirty-three royal levies of troops on the island that swept some fifteen thousand men into military service. Alzina et al., *Història de Mallorca*, 2:11. Mallorcan men were indiscriminately pressed into military service. From 1629 to 1637, some six thousand Mallorcan men left the island as soldiers. In 1637, when a call for two thousand soldiers came up short, adult men were indiscriminately forced into military service.

But not all military service was coerced. When Catalonia rose up against Castilian rule in the 1640s over increasingly heavy taxation and attacks on local privilege, and briefly became a French protectorate, Mallorcans answered the Crown's call for aid and men to fight against the Catalans. Alzina et al., *Història de Mallorca*, 2:10–17. For the origins of this conflict, see also Hugh Trevor-Roper, "The General Crisis of the Seventeenth Century," *Past & Present*, no. 16 (Nov., 1959): 31–64.

43. The result was numerous autos-da-fé, over two hundred reconciliations, and enormous confiscations that staggered the converso community and the island's economy. Henry Kamen, *The Spanish Inquisition: A Historical Revision* (New Haven, Conn.: Yale University Press, 2005), 300–301.

44. In 1720 one final converso was burned in effigy in Mallorca. Picazo, *Els xuetes de Mallorca*, and communication from Picazo to author.

45. To this day, descendants of those executed in 1691 are still sometimes called by the derogatory term *Chueta*.

46. The War of Spanish Succession erupted across Europe in 1701 and resulted from the struggle for the Spanish throne between the Hapsburgs and the Bourbons after the death of the childless Hapsburg king, Charles II of Spain, in 1700. Both the Bourbons and the Hapsburgs had legitimate claims to the throne. When the feeble and weak Hapsburg king Charles II died, he named as his heir Louis XIV's second grandson, Philip, duc d'Anjou. Although Philip was not in line to become king of France (his father, Louis the Dauphin, was), there was grave concern in some corners of Europe that a possible unification of the French and Spanish Crowns in one family—or even one monarch—would overthrow the balance of power in Europe. This concern led to a war that pitted the Bourbon monarchs of France and Spain against England, the Netherlands, and Austria.

47. Alzina et al., *Història de Mallorca*, 2:39–40.

48. In the settlements concluding the War of Spanish Succession, Philip retained Spain and all of its American colonies and agreed to cede the Mediterranean islands of Gibraltar and Menorca to the English.

49. Alzina et al., *Història de Mallorca*, 2:121.

50. Under the Hapsburgs, Mallorca had been ruled by a viceroy who held great power and was free to rule as he saw fit—often independently from the king—and this often meant that the island enjoyed local autonomy. But under the Bourbons, the viceroy was replaced by a captain general who worked for the monarch and represented central authority. The Gran i General Consell—the true autonomous arm of local governance in Mallorca—was dissolved, and its responsibilities passed to the Real Audiencia, which was overseen by the captain general and several other officials, all of whom were from Castile. The captain general also became the supreme legal authority on the island. This reform reached all the way down to the local level, where town councils staffed by royal appointees replaced the *jurats*. The net result of these changes was a tremendous increase in the island's dependence on the Spanish state and a monopolization of political power in the hands of those who supported Philip, the Bourbon monarch.

51. Alzina et al., *Història de Mallorca*, 2:124.

2. PETRA

1. Fray Junípero Serra and Fray Guillermo Rosselló, "Approval of a Funeral Sermon," June 12, 1748, in *The Writings of Junípero Serra*, ed. and trans. Antonine Tibesar (Washington, D.C.: Academy of American Franciscan History, 1955–1966), 4:292–301.

2. Sebastián Rubí Darder, *La Villa Real de Petra: Algunas de sus raices*, 2nd ed. (Petra: Apóstol y Civilizador, 1987), 38.

3. Padre Francisco Torrens y Nicolau, "Censo de población y estadistica de granos y legumbres, en Petra, en el año 1591," in *Apuntes históricos de Petra* (1921; Petra: Apóstol y Civilizador, 1982), 1:63.

4. Ibid., 64.

5. Ibid.

6. Torrens y Nicolau, *Apuntes históricos*, 1:121. See also Antoni Picazo, *Urbanisme i classes socials a Mallorca, 1500–1820* (Palma: El Tall, 2008).

7. The literature on Saint Francis and the Franciscans is enormous. Two recent and illuminating biographies are André Vauchez, *Francis of Assisi: The Life and Afterlife of a Medieval Saint*, trans. Michael Cusato (New Haven, Conn.: Yale University Press, 2012), and Augustine Thompson, *Francis of Assisi: A New Biography* (Ithaca, N.Y.: Cornell University Press, 2012). On Saint Francis and missionaries to Indians, see Ramón A. Gutiérrez, *When Jesus Came, the Corn Mothers Went Away: Marriage, Sexuality, and Power in New Mexico, 1500–1846* (Stanford, Calif.: Stanford University Press, 1991), 66–71.

8. Salustiano Vicedo, *Convento de San Bernardino de Sena: La escuela del Beato Junípero Serra* (Petra: Apóstol y Civilizador, 1991), 87.

9. Ibid., 104.

10. Torrens y Nicolau, *Apuntes históricos*, 2:24–30.

11. Salustiano Vicedo, *La casa solariega de la familia Serra* (Petra: Apóstol y Civilizador, 1984), 25–27.

12. The Serra family genealogy has not been reconstructed further back than the late sixteenth century, for the records make doing so exceptionally difficult. The parish sacramental registers in which the births, marriages, and deaths of Petrans are recorded do not begin until after the Council of Trent mandated that parish priests begin recording the administration of the sacraments in an orderly fashion. The Council of Trent completed its work in 1563.

13. Perhaps it was this common past—or at least the suggestion of a shared Jewish or converso ancestry—that in part accounts for the union of Antonio Abram and Juana Abram y Salom. It is important to note that the Inquisition was active not just in Palma but throughout Mallorca in the sixteenth and seventeenth centuries. Had Serra's ancestors been Jews or conversos suspected of practicing Judaism, they would have been denounced and prosecuted by the Holy Office. Records for the Inquisition do suggest the prosecution of a handful of individuals in Petra for crimes against the Church—blasphemy, solicitation—but there is no indication that any of Serra's ancestors, from his great-grandfather through his parents, were anything other than observant Catholics. See Llorenç Pérez, Lleonard Muntaner, and Mateu Colom, *El tribunal de la Inquisición en Mallorca, relación de causas de fe, 1578–1806* (Palma: Miquel Font, 1986).

14. In her will, Juana Serra y Abram asked that her body be buried in the tomb of the *beatas*. Through most of the nineteenth century, there were no outdoor cemeteries in Petra; all Petrans of good standing within the church were buried in the church, in one of its subterranean vaults. This was done in the belief that it provided comfort to the deceased and their living descendants. Once interred in the church, the remains of the dead would be close to the sacred relics of the church, their souls would be comforted by the recitation of Mass in the church, and their relatives would be near them when they prayed for their salvation. Furthermore, once buried in a church tomb, the bones of the dead would be safe from desecration. In the Convento de San Bernardino, the tombs for the dead are just below the main floor of the church. For a burial, a floor stone covering the tomb was opened, and the body was slid into the tomb. There was no coffin for the body, just a burial shawl and some lime to mask the odors of the entombed. Such was the custom of the day.

15. Vicedo, *La casa solariega de la familia Serra*, 29–35. Primogeniture—the practice of the eldest son inheriting the bulk of an estate so as to preserve and concentrate family wealth and status in a single heir—was not the custom in Mallorca in the seventeenth or eighteenth century, especially among those who were not wealthy.

16. Margarita also inherited a patch of land in Son Homar, but with that too came the requirement that she pay seven *sueldos* each year to the town coffers.

17. In this age marriage was often an elusive goal. See David Sven Reher, *Town and Country in Pre-industrial Spain: Cuenca, 1550–1870* (Cambridge: Cambridge University Press, 1990) and *Perspectives on the Family in Spain, Past and Present* (Oxford: Clarendon, 1997).

18. In all likelihood, this had been true for earlier generations of the family. Juan Serra's own sister—Margarita—died alone and without an heir in 1697. Juana Serra's own marriage prospects may have died with her own mother in 1689, for at that time her father had already died and Antonio and her younger brother were still in their teens. Juana, nearing adulthood herself, may have shouldered the responsibility of raising the younger Antonio and Juan. Doubtless, she would have also relied on extended family—and perhaps charity from the nearby Convento de San Bernardino—for support.

19. Vicedo, *La casa solariega de la familia Serra*, 258.

20. Margarita had only one brother, and most likely the care of the mother had fallen to her. Ibid., 238–39.

21. Fiol, *Història de Mallorca*, 260–61; and Gines Rosa, "Aproximación a la demografia de un pueblo mallorquín: Binissalem, 1700–1867," *Trabajos de geografía* 38 (1981–1982): 41–75.

22. Josep Juan Vidal, "Las crisis agrarias y la sociedad en Mallorca durante la edad moderna," *Mayurqa* 16 (1976): 87–113.

23. Miquel Joseph is Catalan. The family name Serra was written Serre, a common spelling variant in Petra. He was baptized Miquel Joseph Serre.

24. For my analysis of the community of Petra, I have used a census of the town created in 1729 by Bourbon officials. I examined the original in Palma. "Villa de Petra, resumen de su vecindario, " RP-2852, year 1729, signed by Thomas Serre y Martorell, Arxiu del Regne de Mallorca (Archive of Mallorca).

25. He does not appear in the death records in the parish archives of Mallorca, either the main one or the records of the *albats*. How long he lived is not certain, but it is doubtful that he reached his first birthday.

26. Infant deaths were common to this era. In fact, modern studies have shown that in many years it was typical for one in three newborns to die before the first birthday. See, for example, Reher, *Perspectives on the Family in Spain*, 131–42.

27. Given how common it was for children to die in infancy, early modern Catholic society had evolved a cultural response to the deaths of children. Petrans who lost children would typically make extra offerings to either the parish church or the Convento de San Bernardino so that special Masses would be said for the deceased. Yet there is no indication that Antonio and Margarita's grief found expression in this way, if the records of Masses said in Petra in these years are complete. In the parish archive, I examined "Enterros, extremes uncions, drets de campanes i adventicio, 1720–1793," C-3945, and found no record of the Serras making a special donation.

28. For rates of infant mortality in Petra, see Isabel Moll, Antoni Segura, Jaume Suau, and Llorenç Ferrer, *Cronología de les crisis demogràfiques a Mallorca: segles xviii-xix* (Palma: Institut d'Estudis Baleàrics, 1983), 113–16.

29. Maynard Geiger, in his monumental two-volume *The Life and Times of Fray Junípero Serra, O.F.M.; or, The Man Who Never Turned Back (1713–1784)* (Washington, D.C.: Academy of American Franciscan History, 1959), argues that Serra was sickly at birth and thus baptized right away before he could die, but there is no evidence to support this claim. This interpretation is an important jumping-off point for the hagiography of Serra, much of which is rooted in a belief that he spent much of his life overcoming physical challenges, such as his small stature and ulcerated leg. In the year of Miquel Joseph's birth one in three infants in Petra succumbed before age one; it was standard practice to baptize newborns the day of their birth.

30. The girl was named Martina María.

31. For Mallorcan family lineages and their origins, see Onofre Vaquer Bennàssar, app. 2, "Llinatges de Mallorca," in *L'origen dels mallorquins* (Palma: El Tall, 2008), 87–107.

32. See, for example, in the Archive of Mallorca (RP-2853), the *vecindario* (census of heads of households) for Petra in 1732. On the second page at the top is the name "Juan Serra Dalmau," and below him is "Antonio Serra Delmau." Miquel Joseph's father was often referred to in the written records of the town as Antonio Delmau or Antonio Cifre Delmau. And in person he was probably known as Antonio Delmau. How the Serra family acquired these additional names is not known. Cifre and Delmau are both Catalonian family names. Son Delmau, however, was a finca, a small farm, east of Petra, where perhaps Miquel Joseph's ancestors worked or lived.

33. Bartolomé Font Obrador, *El apóstol de California, sus albores* (Palma: Direcció General de Cultura, 1989), 203–6.

34. See, for example, the final page of the "Villa de Petra, resumen de su vecindario." Pages are not numbered.

35. The *vecindario* of 1729 has extensive information on the occupations of the town's residents.

36. He had received the house in the Barracar from his brother, two plots of land from his mother, one from his maternal grandmother, and another from his own brother, Miquel. Moreover, through his wife's family he came to own two more pieces of land and the house in which he had lived during the first years of his marriage. Vicedo, *La casa solariega de la familia Serra*, 243–45.

37. On the houses of Petra, see Jaume Andreu, *Les cases de Son Mieres (Petra): Un apropament històrico-artístic* (Petra: Fundació Jaume Ribot Amengual, 2009).

38. Only 2 percent of the households were fully independent and had sufficient income through land or trade such that they did not have to work during the year. These wealthy individuals were nobles with inherited land, wealth, and titles. Eleven percent of the town's households had income from rents or other means such that their heads had to work only about half the year. And 13 percent of Petra's households survived only through charity. A disproportionate number of these destitute families were headed by widows. "Villa de Petra, resumen de su vecindario."

39. Llibre de Cofrades de 1727, 4, Archives of the Parroquia de San Pedro de Petra.

40. On the interior of the convento—its altar and chapels—see Vicedo, *Convento de San Bernardino de Sena*, 141–215.

41. Torrens y Nicolau, *Apuntes históricos*, 1:53–54.

42. For the demographic data on Petra in these years, see Moll et al., *Cronología de les crisis demogràfiques à Mallorca, segles XVIII–XIX*.

43. "Villa de Petra, resumen de su vecindario."

44. Maynard J. Geiger, trans. and ed., *Palóu's Life of Fray Junípero Serra* (Washington, D.C.: Academy of American Franciscan History, 1955), 3.

45. Torrens y Nicolau, *Apuntes históricos*, 2:66–75.

46. Ibid., 128–31.

3. BECOMING JUNÍPERO

1. Maynard J. Geiger suggested that Serra came to Palma in 1729, but it is not exactly clear when he moved to the capital. Geiger, *Life and Times*, 1:17. Palou, in his *Relación histórica*, says that Serra applied for admission soon after he had arrived in the city and that not long after his rejection he was admitted to the novitiate in September 1730. Palou, *Relación histórica*, 4.

2. Here Serra was emulating Saint Francis, who had left his own family for a life of spirituality, following the Gospel of Saint Matthew, 39:37–39: "Anyone who loves their father or mother more than me is not worthy of me; anyone who loves their son or daughter more than me is not worthy of me. Whoever does not take up their cross and follow me is not worthy of me. Whoever finds their life will lose it, and whoever loses their life for my sake will find it."

3. Palou, *Relación histórica*, 3. The observer here is Francisco Palou, Serra's friend, companion, and fellow Franciscan. Serra and Palou shared a bond and a series of life experiences that began in Palma, and it would be Palou who would craft the first hagiography of Serra. It was published in Mexico City in 1787 under the title *Relación histórica de la vida y apostólicas tareas del venerable padre fray Junípero Serra* and is an exceptionally important source on Serra's life and times, even though it is far from objective. At the Huntington Library, I consulted RB 57251. Palou's hagiography was very ably edited and translated by Maynard J. Geiger, OFM, and published as *Palóu's Life of Fray Junípero Serra*. Note that I adopt the conventional spelling of Palou without an accent over the *o*. That is how Palou rendered his own name.

4. Xamena Fiol, *Història de l'església a Mallorca* (Palma: Moll, 1986), 177–79.

5. Dameto, *Ancient and Modern History of the Balearick Islands*, 19–20.

6. Ibid., 22–23.

7. Ibid., 24.

8. The fifteen lineages are Aguiló, Bonnín, Cortés, Forteza, Fuster, Martí, Miró, Picó, Piña, Pomar, Segura, Tagongí, Valentí, Valleriola, and Valls. Porcel, *Los Chuetas mallorquines*, 56. Cf. Fiol, *Història de Mallorca*, 268, who puts the number of lineages at fourteen. Porcel also provides a list of family names of those accused of Judaizing and those conversos who converted in 1391 and who lived in the Call. Among these family names are Amorós, Dalmau, Noguera, Ripoll, and Serra.

9. Fiol, *Història de Mallorca*, 268.

10. In 1729–1730, Palma's households were enumerated and classified just as Petra's had been in 1729. While the goal was to generate more taxes, the result was a town census that allows us an added sense of what sort of place Miquel Joseph had moved to and where he would make his home for most of the next two decades. See Lleonard Muntaner Mariano, "Un model de ciutat preindustrial: La ciutat de Mallorca al segle XVIII," *Trabajos de geografía 34: Miscelanea* (1977–1978), 47.

11. Santa Cruz parish was also home to 25 percent of the town's poor and, not coincidentally, a high number of widows. See ibid., 32.

12. Josep Juan Vidal, "Notas sobre la población y la vida urbana de la Mallorca moderna," *Mayurqa* 17 (1977): 57–62.

13. Geiger, *Life and Times*, 1:18.

14. Ibid. On this incident, see Palou in Geiger, *Relación histórica*, 4, and Geiger, *Life and Times*, 1:18. There has been some speculation that Serra's acceptance into the order was delayed because of complications resulting from the very high likelihood that conversos were among his ancestors. As discussed in Chapter 2, the given names of some of Serra's ancestors suggest that he descended from conversos, and the family name Serra was in fact associated with one family who converted in 1391. Not long after Serra applied to join the order, all of this would have been known to Franciscan officials, for a formal investigation into the ancestry of all applicants was the norm. By the mid-fifteenth century, applicants for admission to the order

had to be faithful Catholics, not suspected of heresy; they had to be unmarried, healthy, willing to accept religious vows freely, born of married parents, free of debt, not bound in servitude, at least sixteen years of age, of good reputation, and literate. Serra seemingly was all of these. But there was an added hurdle that was imposed in the fifteenth century. As a result of the anti-Semitism that dominated some quarters of Europe and Catholic institutions and the strong belief among many that the conversions of Jews to Catholicism were false, aspirants to the Franciscan order had to demonstrate— through a series of investigations—that they had "pure" blood, as in no Jewish blood, for four generations. Had Serra not been able to demonstrate the "purity" of his blood, he would not have been admitted to the order. There is no indication that his own commitment to Franciscanism and Catholicism was in any way a response to how he or others understood his ancestry. On the origins and procedures of purity of blood investigations and the Franciscan order, see Francisco Morales, *Ethnic and Social Background of the Franciscan Friars in Seventeenth Century Mexico* (Washington, D.C.: Academy of American Franciscan History, 1973), 3–21.

15. Palou, in Geiger, *Relación histórica*, 320n18.
16. Ibid., 5.
17. Ibid., 4. Palou wrote years later that as a result of his careful and impassioned reading of the lives of the saints, in Miquel Joseph there arose "a warm desire from the time of his novitiate to imitate them [the saints] insofar as it was possible." But in all likelihood Palou erred slightly in his judgment, for the novitiate probably fertilized a seed planted years earlier in the Convento de San Bernardino. Miquel Joseph's "growing desire" during his novitiate "to imitate those saints and venerables who had labored for the conversion of souls, especially among the pagans and uncultured peoples," was simply the expression of a desire to follow in the footsteps of San Bernardino, the man whom Perelló had placed high on the main altar at the convent in Petra.
18. Michael B. McCloskey, *The Formative Years of the Missionary College of Santa Cruz de Querétaro, 1683–1733* (Washington, D.C.: Academy of American Franciscan History, 1955), 15–16.
19. Geiger, *Life and Times*, 1:91, has him returning to Spain in 1681.
20. McCloskey, *Formative Years*, 17–18.
21. Ximénez Samaniego was devoted to the writings of the nun María de Jesús de Agreda, whose revelations supported the notion that Indians in northern New Spain were destined to convert to Catholicism.
22. David Rex Galindo, "Propaganda Fide: Training Franciscan Missionaries in New Spain" (PhD diss., Southern Methodist University, 2010), 48.
23. On Solano, see Luis Jerónimo de Oré, *Relación de la vida y milagros de San Francisco Solano*, ed. Noble David Cook (Lima: Pontificia Universidad Católica del Perú, Fondo Editorial, 1998).
24. Diego de Córdova Salinas, *Crónica franciscana de las provincias del Perú*, ed. Lino Gómez Canedo (Washington, D.C.: Academy of American Franciscan History, 1957), 552.

25. Oré, *San Francisco Solano*, 11.
26. Ibid., 17.
27. Juan Domingo de Arricivita, *Apostolic Chronicle of Juan Domingo Arricivita: The Franciscan Mission Frontier in the Eighteenth Century in Arizona, Texas, and the Californias*, translated by George P. Hammond and Agapito Rey, revised and indexed by Vivian C. Fisher, with introduction and notes by W. Michael Mathes. (Berkeley, Calif.: Academy of American Franciscan History, 1996), 1:185–86.
28. Ibid., 94.
29. Ibid., 32.
30. Brother Juniper appears in the Franciscan text *The Little Flowers of St. Francis*, trans. Thomas Okey (New York: Dutton, 1963). See especially pages 134–47. Quotation from Geiger, *Relación histórica*, 321n19.
31. *Little Flowers*, 145.
32. Ibid., 137.
33. Ibid.
34. Geiger, *Life and Times*, 1:21–22.
35. Palou, in Geiger, *Relación histórica*, 5.
36. Ibid. Original reads "estatura mediana." Serra quoted in Palou, *Relación histórica*, Huntington Library, RB 57251, p. 4.

4. PRIEST AND PROFESSOR

1. Photocopy of "Libra de matrícula de los licenciados escotistas desde 1718 anevant," Palma, 1731–1743, naming Serra and his classmates for the above-indicated years. Santa Bárbara Mission Archive-Library (SBMAL), Junípero Serra Collection (JSC), document 14. All SBMAL-JSC documents are photocopies of originals from other archives. Of those in the class who were not Franciscans, nearly all were in their late thirties. Six came from Menorca.
2. Geiger, *Life and Times*, 1:24, 25.
3. Serra, class notes in theology, 1735–1737, SBMAL-JSC 10.
4. Francisco Noguera, "Compendium Scoticum," SBMAL-JSC 34, Palma, 9/9/1740–6/23/1743 and 4/13/1749. This is the notebook of a three-year lecture course in philosophy given by Serra to his students at the Convento de San Francisco, Palma. I examined the original in the Biblioteca de San Felipe Neri, Palma, Mallorca. Serra's notes are in the Biblioteca Pública del Estado in Palma, MS 76.
5. On this point, see James A. Sandos, *Converting California: Indians and Franciscans in the Missions* (New Haven, Conn.: Yale University Press, 2004), 35–38. See also the important forthcoming work by John Dagenais examining the relationship between Serra and Ramon Llull, "Before the California Missions: Junípero Serra's Mallorcan Lecture Notes on Ramon Llull."
6. Transcription of extracts from "Libro sexto de los capítulos, congregaciones y decretos" of the Province of Mallorca, SBMAL-JSC 19, 11/29/1737–10/16/1744, Marquez de Desbrull Collection, Palma; Geiger, *Life and Times*, 1:26.

7. Photocopy of extracts from "Libro sexto de los capítulos, congregaciones y decretos," SBMAL-JSC 21a.

8. Geiger, *Life and Times*, 1:26.

9. Joan Contreras y Ponseu, "Libro de novicios," Franciscan Archive, La Porciúncula, Palma, 1737.

10. Geiger, *Life and Times*, 1:25.

11. Transcript from "Licencia de predicadres y confesores y licencias de oratoriis de 1731–1743," SBMAL-JSC 11, Diocesan Archives, Palma, Mallorca.

12. Transcripts of extracts from several volumes of "Entradas y gastos" of the Convento de San Francisco de Palma, SBMAL-JSC 27, 02/1739–12/1748. I also consulted the originals in Palma, and Geiger, *Life and Times*, 1:26.

13. This preaching was a regular part of his schedule during the year. Most of these sermons were delivered toward the end, if not during the final days, of the month. Transcripts of extracts from several volumes of "Entradas y gastos." I also consulted the originals in Palma. See also AH-C 1089 in the Archive of Mallorca for sermons preached at Petra's Convento de San Bernardino between 1648 and 1761.

14. Benito Vinals de la Torre, *Sermones de los dominicos de Quaresma* . . . (Barcelona, 1713), SBMAL-JSC 33. Serra signed the title page "Del uso de Fr. Junípero Sierra Relig.o Menor."

15. Geiger, *Life and Times*, 1:27, quoting from Noguera's "Compendium Scoticum," SBMAL-JSC 34.

16. On Scotus and Serra, see Sandos, *Converting California*, 37.

17. "No one shall pass through this portal without declaring on his life that Mary was conceived without original sin." Noguera, "Compendium Scoticum," fol. 1a. I examined the original and thank John Dagenais for the page citation.

18. Geiger, *Life and Times*, 1:28.

19. Ibid., 1:30–31.

20. It is not clear who appointed Serra to this position, but most likely the Petrans Homar and Perelló played a role.

21. Geiger, *Life and Times*, 1:31–32.

22. Extracts from the "Actes de bachiller y graus de theologia de la Universidad Litteraria y Estudi General Lulliano desde 1738 fins en 1751," SBMAL-JSC 29. This volume contains the official record of Serra's activities at the university between 1744 and 1749.

23. He often played his part in an exam every week in May, June, and July, and he was also busy with exams in December. Ibid.

24. On processions and other sorts of public celebrations in Mallorca during the seventeenth century, see Antonia M. Perelló, "La festa barroca a la Mallorca del segle XVII," *Pedralbes: Revista d'historia moderna*, no. 6 (1986): 71–82.

25. Nicolás Ferrer de Sant Jordi y Figuera, *Libro de las cosas memorables que han acontecido en Mallorca, desde el año 1730 a 1739*, in Font Obrador, *El apòstol de California*, 132.

26. Ibid., 135.

27. Ibid., 136.

28. The seduction of nuns, while rare, was a common concern with moralists

during the period. They considered the seduction of nuns to be the "worst sin imaginable." To some extent the problem occurred because of the practice of some families of forcing their younger daughters to enter monasteries. For similar concerns in mid-eighteenth-century Mexico City, see Juan Pedro Viqueira Albán, *Propriety and Permissiveness in Bourbon Mexico* (Wilmington, Del.: Scholarly Resources, 1999).

29. The hapless fellow was then led to a specially constructed stage upon which had been erected a crude killing machine apparently of the officer's own design, as he had presided over executions himself and was skilled in engineering.

30. Ferrer de Sant Jordi y Figuera, *Libro de las cosas memorables*, 141–42.

31. On the climate and subsistence crises of the mid-eighteenth century, see John D. Post, *Food Shortage, Climatic Variability, and Epidemic Disease in Preindustrial Europe: The Mortality Peak in the Early 1740s* (Ithaca, N.Y.: Cornell University Press, 1985).

32. Ibid., 67.

33. Ferrer de Sant Jordi y Figuera, *Libro de las cosas memorables*, 143. This was a rarity; snow was routine in the highest mountain elevations, but everywhere else on the island it was unusual for there to be more than an occasional dusting.

34. Ibid., 142–43.

35. Ibid., 151.

36. Alvaro Campaner y Fuertes, *Cronicón majoricense* (Palma de Mallorca: Establecimiento tipográfico de Juan Colomar y Salas, 1881), in Geiger, *Life and Times*, 1:35.

37. Ferrer de Sant Jordi y Figuera, *Libro de las cosas memorables*, 148.

38. Sermons preached by Serra to the Poor Clare nuns of Palma, SBMAL-JSC 16, Palma, 1744. Of all the sermons Junípero Serra delivered during his life, these four are the only ones known to survive. On the sermons and their attribution to Serra, see Font Obrador, *El apóstol de California*, 184–87. These sermons can also be found transcribed and roughly translated in Font Obrador, *El apóstol de California*, 188–217. Note: I have not always followed the translation in Font Obrador but have worked off the transcriptions in Font Obrador, *El apóstol de California*, and SBMAL-JSC 16. For ease of the reader, here I cite only Font Obrador's versions.

39. Serra sermons in Font Obrador, *El apóstol de California*, 190.

40. His refrain was, in Latin, "gustate et videte." The first sermon is in ibid., 188–95.

41. Serra sermons ibid., 199.

42. Serra acknowledged that even Saint Matthew had said that the gates to heaven were narrow. But in quoting Saint Jerome, Serra argued that with love "the way to glory and divine Law are very easy." Serra sermons in ibid., 197.

43. Ibid.

44. Ibid., 203.

45. Ibid., 207, 209.

46. Ibid., 212, 210, 211, 216.

47. Serra cited more than forty different authorities for his points. He relied on the words of the saints, the popes, and many other sources, including the Psalms.
48. Palou, in Geiger, *Relación histórica*, 6.
49. Transcript of record from Alaró municipal archives, 3/31/1748, SBMAL-JSC 24.
50. Palou, in Geiger, *Relación histórica*, 10. Apparently, on all of these trips and others that are now lost to history, Serra left his classes at the university in the hands of a substitute. Ibid., 6.
51. That he would arrive in Petra so early and stay through early April suggests the great difficulties in Palma and even at the Convento de San Francisco during this time of famine. Petra, of course, was hardly a refuge from the crisis: years of bad weather and disease had taken their toll, and there had been no rain for much of the winter, and fears were mounting that the harvest might again fail.
52. Extract from "Llibre de actes de ca'n Riutort," Petra, 3/1749, Private Collection of Francisca Ramis y Riutort, SBMAL-JSC 30.
53. Ibid.
54. For fluctuations in annual totals of births, marriages, and deaths in Petra, see Moll, Segura, Suau, and Ferrer, *Cronología de les crisis demogràfiques à Mallorca*, 150–51.
55. Serra and Guillermo Rosselló, *El phenix obsequiamente luctando en la ciudad de Palma* (Palma, 1749), SBMAL-JSC 25, translated as "Approval of a Funeral Sermon," June 12, 1748, in Tibesar, *Writings of Serra*, 4:293.
56. Ibid.
57. Ibid., 293, 297. Spanish reads: "Tu patria no tan conocido."
58. Here I relied on the original of Palou's *Relación histórica*. For a faithful transcription of the *Relación histórica*, see Miguel Leon-Portilla, *Relación histórica de la vida y apostólicas tareas del venerable padre Fray Junípero Serra* (Mexico: Porrúa, 1970), 16.
59. Palou, in Leon-Portilla, *Relación histórica*, 16.
60. Sermons preached at the Convento de San Bernardino, Petra, 1648–1761, AH-C 1089, Clero Archive of Mallorca, fol. 155A, July 28, 1748.
61. Palou, in Geiger, *Relación histórica*, 9.
62. Ibid.
63. Maynard J. Geiger, "The Franciscan 'Mission' to San Fernando College, Mexico, 1749," *Americas* 5, no. 1 (July 1948): 49.
64. Scholars have written widely about the Spanish Crown's reliance upon missionaries to "pacify" frontier regions. For an introduction to the Bourbons' reliance on missionaries in the mid-eighteenth century, see David J. Weber's *Bárbaros: Spaniards and Their Savages in the Age of Enlightenment* (New Haven, Conn.: Yale University Press, 2005).
65. Geiger, "Franciscan 'Mission,'" 48–49.
66. Fiol, *Història de l'església a Mallorca*, 261.
67. Hugo Storni, *Catálogo de los jesuitas de la Provincia del Paraguay (Cuenca del Plata), 1585–1768* (Rome: Institutum Historicum S.I., 1980).

68. Fiol, *Història de l'església a Mallorca*, 262. See also Josep Amengual i Batle, *Història de l'església a Mallorca: Del barroc a la Il·lustració (1563–1800)* (Palma: Lleonard Muntaner, 2002), 91–93.

69. On Oliver, see Mario Aurelio Poli, "La Virgen de Luján y su cronista franciscano Fray Antonio Oliver Feliu O.F.M. (Palma de Mallorca 1711–Buenos Aires 1787)," *Boletín de la Sociedad Arqueológica Luliana* 64 (2008): 289–308.

70. From an early age she was said to have been particularly religious, and she became a Franciscan nun in her twenties. For more than two decades she was the spiritual adviser of King Carlos IV; in the early 1680s the Catholic Church declared her venerable. In an eight-volume work, *The Mystical City of God* (1670), she recounted what she said was a true revelation she had received directly from Mary about the nature of the life of Jesus as well as life in heaven. Serra and Palou were moved by a widely circulated memorial of her life, her travels across the Atlantic, and a letter composed in 1631 by the Franciscan missionary Alonso de Benavides, who had worked in New Mexico and met with María de Agreda in Spain. So important was this document to the life of Serra that Palou included excerpts of it as an appendix to his hagiography. For more on the influence of María de Agreda on Palou and Serra, and the missionaries of the Southwest, see Anna María Nogar's doctoral dissertation, "La Monja Azul: The Political and Cultural Ramifications of a 17th-Century Mystical Transatlantic Journey" (University of Texas at Austin, 2008).

71. She asserted that she had bilocated and therefore had been in two places at the same time.

72. On these phenomena, see Carlos Eire, "The Good, the Bad, and the Airborne: Levitation and the History of the Impossible in Early Modern Europe," in *Ideas and Cultural Margins in Early Modern Germany*, ed. Robin B. Barnes and Marjorie Elizabeth Plummer. (Burlington, Vt.: Ashgate, 2009), 307–23.

73. Excerpt from a letter written by Fray Alonso de Benavides to the friars of the Holy Custody of the Conversion of Saint Paul in Madrid, 1631, and included as an appendix in Palou's *Relación histórica*. See Palou, in Geiger, *Relación histórica*, 302.

74. María de Agreda wrote that the life of an apostolic missionary was the highest calling, for it "involved suffering." She would have been pleased to have given her blood and life and suffered "cruel martyrdom" if doing so would have saved even a single pagan soul in the New World. Palou, in Geiger, *Relación histórica*, 304.

75. Ibid., 11. Two of those five spots would go right away to Serra and Palou; the other three would eventually be taken by Juan Crespí, Raphael Verger, and Guillermo Vicens, from the Convento de San Francisco in Palma. Native to Mallorca, these five men had no fear of the sea; they had been raised in a culture in which people went to sea and on an island whose history had been shaped by the comings and goings of seafarers for thousands of years.

76. Ibid.

77. Noguera, "Compendium Scoticum," fol. 1a. I thank John Dagenais for this page reference.

5. THE VOYAGE SO FAR

1. See, for example, Palou's statement that Serra during Lent was a sought-after speaker who "was engaged in converting sinners." He continues: "Because of his fervent zeal, great talent, skillful speech and the sonorous voice with which God had enriched him, he [Serra] awakened sinners from the heavy sleep of sin, and they were converted to God." Palou, in Geiger, *Relación histórica*, 6.

2. Ibid., 12.

3. Palou's writing must be central to any biography of Serra, but his biography of Serra—while full of indispensable details on Serra's life—was intended to document Serra's heroic life and his saintly virtues. The facts that Palou presents, I believe, for the most part can be trusted, but I have not always followed his interpretation of Serra's character and motivations. The same can be said about Geiger's magisterial two-volume history of Serra. It is unequaled as a source on Serra's life and everyday activities, but it too is a brief for canonization. For the quotation, see Palou, in Leon-Portilla, *Relación histórica*, 19.

4. Palou, in Geiger, *Relación histórica*, 12.

5. Most likely the delay resulted from a need to secure provisions for the ship and the distance that many friars had to travel from their convents to join the group being assembled there by Pérez de Mezquía.

6. Geiger, "Franciscan 'Mission,'" 54–55.

7. Ages of recruits and their backgrounds are in ibid. and "Misión de San Fernando para el Colegio de San Fernando de Mexico," Contratación, legajo 5546, Archivo General de Indias (Spain).

8. Geiger identifies this priest as Serra's cousin. Geiger, "Franciscan 'Mission,'" 53n7.

9. Serra to Father Francesch Serra, Aug. 20, 1749, Cádiz, in Tibesar, *Writings of Serra*, 1:2–9.

10. Ibid. The Mallorquí reads: "a passar avant, y nunca retrodecer" (2). Here, as in many of his early letters, Serra blends Mallorquí with pure Spanish.

11. Ibid., 5.

12. Ibid., 7.

13. Ibid.

14. On the date of departure, see Serra to Father Francesch Serra, Dec. 14, 1749, Veracruz, in Tibesar, *Writings of Serra*, 1:11.

15. AGI Contratación, 5546, fols. 13a–b.

16. Palou, in Geiger, *Relación histórica*, 263.

17. In 1747, during the War of Austrian Succession, Bonilla and one of his ships had been seized off Cádiz by English privateers. Nevertheless, he won his freedom and traveled round-trip between Cádiz and Veracruz soon thereafter. On the *Guadalupe* and Bonilla, see James A. Lewis, *The Spanish Convoy of 1750: Heaven's Hammer and International Diplomacy* (Gainesville: University of Florida Press, 2009), 8.

18. Serra to Father Francesch Serra, Dec. 14, 1749, 11.

19. Palou, in Geiger, *Relación histórica*, 14.

20. Ibid., 15.

21. Ibid.
22. Ibid.
23. Serra to Father Francesch Serra, Dec. 14, 1749, 13.
24. Ibid., 15.
25. Palou, in Geiger, *Relación histórica*, 16.
26. Serra to Father Francesch Serra, Veracruz, Dec. 14, 1749, in Tibesar, *Writings of Serra*, 1:15–17.
27. Ibid., 17.
28. Palou, *Relación histórica*, 16.
29. Palou, in Geiger, *Relación histórica*, 17.
30. Serra to Father Francesch Serra, Dec. 14, 1749, 17.
31. Michael C. Meyer and William L. Sherman, *The Course of Mexican History* (New York: Oxford University Press, 1979), 169.
32. Alan Knight, *Mexico from the Beginning to the Spanish Conquest* (Cambridge: Cambridge University Press, 2002), 17.
33. Ibid., 20; Meyer and Sherman, *The Course of Mexican History*, 212.
34. Knight, *Mexico from the Beginning to the Spanish Conquest*, 182, 209.
35. Ibid., 22, 27.
36. Ibid., 34.
37. Ibid., 41.
38. On the economy of eighteenth-century New Spain, see D. A. Brading, *Miners and Merchants in Bourbon Mexico, 1763–1810* (Cambridge: Cambridge University Press, 1971). See also P. J. Bakewell, *Silver Mining and Society in Colonial Mexico: Zacatecas, 1546–1700* (Cambridge: Cambridge University Press, 1971).
39. Merchant ships from Cádiz arrived every year or every other year loaded with finished goods and Spaniards who came to the colony by the thousands over the seventeenth and eighteenth centuries. From the early seventeenth century, when the port was moved just to the south of where Cortés had made landfall, Veracruz had been the point of disembarkation for Spaniards coming to New Spain.
40. On Veracruz as Serra saw it, see Jean-Baptiste Chappe d'Auteroche, *A Voyage to California, to Observe the Transit of Venus* (London: Edward and Charles Dilly, 1778). Huntington Library Rare Book 487000:0433.
41. Peter Gerhard, *A Guide to the Historical Geography of New Spain*, rev. ed. (Norman: University of Oklahoma Press, 1993), 360–62.
42. Palou, in Geiger, *Relación histórica*, 17.
43. In 1765, one seasoned traveler described the route between Veracruz and Mexico City as composed of "the worst roads imaginable." Chappe d'Auteroche, *Voyage to California*, 22.
44. Palou, in Geiger, *Relación histórica*, 17.
45. Ibid., 18.
46. Ibid., 19.
47. Ibid.
48. Chappe d'Auteroche, *Voyage to California*, 25–26.
49. Palou, in Geiger, *Relación histórica*, 19–20.
50. The legs and face of Margil de Jesús therefore were often swollen from

bites. See Arricivita, *Apostolic Chronicle*, 1:33, 65, and especially 185–86. In failing to protect themselves from insects, men like Margil de Jesús and, most likely, Serra invited upon themselves physical infirmity and suffering. Serra would not have spent his time trying to determine the insect that caused his affliction, for he knew the cause of his own suffering: his own manifest "unworthiness." He would have believed that his infirmity was as much a part of God's plan as was the man who guided him across the river.

51. Palou, in Geiger, *Relación histórica*, 63.
52. On the likely sights of the journey, see Chappe d'Auteroche, *Voyage to California*, 19–41.
53. On disease and population decline in central Mexico, and Franciscan understandings, see Robert McCaa, "Spanish and Nahuatl Views on Smallpox and Demographic Catastrophe in Mexico," *Journal of Interdisciplinary History* 25, no. 3 (Winter 1995): 397–431.
54. Matthew D. O'Hara, *A Flock Divided: Race, Religion, and Politics in Mexico, 1749–1857* (Durham, N.C.: Duke University Press), 23.
55. José Antonio de Villaseñor, *Theatro americano: Descripción general de los reynos, y provincias de la Nueva-España, y sus jurisdicciones* (Mexico: Imprenta de la Viuda de D. Joseph Bernardo de Hogal, 1746–1748), 1:35. Huntington Library Rare Book 49182.
56. Ibid., 1:36.
57. Viqueira Albán, *Propriety and Permissiveness in Bourbon Mexico*, 98.
58. Chappe d'Auteroche, *Voyage to California*, 40–41.
59. See O'Hara, *Flock Divided*, 96–100.
60. Geiger, *Relación histórica*, 339nn3–4, for the identities of these men.
61. Serra quoted by Palou, in Geiger, *Relación histórica*, 21.

6. THE SIERRA GORDA

1. Geiger, *Life and Times*, 92.
2. The college emerged out of a hospice for friars founded in 1731. See Geiger, *Life and Times*, 1:96, and María Teresa Álvarez Icaza Longoria, "Un cambio apresurado: La secularización de las misiones de la Sierra Gorda (1770–1782)," *Letras históricas*, no. 3 (Fall–Winter 2010): 19–45.
3. Geiger, *Life and Times*, 1:96–97.
4. Serra must have been welcome in the novitiate, for Pumeda had only one novice under his instruction. Ibid., 98.
5. Palou, in Geiger, *Relación histórica*, 22.
6. On the role of libraries in the lives of the apostolic colleges of Mexico, see Rex Galindo, "Propaganda Fide," 214–15. And on the holdings of the library of the College of San Fernando, see Maynard J. Geiger, "The Library of the Apostolic College of San Fernando, Mexico, in the Eighteenth and Nineteenth Centuries," *Americas* 7, no. 4 (April 1951): 425–34.
7. Alonso de la Peña Montenegro, *Itinerario para parochos de indios: En que se tratan las materias mas particulares, tocantes a ellos, para su buena administracion* (Madrid: Joseph Fernandez de Buendia, 1668). At the Huntington,

I examined a 1726 edition printed in Antwerp. Huntington Rare Book 44457.

8. As Montenegro wrote, "If the tongue does not speak words that enter the heart the preacher shall have no hope of winning souls and instead his zeal shall be misplaced." See ibid., bk. 1, treatise 10, secs. vi–vii. Montenegro continued, emphasizing that Indians could not be converted unless they understood the padres' preaching: "It is impossible for faith to enter the interior of the soul unless one preaches in a manner that the heathen can understand; to speak in a language unfamiliar to them is a vain effort, leading to a Babel of confusion and fruitless fervor. Therefore all missionaries shall make every effort to learn the language, although it shall cost them sleepless nights and much sweat, in order to harvest many souls for heaven."

9. William B. Taylor, *Magistrates of the Sacred: Priests and Parishioners in Eighteenth-Century Mexico* (Stanford, Calif.: Stanford University Press, 1996), 216 and 642n62.

10. Serra had his own copy of the *Itinerario* certainly by the mid-1750s, and he presented it to the missionaries at San Juan Capistrano when that mission was founded in the late 1770s. Today, the volume is in the archive of the Archdiocese of Orange, California.

11. This second contingent had sailed from Cádiz on December 31, 1749, and traveled more rapidly than Serra's group, but there is no record of their journey across the Atlantic. Geiger, "Franciscan 'Mission,' " 48–60.

12. Ortés de Velasco was tired of having to beg for missionaries from the other colleges; he wanted to send his own men to the north, men who shared his beliefs and would be more accountable to the college, and since the temporary replacements from the other colleges were only in the Sierra Gorda for six months before others took their places, they had no time to learn the Indians' languages and could make little headway in converting them to Catholicism. Palou, in Geiger, *Relación histórica*, 27.

13. Serra quoted in ibid., 22.

14. One of the padres, Father Melchor Velasco, had left the college a week after he arrived. He was a thin man, in his late twenties, with the mark of a wound in the middle of his forehead, whom the superiors at the college found scandalous. But the other thirty-two, one assumes, were also eager for work on the frontier.

15. Also chosen were Antonio Martínez, Juan Ignacio Gastón, Pascual de Sospedra, Juan Crespí, Antonio Paterna, and Sebastián Sáenz de Insestrillas. Palou, in Geiger, *Relación histórica*, 265.

16. Father Bernardo Pumeda to José de Escandón, June 29, 1751, Fondo Franciscano, doc. 1532, 108-9, Biblioteca Nacional de Antropología e Historia, Mexico, D.F.

17. Palou, in Geiger, *Relación histórica*, 28.

18. On the regions inhabited by the Pames and Jonace, see David Frye, "The Native Peoples of Northeastern Mexico," in *The Cambridge History of the Native Peoples of the Americas*, pt. 2, vol. 2, ed. Richard E. W. Adams and Murdo J. MacLeod (Cambridge: Cambridge University Press, 2000), 95.

19. For representative Spanish views on the Indians of the north, see the sixteenth-century Franciscan chronicle by Fray Gerónimo de Mendieta, *His-*

toria eclesiástica indiana (Mexico: Consejo Nacional para la Cultura y las Artes, 1997), 2:460.

20. Frye, "Native Peoples of Northeastern Mexico," 96.

21. On this sort of resistance, see James C. Scott, *The Art of Not Being Governed: An Anarchist History of Upland Southeast Asia* (New Haven, Conn.: Yale University Press, 2009).

22. On José de Escandón, see Jesús Mendoza Muñoz, *El conde de Sierra Gorda don José de Escandón y la Helguera: Militar, noble y caballero* (Cadereyta: Fomento Histórico y Cultural de Cadereyta, 2005). See also José Antonio Cruz Rangel, *Chichimecas, misioneros, soldados y terratenientes* (Mexico: Archivo General de la Nación, 2003).

23. José de Escandón, "Informe del coronel José de Escandón acerca de su visita a la Sierra Gorda y projecto de reorganización de sus misiones," Feb. 23, 1743, Querétaro, in Margarita Velasco Mireles, coord., *La Sierra Gorda: Documentos para su historia* (Mexico: Instituto Nacional de Antropología e Historia, 1996), 421. For microfilm of original, which I also consulted, see MS 99/378m, 1.4, Bancroft Library.

24. Ibid.

25. And he believed that a new mission there would not cost the Crown much; within eight years, he predicted, the Indians of Jalpan would pay taxes to the Crown. Escandón also reported that the Indians at Jalpan had asked for a resident Franciscan who would say Mass daily and teach the Indians the *doctrina*. Ibid., 422.

26. Lino Gómez Canedo, *Sierra Gorda, un típico enclave misional en el centro de México (siglos XVII–XVIII)* (Querétaro: Ediciones del Gobierno del Estado de Querétaro, 1988), 185–87. The Indians complained that the padres charged them fees to perform sacraments and that they had to carry on their backs twenty-five fanegas of corn nearly fifty miles to the presidio at Zimapan. Escandón assured them that this would change in the future.

27. Monique Gustin, *El barroco en la Sierra Gorda: Misiones franciscanas en el estado de Querétaro, siglo XVIII* (Mexico: Instituto Nacional de Antropología e Historia, 1969), 75.

28. José de Escandón, "Informe," Archivo General de la Nación (hereafter cited as AGN), Provincias Internas (hereafter cited as PI), 249, fols. 89a–103 and 97a for beginning of census, April 22, 1744.

29. Escandón, "Informe," Jalpan, 1744, AGN PI 249, fol. 117a.

30. Escandón registered 402 Indian families at Jalpan mission, but only 18 of them, or 50 people in all, actually lived in the village at the mission. Six hundred and forty-four remained in the hills and the valley of Tancama to the southeast; 580 in the hills of Malila to the east; and 161 in the village of Pisquintla to the west. Sixty of the Indians he counted were descended from the Tlascalans who had been sent into the region as colonists more than a century earlier. In all, he counted more than 1,900 people in and around Jalpan. All of these had Spanish names, suggesting that they had already been baptized and had been affiliated in some way with the former Augustinian mission at Jalpan. It is doubtful, though, that they all spoke Spanish. On Escandón's work congregating Indians at Jalpan, see AGN PI 249, fols. 89a–103a.

31. Escandón, "Informe," Jalpan, 1744, AGN PI 249, fols. 101b–102a.

32. For Escandón's work congregating the Pames to the four other sites, see the *informes* in AGN PI 249, fols. 104a–121b.

33. Father Pedro Pérez de Mezquía, "Informe" on the Sierra Gorda, AGN Documentos para la história de México, 2nd ser., vol. 13, exp. 8, especially fol. 44a. At Tilaco, many of the Indians congregated by Escandón had quickly returned to their villages. Escandón had assigned 750 people to the mission, but only 400 remained. The Indians of the rancherías of El Lobo and El Humo found it necessary to return to their villages ten miles from the mission to cultivate food, and this had set back the padres' efforts to teach them the *doctrina*. The mission harvests had failed, even though a year before, the padres had provided the Indians with four oxen and the tools necessary to work the fields. It was only through a gift of two hundred fanegas of corn from the padres and the civil officials that the Indians had survived. At Tilaco and Tancoyol, while many Indians were living at the mission and were attending catechism and daily prayers, others had "fled" the mission for villages to the north in the jurisdiction of the Villa de los Valles. These Indians continued their custom of *sembrar en rozas*. At Concá too, a good number of Indians continued to live in their native villages, where they farmed in their customary fashion and resisted moving to the mission.

34. Palou, in Geiger, *Relación histórica*, 26–27.

35. Fray José Ortés de Velasco to Fray Juan Fogueras (the *comisario general* of New Spain), "Informe sobre las misiones del Colegio de San Fernando en la Sierra Gorda," Dec. 5, 1746, Querétaro, in Mireles, *La Sierra Gorda*, 483–89.

36. Ibid.

37. Fray José Ortés de Velasco, "Razón de las misiones que tiene el Colegio de San Fernando establicidas en la Sierra Gorda, or Madre, y el estado que a el presente tienen," 1749, MS 99/378m, 1.5, Bancroft Library.

38. One of Serra's first challenges in the Sierra Gorda would have been to settle into his new home, the mission at Jalpan. Throughout the region, securing the necessities—food, water, and shelter—would prove challenging, as would adherence to a regular schedule of observance. Basic foodstuffs—beans, fish, shrimp, chocolate, coffee, sugar, and spices—and religious items, such as baptismal fonts, vestments, tunics, and shrouds, had to be brought into the Sierra Gorda on mule trains from the capital. In addition, Serra did not know anyone other than Palou and the other missionaries from Mallorca. It was all disorienting for him, and he responded by throwing himself into his work. In some ways he was doing in the Sierra Gorda what he had seen the padres do in Petra: build a place of worship and deepen the faith of those who were at least nominally Catholic.

39. At the peak of an epidemic of smallpox or typhus, 199 Pames were buried at the mission in October and November 1748. And certainly scores, if not hundreds, more died away from the mission.

40. Fray José Ortés de Velasco, "Tanto del informe que hizo el padre guardian," Jan. 16, 1751, MS 99/378m, 1.7, 2b–3a, Bancroft Library.

41. For the population at Jalpan, see AGN Indiferente Virreinal (hereafter IV),

vol. 5506, exp. 11; Landa: AGN IV, vol. 5506, exp. 7; Tilaco: AGN IV, vol. 5506, exps. 10 and 12; Concá: AGN IV, vol. 5506, exp. 9; and AGN IV, vol. 5479, exp. 70.

42. Ortés de Velasco, "Tanto del informe que hizo el padre guardian."

43. Ibid., 3b–4a.

44. Census of the mission and summary of baptisms, marriages, and burials at the missions. AGN IV, vol. 5506, exp. 11, Sept. 22 and 24, 1750, two documents, both signed by Father Phelipe Suares Espinosa and Father Junípero Serra. This is the oldest document from the Sierra Gorda with Serra's signature. He signed it Junípero Sierra, a variant spelling of his last name.

45. At Landa, by the fall of 1750 the changes were even more dramatic: over half of the families had no children. One in five of those childless families had living with them either an orphan or an unattached sibling. At Landa, as at Jalpan, there was a large number of dependents: forty-six widows and widowers, sixteen orphans, and twenty unattached siblings. Clearly, even though the padres preached the importance of the nuclear family, their mode of colonization and the diseases that followed in its wake undermined Pames families and communities. At the other Sierra Gorda missions, similar changes in family structure were under way, as spouses and children died in large numbers. Notably, at Tilaco, the number of widows and widowers skyrocketed. In 1744, Escandón had counted only two widowers and one widow; in July 1748, after the epidemics, there were already four widowers and twenty widows. AGN IV, vol. 5506, exp. 12, July 13, 1748, Tilaco, Father Juan Escudero. By fall 1750, Fathers Antonio Martínez and Juan Ignacio Gastón counted seventeen widows, fifty-one widowers, and thirty orphans.

46. Between 1744 and 1758, at Concá, two adults were baptized. At Tancoyol, forty-two adults were baptized. But we know from other sources that more than forty adults had been baptized at Tancoyol between 1744 and 1748. At Landa, twenty-four adults were baptized. At Tilaco, sixty-nine were baptized, and at Jalpan eleven adults were baptized. If we take away those baptized at Tancoyol between 1744 and 1748, only around one hundred adults were baptized in Serra's years. If half of the remaining adult baptisms occurred during Serra's years in the Sierra Gorda, there were maybe fifty adult baptisms in all five missions during Serra's years. Each mission had two Franciscans, making it all the more unlikely that Serra baptized large numbers.

47. Fray Juan Ramos de Lora, "Estado de las misiones franciscanas de Sierra Gorda en 1764," Nov. 21, 1764, in Mireles, *La Sierra Gorda*, 577–80.

48. Palou, *Relación histórica*, 29.

49. Pumeda to Escandón, June 29, 1751, Fondo Franciscano, Doc. 1532, 108a–9a, Biblioteca Nacional de Antropología e Historia, Mexico, D.F. Pumeda notes that Serra had written a melancholy letter about the need to return Indians to their missions.

50. "Estado de las misiones de la Sierra Gorda en 1761," Jan. 11, 1762, in Mireles, *La Sierra Gorda*, 526. The original is missing from the Archivo Franciscano in Mexico's Biblioteca Nacional.

51. Ibid., 536–37.
52. Despite the challenges the missionaries faced in the region, by 1750 the Franciscans had concluded that the Pames were not intractable savages. Left on their own, the missionaries believed, the Pames would choose to live "like wild animals in the woods" ("como fieras en los Bosques"). The Fernandinos had concluded that they would be able to teach the Pames to live and work as Christians, that the Pames were not as "cruel and haughty" as the Jonace, and that in general the Pames respected the missionaries, unlike other "barbarous nations." Ortés de Velasco, "Tanto del informe que hizo el padre guardian," 4a.
53. "Informes sobre las misiones de Concá, Tancoyol, Landa, Tilaco y Jalpan, octubre de 1758," in Mireles, *La Sierra Gorda*, 515–28. Concá at 519, and Tilaco at 525.
54. Palou, in Geiger, *Relación histórica*, 32.
55. Ibid., 33.
56. Father Bernardo Pumeda, observing Serra at work, called Palou over to watch, but Palou could only remark that he had seen Serra work like that before and that "this is what he does every day." Ibid., 265–66.
57. "Estado de las misiones de la Sierra Gorda en 1761," 529–39.
58. Palou, in Geiger, *Relación histórica*, 33.
59. Gustin, *El barroco en la Sierra Gorda*, 121.
60. In the words of Palou, "The Indians, who before were barbarous and savage, became civilized and instructed." Palou, in Geiger, *Relación histórica*, 33.
61. "Informes sobre las misiones de Concá, Tancoyol, Landa, Tilaco y Jalpan, octubre de 1758," especially 517 (Concá), 520 (Tancoyol), and 523 (Landa).
62. Serra to Felipe de Neve, Jan. 7, 1780, Monterey, in Tibesar, *Writings of Serra*, 3:413.
63. "Informes sobre las misiones de Concá, Tancoyol, Landa, Tilaco y Jalpan, octubre de 1758," especially 515 (Concá), 523 (Landa), 525 (Tiláco), and 527 (Jalpan).
64. Ibid., especially 520 (Tancoyol), 523 (Landa), and 525 (Tilaco).
65. Ibid., especially 524 (Landa), 518 (Concá), 512 (Tancoyol), 527 (Jalpan), and 525 (Tilaco).
66. Ibid., especially 520–21 (Tilaco).
67. Ortés de Velasco, "Tanto del informe que hizo el padre guardian," 3a; "Informes sobre las misiones de Concá, Tancoyol, Landa, Tilaco y Jalpan, octubre de 1758," 523.
68. For the story of Cachum, see Palou, in Geiger, *Relación histórica*, 34–35.
69. Serra, Report to the Inquisition, Sept. 2, 1752, Jalpan, in Tibesar, *Writings of Serra*, 1:19.
70. Ibid. On the difference between *brujería* and *hechicería*, see Anna Armengol, "Realidades de la brujería en el siglo XVII: Entre la Europa de la caza de brujas y el racionalismo hispánico," *Tiempos modernos* 3, no. 6 (2002); and Lara Sembolini, "Cacería de brujas en Coahuila, 1748–1751: 'De villa en villa, sin Dios ni Santa María,'" *Historia mexicana* 54, no. 2 (2004): 325–64.
71. These sorts of charges, as fantastic as they may seem to us today, were not uncommon in New Spain in the mid-eighteenth century, and the majority

of accusations of witchcraft, as in this case, were leveled against mixed-race women.

72. Serra's rapid appointment was an indication of the Council of Inquisitors' respect and confidence in him and their concern over the events that he reported in the Sierra Gorda. They could have called upon a *comisario* from a neighboring region to carry out the investigation or appointed one of his superiors at the college to the job, but that would have delayed the inquiry.

73. Escandón, "Informe del coronel José de Escandón acerca de su visita a la Sierra Gorda y projecto de reorganización de sus misiones," 428.

74. Escandón hoped that in granting Saldívar this land, he would demonstrate to the other settlers the advantages of loyalty to the Crown. And he further believed that by putting the Saldívars in this valley, he would discourage Indians from returning to it. Escandón, "Informe," July 28, 1744, Landa, AGN PI 249, fols. 120b–121a.

75. The investigation into this dispute was lengthy and produced extensive documentation. The key source is the "Despacho," by Don Vicente Possada, which contains all the most important documents related to the investigation and resolution of the matter. See AGN Bienes Nacionales, vol. 87, exp. 16, pp. 1–93. Parts of the document carry section numbers, and I cite those when possible. For the number of soldiers involved and a statement of the conflict see Possada, "Despacho," AGN Bienes Nacionales, vol. 87, exp. 16, para. 17, Feb. 5, 1754, pp. 20–21.

76. It is not clear when their complaint was lodged, but it probably occurred during Serra's first year in the Sierra Gorda.

77. "Libro de recibo y gasto perteneciente a la mission de Santiago de Xalpa," Colección de documentos para la historia de México, vol. 22, 2nd Pt., exp. 14.

78. The settlers' ancestors were Indians and Africans; they had moved to the region generations earlier, and in their customs and beliefs and economic pursuits they were not what Serra had in mind for the Indians of Jalpan. The settlers had little wealth; most had a few horses; some had a few mules.

79. Possada, "Despacho," March 21, 1753, AGN Bienes Nacionales, vol. 87, exp. 16, p. 8.

80. Ibid., p. 14.

81. Ibid., para. 13.

82. Ibid., para. 17. This is where Mathías de Saldívar had his own ranch.

83. At this point Juan de Saldívar withdrew his participation from the proceedings and made himself scarce whenever Possada or his assistant, Don Ignacio Vicente de Rubio, sought his cooperation. Rubio was the son-in-law of Mathías de Saldívar and brother-in-law to both Juan de Saldívar and Juan Antonio de Saldívar. Ibid., 8.

84. Ibid., para. 43.

85. Ibid., para. 30.

86. Ibid., p. 75.

87. Ibid., p. 78.

88. Ibid., p. 79.

89. Ibid., p. 80.

90. Ibid., p. 86.

91. On the destruction of the mission, see David J. Weber, *The Spanish Frontier in North America* (New Haven, Conn.: Yale University Press, 1992), 188–91.

92. It would appear that neither Agustín Pérez nor Lorenzo de la Cruz was literate in the Spanish language. Thus, Raphael Mariano de Lima wrote the letter on their behalf, and de Lima seems to have been not just their scribe but someone who believed the Indians' criticisms of the Fernandinos.

93. Raphael Mariano de Lima, AGN Documentos para la historia de México, Colegio de San Fernando, vol. 13, exp. 16, fols. 1a–4a.

94. Ibid., fol. 1b. On the restrictions on punishments of Indians by priests during this period and the continued insistence by priests and missionaries that lashes were crucial to ensure Indian devotion and correct behavior, see Taylor, *Magistrates of the Sacred*, 215–21.

95. De Lima, AGN Documentos para la historia de México, Colegio de San Fernando, vol. 13, exp. 16, fol. 2a.

96. Ibid., fol. 3a. According to de Lima's letter, the Indians had made these complaints before on numerous occasions but without any luck, as whenever the padres learned of the Indians' complaints, they sent out soldiers, and they punished them and sent them to an *obraje*. Agustín Pérez de la Cruz charged that his wife and daughter had also been arrested and tied up (*mancornada*) like "bestias" and put in irons in the house of the fiscal. After two days they were taken to the villa of Cadereyta. Others were also arrested: a sick man and his wife and ten other Pames Indians who were taken to Tancoyol, where, de Lima wrote, they were punished.

97. Joaquín Alexo Rubio, "Informe," AGN Documentos para la historia de México, Colegio de San Fernando, vol. 13, exp. 15, fol. 4b.

98. Ibid., fol. 5a.

99. Ibid., fols. 9a–9b.

100. María Teresa Álvarez Icaza Longoria, "Indios y misioneros en el noreste de la Sierra Gorda durante la epoca colonial" (master's thesis, Universidad Nacional Autónoma de México, 2005), 242. See also "Testimonio de los autos de visita de las misiones de Xalpa, Landa, Tilaco, Tancoyol y Concá, en Sierra Gorda, y otros providencias dadas en ellas, por El Señor Don Joseph de Escandón," AGN PI 249, fols. 336a–417b. According to the concluding documents, Agustín Pérez de la Cruz was jailed (413a), Lobaton was banished for ten years from coming within sixty miles of the missions, Lorenzo de la Cruz was transferred to the Pueblo of Santa María, where his wife was (413b), and Juan Marquez in the villa of Cadereyta was banished for ten years from the missions, the villa of Herrera, and the Real de Escanela (413b). For Fray Ramos de Lora and Osorio's proposed punishments, which were essentially the same, see 400a–402b; for Escandón's opinion, see 402a–406b.

101. Palou, in Geiger, *Relación histórica*, 41.

102. Fray Juan Ramos de Lora, Aug. 28, 1763, Mission Tancoyol, MS 99/378m, doc. 1.9, Bancroft Library; and Ramos de Lora, "Estado de las misiones franciscanas de Sierra Gorda en 1764," Nov. 21, 1764, in Mireles, *La Sierra Gorda*, 577–80.

103. Fray José García, circular letter to the missionaries of the Sierra Gorda, July 6, 1766, Mexico City, in Gómez Canedo, *Sierra Gorda*, 251–67.
104. Calzada to Apodaca, Aug. 7, 1818, Mexico, in *Las misiones de la Alta California* (Mexico, 1914), 2:247–48, in Geiger, *Relación histórica*, 352n16. See also Álvarez Icaza Longoria, "Un cambio apresurado."
105. Padre Domingo Rivas quoted in Geiger, *Relación histórica*, 352–53n16.

7. POPULAR MISSIONS AND THE INQUISITION

1. Geiger, *Life and Times*, 1:148–49. Before his years in the Sierra Gorda, Serra was not elected to any college office, and in fact in the elections of 1752 he garnered only one vote, and in 1755 he tallied not a single vote. It is true that he was not at the college during those years, but members of the college often received large numbers of votes for office while they were posted in the Sierra Gorda or, later, even when they were in Alta California. See also Maynard J. Geiger, "The Internal Organization and Activities of the College of San Fernando, Mexico (1734–1858)," *Americas* 6, no. 1 (July 1949): 3–31.
2. Geiger, "Internal Organization," 15; Palou, in Geiger, *Relación histórica*, 44. Serra received twenty-eight votes.
3. Palou, upon reflecting on Serra's time in that job, could only marvel: "What vistas come before our imagination when we consider how his fervor must have shone forth in his fulfillment of his duties as master of novices!" Palou, in Geiger, *Relación histórica*, 44.
4. Geiger, *Life and Times*, 1:148, gives the names of the four men whose religious observances Serra supervised in these years.
5. Fray Antonio Llinás, who had founded the College of Santa Cruz in Querétaro in 1683, believed that missionaries needed structure in their lives. His reasoning in favor of a rigid and planned life was the same as Serra's own desire to put the Pames to work building churches: so that they "did not have an idle instant and [so] that the enemy would always find them active" and not subject to temptation. Espinosa, *Crónica de los Colegios*, bk. 1, chap. 16, 173, cited in Rex Galindo, "Propaganda Fide," 177n7.
6. On the daily schedule at the college, see Rex Galindo, "Propaganda Fide," 176–83; and Palou, in Geiger, *Relación histórica*, 44.
7. Palou, in Geiger, *Relación histórica*, 279. *Azotarse* is the verb used by Palou.
8. This description of Serra's likely belongings is drawn from Fray Manuel Anfosso Malloral, "Vida exemplar de el religioso, y apostolico varon frai Antonio de Jesús, y Ganancia" (1768), 132a, in manuscript at the Biblioteca Nacional, Instituto Nacional de Antropología e Historia. I thank Karen Melvin for bringing this manuscript to my attention.
9. In this discussion I am indebted to the work of David Rex Galindo and Karen Melvin, as well as Louis Châtellier, *The Religion of the Poor: Rural Missions in Europe and the Formation of Modern Catholicism, c. 1500–1800* (Cambridge: Cambridge University Press, 1993); and Francisco Luis Rico Callado, *Misiones populares en España entre el Barroco y la Ilustración* (Valencia: Institución Alfons el Magnànim, 2006).

10. It also led to the creation of the Inquisition to root out heresies and the growth of Catholic seminaries that trained increasingly orthodox priests.

11. Châtellier, *Religion of the Poor*, 24.

12. Ibid., 46.

13. Reconciliation was among the most important themes of eighteenth-century Spanish preachers. See Charles E. Noel, "Missionary Preachers in Spain: Teaching Social Virtue in the Eighteenth Century," *The American Historical Review*, 90, no. 4 (October 1985): 866–92.

14. Saint Francis Solano, Antonio Llinás, and Antonio Margil de Jesús all spent a good deal of their time and an enormous part of their energy on popular missions. Their efforts were glorified by Franciscan chroniclers, and Serra sought to emulate their deeds. Above all, the chronicles that Serra read emphasized how the missionary could change the lives of Catholics by bringing them closer to their religion.

15. Oré, *San Francisco Solano*, 38; and Cordova Salinas, *Crónica franciscana de las provincias del Perú*, 512.

16. Espinosa, *Crónica de los Colegios*, 152. In Vallodolid, Margil de Jesús's missions brought "innumerable" confessions, and as a result the society's ills were healed. According to Arricivita, after Margil de Jesús's mission "one could see publicly many old licentious friendships were reformed, stolen honor and property restored, and gambling stopped." All arenas of vice apparently were shut down: "The cockfighters gave proof of their reform when the owners themselves killed the roosters." Arricivita, *Apostolic Chronicle*, 1:152.

17. Espinosa, *Crónica de los Colegios*, 291–92.

18. On this and related points, see José Refugio de la Torre Curiel, *Vicarios en entredicho: Crisis y desestructuración de la provincia franciscana de Santiago de Xalisco, 1749–1860* (Zamora, Michoacán: El Colegio de Michoacán, 2001).

19. Rex Galindo, "Propaganda Fide," 261–64.

20. The trip required strenuous travel through remote country, and for eight days Serra and his five companions journeyed through the jungle on a boat down the river Miges, where Palou says they were constantly at risk and suffered from "excessive heat, molestation from mosquitoes," and "the threat of alligators." For a week they stayed in their canoes for fear of being attacked by "tigers, lions, serpents, and other poisonous animals." Palou, in Geiger, *Relación histórica*, 42.

21. Arricivita, *Apostolic Chronicle*, 1:185.

22. Francisco Pangua and Discretorium, College of San Fernando, "Método de misionar," Dec. 5, 1780, translated and published in the *Provincial Annals, Province of Santa Barbara* 7, no. 2 (April 1945): 3–12, and 7, no. 3 (July 1945). Original is in AGN Bienes Nacionales, 1008. Quotation from vol. 7, no. 2, p. 5.

23. Ibid., vol. 7, no. 3, p. 9.

24. They did so, in Palou's words, in order to "prevent the many offenses which are commonly committed against God during the carnival days." Palou, in Geiger, *Relación histórica*, 48.

25. Attendees of the mission could win indulgences by hearing sermons or by participating in devotional acts, such as the Stations of the Cross and the Jubilee of Forty Hours, during which the host was continuously displayed and people were especially encouraged to confess and take Communion. Pangua and Discretorium, "Método de misionar," vol. 7, no. 1, pp. 11–12.

26. Ibid., vol. 7, no. 2, p. 6.

27. Ibid., vol. 7, no. 3, p. 4.

28. Ibid., vol. 7, no. 2, p. 12.

29. Arricivita, *Apostolic Chronicle*, 1:42.

30. Palou, in Geiger, *Relación histórica*, 46–47.

31. Serra, as the leader of this group of Fernandinos, seems to have chosen Jesús y Ganancia to participate in this mission. Jesús y Ganancia, however, would die in Tamiahua long before the mission was completed. His life and virtues were then chronicled by one of his ardent admirers, Fray Manuel Anfosso Malloral. Malloral, though, was not on the mission, and it seems most likely that his source was either Serra or Palou.

32. Malloral, "Vida ejemplar de Ganancia," 124a.

33. Palou, in Geiger, *Relación histórica*, 235.

34. Ibid., 41–42, 280.

35. Ibid., 236.

36. Ibid., 236, 274.

37. Ibid., 49.

38. So important were these events that the leaders of the College of San Fernando called on the padres to record more instances of their amazing accomplishments while on popular missions. Pangua and Discretorium, "Método de misionar," vol. 7, no. 2, p. 15.

39. There had been earlier Inquisition courts in Iberia in the Middle Ages.

40. If Serra's work on popular missions has largely been overlooked, his work for the Inquisition in Mexico has been ignored by scholars who have missed its relevance and downplayed it as detrimental to overall assessments of his career. When the Mexican office of the Inquisition was established in 1571, it was refused the right to hear cases concerning Indians. In reality, though, there was often an overlap in the personnel of those who investigated Indians for the bishop and those who worked officially for the Holy Office. See Richard Greenleaf, "The Inquisition and the Indians of New Spain: A Study in Jurisdictional Confusion," *Americas* 22, no. 2 (Oct. 1965): 138–66, especially 139–41.

41. "Comision que se les da a padres misioneros," AGN Inquisición, vol. 854, 114a–115b.

42. On the Mexican Inquisition, see Solange Alberro, *Inquisición y sociedad en Mexico, 1571–1700* (Mexico: Fondo de Cultura Económica, 1988); and on the early nineteenth century, see Gabriel Torres Puga, *Los últimos años de la Inquisición en la Nueva España* (Mexico City: INAH, 2004). For a recent study of witchcraft in colonial Mexico and the Inquisition, see Laura A. Lewis, *Hall of Mirrors: Power, Witchcraft, and Caste in Colonial Mexico* (Durham, N.C.: Duke University Press, 2003). On the Inquisition as an authoritarian institution, see Irene Silverblatt, *Modern Inquisitions: Peru and the Colonial*

Origins of the Civilized World (Durham, N.C.: Duke University Press, 2004). There is as yet no exhaustive and authoritative account of the Mexican Inquisition during the eighteenth century. The best short treatment is Lewis A. Tambs, "The Inquisition in Eighteenth-Century Mexico," *Americas* 22, no. 2 (Oct. 1965): 167–81; the prosecutions pursued by the Inquisition in the eighteenth century are discussed on p. 180.

43. The cover sheet of the case reads as follows: "Contra Bonifacio de la Ramírez por haver leido una cedula [   ] entrega de su alma al Demonio," Río Verde, 1756. Cited hereafter as "Investigation of Bonifacio de la Ramírez." Not paginated. The original of the case is in the Archivo Histórico Casa de Morelos, but the archive was closed during my research. I consulted microfilm reel 0785787, Inquisición, 1755–1805, Library of the Church of Latter-Day Saints. I thank David Rex Galindo for bringing this case to my attention.

44. As was always the case in these investigations, neither of the witnesses—Joseph Manuel and Alejandro Rodríguez—knew why he had been called to testify. But both told Serra that they presumed they had been called because of the actions of Antonio Bonifacio and their willingness to denounce him.

45. On this policy, see Tambs, "Inquisition in Eighteenth-Century Mexico," 171–72. *Comisarios* rarely called the friends or family of the accused because doing so might alert the accused that he or she was in trouble.

46. Since the document is not paginated, I have assigned my own numbers. Declaration of Ignacio Sánchez, "Investigation of Bonifacio de la Ramírez," Nov. 17, 1755.

47. Ibid.

48. Ibid., 14.

49. Declaration of [Joseph] Alejandro Rodríguez, "Investigation of Bonifacio de la Ramírez," Nov. 17, 1755, 17.

50. Emphasis mine. Ibid., Nov. 17–20, 1755, 17–20.

51. Ibid., Nov. 20, 1755, 20.

52. Unsigned opinion, "Investigation of Bonifacio de la Ramírez," n.d., 22–23.

53. "Investigation of María Pasquala de Nava," AGN Inquisición, vol. 1009, exp. 9, fols. 168–268, 1766. Serra learned of the denunciation of Dominga de Jesús and the arrest of María Pasquala de Nava in late March or early April 1766 when he was in the town of Aquismón east of Mission Tancoyol. Given the distance between Aquismón and Valle del Maíz and his need to return to the College of San Fernando now that his popular mission was done, Serra asked that his preliminary investigation into the charges take place in Villa de los Valles, which was closer to Aquismón and was the largest town in the region. Dominga de Jesús, María Pasquala de Nava, and several other witnesses were then transferred to Villa de los Valles, and Serra traveled there with his fellow Franciscans to conduct the hearing.

54. Declaration of Dominga de Jesús, "Investigation of María Pasquala de Nava," April 14, 1766, AGN Inquisición, vol. 1009, exp. 9, fols. 198a–200b.

55. Declaration of María Pasquala, "Investigation of María Pasquala de Nava," April 26, 1766, AGN Inquisición, vol. 1009, exp. 9, fols. 201b–203a.

56. For both clarity and effect, I have translated this testimony from a third-person narrative into this dialogue.

57. On the differences between *brujería* and *hechicería*, see Sembolini, "Cacería de brujas en Coahuila, 1748–1751"; and Armengol, "Realidades de la brujería en el siglo XVII."

58. My thanks to Rose Marie Beebe for help translating this section of testimony.

59. Declaration of María Pasquala, "Investigation of María Pasquala de Nava," April 26, 1766, AGN Inquisición, vol. 1009, exp. 9, fol. 204a.

60. Ibid., 204b. I thank Rose Marie Beebe for assistance translating this passage.

61. Declaration of María Pasquala, "Investigation of María Pasquala de Nava," April 9, 1766, AGN Inquisición, vol. 1009, exp. 9, fols. 172a–174a.

62. Declaration of María Pasquala,"Investigation of María Pasquala de Nava," April 26, 1766, AGN Inquisición, vol. 1009, exp. 9, fol. 204b.

63. Ibid., fols. 204b–205a.

64. On Spaniards' association of behavior and character with race and ethnicity, see Lewis, *Hall of Mirrors*, 23–24.

65. Gerardo Lara Cisneros, *El cristianismo en el espejo indígena: Religiosidad en el occidente de la Sierra Gorda, siglo XVIII* (Mexico, D.F.: Secretaría de Gobernación: Archivo General de la Nación-México: Instituto Nacional de Antropología e Historia, 2002), 200–201. Surely then, what looks like a prosecution of a hallucinogenic drug was more; it was a Spanish attempt to root out feared Indian beliefs and cults, many of which had proven resistant to previous attempts at eradication and had been central to the Indians' and now apparently the *gente de razón*'s conflation of Spanish and native deities.

66. Ibid., 195–96.

67. Serra to the Inquisidores, May 7, 1766, Tancoyol, "Investigation of María Pasquala de Nava," April 26, 1766, AGN Inquisición, vol. 1009, exp. 9, fol. 168a.

68. Palou, in Geiger, *Relación histórica*, 45–46. Geiger says that this incident occurred when Serra was returning from a popular mission that took him to the Villa de los Valles, and I conclude that this was the same popular mission that ended with the investigation of María Pasquala de Nava. Geiger, *Relación histórica*, 363n1.

69. Antonio Isidro de Pando, "Investigation of María Pasquala de Nava," Dec. 15, 1766, AGN Inquisición, vol. 1009, exp. 9, fol. 267a. The word *pulguero* itself calls to mind María Pasquala's circumstances; it derives from the word *pulga*, flea, and it suggests that the cell in which she was incarcerated was a nasty place.

70. Joseph Miguel Pereli, "Investigation of María Pasquala de Nava," Oct. 13, 1766, AGN Inquisición, vol. 1009, exp. 9, fol. 245b.

71. Decision, signature illegible, "Investigation of María Pasquala de Nava," Dec. 11, 1766, AGN Inquisición, vol. 1009, exp. 9, fol. 265a.

72. Joseph de Ovesso Rabago, Dec. 13, 1766, "Investigation of María Pasquala de Nava," AGN Inquisición, vol. 1009, exp. 9, fols. 266a–b, and Antonio Isidro de Pando, Dec. 15, 1766, fol. 267a.

73. Lewis, *Hall of Mirrors*, 43.
74. Investigations by agents of the Inquisition were not unheard of in Spanish California. In 1787, three years after Serra's death, Father Francisco Lasuén, the father president of the California missions and a *comisario*, investigated a servant, Pedro Joseph Pérez, who was accused of blasphemy. Two years later, Lasuén also investigated on charges of blasphemy and sorcery a sailor, Raphael Rodríguez, who, apparently, had made a love potion out of dead cats.

8. "A WORK SO HOLY"

1. Weber, *Spanish Frontier in North America*, 237.
2. For population figures, see ibid., 90, 195, 206, 209.
3. Gálvez also sent the Marqués de Rubí to inspect the presidios of the northern frontier and plan for their reorganization. Ibid., 204–12.
4. On Gálvez, see Herbert Ingram Priestley, *José de Gálvez, Visitor-General of New Spain (1765–1771)* (Berkeley: University of California Press, 1916).
5. Weber, *Bárbaros*, 109–10.
6. Ibid., 109.
7. Ibid., 110.
8. On the size of the precontact population of Baja California, see Peter Gerhard, *The North Frontier of New Spain* (Princeton, N.J.: Princeton University Press, 1982), 295.
9. On the dates of the Baja California missions, and the relocation and consolidation of some, see Harry W. Crosby, *Antigua California: Mission and Colony on the Peninsular Frontier, 1697–1768* (Albuquerque: University of New Mexico Press, 1994), 179, table 7.1; and Weber, *Spanish Frontier in North America*, 241.
10. Crosby, *Antigua California*, 114–17.
11. Ibid., 121–22.
12. Ibid., 316.
13. Johann Jakob Baegert, *Observations in Lower California* (1952; Berkeley: University of California Press, 1979), 53, 80.
14. Francisco Palou, *Historical Memoirs of New California*, ed. Herbert Eugene Bolton (New York: Russell & Russell, 1966), 1:211.
15. Geiger, *Life and Times*, 184.
16. Geiger, *Relación histórica*, 366n13.
17. Palou, in ibid., 52; cf. Geiger, *Life and Times*, 185.
18. On this mission, see Fray Juan Crespí, in *A Description of Distant Roads: Original Journals of the First Expedition into California, 1769–1770*, ed. and trans. Alan K. Brown (San Diego: San Diego State University, 2001), 157.
19. Serra to Superiors of San Fernando College, Oct. 17, 1767, Tepic, in Tibesar, *Writings of Serra*, 1:33.
20. Ibid.
21. Geiger, *Life and Times*, 1:188–89.
22. Palou, in Geiger, *Relación histórica*, 53.
23. Palou's burial record of Serra puts the number of missions at fifteen. See Zephyrin Engelhardt, OFM, *Mission San Carlos Borromeo (Carmelo): The Father of the*

Missions (1934; Ramona, Calif.: Ballena, 1973), 232. For different totals, see Crosby, *Antigua California*; and Gerhard, *North Frontier of New Spain*.

24. For the population of Mission Loreto in 1768, see Serra, "Report on Condition of the Missions of Lower California," Nov. 3, 1768, Presidio of Santa Ana, in Tibesar, *Writings of Serra*, 4:307–9.

25. Gálvez knew Grimaldi; he had been one of his secretaries in Spain, so he held him in esteem. Charles Chapman suggests that even before the letter from Grimaldi, Gálvez had his sights set on Monterey and Alta California. See Charles Edward Chapman, *A History of California: The Spanish Period* (New York: Macmillan, 1921), 216–19.

26. Weber, *Spanish Frontier in North America*, 83.

27. Chapman, *History of California*, 1–205; and Donald C. Cutter and Iris Wilson Engstrand, *Quest for Empire: Spanish Settlement in the Southwest* (Golden, Colo.: Fulcrum, 1996), 61.

28. Crespí, *Description of Distant Roads*, 163.

29. Palou, *Historical Memoirs of New California*, 38.

30. Ibid., 40.

31. Two missions—Nuestra Señora de los Dolores and San Luis Gonzaga—were closed and eight hundred Indians relocated to Mission Todos Santos hundreds of miles away in southern Baja California. Indians at Todos Santos were to join those already at Mission Santiago el Apóstol. Some families would be moved from Mission San Xavier in central Baja California to San José del Cabo at the southern end of the peninsula. Indians at the overcrowded missions Santa Gertrudis and Nuestra Señora de Guadalupe were to be moved south to La Purísima Concepción and San José del Cabo, two missions with greater land and water resources. Predictably, many Indians deeply resented the Spaniards' intrusion. Ibid., 38–41, 85–87.

32. Ibid., 85, 140.

33. Ibid., 149–50.

34. Ibid., 211.

35. Ibid., 212–13.

36. Serra Diary of the Expedition from Loreto to San Diego, March 28 to July 1, 1769, in Tibesar, *Writings of Serra*, 1:39.

37. Palou, in Geiger, *Relación histórica*, 55.

38. Palou, *Historical Memoirs of New California*, 48.

39. Crespí, *Description of Distant Roads*, 171; Serra Diary, in Tibesar, *Writings of Serra*, 1:41.

40. Gálvez to Serra quoted in Geiger, *Life and Times*, 1:204.

41. Serra Diary, in Tibesar, *Writings of Serra*, 1:39.

42. Ibid.

43. On this expedition, see Harry W. Crosby, *Gateway to Alta California: The Expedition to San Diego, 1769* (San Diego: Sunbelt, 2003); also see Geiger, *Life and Times*, 1:210, for date of departure.

44. Chapman, *History of California*, 222.

45. Serra Diary, in Tibesar, *Writings of Serra*, 1:43.

46. Ibid., 45, 53–55.

47. He spent little time at Mission La Purísima Concepción, where he had

posted his fellow Mallorcan, Juan Crespí. Crespí was not at the mission when he arrived, as he had already gone north with the first overland party. Crespí had delegated a soldier to provide for Serra. Ibid., 45.

48. Ibid., 51.
49. Palou, in Geiger, *Relación histórica*, 62.
50. Palou, *Historical Memoirs of New California*, 1:51.
51. Serra Diary, in Tibesar, *Writings of Serra*, 1:43.
52. On Sancho, see ibid., p. 413n28.
53. Ibid., 49.
54. Ibid., 51–53.
55. Ibid., 53–55.
56. Ibid., 59.
57. On the items that Serra requisitioned from the Baja California missions for those of Alta California, see Serra to Palou, May 8, 1769, Santa María, in Tibesar, *Writings of Serra*, 1:125–31. On May 11, 1769, Serra and Portolá headed north beyond Mission Santa María. Still, they were not breaking new ground, for they were following the route marked out by Rivera y Moncada's group, and he was doing his best to follow the trail blazed years earlier by the Jesuit explorer Wenceslaus Linck. Rivera y Moncada's group was much larger than the one led by Portolá and Serra. The first overland party had some twenty-five to thirty soldiers, Serra's student Juan Crespí, the pilot José de Cañizares, half a dozen muleteers, a vaquero, and perhaps as many as forty Indians from the Baja California missions. In addition, Rivera y Moncada's party had more than one hundred mules, dozens of horses, and nearly two hundred head of cattle. Palou, *Historical Memoirs of New California*, 1:50–52; and Crosby, *Gateway to Alta California*, 54–55. Linck had explored northern Baja California in 1766, and Serra was traveling with a copy of his journal. For Linck, see Crosby, *Gateway to Alta California*, 51–52.
58. Serra Diary, in Tibesar, *Writings of Serra*, 1:59. Translation is mine.
59. Crosby, *Gateway to Alta California*, 50.
60. In this assessment, Serra followed the lead of the Jesuit Wenceslaus Linck, who in 1765 had visited the site. Crosby, *Antigua California*, 350.
61. Palou, in Geiger, *Relación histórica*, 64–65.
62. Ibid., 65.
63. Serra Diary, in Tibesar, *Writings of Serra*, 1:61.
64. Ibid., 63.
65. Palou, in Geiger, *Relación histórica*, 66.
66. Serra Diary, in Tibesar, *Writings of Serra*, 1:63.
67. Portolá in Palou, in Geiger, *Relación histórica*, 66.
68. Four years later, when the mission was turned over to the Dominicans, it had 296 Indians of all ages. Palou, in Geiger, *Relación histórica*, 65.
69. Serra Diary, in Tibesar, *Writings of Serra*, 1:65–67.
70. Portolá in Palou, in Geiger, *Relación histórica*, 67.
71. Ibid., 67–68.
72. These separate coastal peoples lived in small villages of no more than two hundred and had populations of around two thousand. They spoke Yuman languages, unlike the Cochimí.

73. Serra Diary, in Tibesar, *Writings of Serra*, 1:72–73.

74. Ibid., 103.

75. Ibid., 105.

76. Ibid., 109.

77. Ibid., 115.

78. Serra admitted that when he crossed the frontier, his foot and leg had been getting worse but he believed that God had been good to him. He had kept up with the marches, his foot was healed, but his lower leg still had a large wound, one that caused no pain or swelling, just an itch. They had suffered no hardships on the road and had wanted for nothing. Serra to Palou, July 3, 1769, San Diego, in Tibesar, *Writings of Serra*, 1:143.

79. Serra to Father Juan Andrés, July 3, 1769, San Diego, ibid., 1:133.

80. Chapman, *History of California*, 221–22, 223.

81. Serra to Palou, July 3, 1769, 1:141; and Chapman, *History of California*, 223.

82. Serra to Andrés, July 3, 1769, 1:139.

83. Ibid.

84. Sherburne F. Cook, *Population of the California Indians, 1769–1970* (Berkeley: University of California Press, 1976), 20–43; Peter Gerhard, *North Frontier of New Spain*, rev. ed. (Norman: University of Oklahoma Press, 1993), 309.

85. Ohlone is a name that encompasses many groups, some of which are linguistic subdivisions, namely the Chalon, Rumsen, Esselen, Mutsun, Thamien, Awaswas, Chochenyo, and Karkin.

86. Phillip L. Walker, Patricia Lambert, and Michael J. DeNiro, "The Effects of European Contact on the Health of Alta California Indians," in *Archaeological and Historical Perspectives on the Spanish Borderlands West*, vol. 1 of *Columbian Consequences*, ed. David Hurst Thomas (Washington, D.C.: Smithsonian Institution Press, 1989), 355–56; Lisa Kealhofer, "The Evidence for Demographic Collapse in California," in *Bioarchaeology of Native American Adaptation in the Spanish Borderlands*, ed. Brenda J. Baker and Lisa Kealhofer (Gainesville: University of Florida Press, 1996), 56–92; Douglas H. Ubelaker, "Patterns of Disease in Early North American Populations," in *A Population History of North America*, ed. Michael R. Haines and Richard H. Steckel (Cambridge: Cambridge University Press, 2000), 51–97; Phillip L. Walker and Russell Thornton, "Health, Nutrition, and Demographic Change in Native California," in *The Backbone of History: Health and Nutrition in the Western Hemisphere*, ed. Richard H. Steckel and Jerome C. Rose (Cambridge: Cambridge University Press, 2002), 506–23.

87. Thomas Waterman, "Analysis of the Mission Indian Creation Story," *American Anthropologist* 11, no. 1 (Jan.–March 1909): 41–55.

88. On one of California's most ancient sites of human occupation, see John R. Johnson, Thomas W. Stafford, Jr., Henry O. Ajie, and Don P. Morris, "Arlington Springs Revisited," in *Proceedings of the Fifth California Islands Symposium*, ed. David R. Browne, Kathryn L. Mitchell, and Henry W. Chaney (Santa Barbara: Santa Barbara Museum of Natural History), 541–45. On

the thesis that California was in part first settled by maritime peoples, see Kent G. Lightfoot and Otis Parrish, *California Indians and Their Environment* (Berkeley: University of California Press, 2009), 38–41. On evidence for coastal migrations, in particular those to California, see Jon M. Erlandson, Madonna L. Moss, and Matthew Des Laurier, "Life on the Edge: Early Maritime Cultures of the Pacific Coast of North America," *Quaternary Science Reviews* 27 (2008): 2232–45; and Erlandson et al., "The Kelp Highway Hypothesis: Marine Ecology, the Coastal Migration Theory and the Peopling of the Americas," *Journal of Island and Coastal Archaeology* 2, no. 2 (2007), 161–74.

89. Lightfoot and Parish, *California Indians*, 56.

90. Ibid., 6–7. On Indian languages in California, see Michael J. Moratto, *California Archaeology* (New York: Academic Press, 1984), 530–74; and Victor Golla, *California Indian Languages* (Berkeley: University of California Press, 2011). See also Joseph L. Chartkoff and Kerry Kona Chartkoff, *The Archaeology of California* (Stanford, Calif.: Stanford University Press, 1984).

91. Robert F. Heizer and Albert B. Elsasser, *The Natural World of the California Indians* (Berkeley: University of California Press, 1980); Julia G. Costello and David Hornbeck, "Alta California: An Overview," in Thomas, *Archaeological and Historical Perspectives*, 304–8; James T. Davis, *Trade Routes and Economic Exchange Among the Indians of California*, Reports of the University of California Archaeological Survey 54 (Berkeley, Calif., 1961).

92. M. Kat Anderson, *Tending the Wild: Native American Knowledge and the Management of California's Natural Resources* (Berkeley: University of California Press, 2004).

93. Scholars estimate that California Indians burned between 6 and 16 percent of the state, excluding desert areas, or between 7,000 and 18,700 square miles. Lightfoot and Parrish, *California Indians*, 94–122.

94. It would arrive there at the end of the month. Nine more sailors would be buried at sea during its three-week voyage. Palou, in Geiger, *Relación histórica*, 73; Palou, *Historical Memoirs of New California*, 2:275.

95. See Palou, *Historical Memoirs of New California*, 2:279, for who went and who was left behind.

96. According to Palou, the day that Serra chose to found Mission San Diego was a special one for the Franciscans: it was the day observant Catholics set aside to celebrate what they called the Triumph of the Most Holy Cross to honor a Catholic victory over Muslims in the year 1212. Serra believed that just as the raising of the cross had been a prelude to victory in 1212, now by raising a cross in San Diego, they would "succeed in driving out the whole army of hell and subject to the sweet yoke" of Catholicism "the barbarous pagans who inhabited" Alta California. Palou, in Geiger, *Relación histórica*, 75.

97. Ibid., 76.

98. Palou, *Historical Memoirs of New California*, 2:269–70.

99. Palou, *Relación histórica*, 84. Citation to 1787 edition.

100. Serra to Father Juan Andrés, Feb. 10, 1770, San Diego, in Tibesar, *Writings of Serra*, 1:155.
101. Ibid., 151.
102. Palou, *Historical Memoirs of New California*, 2:270–71.
103. Serra to Palou, Feb. 10, 1770, San Diego, in Tibesar, *Writings of Serra*, 1:159.
104. Palou, *Historical Memoirs of New California*, 2:271.
105. Palou, in Geiger, *Relación histórica*, 78.
106. Serra to Palou, Feb. 10, 1770, San Diego, 159.
107. Ibid., 161.
108. Palou, in Geiger, *Relación histórica*, 87.
109. Ibid.
110. The replacement crew for the *San Carlos* sailed on the *San Antonio*.
111. The day before he set out, Portolá sent a report to the viceroy on the status of the expeditions. The Indians carrying the letter left San Diego on April 16, traveled by night, and arrived at Velicatá a mere nine days later. Palou, *Historical Memoirs of New California*, 2:279.
112. Serra to Father Juan Andrés, June 12, 1770, Monterey, in Tibesar, *Writings of Serra*, 1:167.
113. Ibid., 169.
114. For the soldier, see San Carlos Burial, June 3, 1770, Early California Population Project (hereafter ECPP), Huntington Library.
115. Serra to Andrés, June 12, 1770, 171.
116. Palou, in Geiger, *Relación histórica*, 93.
117. Serra to Andrés, June 12, 1770, 175.
118. Ibid., 172–73, 171.

9. SECURING ALTA CALIFORNIA

1. Perhaps hinting at divine intervention, Serra likened the finding of the lanterns to the delivery of a monstrance to another distant and remote frontier, the kingdom of Titlas, "from Spain by the hands of Angels and of the venerable Mother of Agreda." Serra to José de Gálvez, July 2, 1770, Monterey, in Tibesar, *Writings of Serra*, 1:185.
2. Ibid., 183.
3. Serra to Father Guardian [Francisco Pangua] and Discretorium, July 18, 1774, Monterey, in Tibesar, *Writings of Serra*, 2:113.
4. Serra to Father Juan Andrés, July 5, 1770, Monterey, in Tibesar, *Writings of Serra*, 1:193.
5. Serra to Palou, June 21, 1771, Monterey, in Tibesar, *Writings of Serra*, 1:237.
6. Crespí in Serra to Father Rafael Verger, June 20, 1771, Monterey, in Tibesar, *Writings of Serra*, 1:215.
7. Serra to Father Rafael Verger, Aug. 8, 1772, Monterey, in Tibesar, *Writings of Serra*, 1:251.
8. See Steven W. Hackel, *Children of Coyote, Missionaries of Saint Francis: Indian-Spanish Relations in Colonial California, 1769–1850* (Chapel Hill: University of North Carolina Press, 2005), 15–26.

9. In Serra's words, "These poor people knew nothing more of what a Christian ought to know—according to their own account—than that there are devils, that they are bad, and are their enemies. They call them 'Muur.'" Serra to Pangua and Discretorium, July 18, 1774, 115. According to one diarist on a Spanish expedition that stopped in Monterey in 1792, the Rumsen "believed that the sun was of a similar nature to themselves; . . . that he was a man and that he had the power to take over their lives." The Esselen apparently believed that "after this life everyone was transformed into *teclotes*, or owls, a bird to which they showed a singular veneration." See the translation of the manuscript account of the voyage of the *Sutil* and *Mexicana* in Donald C. Cutter, *California in 1792: A Spanish Naval Visit* (Norman: University of Oklahoma Press, 1990), 143.

10. See Hackel, *Children of Coyote*, 74–80.

11. Edith Wallace, "Sexual Status and Role Differences," in *California*, ed. Robert F. Heizer (Washington, D.C.: Smithsonian University Press, 1978), 683–84; Nona Christensen Willoughby, *Division of Labor Among the Indians of California*, Reports of the University of California Archaeological Survey 60 (Berkeley, Calif., 1963), reprinted in *Precontact*, vol. 1 of *Ethnology of the Alta California Indians*, ed. Lowell John Bean and Sylvia Brakke Vane (New York: Garland, 1991), 427–99.

12. Thomas C. Blackburn and Kat Anderson, eds., *Before the Wilderness: Environmental Management by Native Californians* (Menlo Park, Calif.: Ballena, 1993); James A. Bennyhoff and Richard E. Hughes, *Shell Bead and Ornament Exchange Networks Between California and the Western Great Basin*, Anthropological Papers of the American Museum of Natural History 64, pt. 2 (New York, 1987).

13. San Carlos Baptism 0001, Dec. 26, 1770, ECPP.

14. San Carlos Baptisms 0003, Dec. 17, 1779; 0010, Feb. 2, 1771; 0016, March 19, 1771; and 0017, March 19, 1771, ECPP.

15. Serra to Verger, June 20, 1771, 225; Serra to Palou, June 21, 1771, 241–43.

16. Serra to Francisco Teodoro Carlos de Croix, June 18, 1771, Monterey, in Tibesar, *Writings of Serra*, 1:199.

17. Serra to Palou, June 21, 1771, 241.

18. In the late summer and early fall, they harvested grass seeds, collected buckeyes, nuts, and berries, gathered shellfish, and caught fish. Hunters pursued game attracted to dropping acorns. In the late fall, they gathered and stored their most important food, those acorns. Then they set fire to some of their grasslands. During the cool and wet winter, they also collected shellfish and hunted occasionally, but for the most part they subsisted off their stores. Stephen A. Dietz and Thomas L. Jackson, *Final Report of Archaeological Excavations at Nineteen Archaeological Sites for the Stage 1 Pacific Grove–Monterey Consolidation Project of the Regional Sewerage System* (1981), 657–67.

19. Serra to Croix, June 18, 1771, 197.

20. Serra to Verger, June 20, 1771, 217.

21. Rafael Verger to Casafonda (minister of state in Spain), Aug. 3, 1771, Mexico, in Geiger, *Life and Times*, 1:268.

22. Serra to Verger, June 20, 1771, 215.
23. Serra to Palou, June 21, 1771, 241.
24. Geiger, *Life and Times*, 1:275.
25. Ibid., 280.
26. Serra quoted by Palou, in Geiger, *Relación histórica*, 110.
27. Ibid., 111.
28. Geiger, *Life and Times*, 1:281.
29. At Mission San Antonio, ten of the first sixty-one baptisms were of gravely ill Indian children. ECPP.
30. Palou, in Geiger, *Relación histórica*, 112.
31. Geiger, *Life and Times*, 1:282.
32. Palou, in Geiger, *Relación histórica*, 115.
33. Ibid., 116.
34. On the Gabrielino, see William McCawley, *The First Angelinos: The Gabrielino Indians of Los Angeles* (Banning, Calif.: Malki Museum Press; Menlo Park, Calif.: Ballena, 1996); and Bernice Eastman Johnston, *California's Gabrielino Indians* (Los Angeles: Southwest Museum, 1962).
35. Serra to Antonio María de Bucareli y Ursúa, May 21, 1773, Mexico City, in Tibesar, *Writings of Serra*, 1:361.
36. Ibid.
37. Ibid., 361–63.
38. San Gabriel Baptism 0071, Juan Santiago, July 25, 1773, ECPP.
39. San Gabriel Baptism 0081, Matheo María, June 6, 1774, ECPP.
40. Serra to Palou, Aug. 18, 1772, Monterey, in Tibesar, *Writings of Serra*, 1:265.
41. Serra to Father Rafael Verger, Aug. 8, 1772, Monterey, in Tibesar, *Writings of Serra*, 1:259. Those sent to the San Luis Obispo area returned with meat from forty-one bears. Geiger, *Life and Times*, 338.
42. Serra to Palou, Aug. 18, 1772, 269.
43. Ibid., 267.
44. San Carlos Baptism 0015, Juan Evangelista Joseph, March 19, 1771, ECPP.
45. Palou, "Report Made in the Month of December, 1773, to His Excellency the Viceroy, of the State of the Five Missions of Monterey," in *Historical Memoirs of New California*, 3:230.
46. Palou, in Geiger, *Relación histórica*, 128.
47. The first adult baptism at the mission was not until December 1773, San Luis Obispo. Baptism 0023, Pablo Tecum, Dec. 8, 1773, ECPP.
48. Palou to Verger, Loreto, Oct. 2, 1771, quoted in Geiger, *Life and Times*, 1:329.
49. Years later, perhaps aware of the unprecedented nature of Serra's return to Mexico, Palou wrote that Serra had to go because Fages "accomplished nothing but interference and annoyances, a sorrow to the religious and of no benefit to the missions." Palou, *Historical Memoirs*, 2:365.
50. Geiger, *Life and Times*, 1:337.
51. Serra to Father Rafael Verger, Aug. 15, 1779, Monterey, in Tibesar, *Writings of Serra*, 3:337.
52. Geiger, *Life and Times*, 1:353. Evidently, Serra—now something of a veteran of the seas—had composed this summary while on board the *San Carlos*,

when he had time to reflect on his first years in Alta California and the problems that bedeviled the new settlements.

53. Serra to Palou, Nov. 10, 1772, Monterey, in Tibesar, *Writings of Serra*, 1:293.

54. Palou, in Geiger, *Relación histórica*, 136.

55. See Hackel, *Children of Coyote*, 171-79.

56. Palou, in Geiger, *Relación histórica*, 136.

57. Ibid., 137. By the time Serra was sixty, age and years of physical hardship had begun to catch up with him. During his months at the College of San Fernando in 1773, he was prone to fevers and fits of exhaustion. Those around him at times believed he was near death, but soon thereafter he would be nearly fully revived. See ibid., 414-15.

58. Bucareli to Fages, Oct. 18 and Dec. 26, 1772, quoted in Geiger, *Life and Times*, 1:351-52.

59. Serra to Father Fray Miquel de Petra, Aug. 4, 1773, Mexico City, in Tibesar, *Writings of Serra*, 1:393.

60. On Bucareli, see Bernard E. Bobb, *The Viceregency of Antonio María Bucareli in New Spain, 1771-1779* (Austin: University of Texas Press, 1962).

61. Palou, in Geiger, *Relación histórica*, 139.

62. Serra to Antonio María de Bucareli y Ursúa, March 13, 1774, Mexico City, in Tibesar, *Writings of Serra*, 1:295.

63. Ibid., 301.

64. Ibid., 307.

65. Serra to Antonio María de Bucareli y Ursúa, April 22, 1774, Mexico City, in Tibesar, *Writings of Serra*, 1:337.

66. On the various decisions and deliberations of the office of the viceroy in regard to Serra's proposals, see Palou, *Historical Memoirs of New California*, 3:37-114.

67. Serra to Fray Miquel de Petra, Aug. 4, 1773, 388-95.

68. Palou, in Geiger, *Relación histórica*, 143.

69. Geiger, *Life and Times*, 1:401-2, 418n4.

70. Ibid., 405-9.

71. Serra to Father Rafael Verger, Nov. 11, 1773, Guadalajara, in Tibesar, *Writings of Serra*, 2:7.

72. Geiger, *Life and Times*, 1:409.

73. Serra Memorandum, June 22, 1774, Monterey, in Tibesar, *Writings of Serra*, 2:84-89.

74. Serra to Father Guardian [Francisco Pangua], June 14, 1774, Monterey, in Tibesar, *Writings of Serra*, 2:71; Serra to the Franciscans at the College of San Fernando, July 1, 1774, Mission San Carlos, in *Diario del capitán comandante Fernando de Rivera y Moncada, con un apéndice documental*, ed. Ernest J. Burrus (Madrid: J. Porrúa Turanzas, 1967), 2:393-97.

75. Serra to Antonio María de Bucareli y Ursúa, May 29, 1774, Monterey, in Tibesar, *Writings of Serra*, 2:59.

76. Serra to Antonio María de Bucareli y Ursúa, June 21, 1774, Monterey, in Tibesar, *Writings of Serra*, 2:79.

10. BUILDING A "LADDER" OF MISSIONS

1. On the totals of baptisms and residents, see the ECPP; Palou, *Historical Memoirs of New California*, 3:239; and Serra to Antonio María de Bucareli y Ursúa, Feb. 5, 1775, Monterey, in Tibesar, *Writings of Serra*, 2:222–49.

2. Serra to Bucareli y Ursúa, Feb. 5, 1775, 222–49, especially 241–49.

3. Hackel, *Children of Coyote*, 139–54.

4. On music in the missions—and Indian choristers—see the important work of Sandos, *Converting California*, 128–53; and Sandos, "Identity Through Music: Choristers at Mission San José and San Juan Bautista," in *Alta California: Peoples in Motion, Identities in Formation, 1769–1850*, ed. Steven W. Hackel (Berkeley: Published for Huntington-USC Institute on California and the West by University of California Press and Huntington Library, 2010), 111–28; and Craig H. Russell, *From Serra to Sancho: Music and Pageantry in the California Missions* (New York: Oxford University Press, 2009).

5. See Taylor, *Magistrates of the Sacred*, 215–21.

6. Serra to Antonio María de Bucareli y Ursúa, May 21, 1773, Monterey, in Tibesar, *Writings of Serra*, 1:357.

7. Serra to Fernando Rivera y Moncada, Jan. 22, 1775, Carmel, in Tibesar, *Writings of Serra*, 4:421.

8. Hackel, *Children of Coyote*, 337–38.

9. Serra to Rivera y Moncada, July 24, 1775, Monterey, in Tibesar, *Writings of Serra*, 2:285.

10. Serra to Rivera y Moncada, July 31, 1775, Monterey, in Tibesar, *Writings of Serra*, 4:425. The Indians punished were Carlos Juan, San Carlos Baptism 0079, March 19, 1773; Geronimo Joseph, San Carlos Baptism 0120, May 29, 1773; Christobal Joseph, San Carlos Baptism 0122, June 6, 1773; and Ildefonso Joseph, San Carlos Baptism 0303, Feb. 24, 1775, ECPP.

11. Burrus, *Diario del Rivera y Moncada*, 1:166.

12. Serra to Felipe de Neve, Jan. 7, 1780, Monterey, in Tibesar, *Writings of Serra*, 4:413, 415.

13. Serra to Father Guardian [Francisco Pangua] and Discretorium, July 18, 1774, Monterey, in Tibesar, *Writings of Serra*, 2:111.

14. By the time Rivera y Moncada arrived in Monterey with a portion of fifty-one new recruits for Alta California from Sonora, Serra had reconciled with Fages. Fages was crestfallen by his removal from office, and Serra seemed remorseful for the role he played in Fages's downfall, especially when he realized that some of what he had reported to the viceroy about Fages might not have been true. Serra, perhaps wishing to make amends, asked Bucareli to treat Fages with respect and honor. In one of his most awkward moments of false modesty, Serra stated that he thought he himself had played a role in the conquest of Alta California, that he had, along with soldiers, suffered danger and deprivation. If his contributions were worth anything to the military, Serra told Bucareli, he would now "renounce it all in favor of Don Pedro

Fages." Serra to Antonio María de Bucareli y Ursúa, July 19, 1774, Monterey, in Tibesar, *Writings of Serra*, 2:129.

15. Serra to Bucareli y Ursúa, July 19, 1774, Monterey, ibid., 131.
16. Serra to Pangua and Discretorium, July 18, 1774, 101.
17. Serra to Father Guardian [Francisco Pangua] and Discretorium, Jan. 8, 1775, Monterey, in Tibesar, *Writings of Serra*, 2:207.
18. Serra to Bucareli y Ursúa, Aug. 17, 1775, Monterey, in Tibesar, *Writings of Serra*, 2:301.
19. Serra to Pangua, Oct. 29, 1775, Monterey, in Tibesar, *Writings of Serra*, 2:387.
20. Ibid., 389.
21. Ibid.
22. Lasuén to Pangua, in Tibesar, *Writings of Serra*, 2:478n133.
23. Lasuén to Fray Francisco Pangua, Aug. 17, 1775, Presidio of Monterey, in *Writings of Fermín Francisco de Lasuén*, trans. and ed. Finbar Kenneally, 2 vols. (Washington, D.C.: Academy of American Franciscan History, 1965), 1:57.
24. Serra to Pangua, Oct. 29, 1775, 393.
25. Burrus, *Diario de Rivera y Moncada*, 1:170–71.
26. Lasuén to Pangua, Aug. 17, 1775, Monterey, in Kenneally, ed., *Writings of Lasuén*, 57.
27. Burrus, *Diario de Rivera y Moncada*, 1:171.
28. Serra to Pangua, Oct. 29, 1775, 395.
29. Ibid., 393.
30. Ibid., 395.
31. Geiger, *Life and Times*, 2:58–59.
32. Palou, in Geiger, *Relación histórica*, 167; and Geiger, *Life and Times*, 2:68.
33. Father Fuster to Serra, Nov. 28, 1775, San Diego, in Tibesar, *Writings of Serra*, 2:449–50, 451, 452.
34. Ibid., 452–54.
35. Serra to Bucareli y Ursúa, Dec. 15, 1775, Monterey, in Tibesar, *Writings of Serra*, 2:400–401. The phrase "valley of tears" refers to the tribulations of life and is likely drawn from the Catholic Marian hymn "Salve Regina," one that Serra sang on feast days and notable occasions.
36. Serra to Bucareli y Ursúa, Dec. 15, 1775, Monterey, in Tibesar, *Writings of Serra*, 2:403.
37. Fuster to Serra, Nov. 28, 1775, 457.
38. Serra to Father Francisco Pangua, July 30, 1776, San Diego, in Tibesar, *Writings of Serra*, 3:21.
39. Ibid.
40. Serra to Bucareli y Ursúa, Dec. 15, 1775, 2:405.
41. Serra to Father Francisco Pangua, April 13, 1776, Monterey, in Tibesar, *Writings of Serra*, 2:422–43.
42. Serra to Father Francisco Pangua, Feb. 26, 1777, Monterey, in Tibesar, *Writings of Serra*, 3:93.
43. Geiger, *Life and Times*, 2:99–100.

44. Serra to Father Francisco Pangua, Sept. 24, 1776, Monterey, in Tibesar, *Writings of Serra*, 3:29.

45. While the governor remained in Loreto, Fages and Rivera y Moncada were given the authority to work directly with the viceroy rather than through Barri.

46. On Neve's early career, see Edwin A. Beilharz, *Felipe de Neve: First Governor of California* (San Francisco: California Historical Society, 1971), 8–19.

47. Ibid., 52; Weber, *Bárbaros*, 102.

48. On the New Method, see Weber, *Bárbaros*, 102–7.

49. Neve to Croix, June 4, 1779, Monterey, quoted in Beilharz, *Felipe de Neve*, 51–52.

50. On the Comandancia General of the Interior Provinces, see Weber, *Spanish Frontier in North America*, 224–27.

51. Serra to Father Rafael Verger, Oct. 29, 1779, San Francisco, in Tibesar, *Writings of Serra*, 3:399.

52. According to Neve, "With the elections and the establishment of a new República, His Majesty's designs will have been carried into effect, as far as these countries are concerned. And, guided by our more seasoned experience, the natives of these parts will, in the course of time, develop into useful vassals for our religion and for our State." Felipe de Neve to Serra, quoted in Serra to Neve, Jan. 7, 1780, Monterey, in Tibesar, *Writings of Serra*, 3:410–11.

53. The only record of Neve's original order is Lasuén's response, Jan. 25, 1779, in Kenneally, *Writings of Lasuén*, 1:75–77. Neve notified Teodoro de Croix, commander general of the Interior Provinces, of his directive, Feb. 24, 1779 (copy certified in Monterey, Nov. 15, 1796), AGN Californias, vol. 65, exp. 7, fol. 303r. Croix sent his approval, July 28, 1779, AGN Californias, vol. 65, exp. 7, fol. 304r. The already established missions at San Francisco (1776), San Juan Capistrano (1776), and Santa Clara (1777) were exempt from the governor's orders.

54. This process is described in Lasuén to Neve, Jan. 25, 1779, in Kenneally, *Writings of Lasuén*, 1:75.

55. Serra to Father Guardian and the Discretorium, Aug. 13, 1778, Monterey, in Tibesar, *Writings of Serra*, 3:215–25.

56. Taylor, *Magistrates of the Sacred*, 83–86.

57. *Recopilación*, bk. 6, title 3, law 15.

58. Serra to Father Guardian and the Discretorium, Aug. 13, 1778, 219.

59. Lasuén stated the Franciscans' case clearly: "We, Sir, are not parish priests; we are apostolic missionaries bound by papal bulls to depart from the missions as soon as we recognize that the neophytes, whom we have brought together by our missionary efforts, are sufficiently instructed in the divine law, and sufficiently competent to care for the economic welfare of their families and for the political government of their pueblos. When that stage is reached, they may then come under the jurisdiction of the parish priests sent by the bishops to whose care they are to be entrusted." Lasuén to Neve, Jan. 25, 1779, 1:76–77.

60. Serra to Lasuén, [March 29], 1779, in Tibesar, *Writings of Serra*, 3:294–95.

61. Matt. 10:16; Serra to Lasuén, [March 29], 1779, 3:294–95.
62. Serra to Lasuén, ibid.
63. Genesis 2:4; Serra to Lasuén, [March 29], 1779, 296–97.
64. Serra to Lasuén, Aug. 16, 1779, in Tibesar, *Writings of Serra*, 3:364–65.
65. Serra to Neve, Jan. 7, Monterey, ibid., 3:408–9.
66. Neve's instructions to Serra on the election of the officials have not survived, but they were paraphrased by Serra, ibid. The restriction of the franchise to a select few was consistent with practices in Spain and its colonies.
67. Serra to Lasuén, [March 29], 1779, 296–97.
68. Serra to Neve, Jan. 7, 1780, 409, 411.
69. Serra to Lasuén, Aug. 16, 1779, 367.
70. Neve to [Commander General] Croix, March 26, 1781, Monterey, quoted from Beilharz, *Felipe de Neve*, 153–55.
71. Serra to Father Francisco Pangua, Dec. 8, 1782, Monterey, in Tibesar, *Writings of Serra*, 4:169.

11. TWILIGHT

1. On Serra's concern that the Fernandinos might lose the California missions, see Serra to Father Juan Sancho, Aug. 6, 1784, Monterey, in Tibesar, *Writings of Serra*, 4:284–87. See also Geiger, *Life and Times*, 2:367–69.
2. On Neve's *reglamento*, see Beilharz, *Felipe de Neve*, 85–96; Weber, *Spanish Frontier in North America*, 261–62; Chapman, *History of California*, 361–62; and Felipe de Neve, *Reglamento para el gobierno de la provincia de Californias, 1781*, ed. Salvador Bernabéu Albert (Aranjuez, Madrid: Doce Calles; La Paz, B.C.S.: Ayuntamiento, 1994).
3. William M. Mason, *The Census of 1790: A Demographic History of Colonial California* (Menlo Park, Calif.: Ballena, 1998).
4. Serra to Father Francisco Pangua, Aug. 22, 1775, Monterey, in Tibesar, *Writings of Serra*, 2:321, and Serra to Pangua, Oct. 29, 1775, Monterey, ibid., 395. Writing letters is how Serra fended off the governor's encroachments on missionary privilege, promoted the missions, gave directives to Franciscans across California, and carried out his other considerable responsibilities as father president. But all of this took huge amounts of time since those letters would have to be carefully composed and then copied.
5. Serra to Father Francesch Serra, Aug. 20, 1749, Cádiz, in Tibesar, *Writings of Serra*, 1:5.
6. A small number of others were baptized, but the records of those baptisms have been lost from the archives.
7. Palou, in Geiger, *Relación histórica*, 157, 234, 238.
8. San Carlos Baptism 0350, Miguel Gregorio Pach-hepas, May 9, 1775, ECPP.
9. On the role of the confessional in mission life, see Hackel, *Children of Coyote*, 143–47; and James A. Sandos, "Levantamiento! The 1824 Chumash Uprising Reconsidered," *Southern California Quarterly* 67, no. 1 (Summer 1985): 109–33.
10. See also Hackel, "Junípero Serra's California Sacramental Community," in

"To Toil in That Vineyard of the Lord": *Contemporary Scholarship on Junípero Serra*, ed. Rose Marie Beebe and Robert M. Senkewicz (Berkeley: Academy of American Franciscan History, 2010), 75–93.

11. San Carlos Baptism 1000, Millan Deogracias, June 3, 1784, ECPP.

12. San Carlos Baptisms 1003–1006, June 8 and 12, 1784, ECPP.

13. First, the pope had to grant the permission, and then the Council of the Indies in Spain and the viceroy in New Spain had to approve of the appointment. Finally, the College of San Fernando had to appoint one Franciscan as the one to administer the sacrament, all the paperwork had to be approved by high-ranking officials in New Spain, and the copies had to be forwarded on to Serra in Monterey.

14. On date of expiration, see Palou, in Geiger, *Relación histórica*, 204, and 449n15.

15. Geiger, *Life and Times*, 2:166.

16. Palou, in Geiger, *Relación histórica*, 205. The date in the *Relación histórica* is incorrect on this point. See Geiger, *Life and Times*, 2:170.

17. Palou, in Geiger, *Relación histórica*, 205.

18. Serra to Lasuén, Aug. 16, 1779, Monterey, in Tibesar, *Writings of Serra*, 3:365.

19. Serra to Lasuén, Sept. 24, 1779, Monterey, in Tibesar, *Writings of Serra*, 3:383.

20. Serra to Lasuén, Sept. 28, 1779, Monterey, in Tibesar, *Writings of Serra*, 3:391.

21. Palou insists that he walked. See Palou, in Geiger, *Relación histórica*, 208.

22. Ibid.

23. Ibid., 209, 452n21.

24. Ibid., 213.

25. Serra to Lasuén, Dec. 8, 1781, Monterey, and Serra to Father Francisco Pangua, July 17, 1782, Monterey, in Tibesar, *Writings of Serra*, 4:99, 145–46.

26. Serra to Pangua, July 17, 1782, in Tibesar, *Writings of Serra*, 147.

27. Serra to Pangua, Dec. 8, 1782, Monterey, in Tibesar, *Writings of Serra*, 4:167.

28. Serra to Pangua, July 17, 1782, Monterey, in Tibesar, *Writings of Serra*, 4:155.

29. Serra to Father Juan Sancho, Oct. 27, 1783, San Gabriel, in Tibesar, *Writings of Serra*, 4:197.

30. Geiger, *Life and Times*, 2:286.

31. Serra to Father Francisco Pangua, July 17, 1782, Monterey, in Tibesar, *Writings of Serra*, 4:151.

32. Geiger, *Life and Times*, 2:288.

33. Serra to Teodoro de Croix, April 28, 1782, Santa Barbara, in Tibesar, *Writings of Serra*, 4:135, and for quote, see Geiger, *Life and Times*, 2:288.

34. Palou, in Geiger, *Relación histórica*, 230.

35. Serra to Pangua, July 17, 1782, 153. Neve, in December 1783, when he was near the end of his governorship in California, came to believe that the Franciscans' work in California had surpassed his expectations, but he stopped short of praising Serra. See Geiger, *Life and Times*, 2:368–69.

36. Serra to Father Juan Sancho, Oct. 29, 1783, San Gabriel, in Tibesar, *Writings of Serra*, 4:205. Soon thereafter Croix would be named the viceroy of Peru.

37. Serra to Father Francisco Pangua and the Discretorium, Dec. 8, 1782, Monterey, in Tibesar, *Writings of Serra*, 4:171.
38. Serra to Sancho, Oct. 29, 1783, 205.
39. Palou, in Geiger, *Relación histórica*, 236.
40. Ibid., 237.
41. Ibid.
42. Geiger, *Life and Times*, 2:337.
43. Palou, in Geiger, *Relación histórica*, 237.
44. Serra to Sancho, Oct. 27, 1783, 193.
45. Ibid.
46. Serra to Sancho, Oct. 29, 1783, 199.
47. Ibid., 205.
48. Serra to Father Fermín Francisco de Lasuén, April 17, 1784, Monterey, in Tibesar, *Writings of Serra*, 4:223.
49. Palou, in Geiger, *Relación histórica*, 239–40.
50. Ibid., 241.
51. Serra to Father Juan Sancho, Feast of the Sacred Heart, Monterey, in Tibesar, *Writings of Serra*, 4:243–45.
52. Palou, in Geiger, *Relación histórica*, 241.
53. Serra to Father Juan Sancho, Monterey, Aug. 6, 1784, in Tibesar, *Writings of Serra*, 4:284–85.
54. Serra's whole penitential life, his countless sermons on popular missions, and his insistence on the importance of confessions had all been motivated by his profound sense that a death without a recent confession and the final sacraments might undo a life of Catholic devotion and observance and thereby undermine the state of his soul and the likelihood that he would go to heaven.
55. Palou, in Geiger, *Relación histórica*, 243–44.
56. Ibid., 245.
57. Ibid., 247.
58. Ibid., 247–48.
59. Sancho, quoted in Geiger, *Life and Times*, 2:392.
60. Ibid., 2:393.
61. "Libro de gastos y entradas," Convento de San Bernardino, Petra, fol. 68a, C-1084, Archive of Mallorca.
62. On the death of Juana María, see Vicedo, *La casa solariega de la familia Serra*, 260.

EPILOGUE

1. Serra and Mathías Antonio Noriega, "Report on the Missions," July 1, 1784, Monterey, in Tibesar, *Writings of Serra*, 4:271.
2. Hackel, *Children of Coyote*, 65–80.
3. Ibid., 96–118.
4. Hackel, "From Ahogado to Zorillo: External Causes of Mortality in the California Missions," *The History of the Family*, 17, no.1 (2012): 77–104.
5. Randall Milliken, *A Time of Little Choice: The Disintegration of Tribal Culture in the San Francisco Bay Area, 1769–1810* (Menlo Park, Calif.: Ballena, 1995).

6. Payeras to Reverend Father Guardian [Baldomero López] and Venerable Discretorio, Feb. 2, 1820, in *Writings of Mariano Payeras*, ed. Donald C. Cutter (Santa Barbara, Calif.: Bellerophon Books, 1995), 225–28.

7. Population estimates are for 1820. Gerhard, *The North Frontier of New Spain*, 309. Mission San Francisco Solano would be established in 1823.

8. Hackel, "From Ahogado to Zorillo," 82, and burial records in the ECPP.

9. Cook, *The Population of the California Indians, 1769–1970*, 42–45.

Further Reading

PRIMARY SOURCE MATERIALS

The sources on Junípero Serra's life are dispersed throughout California, Mexico, Mallorca, and Spain. The most complete assemblage is found in the Junípero Serra Collection of the Santa Bárbara Mission Archive-Library. Nevertheless, extensive and important documents relating to Serra and his life's work are available only in Mexico's Archivo General de la Nación, UC Berkeley's Bancroft Library, the Henry E. Huntington Library, and Spain's Archivo General de Indias, as well as the other archives cited in the notes.

Many of the most important primary sources on the exploration of California and the establishment and administration of the missions have been published in translation. Henry R. Wagner's *Spanish Voyages to the Northwest Coast of America in the Sixteenth Century* (Amsterdam: N. Israel, 1966) contains narratives of the most important early explorations of California and the Pacific Coast. In Juan Crespí's *Description of Distant Roads: Original Journals of the First Expedition into California, 1769–1770* (San Diego: San Diego State University Press, 2001), Alan K. Brown has provided an extraordinary translation of Crespí's narrative of the first overland expedition to Alta California and then as far as Monterey. Serra's own narrative of his overland journey from Loreto to San Diego can be found in volume 1 of the Tibesar volumes cited below. For the journals of Juan Bautista de Anza's expeditions to California from Sonora, see Herbert Eugene Bolton, ed., *Anza's California Expeditions*, 5 vols. (Berkeley: University of California Press, 1930).

Nearly all of Serra's known writings have been compiled and edited by Antonine Tibesar in a four-volume set, *Writings of Junípero Serra* (Washington, D.C.: Academy of American Franciscan History, 1955–1966). Francisco Palou's letters from his tumultuous years in Baja California appear in transcription in *Cartas desde la península de California, 1768–1773*, transcribed and ed. José Luis Soto Pérez (Mexico: Porrúa, 1994). The letters of Fermín Francisco de Lasuén, Serra's successor as father president, contain much on the expansion of the missions after Serra's death. See Finbar Kenneally, ed., *Writings of Fermín Francisco de Lasuén*, 2 vols. (Washington, D.C.: Academy of American Franciscan History, 1965). Although fewer in number, the letters of Father President José Francisco de Paula Senán are also very informative. See Lesley Byrd Simpson, ed., *The Letters of José*

Señán, O.F.M., Mission San Buenaventura, 1796–1823, trans. Paul D. Nathan, ed. Lesley Byrd Simpson (San Francisco: J. Howell Books for the Ventura County Historical Society, 1962). Father President Mariano Payeras's writings are an exceptional source on the administration of the missions and Indian life in them. See Donald Cutter, ed., *Writings of Mariano Payeras* (Santa Barbara, Calif.: Bellerophon Books, 1995). Bolton's four-volume edition of Palou's *Historical Memoirs of New California* (Berkeley: University of California Press, 1926) contains translations of some of the most important documents relating to the settlement of Alta California and the establishment of missions during the life of Serra.

The writings of California's Spanish governors are of great importance, but they have not attracted sustained interest from publishers or translators. For a transcription of the diary of Fernando de Rivera y Moncada, see Ernest J. Burrus, ed., *Diario del capitán comandante Fernando de Rivera y Moncada: Con un apéndice documental*, 2 vols. (Madrid: J. Porrúa Turanzas, 1967). Governor Pedro Fages's narrative description of California provides material on California Indians not available elsewhere and reveals Fages to be an astute observer. See Pedro Fages, *A Historical, Political, and Natural Description of California*, trans. Herbert Ingram Priestley (Berkeley: University of California Press, 1937). *Lands of Promise and Despair: Chronicles of Early California, 1535–1846*, ed. Rose Marie Beebe and Robert M. Senkewicz (Berkeley: Heyday Books, 2001), contains translated excerpts of important documents across the span of much of early California history. Information on individuals baptized, married, and buried in the California missions has been made available online and searchable by the Huntington Library's Early California Population Project. See http://www.huntington.org/information/ecppmain.htm.

SPAIN AND MALLORCA

Befitting a place with a deep and complicated history, Mallorca has been the subject of extended historical inquiry. For a synthesis of the history of the island, consult Pere Xamena Fiol, *Història de Mallorca* (Palma: Moll, 1991). A more detailed overview of particular moments and periods in Mallorcan history can be found in an outstanding two-volume work, *Història de Mallorca*, 2nd ed., ed. Jaume Alzina et al. (Palma: Moll, 1989 and 1994). Josep Amengual i Batle's *Història de l'església a Mallorca: Del barroc a la Il·lustració (1563–1800)* (Palma: Lleonard Muntaner, 2002) covers the history of the Catholic Church in early modern Mallorca. See also Pere Xamena Fiol, *Història de l'església a Mallorca* (Palma: Moll, 1986).

Mallorcan history has been marked by immigration, expulsions, and epidemic disease. Onofre Vaquer Bennàssar has studied the origins of those who resettled the island after the conquest of 1229, *L'origen dels mallorquins* (Palma: El Tall, 2008). Bennàssar's volume has a particularly useful appendix on the origins of the island's family lineages. On the expulsion of the Moriscos, see Julián García de la Torre, "Repercusiones en el reino de Mallorca, de la expulsión de los moriscos," *Mayurqa* 21 (1985–1987): 191–95. On Islam and the island, see Guillermo Rosselló Bordoy, *Mallorca musulmana* (Palma: J. Mascaró Pasarius, 1973). On the population of Mallorca and the prevalence of epidemic disease, see Antonio Contreras Mas, "Epidemiologia rural mallorquina a fines del siglo XVIII," *Treballs de geografía*, no. 37 (1980–1981): 83–90; Gines Rosa, "Aproximación a la demografía de un pueblo mallorquín: Binissalem, 1700–1867," *Trabajos de geografía* 38 (1981–1982): 41–75; and Jaume Suau Puig, "Demografía rural mallorquina del segle XVIII," *Mayurqa*, no. 16 (1976): 137–79.

A discussion of Mallorca's waxing and waning political autonomy and its complex relationship with the Crown of Aragon is provided by J. N. Hillgarth, *The Spanish Kingdoms, 1250–1516* (Oxford: Clarendon, 1976–1978), and Thomas Bisson, *The Medieval Crown of Aragon* (Oxford: Clarendon, 1986).

An excellent study of Mallorca during the Middle Ages, in particular its place in the economy of the Mediterranean, is David Abulafia, *A Mediterranean Emporium: The Catalan Kingdom of Majorca* (Cambridge: Cambridge University Press, 1994). Josep Juan Vidal, a leading historian of Mallorca who has published widely, provides an overview of the economic and political trials of Mallorca during the late fifteenth and early sixteenth centuries with the opening of transatlantic trade in *Mallorca en tiempos del descubrimiento de América* (Palma: El Tall, 1991). On the meaning for Mallorca of Hapsburg rule, the ascendance of the Bourbons, and the imposition of imperial authority, see John Lynch, *Spain Under the Habsburgs* (Oxford: B. Blackwell, 1964) and *Bourbon Spain, 1700–1808* (Oxford: B. Blackwell, 1989).

A central concern of historians of Mallorca has been the inability of the island to produce an adequate food supply. For an overview of the subject, see Isabel Moll Blanes, "Los estudios de historia agraria en Mallorca," *Historia agraria: Revista de agricultura e historia rural* 1 (Feb. 1990): 29–38. Mallorca's historical reliance on North Africa for food is the subject of Josep Juan Vidal, "El comercio de trigo entre Mallorca y Africa del Norte en los siglos XVI y XVII," *Mayurqa* 15 (1976): 73–92. For analysis of the food deficit on the island, see Ubaldo de Casanova i Todolí, "El déficit alimenticio del reino de Mallorca a lo largo del siglo XVII y sus problemas de abastecimiento," *Mayurqa* 21 (1985–1987): 217–32. Scholars have linked the inadequate food production on the island to Mallorca's rigid and inequitable distribution of landownership. See Josep Juan Vidal, "Las crisis agrarias y la sociedad en Mallorca durante la edad moderna," *Mayurqa* 16 (1976): 87–113; and especially Isabel Moll and Jaume Suau, "Senyors i pagesos a Mallorca (1718–1860/70)," *Estudis d'història agrària*, no. 2 (1979): 95–170.

Lleonard Muntaner Mariano has studied the urban geography of Palma, Mallorca's largest city, as it appeared in 1729 and thus as Serra saw it. See "Un model de ciutat preindustrial. La ciutat de Mallorca al segle XVIII," *Trabajos de geografía 34: Miscelanea* (1977–1978). For another look at the urban population of Palma, see Josep Juan Vidal, "Notas sobre la población y la vida urbana de la Mallorca moderna," *Mayurqa* 17 (1977): 62–75. See also the very useful Antoni Picazo, *Urbanisme i classes socials a Mallorca, 1500–1820* (Palma: El Tall, 2008).

The Spanish Inquisition greatly affected Mallorca, and scholars have devoted enormous energy to its exploration. For an entry into this literature, see Kimberly Lynn Hossain, "Unraveling the Spanish Inquisition: Inquisitorial Studies in the Twenty-First Century," *History Compass* 5, no. 4 (2007): 1280–93. Henry Kamen's *Spanish Inquisition: A Historical Revision* (New Haven, Conn.: Yale University Press, 1998) touches on events in Mallorca. See also Joseph Pérez, *The Spanish Inquisition: A History* (New Haven, Conn.: Yale University Press, 2005).

Few topics have garnered more interest among scholars interested in Mallorca than the persecution of the island's Jews and conversos. Important early works in English are Baruch Braunstein, *The Chuetas of Majorca: Conversos and the Inquisition of Majorca* (New York: Ktav, 1972); and Kenneth Moore, *Those of the Street: The Catholic-Jews of Mallorca: A Study in Urban Cultural Change* (Notre Dame, Ind.: University of Notre Dame Press, 1976). For an overview of this tangled and sad history, see Baltasar Porcel, *Los Chuetas mallorquines: Quince siglos de racismo* (Palma: Miquel Font, 1986). A richly illustrated survey is Miquel S. Font Poquet, *La fe vençuda: Jueus, conversos i xuetes a Mallorca* (Palma: Miquel Font, 2007). On the Jews of Palma in the Middle Ages, see José María Quadrado, *La judería de Mallorca en 1391* (Palma: Lleonard Muntaner, 2008). On the persecutions of the seventeenth century, the indispensable work is Antoni Picazo's *Els Xuetes de Mallorca: Grups de poder i criptojudaisme al segle XVII* (Palma: El Tall, 2006). For a summary of particular cases the Inquisition investigated in Mallorca, see Llorenç Pérez, Lleonard Muntaner, and Mateu Colom, *El tribunal de la Inquisición en Mallorca, relación de causas de fé, 1578–1806* (Palma: Miquel Font, 1986).

Much of what we know about the village of Petra is the result of work by local historians. Sebastián Rubí Darder's *La villa real de Petra: Algunas de sus raíces*, 2nd ed. (Petra: Apóstol y Civilizador, 1987), provides an overview of the village's past with excerpts from primary sources describing key moments in the life of the community. It is similar to the very useful two-volume study by Padre Francisco Torrens y Nicolau, *Apuntes históricos de Petra* (Petra: Apóstol y Civilizador, 1982), which was completed by the author in 1921 and enriched by the inclusion of numerous historical documents. The history of Junípero Serra's childhood home, still preserved today in Petra, is the subject of Fray Salustiano Vicedo's *La casa solariega de la familia Serra* (Petra: Apóstol y Civilizador, 1984). The institution that gave Serra his early education and put him on the path of the priesthood is the focus of Fray Salustiano Vicedo's *Convento de San Bernardino de Sena* (Petra: Apóstol y Civilizador, 1991).

The work of historical demographers and social science historians has allowed new generations of scholars to rewrite the history of early modern Europe with a greater emphasis on the structures that shaped daily life, especially patterns of marriage and reproduction, and rates of mortality. For Spain during the early modern period, consult the work of David Sven Reher, *Town and Country in Pre-industrial Spain: Cuenca, 1550–1870* (Cambridge: Cambridge University Press, 1990) and *Perspectives on the Family in Spain, Past and Present* (Oxford: Clarendon, 1997). The relationships among climate, food production, and disease have also been the focus of an outpouring of excellent scholarship. The seminal article is Andrew B. Appleby, "Grain Prices and Subsistence Crises in England and France, 1590–1740," *Journal of Economic History* 39, no. 4 (Dec. 1979): 865–87. See also Andrew B. Appleby, "Epidemics and Famine in the Little Ice Age," *Journal of Interdisciplinary History* 10, no. 4 (Spring 1980): 643–63. For the late 1740s, when Mallorca was in food deficit and demographic crisis, see John D. Post, *Food Shortage, Climatic Variability, and Epidemic Disease in Preindustrial Europe: The Mortality Peak in the Early 1740s* (Ithaca, N.Y.: Cornell University Press, 1985). For Mallorca and the community of Petra, the most exacting study of fluctuations in annual totals of births and deaths across the island remains Isabel Moll, Antoni Segura, Jaume Suau, and Llorenç Ferrer, *Cronología de les crisis demogràfiques à Mallorca, segles XVIII–XIX* (Palma: Institut d'Estudis Baleàrics, 1983).

INTELLECTUAL AND SPIRITUAL INFLUENCES ON SERRA

The religious and intellectual world of Junípero Serra largely was shaped by Franciscan men, many of whom lived centuries before him. The life of Saint Francis is revealed by his most important early chronicler, Saint Bonaventure, in *Bonaventure*, trans. Ewert Cousins (New York: Paulist Press, 1978). For an academic study of the life of Saint Francis and the order he founded, see André Vauchez, *Francis of Assisi: The Life and Afterlife of a Medieval Saint*, trans. Michael F. Cusato (New Haven, Conn.: Yale University Press, 2012). Saint Francis and much of his appeal to his followers are chronicled in *The Little Flowers of Saint Francis*, a volume that has been reprinted and republished many times over the centuries. On Ramon Llull, the great Mallorcan missionary and intellectual whose own writings are nearly impenetrable, begin with Anthony Bonner's *Doctor Illuminatus: A Ramon Llull Reader* (Princeton, N.J.: Princeton University Press, 1993), and Amador Vega's *Ramon Llull and the Secret Life* (New York: Crossroad, 2003). Additional details on Llull and his important years in France are found in J. N. Hillgarth, *Ramon Llull and Llullism in Fourteenth-Century France* (Oxford: Clarendon Press, 1971).

Serra was greatly influenced by Franciscan missionaries of the seventeenth and early eighteenth centuries. Still useful and readable is Juan Domingo Arricivita's late-eighteenth-century chronicle of the Franciscan missionaries of the College of Santa Cruz in Querétaro, *Apostolic Chronicle of Juan Domingo Arricivita: The Franciscan Mission Frontier in the Eighteenth Century in Arizona, Texas, and the Californias* (Berkeley, Calif.: Academy of American Franciscan History, 1996). There is no modern biography of Saint Francis Solano, let alone one in English. Nor is there one on Fray Antonio Llínas. The life of Fray Antonio Margil de Jesús, however, is the subject of Peter Forrestal's short biography, *The Venerable Padre Fray Antonio Margil de Jesús* (Austin: Texas Catholic Historical Society, 1932), and Eduardo Enrique Rios's *Life of Fray Antonio Margil, O.F.M.* (Washington, D.C.: Academy of American Franciscan History, 1959). Margil de Jesús's spiritual and devotional writings have been published by Marion A. Habig, ed., and Benedict Leutenegger, trans., *Nothingness Itself: Selected Writings of Ven. Fr. Antonio Margil, 1690–1724* (Chicago: Franciscan Herald Press, 1976).

Other than Serra's own mother and the Virgin Mary, it would seem that the only woman who shaped Serra's life was the nun María de Jesús de Agreda, who had numerous visions, all of which inspired him. Clark Colahan provides an approachable discussion of her life and the revelations she received in *The Visions of Sor María de Agreda* (Tucson: University of Arizona Press, 1994). Anna María Nogar presents the most perceptive discussion of the influence of María de Agreda on Palou and Serra, and the missionaries of the Southwest, in her PhD dissertation, "La Monja Azul: The Political and Cultural Ramifications of a 17th-Century Mystical Transatlantic Journey" (University of Texas at Austin, 2008).

TRANSATLANTIC FRANCISCANISM

Junípero Serra was hardly unique in his decision to leave Mallorca for the New World. On the movement of Spanish missionaries to New Spain, see Pedro Borges

Morán, *El envío de misioneros a América durante la época española* (Salamanca: Universidad Pontificia, 1977) and "Expediciones misioneros al Colegio de Querétaro," *Archivo ibero-americano*, 2nd ser., 42, nos. 165–68 (1982): 809–58. For the period after Serra, and the origins and qualifications of emigrant missionaries, see Carlos José de Rueda Iturrate, "Envío de misioneros franciscano a Nueva España, 1790–1830," *Archivo ibero-americano*, 2nd ser., 57, nos. 225–28 (1997): 421–32. On the backgrounds of the Spanish Franciscans who went to Mexico, see Francisco Morales, *Ethnic and Social Background of the Franciscan Friars in Seventeenth-Century Mexico* (Washington, D.C.: Academy of American Franciscan History, 1973).

The College of San Fernando became home not only to Serra but also to many other Mallorcans. On the Mallorcan contribution to the college, see Maynard J. Geiger, "The Franciscan 'Mission' to San Fernando College, Mexico 1749," *The Americas* 5, no. 1 (July 1948): 48–60; and for the college itself, see also Geiger's "Internal Organization and Activities of San Fernando College, Mexico (1734–1858)," *The Americas* 6, no. 1 (1949). By far the most probing, detailed, and expansive study of the College of San Fernando, and by extension the other apostolic colleges in Spanish America, and the life of the padres affiliated with them, is David Rex Galindo's recent PhD dissertation, "Propaganda Fide: Training Franciscan Missionaries in New Spain" (Southern Methodist University, 2010). On the college out of which the College of San Fernando emerged, see Michael B. McCloskey, *The Formative Years of the Missionary College of Santa Cruz of Querétaro, 1683–1733* (Washington, D.C.: Academy of American Franciscan History, 1955).

COLONIAL MEXICO

As one would expect, there is an enormous body of scholarship on colonial Mexico, where Serra lived for close to two decades. Alan Knight ably synthesizes what is known about indigenous societies in Mesoamerica on the eve of the Spanish conquest in *Mexico: From the Beginning to the Spanish Conquest* (Cambridge: Cambridge University Press, 2002). Charles Gibson's *Spain in America* (New York: Harper & Row, 1966) is a brief and standard introduction to Spain during the age of exploration and colonization, and to its American colonies. For an illuminating comparison of the transatlantic colonies of Spain and England, see J. H. Elliott, *Empires of the Atlantic World: Britain and Spain in America, 1492–1830* (New Haven, Conn.: Yale University Press, 2006). Spanish motivations and Indian life during the conquest are the subject of Ross Hassig's *Mexico and the Spanish Conquest* (New York: Longman, 1994). Indian responses and accommodations to Spanish colonial society, in particular in language and culture, are the subject of James Lockhart, *The Nahuas After the Conquest: A Social and Cultural History of the Indians of Central Mexico, Sixteenth Through Eighteenth Centuries* (Stanford, Calif.: Stanford University Press, 1992). Lesley Byrd Simpson studied the early economic institutions that supported the conquering class in *The Encomienda in New Spain: The Beginning of Spanish Mexico* (Berkeley: University of California Press, 1966). For a discussion of the debates that have characterized scholars' attempts to quantify the scale of the Indian population decline in the Americas, and in particular in Mexico, in the wake of 1492, see David P. Henige, *Numbers from Nowhere: The American Indian Population Debate* (Norman:

University of Oklahoma Press, 1998). The best guide to the extremely complex human landscape of colonial Mexico is Peter Gerhard's *A Guide to the Historical Geography of New Spain*, rev. ed. (Norman: University of Oklahoma Press, 1993). For early Franciscan attempts to convert Indians, see Inga Clendinnen, *Ambivalent Conquests: Maya and Spaniard in Colonial Yucatan, 1517–1570* (Cambridge: Cambridge University Press, 1987).

The history of Bourbon New Spain has spawned a vast literature. On the church-state tensions that characterized the years Serra was in Mexico, see Nancy M. Farriss, *Crown and Clergy in Colonial Mexico, 1759–1821: The Crisis of Ecclesiastical Privilege* (London: Athlone, 1968). For the military during these years, see Christon I. Archer, *The Army in Bourbon Mexico, 1760–1810* (Albuquerque: University of New Mexico Press, 1977). On Spaniards' views of Indians, in particular the views of government officials and missionaries during the eighteenth century, see David J. Weber's *Bárbaros: Spaniards and Their Savages in the Age of Enlightenment* (New Haven, Conn.: Yale University Press, 2005). William B. Taylor examined the role of the Catholic Church and its officials in everyday life in late colonial Mexico in *Magistrates of the Sacred: Priests and Parishioners in Eighteenth-Century Mexico* (Stanford, Calif.: Stanford University Press, 1996). D. A. Brading has studied the intellectual currents swirling about New Spain in *The First America: The Spanish Monarchy, Creole Patriots, and the Liberal State, 1492–1867* (Cambridge: Cambridge University Press, 1991). Viceroy Antonio María de Bucareli y Ursúa and Visitor General José de Gálvez were exceptionally important in Serra's years at and his administration of the California missions. On these two men, see Bernard E. Bobb, *The Viceregency of Antonio María Bucareli in New Spain, 1771–1779* (Austin: University of Texas Press, 1962); and Herbert Ingram Priestley, *José de Gálvez, Visitor-General of New Spain (1765–1771)* (Berkeley: University of California Press, 1916).

During his years in central Mexico, Serra came to know the capital well, although he seems to have never written about his life there. The thriving street culture and class and ethnic tensions that were so much a part of Mexico City in the mid-eighteenth century are vividly rendered in Juan Pedro Viqueira Albán's *Propriety and Permissiveness in Bourbon Mexico* (Wilmington, Del.: Scholarly Resources, 1999). Matthew D. O'Hara's *A Flock Divided: Race, Religion, and Politics in Mexico, 1749–1857* (Durham, N.C.: Duke University Press, 2010) captures the degree to which Indians and non-Indians lived and worshipped separately in Mexico City during Serra's day.

Scholars over the past several decades have turned the study of Spain's settlement of the region from Florida to California into a robust field. David Weber's *Spanish Frontier in North America* (New Haven, Conn.: Yale University Press, 1992) blends synthesis and archival research in a sweeping narrative of Spanish exploration and colonization of its northern frontier. See also John L. Kessell's *Spain in the Southwest: A Narrative History of Colonial New Mexico, Arizona, Texas, and California* (Norman: University of Oklahoma Press, 2002). For military policy and the lives of soldiers on the northern frontier, see Max L. Moorhead, *The Presidio: Bastion of the Spanish Borderlands* (Norman: University of Oklahoma Press, 1975).

THE SIERRA GORDA

Serra's first stint as a missionary to Indians was in the Sierra Gorda, a region about which only a handful of specialists have written, and one for which there are only a few documents in Serra's hand. María Teresa Alvarez Icaza Longoria's master's thesis, "Indios y misioneros en el noreste de la Sierra Gorda durante la epoca colonial" (Universidad Nacional Autónoma de México, 2005), is the most detailed examination of Indian-missionary relations in the region based on archival materials. Monique Gustin's *El barroco en la Sierra Gorda: Misiones franciscanas en el estado de Querétaro, siglo XVIII* (Mexico: Instituto Nacional de Antropología e Historia, 1969) illuminates the architecture and religious iconography of the Sierra Gorda missions. Lino Gómez Canedo puts the Franciscans at the center of events in his *Sierra Gorda, un típico enclave misional en el centro de México (siglos XVII–XVIII)* (Querétaro: Ediciones del Gobierno del Estado de Querétaro, 1988). Canedo's magnum opus, *Evangelización, cultura y promoción social* (Mexico: Porrúa, 1993), contains two valuable essays on Serra's years in the Sierra Gorda. The interactions of soldiers, settlers, missionaries, and Indians in the Sierra Gorda are examined in José Antonio Cruz Rangel's *Chichimecas, misioneros, soldados y terratenientes: Estrategias de colonización, control y poder en Querétaro y la Sierra Gorda, siglos XVI–XVIII* (Mexico: Archivo General de la Nación, 2003). José de Escandón was the most important military official in the Sierra Gorda. His life and rise to power are discussed by Jesús Mendoza Muñoz, *El conde de Sierra Gorda don José de Escandón y la Helguera: Militar, noble y caballero* (Cadereyta: Fomento Histórico y Cultural de Cadereyta, 2005). For transcriptions of some of the most important documents relevant to the history of the Sierra Gorda during Serra's years there, see Margarita Velasco Mireles, coord., *La Sierra Gorda: Documentos para su historia* (Mexico: Instituto Nacional de Antropología e Historia, 1996), vol. 1.

POPULAR MISSIONS AND THE MEXICAN INQUISITION

Serra's important work with popular missions in the Mexican countryside during the 1750s and 1760s is best understood in the tradition of the itinerant missionaries who spread throughout the European countryside to bring Catholicism to rural people who had neither a parish priest nor a firm commitment to the religion. This aspect of European Catholicism has been thoroughly explored by Louis Châtellier in *The Religion of the Poor: Rural Missions in Europe and the Formation of Modern Catholicism, c. 1500–1800* (Cambridge: Cambridge University Press, 1993). Franciscan popular missions in Mexico are examined in Karen Melvin's *Building Colonial Cities of God: Mendicant Orders and Urban Culture in New Spain* (Stanford, Calif.: Stanford University Press, 2012).

Philip II formally established the Mexican Inquisition in 1571, and missionaries like Serra were often quite active in its prosecutions. The Inquisition was less active in the eighteenth century in Mexico than in previous centuries, and the most rigorous scholarship has been focused on the earlier period. Solange Alberro provides a detailed study of the concerns and victims of the Mexican Inquisition during its most active years in *Inquisición y sociedad en México, 1571–1700* (Mexico: Fondo de Cultura Económica, 1988). Irene Silverblatt's *Modern Inquisitions: Peru and the Colonial Origins of the Civilized World* (Durham, N.C.: Duke University Press, 2004) suggests the terrorizing aspects of the institution. Many, if not most, of the victims of the Mexican Inquisition during the eighteenth century were women accused of witchcraft. Laura A. Lewis explains why this is so in *Hall of Mirrors: Power, Witchcraft, and Caste in Colonial Mexico* (Durham, N.C.: Duke University Press, 2003).

BAJA CALIFORNIA
Historians have paid little attention to Serra's years in Baja California in the late 1760s, seeing them as only a stepping-stone to his later work in Alta California, but he left an important mark on the region. The most thorough work on the history of the Jesuits' long presence in the region is Harry W. Crosby's *Antigua California: Mission and Colony on the Peninsular Frontier, 1697–1768* (Albuquerque: University of New Mexico Press, 1994). Miguel León-Portilla's writings on Baja California have been compiled in *La California mexicana: Ensayos acerca de su historia* (Mexico: Universidad Nacional Autónoma de México, Instituto de Investigaciones Históricas, 1995). The Jesuit missionary Ignacio Tirsch created beautiful, if idealized, views of the peninsula in the years just before Serra arrived. See *The Drawings of Ignacio Tirsch, a Jesuit Missionary in Baja California* (Los Angeles: Dawson's Book Shop, 1972). On the route and overland expedition from Baja California that carried Spaniards to San Diego in 1769, see Harry W. Crosby, *Gateway to Alta California: The Expedition to San Diego, 1769* (San Diego: Sunbelt, 2003).

CALIFORNIA INDIANS AND THE MISSIONS
For more than a century now anthropologists and historians have been studying California Indians. The best one-volume overview of many of the peoples that Serra anticipated converting is volume 8, *California*, of the Smithsonian's *Handbook of North American Indians*, ed. William C. Sturtevant (Washington, D.C., 1978). Kent G. Lightfoot and Otis Parish have refocused the attention of scholars on the important role of fire in California Indians' management of their land. See Lightfoot and Parish, *California Indians and Their Environment* (Berkeley: University of California Press, 2009). Randall Milliken's important book, *A Time of Little Choice: The Disintegration of Tribal Culture in the San Francisco Bay Area, 1769–1810* (Menlo Park, Calif.: Ballena, 1995), was the first monograph to fully exploit mission sacramental records with an eye toward understanding Indians and their relations with the missions. On mission registers as sources for the writing of California history, see John R. Johnson, "Mission Registers as Anthropological Questionnaires: Understanding Limitations of the Data," *American Indian Culture and Research Journal* 12, no. 2 (1988): 9–30; and Steven W. Hackel and Anne Marie Reid, "Transforming an Eighteenth-Century Archive into a Twenty-First Century Database: The Early California Population Project," *History Compass* 5 (2007): 1013–25. Robert H. Jackson and Edward D. Castillo showed the detrimental effects of the missions on California Indians in *Indians, Franciscans, and Spanish Colonization: The Impact of the Mission System on California Indians* (Albuquerque: University of New Mexico Press, 1995). Lisbeth Haas examines landholding and identity among the Acjachemen in the wake of Spanish colonization in *Conquests and Historical Identities in California, 1769–1936* (Berkeley: University of California Press, 1995). In my earlier work, I examined the destructive

role of disease and environmental change in Spanish California, as well as religious indoctrination and labor practices in the California missions. See Steven W. Hackel, *Children of Coyote, Missionaries of Saint Francis: Indian-Spanish Relations in Colonial California, 1769–1850* (Chapel Hill: University of North Carolina Press, 2005).

ALTA CALIFORNIA

The scholarship on Spanish settlement in Alta California is voluminous. For an encyclopedic overview of early California history, see volume 1 of Hubert Howe Bancroft's 1884 seven-volume *History of California* (San Francisco: The History Company). The experiences of women in Spanish California are still largely un-written, but the most comprehensive study is by Virginia Marie Bouvier, *Women and the Conquest of California, 1542–1840: Codes of Silence* (Tucson: University of Arizona Press, 2001). Sylvia L. Hilton examines the settlement of Alta California within the context of Spanish imperial ambitions in *La Alta California española* (Madrid: MAPFRE, 1992). On the economy of the California missions and the whole province, the best book is still the only one on the topic, Robert Archibald's excellent *The Economic Aspects of the California Missions* (Washington, D.C.: Academy of American Franciscan History, 1978). On the arrival of Spanish settlers in Alta California, see Vladimir Guerrero, *The Anza Trail and the Settling of California* (Berkeley, Calif.: Heyday Books, 2006). On the race, caste, ethnicity, and origins of the soldiers and settlers who came to California, see William M. Mason, *The Census of 1790: A Demographic History of Colonial California* (Menlo Park, Calif.: Ballena, 1998).

EARLY INTERPRETATIONS OF SERRA

Serra might have drifted into semi-obscurity had his student and colleague Fray Francisco Palou not written his hagiographical *Relación histórica de la vida y apos-tólicas tareas del venerable padre fray Junípero Serra* (Mexico, 1787). The *Relación histórica* is a classic Franciscan chronicle in the tradition of the lives of the saints, and its publication shaped nearly everything subsequently written about Serra and the California missions. Monsignor Francis J. Weber discussed the publication history of the *Relación histórica* and other important Serrana publications through the 1960s in his article "California's Serrana Literature," *Southern California Quar-terly* 51, no. 4 (Dec. 1969): 325–42. For Palou's goals in writing his life of Serra, and other views on Serra since, see Robert M. Senkewicz's essay "The Representation of Serra in California History," in *"To Toil in That Vineyard of the Lord": Contem-porary Scholarship on Junípero Serra*, ed. Rose Marie Beebe and Robert M. Senkewicz (Berkeley, Calif.: Academy of American Franciscan History, 2010), 17–52. Palou's other great historical work, *Historical Memoirs of New California* (Berkeley: Uni-versity of California Press, 1926), was not published until the twentieth century, yet it too sheds much light on Serra's life and times. Both of Palou's studies depicted Serra's deep piety, religious orthodoxy, virtuous temperament, and exemplary commitment to the mission enterprise as seen through the eyes of Serra's greatest admirer.

The degree to which Palou's vision of Serra took hold in the literature on Serra and Alta California can be seen in the writing of Hubert Howe Bancroft. In volume 1 of his *History of California*, Bancroft maintained that Serra could be stubborn in his dealings with Alta California's governors and concluded that Serra was "kind-hearted and charitable to all" and that his faults—his strict and narrow belief that the Franciscan way was the only way—"were those of his cloth" (414–16).

The Franciscan Zephyrin Engelhardt could tolerate not even the slightest criticism of Serra, and thus he considered Bancroft's writings a vicious and unprincipled attack. In *The Franciscans in California* (Harbor Springs, Mich.: Holy Childhood Indian School, 1897), i, he accused Bancroft of "bigotry" and demonstrating "ignorance of Catholic affairs." Engelhardt went further in his monumental four-volume *Missions and Missionaries of California* (San Francisco: James H. Barry, 1912–1929), arguing that Bancroft's criticisms of Serra were part of an "agitation against the founder of Christianity and civilization in California." Putting his own mark on Serrana, Engelhardt added a strong dose of late-nineteenth- and early-twentieth-century racism to Palou's hagiography, and as a result California Indians in Engelhardt's works appear far more savage than in Serra's correspondence or in Palou's writings about Serra or Alta California.

Engelhardt cast a long shadow over Serra studies and examinations of Alta California. He was the most important Franciscan scholar of his generation working on California, and he served for many years as director of the important Santa Bárbara Mission Archive-Library. Engelhardt's work, at least until the middle of the twentieth century and the publication of Geiger's edition of the *Relación histórica*, remained by default the most important source for many historians of Serra, especially those who did not read Spanish or who had no access to Serra's then unpublished correspondence.

Alongside the Catholic tradition of Serra admiration there is a body of secular writing that borders on hagiography. Perhaps the earliest and most important secular admirer of Serra was Charles F. Lummis, who arrived in Southern California in 1885, took a keen interest in the life and legacy of Serra, and founded the Landmarks Club, which he devoted in part to the preservation and conservation of the California missions. Lummis's early statements about Serra were nearly indistinguishable from those of Catholic historians like Engelhardt and were extremely influential in California and beyond. Lummis, however, was far less dismissive of the Indians Serra worked with than Engelhardt and his followers had been. In *The Spanish Pioneers and the California Missions* (Chicago: A. C. McClurg, 1929), Lummis maintained that Serra—"The Apostle of California—Founder of Civilization"— was first and foremost among the Franciscan missionaries. Serra, he wrote, "made a deeper and more lasting dent on the history and the ideals and the future of California than any other man of any race who ever lived within these boundaries."

SERRA AND MALLORCAN HISTORIANS
While Serra has cast a long shadow over the history and historiography of Spanish California and been a figure of interest to American scholars of the borderlands, he remains obscure in Spain and Mexico. As with many historical figures, interest in Serra has often increased in conjunction with anniversaries of his birth (in 1713) and death (in 1784). In Petra and Mallorca, the memory of Serra was revived in the late nineteenth century by Francisco Torrens y Nicolau, who, while studying for the priesthood in Palma, came across Palou's *Relación histórica* in a bookshop.

From that point forward he dedicated his life to the commemoration of Serra. In 1913, on the bicentennial of Serra's birth, Torrens y Nicolau published his own hagiography of Serra, *Bosquejo histórico del insigne franciscano, V.P.F. Junípero Serra, fundador y apóstol de la California septentrional* (Felanitx: B. Reus, 1913). Torrens y Nicolau's volume is largely an abbreviation of Palou, but it rekindled the memory of Serra on Mallorca.

The most important Mallorcan Serra scholar since Torrens y Nicolau was Bartolomé Font Obrador, author of the richly illustrated *Fra Junípero Serra: Mallorca, México, Sierra Gorda, Californias* (Palma: Comissió de Cultura, Consell Insular de Mallorca, 1992). Coauthored with the art historian Norman Neuerburg, this volume captures the full arc of Serra's life in brief fashion and provides an illuminating discussion of various intellectual influences on Serra. Two of Font Obrador's books present significant overviews of Serra's life as well as important documents related to Serra: *Juníper Serra: L'emprenta mallorquina a la Califòrnia naixent* (Palma: Ajuntament de Palma, 1988) and *El apóstol de California, sus albores* (Palma: Direcció General de Cultura, 1989). Font Obrador's *Fray Junípero Serra: Doctor de gentiles* (Palma: Miquel Font, 1998) contains a transcription of various prayers possibly authored by Serra and concludes with tributes and prayers on behalf of Serra's candidacy for sainthood. Lorenzo Galmés, a native of Mallorca, has written a fine, readable biography from a Catholic perspective, *Fray Junípero Serra: Apóstol de California* (Madrid: Biblioteca de Autores Cristianos de la Editorial Católica, 1988).

In Mexico today, Serra is all but unknown outside academic circles and the Sierra Gorda. A small group of scholars has examined the missions of the Sierra Gorda as objects of local interest. Mexican historians have studied Serra as they would any other important Franciscan missionary, but they have not embraced him to the extent that those in Mallorca have. On Serra's treatment by Mexican historians, see the section on the Sierra Gorda above.

THE SERRA CAUSE FOR CANONIZATION

In 1934 the Catholic Church formally initiated proceedings to investigate the worthiness of Serra for canonization and recognition as a saint. The Church established a historical commission composed of the historian Herbert Eugene Bolton, Father Maynard J. Geiger (archivist of the Santa Bárbara Mission Archive-Library), and Monsignor James E. Culleton (chancellor of the diocese of Fresno-Monterey). The three testified before an ecclesiastical court convened to examine Serra's life. In 1949, the testimony given in the investigation and nearly seventy-five hundred pages of documents relating to Serra's life were sent to Rome for further scrutiny. Thirty-six years later, in 1985, Pope John Paul II declared Serra venerable, and three years later he beatified the Mallorcan missionary, leaving Serra one miracle short of qualifying for sainthood. As part of the campaign to demonstrate Serra's virtues, Geiger translated and edited Palou's biography of Serra in 1955. See Geiger, ed., *Palóu's Life of Fray Junípero Serra* (Washington, D.C.: Academy of American Franciscan History, 1955). Geiger also wrote a monumental two-volume biography of Serra, *The Life and Times of Fray Junípero Serra, O.F.M.; or, The Man Who Never Turned Back (1713–1784)* (Washington, D.C.: Academy of American Franciscan History, 1959). Although long out of print, a half century after its publication *The Life and Times of Junípero Serra* remains the definitive cradle-to-grave biography of Serra and the starting point for all serious research on the missionary from Mallorca.

Geiger's biography of Serra has company in an array of kindred studies. Charles J. G. Maximin Piette's *Évocation de Junípero Serra: Fondateur de la Californie* (Washington, D.C.: Academy of American Franciscan History, 1946) presents Serra's life and a very useful chronological list of Serra's known correspondence. Piette's posthumously published two-volume *Le secret de Junípero Serra: Fondateur de la Californie-Nouvelle, 1769–1784* (Washington, D.C.: Academy of American Franciscan History, 1949) was the first modern biography of Serra (complete with extended excerpts from much of Serra's correspondence). The Franciscan Omer Englebert's *Last of the Conquistadors: Junípero Serra, 1713–1784* (New York: Harcourt, Brace, 1956) was included in the Catholic Book of the Month Club, but Father Eric O'Brien, OFM, bemoaned the book's "many errors." Don DeNevi and Noel Francis Moholy broke little new ground in their *Junípero Serra: The Illustrated Story of the Franciscan Founder of California's Missions* (San Francisco: Harper & Row, 1985), but the volume does contain numerous useful illustrations and photographs relating to Serra's life and work. Monsignor Francis J. Weber has authored many works on Father Serra, the most recent and enduring of which is *Blessed Fray Junípero Serra: An Outstanding California Hero* (Strasbourg, France: Éditions du Signe, 2007). Finally, M.N.L. Couve de Murville, archbishop of Birmingham, England, has provided a short, clear, learned, and richly illustrated biography of Serra squarely within the Catholic tradition. In *The Man Who Founded California: The Life of Blessed Junípero Serra* (San Francisco: Ignatius, 2000), Couve de Murville acknowledged a wide range of views of Serra, some of them critical. Martin J. Morgado's two pictorial illustrations of Serra's life, *Junípero Serra's Legacy* (Pacific Grove, Calif.: Mount Carmel, 1987) and *Junípero Serra: A Pictorial Biography* (Monterey, Calif.: Siempre Adelante, 1991), contain spectacular photographs by Patrick Tregenza.

Beyond public proclamations, commemorative statues, hagiographic texts, and richly illustrated volumes, the celebration of Serra found its place during the second half of the twentieth century in children's literature. Nearly all children's books on Serra discuss his small stature and teach that he overcame his size and his sore leg to accomplish great things. Typical of this genre is Leo Politi's *Mission Bell* (New York: Scribner, 1953), which dwells on Serra's "lame leg," kindly nature, and love for Indians. The same didactic prose, minus the lame leg, can be found in Donna Genet's *Father Junípero Serra: Founder of California Missions* (Springfield, N.J.: Enslow, 1996). Similar books have also appeared in Spanish.

THE SERRA CONTROVERSY

Just as the Serra cause was gaining momentum in the decades after World War II, American society underwent dramatic transformations that led many to call into question the rosy and dominant accounts of the Spanish colonization of California, the peaceful Franciscan missions, and the benign nature of Serra's life and work. Some observers claimed that pro-Serra scholarship willfully neglected to take into account Indian life within the mission system and asserted that some Indian cultures had been all but destroyed as a result of policies implemented by

Serra and his followers. The scholar Sherburne F. Cook brought to light accusations of cruelty against the missionaries in a series of essays that were later reprinted as *The Conflict Between the California Indian and White Civilization* (Berkeley: University of California Press, 1976), but Cook did not explicitly criticize Serra, even though he portrayed the missions and missionaries in a highly unfavorable light.

In a series of articles in the *Southern California Quarterly*, Francis F. Guest, OFM, attempted to rebut Cook by describing the intellectual and religious worlds from which Serra had come; he argued that Franciscan missionaries did not force Indians to convert to Catholicism. See Guest, "An Examination of the Thesis of S. F. Cook on the Forced Conversion of Indians in the California Missions," 61, no. 1 (1979): 1–77; "Cultural Perspectives on California Mission Life," 65, no. 1 (1983): 1–65; "Junípero Serra and His Approach to the Indians," 67, no. 3 (1985): 223–61; "An Inquiry into the Role of the Discipline in California Mission Life," 71, no. 1 (1989): 1–68; and "The California Missions Were Far from Faultless," 76, no. 3 (1994): 255–307.

Guest's attempt at refutation may have played well with Serra's supporters, but it was of limited impact elsewhere. In "Junípero Serra's Canonization and the Historical Record," *The American Historical Review* 93, no. 5 (Dec. 1988): 1253–69, James A. Sandos summarized the role that historians have played in the burnishing of Serra's image. He criticized Bolton for his unflagging and seemingly politically motivated support of Serra and urged historians to regain their independence and objectivity in their scholarship on Church figures like Serra. In the tradition of Cook, the scholars Robert H. Jackson and Edward D. Castillo called attention to the oppressiveness of the missionaries and the degree to which the padres' rule led neophytes to despair and to demographic collapse. See Jackson and Castillo, *Indians, Franciscans, and Spanish Colonization: The Impact of the Mission System on California Indians* (Albuquerque: University of New Mexico Press, 1988). The causes and effects of Indian population decline in the California missions have been examined by Robert H. Jackson, *Indian Population Decline: The Missions of Northwestern New Spain, 1687–1840* (Albuquerque: University of New Mexico Press, 1994).

While Cook and his followers directed their fire at the whole mission enterprise, a group of academics and Indian activists pointed their fingers directly at Serra. California Indians, political activists, and academic scholars blasted the Church's declaration in 1985 that Serra was worthy of veneration. In response, the bishop of Monterey published "The Serra Report," a defense of Serra that fueled the controversy by pulling into the debate some of California's leading scholars on Spanish colonization and Indian life. Then, on the eve of Pope John Paul II's visit to Monterey in 1987, Rupert Costo and Jeannette Henry Costo published a polemical attack on Serra and the missions. The Costos' *Missions of California: A Legacy of Genocide* (San Francisco: Indian Historian Press, 1987) accused academic historians of falsifying California history and California missionaries of enslaving and killing California Indians. While some critics dismissed this book out of hand, it unquestionably gave new prominence to the growing critique of Serra and the missionaries, and it added Native voices to the debate for the first time. A more sober yet presentist critique of Serra and the California missions can be found in Daniel D. Fogel's *Junípero Serra, the Vatican, and Enslavement Theology* (San Francisco: Ism Press, 1988). Fogel sought to shift the debate from Serra's saintly qualities to the political motivations of the Catholic Church in promoting his canonization. Recently, in *Converting California: Indians and Franciscans in the Missions* (New Haven, Conn.: Yale University Press, 2004), James A. Sandos tried to move beyond the controversy over Serra and situated his life and work in the ideas and writings of three figures who inspired Serra: Saint Francis of Assisi, John Duns Scotus, and María de Agreda. Serra studies will continue to evolve as successive generations examine his life anew.

Acknowledgments

In writing this book, I incurred debts to institutions, colleagues, friends, and family. I have been very fortunate to have received strong institutional support for my research throughout my career. I began in earnest working on the life of Serra when I was on the faculty at Oregon State University, although as a California native and historian of early California I had been thinking about him in one way or another for a long time. OSU's College of Liberal Arts and its Center for the Humanities supported my early research on this book. At OSU my thoughts on Serra were sharpened by encouraging colleagues. Paul Farber, Robert Nye, Mary Jo Nye, Jeff Sklansky, Ben Mutschler, Nicole von Germeten, Lisa Sarasohn, Maureen Healy, and the late Peter J. Copek helped me conceptualize this book. At the University of California, Riverside, I also enjoy an extraordinarily supportive group of colleagues and administrators. Thomas Cogswell, Randolph C. Head, and James P. Brennan—all ideal department chairs—and my dean, Stephen E. Cullenberg, facilitated the leave time that allowed me to complete this book. Catherine Gudis helped me see more clearly the enduring legacies of Serra and the California missions. At UCR our outstanding undergraduates, especially those enrolled in History 30, helped me think through Serra's life and its importance. Three graduate students in particular—Seth Archer, George Curley, and Ea Madrigal—helped me clarify my understanding of Alta California and the Spanish borderlands.

For more than two decades now the Huntington Library has been my steadiest intellectual home outside of the university, and it was there I carried out much of the research and writing of this book. A faculty fellowship from the John Randolph Haynes and Dora Haynes Foundation in 2009 and before that a Huntington Library summer fellowship gave me added time at the library to work on Serra. Even as the digital revolution transforms how historians gather and analyze documents and then write and edit manuscripts, I still do my best writing in a quiet room with paper and pencil. For that quiet office, and so much more over the years, I thank Robert C. Ritchie, retired Director of Research and mentor to so many of us at the library, and Steve Hindle, the Huntington's W. M. Keck Foundation Director of Research. Bill Frank, Curator of Hispanic, Cartographic, and Western Historical Manuscripts at the Huntington, guided me to innumerable valuable materials related to Serra and Spanish California. Carolyn Powell, Susi Levin, Juan Gómez, and Kadin Henningsen have made my life as a reader more pleasant and efficient through their generous assistance.

A Huntington NEH long-term fellowship in 2010–2011 allowed for a year of uninterrupted writing. My thinking about Serra during that year was advanced by Marcy Norton, Daniel and Helen Horowitz, Seth Rockman, Martha Sandweiss, and David W. Blight. Ramón A. Gutiérrez, a fellow at the Huntington in 2011–2012, helped me understand aspects of Franciscan practice during the colonial period. Hal Barron, Bill Deverell, Janet Fireman, David Igler, Peter Mancall, Doug Smith, and many other long-term readers helped me refine my thoughts on Serra. My understanding of Serra's life and of the tremendous interest in his legacies in California and elsewhere has been greatly enriched by my work on a Serra exhibition that will show at the Huntington in the fall and winter of 2013. While the exhibition and this book have remained distinctly separate projects, I thank David Zeidberg, Avery Director of the Library, and Steven Koblik, President of the Huntington, as well as Susan Turner-Lowe, Randy Shulman, and Kristy Peters, for their deep commitment to bringing the story of Serra and his legacies to a wide and diverse public.

Without the help of librarians, archivists and curators, I would not have been able to dig so deeply into Serra's life and the worlds in which he lived. At UCR's Tomás Rivera Library, the reference staff and Interlibrary Loan Services were exceptionally helpful. At the Bancroft Library, Walter Brem, Theresa Salazar, and David Kessler were enormously helpful locating documents. At the Santa Bárbara Mission Archive-Library, Monica Orozco provided me with a steady stream of photocopies of Serra materials from the archive's invaluable collection. In Mexico, the staff of the Archivo General de la Nación were always helpful and genial. After I had completed an exhausting visit to the Sierra Gorda, Robert H. Jackson showed me great hospitality. My desire to see the Sierra Gorda and learn more about Serra was inspired by long conversations with the late Dionisio Chavarría Cárdenas and his lovely wife, Marcela González. Loren Chavarría and Bruce Bechtel also greatly encouraged my work on Serra and my interest in colonial Mexico.

During my first visit to Mallorca, the late Bartolomé Font Obrador not only showed me all the sights but also took me to numerous archives that held important Serra materials. I am grateful to him for doing so. On my return to the island, Amy Christiansen, Catalina Font, and Tumi Bestard gave me a taste of Mallorcan hospitality that I will never forget or be able to repay. Their commitment to Serra's legacy—and its meaning for Mallorca—is testament to the padre's vision. Fray Joan Martí Gandía gave me access to the parish archives in Petra, and Catalina Font arranged for me to visit Petra's municipal archives. The staff at the spectacular Arxiu del Regne de Mallorca was unfailingly helpful. Without their assistance I would have a far thinner understanding of Serra's years in Petra and Palma. In Madrid, Sylvia Hilton greatly facilitated my research in museums and archives.

Participants in the USC–Huntington Library Early Modern Studies Institute Borderlands Seminar have vastly improved my understanding of the Spanish frontier in North America. I also thank Christopher Grasso, Karin Wulf, and Peter Mancall for the opportunity to present an early draft of the epilogue to a lively group of biographers gathered by the EMSI and *The William and Mary Quarterly*.

I thank David Igler, Peter Mancall, Gary B. Nash, and Robert M. Senkewicz for their support of this project at critical moments.

Over the years, I learned much about Serra and missionaries through conversations with Amy Turner Bushnell, Inga Clendinnen, Andy Galvan, Malcolm Margolin, Vincent Medina, Cynthia Radding, James Sandos, Bob Senkewicz, Monsignor Francis J. Weber, and the late David J. Weber. On numerous occasions, John R. Johnson and John G. Douglass guided me through the vast anthropological literature on California Indians. In addition, Jeanette Zerneke helped me to see the spatial dimensions of Serra's life.

Many friends and colleagues have read my work on Serra, and their comments and suggestions have greatly improved this book. John Dagenais, Teofilo F. Ruiz, and Antoni Picazo Muntaner lent their expertise to my interpretation of Serra's years in Mallorca. David Rex Galindo gave me superb comments on the first half of the book. José Refugio de la Torre refined my chapters on colonial Mexico. David Igler read the whole manuscript, helped me reframe the final argument, and wisely encouraged me to be done with it. William B. Taylor read the manuscript in its entirety, offering comments that only an expert can provide, and he did so with the gentle persuasiveness of a master mentor. His reading improved the manuscript and reminded me yet again of how much we depend upon our fellow scholars for the precision of our own work.

At Hill and Wang, Thomas LeBien was always encouraging and pushed me to begin writing those early chapters. More recently, Alex Star helped shape the manuscript into its final form, and then he moved mountains to see the book to publication on schedule. Dan Gerstle improved my writing and argument through his attention to detail, logic, and brevity. He and Christopher Richards shepherded the book through production. Ingrid Sterner provided superlative copyediting.

My parents—Al and Brenda Hackel, and Jackie Hackel and David Rubsamen—and my siblings—Jamie and Daniel—encouraged me as I wrote this book, and for that I am very grateful. I wish that David had seen it in print.

Heidi Brayman Hackel has helped me in every way possible at every stage of this project from beginning to end. Most of all, at the crucial moment, she instilled in me the hope and confidence that I could complete this book in a timely fashion. And then she gave me the time and the support to do so. Without her this book would not be. Anna and Gabriel, already too expert for their tender years on the life of Serra and the history of the California missions, encouraged me in their own ways to finish this project. It is to Heidi, for her loving support, and to Anna and Gabriel, in partial recompense for their patience with their father, that I dedicate this book.

Index